OCT. 2 2 1993

W9-DDX-124

The President's Private Eye

The President's Private Eye

THE JOURNEY OF DETECTIVE TONY U.
FROM N.Y.P.D. TO
THE NIXON WHITE HOUSE

Tony Ulasewicz

with Stuart A. McKeever

MACSAM Publishing Company, Inc.

Westport, Connecticut

LIBRARY OF CONGRESS Catalog Card Number: 90-61514 ✓

ISBN 0-9626154-0-4

Published in the United States by
MACSAM Publishing Company, Inc.
155 Post Road East
Westport, Ct. 06880

Distributed to the trade by
Publishers Group West
4065 Hollis
Emeryville, CA 94662

Manufactured in the United States of America

10   9   8   7   6   5   4   3   2   1

363.2

To my Mary, with love.

All these years she could only stand on the sidelines and watch. Now, at last, she can step into my journey. I pray we continue this journey together, hand in hand, wherever the road will lead.

T.U.

To Nancy, Sean, Darin and Kara

Your loving care and understanding made this writer's journey possible. I can only say thank you again and again.

S.A.M.

Acknowledgments

MANY thanks to my brother and sister detectives of BOSSI for their aid and recollections. Grateful appreciation is extended to all the members of my family and to the family of my co-author for their unending support and encouragement. Thanks also to everyone who believed in the telling of this story, and to all those who have helped bring it to the surface, especially, in alphabetical order, Toby Greenberg, Charlie Hacker, Norma Jean Inman, Herb Kalmbach, John Murphy, Betty Pessagno, Jon Riffel, Harriet Ripinsky, Linda Ripinsky, Steve Tilley, and Charlie Winton.

Contents

The
President's
Private Eye

Surfacing

TODAY I live in firewood country, in the foothills of the Adirondack Mountains, north of Albany, New York, on a hillside overlooking Great Sacandaga Lake. Stacked cords of maple, yellow and white birch, mountain ash and elm stand in rows among the trees behind my home. I cut, haul, and split the wood myself. I love the work. I even raise some chickens. I share the eggs with my neighbors. Before I knew better, I once had four roosters. I named them Haldeman, Ehrlichman, Dean, and Sirica. Rooster Haldeman had a cropped comb; rooster Ehrlichman had a high brow and a jutting chin; rooster Dean walked with a little swish; and Rooster Sirica looked judicious. Roosters Haldeman, Ehrlichman, and Dean are gone now. I gave them away when they began fighting with each other and created havoc in the hen house. There can only be one king of the roost. That's rooster Sirica, and he remains firmly in control. "Why Sirica as the name of a rooster?," a reporter once asked me. "Because," I answered, "he's the oldest and the wisest."

The main road below my home is called Star Route. It is a fitting label. At night, when it's dark and clear, I can watch the stars burst out of their sockets; in daylight, I can see across to the horizon. The seasons change here with dramatic fury. In the winter, ice storms and deep snow spread across the landscape. In the spring and summer, massive bolts of lightning occasionally knock out my phone when thunderstorms roar across the hills.

I always know the coming of a visitor. I should; I spent twenty-seven years looking for things as a cop with the New York City Police Department. Seven years (interrupted by my service with both the Army and the Navy in the Second World War) were spent as a patrolman in Harlem's Twenty-fifth Precinct. I walked a beat, swung a bat, rode shotgun in hospital ambulances, blew my whistle until my lungs almost burst, and risked my life arresting armed felons in dark hallways. I battled for a promotion and when I won it, the Police Commissioner, in a complete switch from my beat in Harlem, assigned me to the Bureau of Special Service and Investigation. This was the intelligence unit of the NYPD. In my time this unit was known as "BOSSI." In the Justice and State Departments in Washington, it was known as the little FBI and the little CIA. BOSSI and its ancestors were in existence long before the FBI and the CIA were born. I spent twenty exciting years with BOSSI.

I had many unique and challenging assignments as a BOSSI detective. One was guarding the leaders of the world—kings and queens, premiers and presidents, chancellors and shahs, emperors and dictators—when they or their wives and children came to New York to attend sessions of the United Nations or just to go out on the town for a good time. Another assignment was recruiting, organizing, training, and supervising undercover agents who infiltrated some of the most radical, dangerous, and violent groups ever to confront intelligence operations in the history of this country.

In 1969, I left the sanctuary of BOSSI and the New York City Police Department to become President Richard Nixon's confidential, personal, private investigator. My career as a detective and later as a private eye for the White House involved me in some of the biggest plots and coverups of the twentieth century.

My first assignment for President Nixon was investigating Senator Ted Kennedy's trip over the bridge on Chappaquiddick which killed Mary Jo Kopechne. One of my last assignments was delivering White House cash payments to families of the Watergate burglars. Chappaquiddick and Watergate are the bookends of my career as the first private investigator ever hired to work for a President of the United States. Some bookends!

I keep some souvenirs of Chappaquiddick and Watergate around my house. A discarded "NO TRESPASSING" sign from Chappaquiddick hangs in my garage as a reminder of my many visits there. I was on Dike Bridge less than twenty-four hours after Kennedy's car failed to negotiate its planks, flipped over, and landed bottoms up in the waters of Pocha Pond. My Watergate souvenir is a chrome busman's money changer which sits on a bookshelf in my den and glints in the afternoon sun. In the summer of 1972, after the Watergate break-in at Democratic National Committee headquarters, I almost wore out my pants pockets carrying the change I needed to call lawyers and some of their burglar clients to whom I was trying to deliver chunks of cash the White House wanted passed around. I bought the money changer to save my pants and clipped it on my belt. The money changer remains tagged with a label that marked it as "Exhibit 112" in the Watergate conspiracy trial held before Judge John Sirica in November 1974. I carried most of the cash around in a brown paper bag. I called it my "lunch." Thumbtacked to a bulletin board in my kitchen is a lunch bag imprinted with the words "TONY's BAG." My wife gave it to me for my birthday.

Some of the visitors who have come to my home have been unknown and uninvited. The dropping of a sawbuck down the road at one of the local watering holes tells them the way up my hill. They come to pick at my mind like children on a treasure hunt. "Tony," they ask me, "where do we go from here? You're the last stop. We can't go any further unless you can help us verify . . ." I'm polite and invite them in if the weather is bad, but the most direction I'll give a stranger is the way back down the hill. Others have saved themselves the trip north and have instead used the telephone to offer me a spot on a payroll to find out what I know; one offered me a free trip south to Florida, just for a little chat, to find out what I knew about Chappaquiddick. I have been promised status and anonymity as a most reliable source. "What's the real story, Tony?," I've been asked at all hours of the day and night. After the Watergate scandal broke, scavengers with buzzing gadgets and government badges came to my home like the gnats of summer hoping to find buried treasure beneath the frost line. I had to shoo others away who were hiding in my garden, popping up like jack-in-the-boxes to snap my picture through the kitchen window. In my yard, camera crews with their floating eyes sometimes tripped on their cables as they tried to get out of the way of my chickens.

In early 1977, I ran into H. R. Haldeman, former White House Chief of Staff under President Nixon, at New York's La Guardia Airport. It was on the very day Haldeman had been released from prison after serving his sentence for conspiring to obstruct the government's Watergate investigation. My wife Mary was with me; she was on her way to Florida to visit her brother. Haldeman was also accompanied by his wife. After greetings and handshakes, we all headed for the airport coffee shop. During our conversation Haldeman paused once and said, "You know, Tony, the problem is we needed someone with street smarts, someone to guide us through all of this. You were there all the time, right under our noses. We didn't realize what we had. We couldn't see."

The now famous Nixon White House tapes reveal that in March 1973, then White House Counsel John Dean told the President that I was "probably the most knowledgeable man in the country" with regard to the Chappaquiddick affair. Dean was describing my work investigating Chappaquiddick. Dean told Nixon that he thought I "ran up against walls and they closed the records down." This was said at a time when the White House was stonewalling the investigation into its own conduct and shredding its own records. My work for President Nixon took me inside Kennedy's coverup of Chappaquiddick and, after three years on the job, into the President's own coverup of Watergate. Dean also told the President that there were some things I couldn't find out, but that as a twenty-year detective I could ask the right questions. "But we don't want to surface him right now," Dean said to Nixon. "If he is ever surfaced, this is what they will get."

When I finally surfaced as "the mystery voice with the New York accent," before the United States Senate Watergate Committee in May 1973, the press described me as a "secret agent," a "sly fox," a "bagman," a "gumshoe"; as "droll," "cuddly," "Runyonesque" and "Shakespearean." That's enough to stuff an attic.

"Who thought you up?," Senator Howard Baker of Tennessee asked

6

me at one point during my testimony at the Watergate hearings. The audience in the Senate Caucus Room roared. Baker's question seemed more appropriate as a cartoon caption than in the gloom and doom staging of President Nixon's fall from power. Baker's question bothered me. It made me feel more like a vaudeville comedian than a subpoened witness at a Senate hearing. I didn't intend my answer to Baker's question to trigger another burst of laughter—it was actually a throwaway line—when I said, "I don't know, but maybe my parents." The audience roared again. What I wanted to say was, "Senator, do you really want to know who I am, where I come from, what I think of all this? Do you have all day? I'll tell you, Senator. I'll tell you my story."

M Y parents were Polish immigrants. My father, Joseph Ulasewicz, came to America in 1910 from the Polish sector of southern Russia, near Minsk, by the Black Sea. My mother, Leokadia Smolski, came in 1914 from a depressed mining area in southeastern Poland with her only brother. My parents met at one of the many Polish gatherings sponsored for new immigrants by St. Stanislaus Catholic Church on East Seventh Street on New York's Lower East Side. Churches like St. Stanislaus, as well as Jewish synagogues, brought immigrants together and also helped them find jobs and places to live. My mother and father were married in St. Stanislaus Church in 1915. As for having children, I wasn't my parents' first idea; that was reserved for my brother Leo, named in tribute to my mother. I was born at home on December 14, 1918, right after the end of World War I. I was named after my father's brother, Antoni. There were no scales then to weigh babies, but the betting line in the neighborhood said that I entered the ring at fourteen pounds. "You were some Jabka!" (a big apple), my mother used to tell me. Eight years later, in 1926, my younger brother, Joseph, Jr., was born.

We lived in an apartment house at 718 East Fifth Street. We had the first floor living quarters because my mother was the janitor of the building. She had been a charwoman, cleaning uptown office buildings, when she married my father. He was a tailor who worked downtown in the sweatshops of the garment industry. Our home was in a Jewish

7

neighborhood situated just shy of the Polish-Ukrainian sector on the Lower East Side. We were the only Christians on the block. On the Sabbath, Christian "shabus" kids like me scurried up fire escapes to turn on the lights and the heat for our Jewish neighbors while they prayed at Temple. Each family paid us a penny for the task.

There was no firewood on the Lower East Side of New York. Except for the burning of furniture and food crates during the Great Depression, coal heated everything. It cost fifty cents a ton. A man could earn a buck a day delivering coal. That was a lot of money then. Hauling coal was back-breaking, dirty work. At the end of a day, when exhaustion or the effects of too many swigs of booze caused the deliveryman to misdirect the coal onto the sidewalks of my neighborhood, my older brother and I would hustle out with our brooms to clean up the mess. The owner of a speakeasy and the madams of several tenement brothels in the neighborhood paid us to keep the entrances to their establishments spotless. The brothel madams were the best tippers. My mother yanked us out of the butcher shop by our ears, however, if one of them walked in while she was shopping. They were always dressed and made up like they were ready to go on stage. Most of them wore heavy, brocaded, colored fabrics. (I used to think they wrapped themselves up in living room drapes.) What I learned in the streets and what my mother wanted me to know didn't always match.

To make an extra buck on weekends, I planted myself with my shoeshine kit on the steps of the Clinton Street Station House near the Williamsburg Bridge, or outside the Ninth Precinct on Fifth Street. There, when the police changed shifts, I caught tips shining shoes for cops, especially the ones who wore a suit, not a uniform, a big hat, and a diamond ring on the pinky. Plainclothes detectives liked to get their shoes shined posing on the steps of the precinct. It made them feel like a big deal, and some of them tipped accordingly. Uniformed patrolman had their shoes shined inside the precinct by a man paid to shine shoes. Money was deducted every month from a cop's paycheck to pay the shoeshine man along with the maids who cleaned and changed the beds in the precinct's dormitory. I had to carry my shoeshine kit to the precincts in a muslin flour bag because my father wanted it hidden. He was a proud man and didn't want it known that his family needed every cent we could scrape together.

My father would never go near a police station. He would cross to the other side of the street rather than pass directly in front of one. Uniforms meant soldiers to him, and they symbolized bloodshed or war, not the management of peace. When he was ten years old, a wild, roving band of Russian Cossacks plucked him off his family's farm while he was working in the field. He was taken to a Cossack camp and thrown on a pile of dung. He never saw his mother and father or his brothers and sisters again. My father traveled with the Cossacks for ten years, caring for their horses, repairing their uniforms and stitching and polishing their boots. In the process, he learned the skills of a tailor. He also learned to play an accordion. With it, my father escaped from the Cossacks with the help of a traveling circus he joined. He headed southwest across Europe until he came to the sea and crossed to America. My father told me that he had seen too many examples of Cossack violence and pillage, of the cheapness made of life, to trust a gendarme's uniform. "Pop, they're called cops in America," I used to tell him. "A gendarme is a gendarme," he'd always respond. There was no changing my father's opinions. During his life with the Cossacks, he said he saw men in uniforms kill and burn and rape until they collapsed in heaps of stained and drunken silence. My father thought the purpose of the police was to protect him, his family, and his property. He didn't like the idea of people in uniforms telling people where to walk, how to behave, or where they could gather to speak their minds. He never forgot the loss of his parents. He kept his vigil and stayed away from uniforms.

While my father may have avoided contact with the police, he didn't know how to avoid trouble. His tailoring expertise, learned from his years with the Cossacks, kept him working six days a week, sometimes seven, for the pay of five. In the basement of St. Stanislaus Church, my father met with other workers from the garment industry to help organize a clothing workers union. Returning home from school one day, I found him bloodied and battered in the hallway outside our apartment. He was hanging onto a bannister. I could hear my mother crying inside the apartment. My father had told her to stay inside and keep the door

9

locked. Management's union busters—then the same gangsters who enforced the underworld's protection rackets—beat a message into his face to stop trying to organize a union. These goons had wanted to beat him up inside our apartment so they wouldn't be seen or be caught in the act, but my father wouldn't let them in. His home was a sacred place, and he would have fought to his death to protect it.

It never crossed my father's mind that the establishment of a union had anything to do with politics, naive as that may sound today. He simply wanted better working conditions for himself and his fellow workers. He told my brothers and me that before coming to America he had heard stories repeated over and over that America's streets were paved with gold. When he got here, he told us he found the cobblestone streets were paved with "konskie gowno" (horse shit), not gold; instead, he looked to opportunity, and he was determined that no one would deprive him of it.

At first, my father's battle and those of others like him were fought one on one with industry management; it was little David (without a slingshot) against a growing Goliath. Glib spokesmen moved on the scene and began rallying workers to their cause: capitalism was evil, adults and children were being made slaves to labor, it was time to rise up and revolt. Some of these men carried the banner of communism. Not that they were necessarily members of the Communist Party in the United States—that came later, after Russia's Bolshevik Revolution in 1917. Rather, my father knew these men to have been communists or anarchists in Europe before coming to America. They were immigrants like himself. Once here, they made no bones about their true beliefs. They used their newfound freedom to say anything they wanted, anytime, anyplace. They talked at work, at church gatherings, in the synagogues, on street corners, and at rallies in Union Square. Freedom, however coveted, made people vulnerable, gullible, and trusting. Men who wanted to satisfy their greed for power played with freedom of speech like it was a toy. My father was a fighter, not a communicator. He simply believed that a workers union was the best way to improve the conditions under which he labored. He hated to see the purpose of a union twisted out of shape. He was a charter member of the Amalgamated Clothing Workers Union of America. His beating made him fight even harder to improve the quality of his life and of his fellow workers.

POLICE precincts on the Lower East Side were positioned like outposts on an immigrant plantation. I did not share my father's distrust of uniforms: For me, a cop was a walking, breathing, mobile buffer zone. He was The Man, The Prosecutor, The Defender, The Judge, The Jury, and, thank God, The Redeemer. He chased us back to where we belonged if we crossed the boundaries of our turf and tried to sneak uptown past Fourteenth Street. That was another world where we were told we didn't belong; if a gang from another neighborhood invaded our territory and there was a fight, a cop was always around to break it up. He helped clear the streets for neighborhood stickball games; he broke up our crap games in the alley and the five card stud we played on tenement stoops; on Sunday he stood like a shepherd in the back of the church. He kept our streets secure.

To have a cop's badge was to have a ticket out of the immigrant plantation; it provided a clear passage north, south, east, and west. When the police came out of a precinct and stopped for a shine, I felt that with the badge they carried, they owned the world. A badge commanded respect. It had the power to stop things from happening. Why, it could stiffen us up in a pool hall as straight as a cue stick. I wanted a round-trip ticket—to someday stand on the steps of a precinct in my neighborhood and have my shoes shined; I wanted to wear a big hat and someday see a kid smile when I tossed him two bits; I wanted to help protect the people and property of my neighborhood. I wanted to be a cop.

Before I was old enough to think seriously about wearing a uniform and a shield, however, I was running in the streets of the Lower East Side where I was Captain of the Meteors, a gang of kids from East Fifth Street. The Meteors were made up of Ukrainians, Lithuanians, Gypsies, Poles like me, and one black kid named Nicodemus. He and his family seemed to have been stranded on the Lower East Side; most black families had already migrated north toward Harlem. In 1933, my Meteors won second place honors and a trophy (I still have it) when the

11

Boys Club of New York sponsored the citywide Olympics of the Streets. We swam and ran track; we played basketball, baseball, stickball, tiddlywinks, and every other game imaginable, except football; we pitted our street skills against the Irish, the Italians, the Germans, the rich and the poor—kids from all over the city.

Any chance to play was a chance for us to triumph. Life was cheap in the streets; risking it was fun. We pressed against the edge. Sometimes the challenge ended in death, like the time a friend drowned when he got stuck in the ooze and debris at the bottom of the East River after diving off a pier, or the time I lost another member of the Meteors when he plunged down an areaway, between buildings, while running a foot race across tenement roofs. In the heat of the summer we had the choice of fire hydrants opened in the streets or a dive in the East River to cool us off; I preferred the river. I used to swim across to Brooklyn, then walk back home across the Williamsburg Bridge. My mother dreaded my swimming in the East River with its punishing currents and its traffic of tankers and tugboats.

In most of our homes, churches, and synagogues, we were told to shut up, learn, and be grateful for what we had. If I got a little wise at St. Stanislaus parochial school, a Felician Sister would whack me on the head with her crucifix. If I complained about it at home, I would get whomped again for causing trouble in the first place; my father's razor strap was always available.

Crime on the Lower East Side was commonplace. Stickups were tried by boys I knew, with guns they had stolen or won in a fight. For their efforts, most of them got a free trip north, in handcuffs and shackles, to Sing Sing Prison. A few even made it to the electric chair. As a kid I remember racking billiard balls one Friday night in a pool hall on the corner of Fifth Street and Avenue B when the crack of a pistol shot spread-eagled a pool shark up against a wall. Everyone ran for cover. A men's room big enough for only one person was suddenly stuffed with a dozen; I dove under one of the pool tables. That's where I was, looking at the hit man's spats, when he fired off another shot. The pool shark slithered down the wall. I stared at the dead man's head. I was so stunned I couldn't tell whether the color of his blood was red or gray; the man's brains were mixed in with the sawdust on the pool room floor. When the spats moved out of view, someone grabbed hold of my apron strings and began pulling me out from underneath the table. "Oh, my God," I thought, "I'm gonna get shot!" It was worse than a bad dream. I waited for the bullet. "Hey, kid," one of the pool hall owners yelled at me as my head came out from under the table. "You better get out of here. We'll take you home. There's a limousine outside. Get in it and keep down. We don't want any trouble. You're under age." Under age?! The pool owners were more worried about cops shutting them down because I was working there under age than they were about the shots and the mess and the body and the guy with the spats.

My mother died the same year my Meteors competed for the trophy in the Olympics of the Streets. She was stricken with viral pneumonia and taken to the hospital. Because neither sulfa drugs nor penicillin were available then, she didn't make it. My mother's death was one of the saddest times of my entire life. When she went to the hospital, the thought never crossed my mind that she wouldn't be coming back. That was a terrible shock to me. Because of my father's long hours of work, my brothers and I would spend most of our time with our mother when we weren't in school or out hustling for a buck with our brooms or shoeshine kits. She used to ask me to brush her hair. It was long and blond and hung down to her waist when she let it fall. She had no daughters to help her with her chores. When my father came home, we would have dinner. When we finished, he would ask my brothers and me to report what had happened to us during the day. We had a disciplined household. My mother's advice combined with my father's strap taught me that you couldn't win, you couldn't survive if you got into trouble. "Keep your wits about you, have fun and behave yourself," they told me. "Don't become a man until you finish being a boy. You'll be a man soon enough." These were my parents' commandments.

On the day of my mother's funeral, there was a procession from our home on Fifth Street to St. Stanislaus Church. Our Jewish neighbors helped clean up the streets. Every organization in the church marched in the procession in honor of my mother. They carried banners draped with colored ribbons. Friends and neighbors dressed up in their finest clothing, the dress of their native lands. The procession seemed to blossom like a flower garden. Even with the awful emptiness I felt with

13

her loss, care and hope and beauty were in the air on the day she was buried. The day of her funeral was like a rainbow in the dark. After her burial, I remember being alone for awhile in our apartment. I looked at the kitchen floor and saw that it needed to be cleaned; that was one of my chores. It was time to go back to work, I thought, time to move on, to go forward and never look back. Shed your tears and keep going. If I've ever had a motto in life, that's it. I got out the pail and mop and scrubbed the floor spotless.

I N 1937, after I graduated from Peter Stuyvesant Public High School, I joined the Army National Guard. I was eighteen at the time, too young to join the New York City Police Department, but not too young to harvest credentials for my record when I applied for the right to wear a shield. The year I graduated, my dream of being a cop was almost beaten out of me by two Ukrainian hoods. It happened after I had gone to a dance at the Ukrainian Hall on East Sixth Street with my girl (now my wife) Mary Dumiak. Mary and her family were Ukrainian. She moved into my neighborhood in 1931. Most of our dates were spent holding hands on the Williamsburg Bridge. We used to walk halfway across, then stop and scan the world around us. It was an inexpensive, beautiful time together. It didn't cost us a dime to look back at the horizon of New York, as the sun set on a summer night.

Going to a church-sponsored dance on a weekend was a big treat for the kids in our neighborhood. If Mary and I weren't out taking a walk and holding hands, we usually headed for the Ukrainian Hall on East Sixth Street. The dance hall was upstairs, and a pool hall and a bar were downstairs. One night while we were upstairs dancing the polka, a fight broke out below. The manager of the Ukrainian Hall was badly beaten over the head with a cue stick. Demetrius Gula and Joseph Sacoda, two Ukrainian tough guys, came upstairs and asked me to step outside. It was more of an order than a request. Gula's father had been the one who absorbed the blows, and his son and buddy, Sacoda, thought I knew who did it. Gula and Sacoda told me somebody had squealed and said the blows were struck by one of the members of the "Fifth Street Gang." That meant one of my boys from the Meteors. Gula and Sacoda grabbed me by my arms and hauled me out of the Hall into a nearby alley. "Tell us who did it, kid, or you're not going back inside." I told them I didn't know anything about the beating and that I was with my girl the whole time. (I had a pretty good idea who put the dent in old man Gula's noggin, but I sure wasn't about to share my opinion.)

When I didn't tell them what they wanted to know, Gula and Sacoda began tearing me up. They pounded my gut with their fists; they broke one of my teeth and cut my mouth. I was dazed and bloodied. They walked me around the block, telling me more would come my way if I didn't own up to who did it. Life and death on the Lower East Side depended on how much you kept your mouth shut. Sometimes it became a losing proposition, either way you called the shot. After beating me up, these goons tried to soften me up by buying me an egg cream. They asked me if I wanted to join up with them. They said they had a good thing going. I drank the egg cream and said no thanks. Finally, after a parting swipe at the side of my head, Gula and Sacoda gave up and left me sitting alone on a tenement stoop. I could hardly stand up. I held a bloody handkerchief to my face and wondered what I was going to tell my father about what happened to my new suit. Before Gula and Sacoda changed their minds and came back after me, I headed back to the dance hall to pick up Mary and take her home. In those days, if you took a girl to a dance you brought her home. If you didn't, you'd never hold her hand again. When she spotted me coming she looked startled and scared. "Don't say a thing, Mary," I said. "Let's get out of here. I'll tell you later."

A few years later, on January 11, 1940, Gula and Sacoda were executed at Sing Sing Prison for kidnapping a businessman from Westchester County named Arthur Fried. It was the first execution in New York under the "Little Lindbergh" law that was passed after Congress made kidnapping a federal offense punishable by death. Fried's body was never found, but the word in the streets was that after Fried was snatched, he was shot in the head, his body hacked into pieces and then stuffed in the furnace in the basement of the Ukrainian Hall (where I went to dance with Mary). Gula and Sacoda led the "Ukrainian Hall Gang" (the one they wanted me to join) that was suspected of murdering Bowery derelicts in order to collect on insurance policies they forced

15

these bums to take out in exchange for getting them a job. A member of Gula and Sacoda's gang took turns being named as the beneficiary. Once they buried the bones, it was time to collect.

Having survived my ordeal at Gula and Sacoda's hands, I reported for duty as a "Buck" Private in the Army National Guard. I was assigned to the 102nd Engineers Corps, stationed at the 168th Street Armory, in Manhattan. Because of some bureaucratic foul up, part of my last name got chopped off on my induction papers. I was known officially as Anthony Ulas instead of Ulasewicz. Soon, my buddies in the service reduced the Ulas to just "U"—a name, along with Tony, that has stuck to me all my life. Whenever I hear someone yell, "Hey, you," I always turn around.

In high school, I developed a keen interest in photography. After graduation, while still waiting to hear from the National Guard, I started my own business called Ulas Photo Service. My brochures read: "Snappy, Intelligent Service. Everything Legal." As soon as I was inducted into the Guard, I put in an application for a transfer to the 102nd Observation Squadron located at Miller Field on Staten Island. (There was no separate United States Air Force at the time; the Air Force was a wing of the Army.) My application was granted, and I was assigned to duty as an aerial photographer; once I was in the air, I took photographs for use in making aerial maps and surveys of the Atlantic coastline from Maine to the Carolinas.

Sometimes, I flew over the entire city of New York. I was no longer out of bounds; there was no cop in the sky to tell me to get back to Fifth Street where I belonged. I flew north of Fourteenth Street and over Central Park; I flew west, over the Hudson River, and then across the currents of the East River, where I had learned to swim. Below me, life in the city was changing rapidly. Prohibition had been given a one-way ticket into history; the Depression of the 1930s was under the demolition ball of the National Recovery Act, the Civilian Conservation Corps, and the promises of Franklin Delano Roosevelt. South of Fourteenth Street, empty egg crates and fruit boxes that had been stacked for shelter gradually disappeared. The furnishings of evicted families no longer blocked the sidewalks. In their place, stoves, refrigerators, washing machines, and radios stood waiting to be hauled up tenement stairs.

In September 1940, Mary and I got married. While the Germans were starting World War II, the Ulasewicz and Dumiak families were busy with a battle of their own over which church, Polish or Ukrainian, would house the wedding ceremony. My father, claiming immigrant seniority over the Dumiaks, insisted that we be married in St. Stanislaus Church where he and my mother were married in 1915. The Dumiak clan arrived in America several years after my father. Mary's father claimed the tradition of the bride's right of choice but kept the choice for himself. Mary wanted to be married in St. Stanislaus; her father refused to permit it. He said that we had to be married in the Ukrainian Church. Both fathers became stubborn mules and would have let our dreams rot if we hadn't threatened revolt. We told them that they could come to City Hall if they wanted to witness the ceremony. If they stood their ground, we were going to stand ours. We weren't going to get married in either church. It was defiance, but Mary and I loved each other. Finally, in one desperate attempt to salvage the family peace, Mary and I knocked on the door of the Pastor of Our Most Holy Redeemer, a German Catholic Church on East Third Street, and begged him to intervene. The pastor, sympathizing with our plight, arranged for a dispensation from the strict jurisdictional rules of the Catholic Church that prohibited us from switching parishes. (That was our respective fathers' last card in the deck to play, but we beat them to it.) The Pastor married us with our fathers in attendance.

Our wedding reception was a disaster. Not because our families fought or wouldn't speak to each other, but because gate crashers invaded the party. On the Lower East Side, a good party was a target for freeloaders; anyone willing to pay the freight risked having their affair invaded. Plenty of gate crashers forced their way inside our reception, and within minutes the bar that had been specially set up was torn loose from the floor and shoved through a plate glass window; we were on the second floor. Fortunately, the bar got stuck in the frame of the window; otherwise, it would have landed on the sidewalk below or on someone's unsuspecting head. Mary and I dashed from the debris of broken glass and broken noses to try to start a peaceful life together despite all the trouble involved in starting it.

On February 23, 1941, I was honorably discharged from the Army

National Guard with the rank of Specialist First Class, which was the equivalent of being a Buck Sergeant in the regular army. During my tour of duty with the Guard, when I had time off I signed up and took every New York City civil service exam listed, regardless of the job category, as practice for the Police Department test. After my discharge from the Guard, I took so many exams and fit so many categories that the Civil Service Commission didn't know where to put me or what my pay classification should be. I took the police exam and passed it, but there were no openings in the Department then. The closest I could get to being a policeman was to join the New York City Transit Department— again as a photographer, assigned to take pictures of accident scenes anywhere a moving target belonging to the City of New York got clobbered.

Two years later, I received my notice to appear for my appointment as a probationary policeman. I was sworn in on February 17, 1943. Recruits were then in short supply because of the war, and attendance at the Police Academy lasted as long as it took the tailor to scrape together enough material to make a uniform. Because of the war, cloth for police uniforms was in short supply. Sometimes the coat and pants didn't match the season; winter wool, for example, had to be worn in the summer. I had to take out a loan from the Police Department to pay for my uniform. It was ready right before the St. Patrick's Day parade on March 17. Marching orders for rookies put us in the front ranks of the Department's veteran contingent, right behind the cavalry. "It's your job to pave the way," said a wisecracking sergeant. When the whistle blew, the trumpets blared, the bass drum boomed, and the drum major signalled for us to step off, the horses in front of me whinnied and my freshly shined black shoes quickly turned a dull brown as we marched off into glory.

After the parade, I might just as well have kept on marching. My precinct assignment was north to Harlem, an area I'd never explored before; it was talked about below Fourteenth Street but never visited. The only black I had ever known was my friend Nicodemus from the Meteors. I was sent to the Twenty-fifth Precinct where I joined a curdled mixture of top-grade cops, rookies like myself, and a variety of busted plainclothesmen who were exiled to a Harlem precinct for recycling.

Harlem was the purgatory of the Police Department. Make a mistake, goof off, get caught with your hand in the cookie jar and it was off to Harlem you went—if you didn't get canned from the job altogether. Without an Irish Hook or a Jewish Rabbi to put in the good word at police headquarters on Centre Street, a name like Ulasewicz didn't qualify for a preferred downtown precinct assignment. Geographically, the Twenty-fifth Precinct covered the smallest territory of the four precincts making up the Police Department's Seventh Division. Its jurisdiction stretched north from 116th Street to where the East and Harlem rivers met under the Triborough Bridge, then west to Fifth Avenue and north again to 139th Street. The boundaries of my precinct followed the contour of the East and Harlem rivers as they curved around the northern tip of Manhattan.

On my first walking tour of duty, someone threw a milk bottle at me from a tenement window. It smashed at my feet, and the milk splattered my shoes and pants. "At least you were worth a full bottle," the desk sergeant quipped when I returned to the safety of the precinct. On the Lower East Side, we had our ethnic jealousies, our battlegrounds and our territories, but nobody exhibited the outright hatred for the man with the badge that I witnessed in Harlem; the air was full of suspicion, we were to be avoided at all costs, the badge was a symbol of doom and gloom. And yet I liked Harlem; the sound of its heartbeat seemed put through an amplifier. From the Gospel singing in churches, to shows at the Apollo Theater, to the playing of jazz far into the night at the Cotton Club and after-hour joints, Harlem was always alive with song and dance. There was violence and crime all around me, but there were also decent, hard-working families trying to raise kids, make a buck, and survive to live another day. In Harlem, I had all the action I wanted or could ever handle.

I had about as much time to prepare for my first arrest as I had to duck the bottle of milk that landed at my feet. I was on foot patrol one night when a big, drunken Finnish sailor came out of the Viking Restaurant and Bar on 125th Street between Lexington and Park Avenues. The bar was across the street from a firehouse. The Finn was three times my size, and I was a big cop. He swayed and lurched, back and forth, then stumbled into the middle of the street where he began yelling at the sky;

19

it sounded like he was trying to call one of his Viking gods into action. I told him to quiet down. "Quiet down?," the huge Finn asked me and kept looking at me with a face full of disbelief. "I show you how I quiet down," he said. He picked up an iron "NO PARKING" stanchion from in front of the firehouse and threw it all the way across the street right through the Viking Bar's plate glass window. "What the hell do I do now?," I said to myself. "Arrest him? Forget about him? Check if anybody's hurt? Call the precinct?" In the Police Academy you're told that if you see a crime occurring, you have a duty to make an arrest. How do you arrest a man who could pick you up by the ankles and throw you over the roof? I decided to leave the Finn for awhile and went into the bar. The bartender, acting as if it was business as usual, moved the stanchion out of the way and brushed the shards of glass into a pile. "Happens all the time," he said. "These Finns get off their ships after six months and go crazy. I don't let anyone sit next to the window. I reserve the space for broken glass." He said that he knew what was coming when the Finn left the bar. "I already called the precinct before you showed up."

When I went back outside to check on the Finn, I saw that a patrol car had already arrived at the scene. The officer was out of the car, stalking him like a hunter after big game. "I'll show you how to take care of this kid," the officer said as he took my night stick and flattened the Finn with one shot. "That settles that," he said. "Let's pick 'im up and haul him in." By the time I made the rounds on my patrol the next night, the window of the bar had been fixed and made ready for the next missile to be hurled its way.

On the hot Sunday night of August 1, 1943, during my rookie year, Harlem exploded into one of the worst riots New York City has ever seen. On the night of the riot, I was working the four-to-midnight shift and was just returning to the precinct from night court when I spotted a flatbed truck parked in front loaded with parade barriers. Other patrolmen wearing civil defense helmets were climbing on board. I had barely got my foot inside the precinct when I was ordered to grab a helmet and get on the truck. All I knew then was that we were going across town to the Twenty-eighth Precinct to help break up a riot. On the way over there, the truck stalled at an intersection. Within seconds all of us on

20

board had to dive for cover as a shower of bottles, rocks, pieces of furniture, garbage, slop pots and the limbs of some store front mannequins began landing on our heads. We were suddenly surrounded by scores of angry rioters who began pulling the parade barriers off the truck and started using them as battering rams to smash store front windows. The rioters would have smashed our heads, too, if we hadn't started running for our lives. As soon as I reached the "Two-eight," I was sent back into the streets to break up the rioters on Seventh Avenue between 116th and 125th Streets. I was sent out as part of a three-man team, one of several that was ordered to break up the rioters into smaller groups and keep them from gathering strength until reinforcements arrived from downtown precincts. I spent almost five hours desperately trying to scatter the rioters and quiet things down; but it was no use, they just got louder and louder, more threatening and violent as they grew in number. The only thing I was able to break apart was my night stick. By 5 a.m., I and my other team mates had managed to move only two blocks. We threw away our helmets as too unwieldy, had our uniforms torn, garbage thrown at us, and were shot at. Bullets were being fired from every direction. We couldn't see who was firing the shots. The warning shots we fired into the air had no effect on the roving mobs. Each of us had been issued sixty extra rounds of ammunition but they may as well have been a thousand. At one point, I watched a blockade of rioters stop a fire engine clanging up Seventh Avenue dead in its tracks. Just as we had done when the flatbed truck stalled at the intersection, the firemen jumped off the firetruck and ran for their lives. The rioters pulled a ladder off the truck and, using it like a crowbar, bent open the steel gates protecting the front of a liquor store, then shattered the glass, swishing the ladder back and forth like the tail of a frenzied shark.

When I finally made it back to the "Two-eight," the riot was still out of control and I still didn't know exactly what started it. A hot night in Harlem was like heating gasoline on a stove. It could explode at any time, but this was more like a war that no one was going to win. At the time of the riot, Fiorello LaGuardia, "The Little Flower," was Mayor of the city. At the height of the riot, he showed up at the Twenty-eighth Precinct with a bull horn and a sound truck. He rode the streets for awhile trying to preach calm to everyone, but nobody was listening. He, too, was pelted with debris and soon headed back to the precinct for cover, which became his operating headquarters. Preceding the Mayor to Harlem were some spit and polish police brass wearing braided hats, shiny buttons, and white gloves. A carrot-topped sergeant from some downtown precinct, oblivious to the rioting world outside, kept yelling at me and the other members of my team, "You're all out of uniform!" which was a stunning statement to our battered group, some of us bloodied, all of us with our uniforms shredded, and none of us wearing hats or helmets. Suddenly, we were ordered into a back room and told to sit on the floor and wait; we were locked in, and the brass began taking our names. First, they took our shields and guns away, and then they began sniffing the barrels, asking us how many times our guns were fired. The carrot-topped sergeant, with his white gloves still spotlessly clean, hollered at us in disbelief, "You fired sixty shots?" as if he had never heard of a bullet.

For what seemed like hours, we paced the floor wondering what the confinement was all about and what in the world had started the riot. "Why were we being isolated?," we asked each other. Cops were coming into Harlem from all over the city. Why weren't we being asked to join them? The questions they asked us earlier in the night clearly suggested that charges of police brutality had already been leveled at the Department. People had been shot, and some were dead. As we found out, black leaders were accusing cops of being trigger happy. Not everybody, they said, had shot their guns into the sky to warn and scatter the rioters. Not liking the way we were being treated, we asked the Police Benevolent Association to step in. We specifically asked John Chanda, our PBA delegate, to get us out of this back room. The police brass from downtown were adopting the politicians' claim that we had somehow mishandled the riot. Both groups were looking for a scapegoat to take the blame. We made up our minds it wasn't going to be us. It was the first time that my life as a cop had become wedded to politics. I didn't like the feeling.

The riot was a bad break for Harlem. It happened on a Sunday night when the better brains in the Police Department, the men in command in Harlem, weren't around. The riot started as the result of a false rumor that a white cop had killed a black soldier who was home on leave from the Army. Patrolman James Collins, a white cop from the Twenty-eighth Precinct, was walking his beat near the Hotel Braddock on 126th Street when a woman patron of the hotel stopped him. She complained that after she had checked the quality of her accommodations and rated them lousy, the desk clerk refused to give her a refund. Collins and the woman went back inside the hotel. There, in front of the desk clerk, the woman let loose with a barrage of profanity loud enough to pummel Brooklyn. Collins tried to quiet her down. When she refused, he warned her that if she kept it up she was going to get herself arrested for disorderly conduct (breaching the peace). When she kept up her yelling and cursing, he tried to place her under arrest. The woman now started swearing at Collins as well. Hearing the commotion, Robert Bandy, a black soldier on leave from the Army, came on the scene, took the woman's side of the story, and began arguing with Collins. They began to struggle; Bandy took away Collins's night stick and hit him over the head with it. As Bandy fled the hotel, Collins fired his service revolver and shot him in the shoulder. Within minutes, both were on their way to Sydenham Hospital. While all the shouting and shoving had been going on inside the hotel, a crowd had gathered outside; it soon grew ugly and menacing. When a shout was heard above the grumbling that the black soldier was probably dead, the crowd erupted like a volcano and the riot was on. Before it stopped, it would burn even the sunrise.

To squelch the rumor spreading in the streets that Bandy had been killed, many key people—Harlem precinct captains, church leaders, detectives with important connections in the legitimate and illegitimate worlds of Harlem—couldn't be brought back to the job fast enough to take control and turn down the heat. The only people left in Harlem that hot August night were the ones who suffered there every day; the ones who were broke all the time, living off their welfare checks, having nowhere to go. For many of these people, Harlem was a land of dried up dreams. Big, strong black men from the South rode the rails to New York hoping to earn enough money that would allow them to bring their families out of the South. Instead, many of them ended up shriveled in the streets, carved up in ugly fights, blistered by lye thrown in their faces, and crusted over with plenty of jail time. Those who did find jobs usually ended up cleaning up someone else's mess, handing out towels in

23

a men's room, scrubbing floors, carrying luggage, or shining shoes. On the night of the riot, those left in Harlem were stuck in a smoldering pot. They were the ones left to explode. The rumor, the heat, the booze pouring down throats, the sight of fire trucks, clanging bells, sirens, the barriers, the sight of a white cop firing his gun at a black man—all proved too much. A war was started that nobody could win. The meager trust that we had worked so hard to build in Harlem was shattered for a long time to come.

Harlem's Seventh Division was a unit that worked by itself. The brass from downtown ignored it—like Harlem was some kind of Devil's Island—as long as it didn't interfere with anybody else's way of life. As long as nothing spilled over from Harlem's bowl to stain the rest of the city, the brass didn't care what happened there. When the brass had to react, as they did during the riot, every cop in Harlem became a sacrificial lamb. In the eyes of our fellow cops in Harlem, we were given credit for being out there risking our lives in a runaway riot, but in the hearts and minds of politicians and some of the police brass, we were the cause of it all. I didn't like the feeling. It took a long time for us to calm the hostile feelings we felt towards our superiors as well as the feelings the people of Harlem had towards anyone wearing a uniform. Even though we were exonerated from causing the riot and overreacting once it started, nothing would ever be the same for me in Harlem. But then again nothing ever seemed to change there, and I regretted that because there's no way a community can work together when there's nothing but hatred and suspicion on the streets.

While Harlem was almost self-destructing that summer, friends I had flown with in the National Guard were being killed in the war in Europe, flying aerial reconnaissance missions over Germany. In June 1944, I volunteered to return to military service. This time it was in the Navy. I didn't have to go because as a policeman I was exempt from the draft, but, like many others drawn to service, I joined up again. For the next year and a half I flew on reconnaissance missions as an aerial photographer over the Atlantic, Caribbean, and Pacific oceans. The orbit of my world was growing wider. I was stationed for a time in Norfolk, Virginia; Pensacola, Florida; and on a base in Alaska's Aleutian Islands. This time my hunt was for German and Japanese submarines and for Japanese task forces roaming near the Aleutian Islands.

On January 17, 1946, I received my second Honorable Discharge. A month later, I pinned my police shield back on and returned to the streets of Harlem. Upon my return to the Twenty-fifth Precinct, the number of arrests I made catapulted. It wasn't so much that crime was on the increase but that my time in the Navy had strengthened my chances of becoming a detective, which was what I wanted most. The more arrests a cop made, the better chance for a promotion. I became something of a nuisance to the Detective Bureau—to the "Brains" as we called them. A detective's opportunity to advance in grade from third to second to first (the gold shield) was governed in part by the number of felony arrests he made each month. If a uniformed cop like me made more key arrests than one of the "Brains" in a precinct, an irritating competition between ranks inevitably developed. The "Brains" and I started rubbing each other the wrong way. At times, I got tangled in so much paper work and made so many trips to the courthouse I was off patrol more than I was on. As a compromise with the "Brains," I began sharing credit with them for some of my arrests. It was like plucking petals off a daisy: one for you, one for me.

In Harlem, there was so much action every cop had his story for the day, and some days never seemed to end. I still vividly remember the end of one eight-to-four day shift in 1946, when I stopped to report in to the precinct from the call box on 125th Street next to the railroad station. A foot patrolman had to report in to the precinct every hour (or if he stopped to eat). If he didn't, a patrol car would be on the streets in minutes tracking down his whereabouts. Every call was logged in the police blotter. At the call box, I met a rookie cop who was making his last call to the precinct before coming off his beat. A taxi cab suddenly screeched to a halt at the curb right in front of us. The cabbie yelled, "Hold-up!, there's been a hold-up!, watch out for the cab behind me, there's two gunmen in it, they just nailed us, watch out, they're coming!" The cabbie then sped away, never to be seen again. As we turned our heads back in the other direction, another cab pulled up to the curb. The back door of the cab flew open, and a guy with a package under his arm lurched out onto the sidewalk. The rookie cop pulled out his service revolver and started firing. He plugged the guy with three shots—smack in his bellybutton—three cigarette burns Robin Hood couldn't match. Suddenly, I found myself in the middle of the street with my finger squeezing the trigger of my gun and pointing at the guts of a second man who bolted out the other side of the cab when the rookie fired his shots. "Don't shoot, don't shoot," the second man started yelling. "We're guards, we're guards from Rikers." The rookie cop had shot a prison guard from the New York City Penitentiary on Rikers Island. The guards were simply on their way home. I remember taking the pressure off the trigger, and I can still hear the screams of bystanders and the sounds of horns blowing and a train passing overhead, pounding the noise into my ears. "Assist patrolman! Assist patrolman!" echoed in every patrol car in Harlem. The sound of sirens became deafening. The rookie had shot and killed an innocent man. The wrong cab had pulled up to the curb. The right cab with the stick-up men just drove on by with their eyes glued to the frozen rookie and the dead guard on the sidewalk.

I don't know what time I got home. After the shooting came the questioning back at the precinct from the detective squad; then came the "Q & A" interrogation by an Assistant District Attorney from the D.A.'s homicide bureau; a grand jury investigation followed in a few days. I was asked the same questions over and over: "Why didn't you shoot? You were right next to him, couldn't you have stopped him?" I tried to explain that time didn't permit hesitation. The rookie was right next to the car door when it opened. The guard who was killed came out in a hurry, holding something under his arm that could have concealed a gun. The rookie reacted with an instinct for survival. Why didn't I shoot? Maybe it was just an extra edge of experience I wore with my uniform. Maybe but for the grace of God there go I. I wasn't standing on top of the door when it opened. What I thought was a predictable end of a day ended with an unpredictable shooting and the death of an innocent man. A cop lives his life on the job holding his breath; anything can happen at any given time.

Captain Walter Harkins, commanding officer of the Twenty-fifth Precinct, recommended me for the Police Department's Detective

School three different times, but his recommendation amounted to nothing more than a captain's salve rubbed on a patrolman's ego. Downtown, not uptown captains, controlled promotions. Even so, I took the Detective's exam every chance I had. My ears burned every time I was told, "Maybe next time" or "Give it another try." The examiners would never tell me my grade. I was getting shut out of an opportunity to advance, and I didn't intend to let the promotional hierarchy ignore me and think I would just go away. My one chance to find out my grade, without breaking into Police Headquarters and finding the answer myself, was through my partner in Harlem, Officer Frank Crowley. Crowley didn't have a hook or a Rabbi either; all he had was a cousin somewhere inside the Department's administrative bureaucracy who wasn't able to get him out of Harlem—and was Crowley teed off!

No matter how hard Crowley and I tried to get through the promotional barrier, nothing seemed to work. We even got our pictures in the paper and were awarded Honorable Mention as cops of the month for arresting three stickup men we had chased on foot all over Harlem. Crowley's downtown cousin finally came through with our exam grades; I had missed only one answer, but that still wasn't enough to get me through the promotional pecking order. I got a gold star for effort but not the shield of a detective.

I finally decided that the only person who could move me up in rank was the Police Commissioner of the city. The rule book— the Police Department's Manual of Procedures—said that any policeman could contact the Police Commissioner directly on any matter of importance. Well, it was important for me to be a detective. On January 5, 1949, I wrote a letter to Police Commissioner Arthur W. Wallender. It read:

Dear Commissioner Wallender:

At your convenience I would appreciate your granting me a personal interview relative to assignment to the Detective Division.

Respectfully,
Ptl. Anthony T. Ulasewicz
Shield 18076
25th Precinct

"You did what?!" Captain Harkins screamed when he found out about the letter. "You don't leapfrog over me and write a letter to the Commissioner!" Harkins wanted my head assigned to the steps of the precinct, skewered on a night stick. My letter was a one-man revolt against the promotion system. My partners in uniform told me I might as well have written to Santa Claus. But Police Commissioner Wallender surprised them all and granted me the interview. I was to report to his office the following week. I went there with pride in my record as a cop. I had already received four Police Department citations for excellent and meritorious duty, together with a commendation for disarming a felon who turned on me with a loaded gun after I had chased him into a hallway. The interview with Wallender was short, sweet, and to the point.

"Patrolman Ulasewicz," the interview began.

"Yes, sir?" I replied.

"I have reviewed your record. It's excellent. What can I do for you?"

"I want to be a detective," I said.

On February 1, 1949, less than a month after I wrote my letter to the Commissioner, I was back in his office. I stood there with eight other men who were also being raised to the rank of detective. This was Wallender's day for the swearing in of new recruits, of moving Division Commanders sideways and upwards, of appointing new Deputy Inspectors, of making the whole damn Police Department feel good about itself. He had shocked the political establishment a few days earlier with the announcement of his retirement, effective March 1. Wallender said he was going to start his last vacation as Commissioner the day after my appointment. Arthur Wallender was a man from the ranks who had made it to the top. In leaving, he wasn't going to let anyone think he had forgotten where he started.

As I stood waiting for my name to be called, I hoped my assignment would be back downtown in my old neighborhood; I wanted to get my shoes shined on the steps of a precinct and toss a kid two bits, but there were other plans for me.

"Ulasewicz!" the Chief Clerk of the Department called out crisply.

"Yes, sir?"

"Report to Special Services."

"Where?," I asked the clerk. I had never heard of Special Services.

"Ulasewicz," the clerk said as he looked at me in disbelief, "do you see that door over there? Go out and ask the man at the desk. He'll tell you."

When I went out that door I stepped into a career, first as a detective and later as the private-eye for the President of the United States, that would get me involved in one of the biggest conspiracies and coverups of the twentieth century.

BOSSI

THE door to Special Services was unmarked. It opened into the headquarters of the intelligence squad of the New York City Police Department. This brick and mortar unit helped build every other intelligence agency this country has ever known. Special Services was given a lot of different names over the years, but when I first joined, it was known as BOSSI, the Bureau of Special Service and Investigation.

Before I reported for duty, BOSSI's then Commanding Officer, Lieutenant Thomas F. Crane, gave me two days to clear up my precinct paper work. I took a good part of this time to find out as much as I could about Crane's command.

"BOSSI gets dumped on with all the investigations nobody else knows what to do with," an oldtimer in the Department told me. "If they show up at a precinct, nobody questions what they want. They wouldn't get an answer if they did. You're a BOSSI man, now, Tony. It's something different—I mean being a BOSSI man, well, that's something special. There's nothing else like it in 'the job.' " There wasn't and, as far as I'm concerned, there never will be.

Before I joined its ranks, BOSSI and its predecessors had been in operation for almost half a century. The squad was conceived at the turn of the century when police and immigration officials realized that once an immigrant had passed through the entry checkpoint on Ellis Island, no intelligence mechanism existed to keep track of the radical or criminal intentions aliens might have brought along with their luggage. While Immigration officials tried their best to ferret out anarchists, terrorists (they were around then, too), and gangsters through brief interrogations, the flood of immigrants kept them so busy trying to figure out the names of those coming here from so many different countries, they had little time for security checks, crude as they might have been. (My mother's first name was Leokadja, and the best they could make out of her Polish handwriting was to name her Lillian.) If anyone was pulled out of line, it was usually because they didn't have a passport, in which case their immigrant visa was then stamped WOP, With-Out-Passport. The Italians got branded with that logo more than any other nationality. Calling an Italian a WOP was cause for a fist in the teeth. Health officials were also concerned that an immigrant might be a carrier for one of Europe's devastating plagues.

In those early days, there were no sophisticated computer systems in place to match the profiles of suspected terrorists or violent radicals, no centralized fingerprint bureau to check an alien's arrest record, or any nationwide network in place to cross-check information with other intelligence agencies. Law enforcement on the federal level was still in its infancy. To develop information about alien ties to radical groups that might resort to violence in order to change our form of government, the Police Department established a citywide clearinghouse for information about any alien placed under arrest. The nature of the charge didn't matter. If convicted, the alien then faced possible deportation. Any radical organization suspected of promoting violence was put under surveillance. Unlike today's terrorist underground, attempts to recruit new immigrant blood into these organizations were all made out in the open. The roof tops I ran across as a kid were used as platforms for throwing propaganda leaflets to the people walking on the sidewalks below. The leaflets were produced in tenement basements converted into makeshift printing shops. We had to attend meetings and the rallies of these organizations, take pictures, and comb newspapers and magazines for any leads that might provide information about radical plans and activities.

BOSSI was first named the Italian Squad because one of its first tasks was to bust up the extortion rackets that flourished in Little Italy. The "Black Hand" from Sicily, exported to the streets of New York, spread fear, blackmail, extortion, and violence throughout the Italian immigrant population. Members of the Black Hand, known officially as the Camorra in Sicily, terrorized families and shopkeepers in New York's Little Italy. If payoffs weren't made on time, threats of kidnapping an immigrant's young daughter and turning her into a prostitute chilled the heart of many a struggling young father trying to support his family. After the Camorra was split apart in Sicily, the Mafia, or its fancier name, the Cosa Nostra, followed in its footsteps. (Unlike the Camorra, the Mafia has always been territorial in its operations—setting up little racket kingdoms that, given time, have blossomed into the equivalent size of a separate continent.)

The success of these rackets—whether sponsored by the Black Hand or the Mafia—soon spread to other parts of New York's Lower East Side. Racketeers began importing strong-arm enforcers to make sure the shakedown worked. By October 1912, the Italian Squad had broadened its role into monitoring the conduct of political radicals. The greed for political power matched the greed for money. The Italian Squad changed its name to the Radical Squad. The name changed again in 1914, when, partly because of President Wilson's efforts to form a League of Nations, BOSSI became known as the Neutrality Squad. This name also reflected political elements that didn't want America spreading itself so thin that it couldn't handle its own problems on its own shores. The "Neutrality" label was short-lived: we soon found ourselves sending troops overseas to fight the Germans in Europe during World War I. After the war, BOSSI switched its name back to the Radical Squad. Washington had to wake up to the fact that saboteurs and espionage agents were burrowing into our political soil. (On July 30, 1916, two years before I was born, a huge cache of explosives that had been stored on an island in New York Harbor were detonated by a saboteur. Almost fifty years later, militants

33

from the Black Liberation Front tried to blow up the Statue of Liberty. I was in BOSSI then, assigned to work undercover in an effort to stop things like that from happening.)

The Radical Squad (or the "Red Squad" as it came to be called) concentrated most of its efforts on Communist Party activities. The Bolshevik Revolution in Russia had stirred and idealized everyone's radical pot, and in November 1919, a massive effort was launched to try and put a lid on it. Seventy-three locations spread around the five boroughs of New York City were raided by a combined force of police, agents of the Department of Justice (J. Edgar Hoover was one of them), inspectors of the Immigration Service, and detectives from the Radical Squad. Tons of seditious literature advocating violent revolution were seized from printing shops, meeting rooms, editorial offices, and tenement basements. Hundreds were arrested, the largest number from a building on East Sixth Street, one block away from my home on East Fifth Street. Over the years, BOSSI's surveillance of Communist Party activities became something of a cat and mouse game. It was suspected that Party members kept BOSSI headquarters under surveillance, just as we did of their front organizations, taking pictures of everyone who entered the front door and then matching the faces against anyone thought to be a BOSSI agent. Sometimes we even gave the party back the records we obtained (after copies were made) by leaving them on the doorstep of *The Daily Worker*.

In 1924, three other intelligence units of the Police Department were put under BOSSI's umbrella: the Bomb Squad (to hunt down nuts and radicals trying to blow things up); the Industrial Squad (to investigate labor agitation, strikes, and boycotts and to help the city survive all three); and the Gangster Squad (to keep track of underworld movements and the wars over the control of territory). The Bureau was also given responsibility for protecting visiting dignitaries, both foreign and domestic, and for conducting other investigations as directed by the Chief of Detectives. That meant investigations conducted undercover. Effective January 1, 1931, all BOSSI units were placed under the jurisdiction of the Bureau of Criminal Alien Investigations. The Bureau's undercover operations functioned as a unit called Special Squad I. For a while, the Alien Squad and Special Squad I operated independently of each other, especially during the years Hitler was building his Nazi support base in Germany, and the German American Bund was feeding off the frustrations of German immigrants in this country. During the Second World War, these units merged. Undercover operators working in military defense establishments, such as the Brooklyn Navy Yard, had to have one chain of command. They worked side by side with regular shipyard employees as welders and sheet metal workers. They made more money in these jobs than they did as cops, but they couldn't keep it. They had to turn in their paychecks to the Police Department.

In 1939, at the outbreak of World War II, a working relationship was established between the FBI, the Bureau of Criminal Alien Investigations, and Special Squad I. This relationship was cemented by President Roosevelt's Executive Orders that called for all law enforcement agencies to pool their information in order to prevent sabotage at military defense installations. In New York, Presidential Search Warrants authorizing the search of homes of German and Japanese nationals were carried out by two-man teams consisting of one FBI agent and one detective from the Bureau of Criminal Alien Investigations. At the start of the war, the number of FBI field agents was limited. The FBI had no choice but to ask the Bureau of Criminal Alien Investigations for help in its investigations.

BOSSI's office was downtown on the third floor of a building at 400 Broome Street, just north of Police Headquarters on Centre Street. Even though I wasn't being assigned to an old neighborhood precinct, this was still the territory of my youth. Uptown had been off limits to me as a kid but not downtown. Centre Street bordered Little Italy, and that bordered the Bowery and was right around the corner from Fifth Street, where I was born and raised. I knew all the streets and alleys in the area from the banks of the Hudson to the banks of the East River. Besides being the home for BOSSI, 400 Broome Street also housed the command posts for special units of the Police Department such as the Safe and Loft (burglary) Squad and the Bureau of Criminal Identification (rap sheets and fingerprint records). The building ran a full block between Broome and Kenmare Streets.

Entering its ground floor, I showed my shield and headed for the elevator. After riding it a few times, I switched to taking the stairs when I

35

came in to work. The elevator was too slow. It creaked and groaned so much I thought each ride was a test to see if it could still make it up and down. I had more trust in airplanes than I did in this elevator. Once inside BOSSI's unmarked door, I had to show my shield again and then had to pass around a long table called "The Rack." It acted as a barrier to anyone who didn't have the right credentials and was BOSSI's telephone nerve center. Phones were stretched out on it from end to end. Given the green light to pass around it, I headed down the hall to meet my new boss. When I walked into Lieutenant Crane's office, I felt I had just entered the province of a father confessor—a Bishop in street clothes sitting behind a desk. He looked deep in thought, as if praying, maybe about what he was going to do with me. Crane, was, in fact, a very religious man, a daily communicant who attended mass every day at St. Andrew's Catholic Church in Foley Square, a few blocks south of BOSSI headquarters. He was the heartbeat of BOSSI. During that first meeting he told me he played no part in the selection of the people sent to him, but as I was to find out, once you were in his clutches and under his thumb, your future was in his hands. He said there were no guarantees I would stay in Special Services. If I wanted to remain a BOSSI detective, he made it clear to me that he had only one standard—you had to be the best. Crane was one tough cop, a master craftsman in the field of intelligence, dedicated to serving his city and his country. He made sure everybody in the house of BOSSI knew he was the one who ran the show.

When I first joined this squad, however, I didn't feel I was part of anything special at all. The contrast between my years patrolling the streets of Harlem and my new assignment was as great as, and initially bleaker than, anything I could have imagined. After what I had heard about Special Services' operations, I was at first excited about the kind of challenge intelligence presented, but the excitement quickly disappeared. I felt I had been exiled into oblivion. There would be no more beats to walk or uniforms to wear, no more patrol cars to bang up or "shotgun" rides in a speeding ambulance, no more chasing armed felons into dark hallways or feeling the rythmic, sometimes violent pulse of Harlem life. I now wore civilian clothes and a big hat. I felt like a clerk. I couldn't even find a kid to shine my shoes. With my hours now nine to five, I was home for dinner every night. While I loved my family, I had a hard time getting used to civilized hours. For the first three months on the job, Lieutenant Crane stuck me in a file room, starting me off reading old files, learning BOSSI's filing system, cross-checking names alphabetically, cutting out newspaper and magazine articles, and reading papers like *The Daily Worker, The Workers World,* and other publications of the "ists" in New York—the communists, the socialists, and the anarchists. I read about other known radical groups, too, and about the nuts and terrorists who periodically threatened to blow up buildings and shoot people. BOSSI's most sensitive files were kept in Crane's office, and nobody was allowed to see them without his invitation.

I didn't know what to do with all the information Crane was cramming into my head. It was the Police Academy experience all over again, and I couldn't wait to get out of it. The plain fact is that I was born to the streets, and that's where I felt I belonged. Every time I heard the clanging bell or the siren of a fire engine roaring up Centre Street, I wanted to jump on its tail and hitch a ride back to Harlem. At home, I kept waiting (and hoping) for the phone to ring from the desk sergeant at the Twenty-fifth Precinct to tell me to come back; that my assignment to Special Services had been a mistake; that it was all a big joke—played on me. I was convinced someone had blindsided me; I thought it had to be Captain Harkins's revenge for going over his head and writing to the Police Commissioner. The talk at the bar at Patrissy's Restaurant on Kenmare Street or around the corner at "Tony Tens" on Mulberry Street didn't help me deal with the situation either. Whenever I went for a beer and a sandwich, I had to hear about the action of every other squad but mine. I couldn't talk about what I did. I was drowning in a file room with the alphabet. I began looking at my shiny new detective's shield and saying to myself, "Congratulations, Ulasewicz, you just buried yourself." In the office, I filled out a card for myself, my tombstone, I thought, for my life as a cop.

> "Detective Tony Ulasewicz, Shield
> Number 1719. Wears Plain Clothes
> And Big Hat. His Assignment:
> Learn His ABC's."

I took the subway to work. My big hat and I traveled to Special Services from my new home in Flushing, Queens. I had bought the house with the help of the G.I. Bill. Besides my wife and me, there were now four little "U"'s occupying the House of Ulasewicz. Mary and I were proud parents of three daughters—Antonette, Alice, and Manya— and a son, Thomas. We added a fifth to our brood, a son named Peter, in 1954. Whatever frustrations I felt as I picked up my new shield each morning, I never brought the job home with me. As it was with my parents, and especially after my mother died, home was a special place in the universe, at times my only oasis. I was lucky to be both a husband and a father and I wasn't going to let my Police Department career interfere with that bit of good luck.

Toward the end of April 1949, Lieutenant Crane called me into his office. "Get your camera ready, Tony," he ordered. "You're going to the May Day parade." The parade, held annually on May 1, was primarily a Communist Party celebration. It was followed by a rally in Union Square. Socialists and trade unionists customarily joined the marchers, but historically, at least as far as the Police Department was concerned, it was the Communist Party that sought the parade permit from City Hall. "I'm pressing that ULAS Photo Business of yours into service," Crane said. My assignment was to take pictures of all the marchers, the stewards of the parade who would be wearing arm bands, anyone sitting in the parade reviewing stand, marchers carrying the signs and banners of the Communist Party that read, "Workers of The World Unite," and the speakers on the rally platform at Union Square. Crane said that not all the marchers would be communists, but some marchers were going to repeat the trip down Broadway to make it look like the line of the parade was endless. The idea was to create the illusion that there was greater Communist Party membership than actually existed. The more numbers the communists could show were supporting their cause, the more chance they had of recruiting new members, raising more money, and lessening the risk that their parade permit wouldn't be renewed the following year. The Police Department and the FBI, Crane lectured me, were joining forces to count the number of Communist Party members in New York. Heads in the parade repeating their journey were not to be counted twice. The parade route itself stretched from Eighth Avenue and

Fortieth Street to Union Square. To get back to the starting gate, marchers would scurry to the nearest subway station and ride back uptown. Then they would tack themselves onto the back of the parade and start walking again toward Union Square. I groaned a little when Crane told me I was going to cover both ends of the parade.

This first assignment out of my file room purgatory didn't relieve my earlier frustrations. Now I thought my expertise with a camera was going to imprison me in a dark room. I felt my detective's shield was no more valuable than a prize from a cereal box. I would become known as Tony the Bulb, Tony the Click, Tony Makes a Very Glossy Print. "Ah, nuts!," I said to myself as I left Crane's office.

On May 1, I journeyed up and down the parade route taking closeups, span shots, and poster-size shots. I developed them myself and sent copies to FBI and Justice Department officials. I wasn't going to let my ULAS Photo Company's "Snappy Intelligent Service" get a black eye or get bounced out of BOSSI because I took lousy pictures. They apparently passed the test because the day after the parade, Crane told me my assignment to Special Services was permanent. "You can forget about going back to Harlem," he said. (Six years later, in June 1955, I was subpoened by Attorney General Herbert Brownell, Jr., and directed to produce negatives and one print each of the photographs I had taken at the 1949 and 1953 May Day celebrations. Together with other BOSSI detectives, I traveled to Washington to testify as a witness before the Subversive Activities Control Board in a proceeding initiated to prove that the United May Day Committee was a Communist Party front organization.) When I left Crane's office the day after my first assignment was completed, I had mixed feelings—not about the job I did, but about how the orbit of my life as a BOSSI detective was going to widen. There was no turning back.

In that same spring of 1949, the first major Communist conspiracy trial in the history of the United States was taking place in the U.S. District Courthouse for the Southern District of New York. Twelve top leaders of the Communist Party were indicted in July 1948 for conspiring to overthrow the American government by force and violence. A few months after the trial started, Lieutenant Crane sent me on my next assignment to the cavernous courtroom of Federal District Judge Harold

39

R. Medina, the trial's presiding judge. In my briefing before heading to the courthouse, Crane said the defendants in the case were hell bent to bust up the trial, aggravate the judge so much that he'd blow a ruling, and, as a result, louse up the government's case. If convicted, the defendants wanted to make sure the verdict wouldn't stand up on appeal. Demonstrations, Crane told me, were being carefully orchestrated. Outside the courthouse, pickets were on the border of violence every day. Inside the courtroom, every ruling Judge Medina made was being met with a barrage of protest. Crane explained that the Justice Department wanted Special Services to help pin down the identity of the leaders of the disruptions. My job was to make a list of every name mentioned during the trial and to summarize the day's proceedings. At the end of each day, the list of names was to be matched against BOSSI records. If one of the files indicated a cross-reference to the report of one of Special Services' undercover operators inside the Communist Party, that report was to be pulled from under lock and key in Crane's office and checked for past evidence of potential future violence. Photographs of those with prior criminal records were to be ordered from the Bureau of Criminal Identification (BCI).

Before the trial resumed the next morning, I was directed to prepare a summary of the records and deliver it, together with any photographs, to the team of Justice Department lawyers trying the case. Several times during this assignment, I was escorted through the back channels of the courthouse and up a private elevator to Judge Medina's chambers to help him deal with the demonstrators scattered inside his courtroom who were causing him so much grief. The Judge had a hard time pronouncing my name so he began calling me "Mr. Ulysses."

Inside the courtroom, by pre-arrangement, I sat in the Foreign Correspondents section reserved for foreign journalists covering the trial. "Don't speak any English," Crane ordered. "If you have to open your mouth, make sure what comes out is some of that Polish or Russian you know." I pretended to be an observer for a fictitious foreign writers' association. I was actually a replacement for a former Special Services undercover operator, Frank Hlvasa, who had spent almost a decade inside the Communist Party organization. One day during the trial, Hlvasa showed up wearing a wool muffler. It was summertime and it was hot outside. Hlvasa kept the muffler on while he sat watching the trial from a seat right behind the defense counsel's table. One of the defendants' attorneys, Harry Sacher, went bananas as Hlvasa sat there stonefaced. He demanded to know who Hlvasa was and why he was allowed to sit so near the defendants. But since Hlvasa wasn't bothering anybody, Judge Medina let him stay where he was.

Then one day Hlvasa was gone. The multilayered loneliness and isolation that resulted from his role as an undercover operator, plus an accident he had suffered near his home, precipitated his rise to the surface and his presence in the well of Judge Medina's courtroom. Special Services felt that Hlvasa's muffler was a symbol of the double life he had led. It was a contradiction: he was a cop who had faked his role as a member of the Communist Party that itself thrived on double meaning language. After he left Judge Medina's courtroom, Hlvasa was assigned to clerical posts, mostly answering the phones at "The Rack." When the phones were silent, he could be seen reading books on farming and raising cattle. Then one day he was gone. He changed his name, retired on disability, and moved to Maine where he could breathe in the great outdoors.

A few days after I started attending the trial, during one of the recesses I found myself standing next to Harry Sacher in the men's room. I was a new face in the courtroom. Sacher said something to me in English, but I responded in Polish. I wanted to make sure he had nothing more to say to me—or I to him.

As I sat in the courtroom watching the trial, the thought crossed my mind that the battle I was witnessing was just like the street brawls I used to get into as a kid, only this one was being fought with words instead of fists. I watched Judge Medina trying to keep control of his courtroom. It was an explosive atmosphere. From start to finish, the defendants' tactics were designed to attack the entire machinery of the judicial process. The defendants blasted the manner of jury selection as discriminatory ("not a jury of their peers"); they argued that the Justice Department was run by a bunch of mad dog fascists and that the Police Department was being run on their leash. The defendants had no use for the press either and, while they were at it, none for the President of the United States. When the Communist conspiracy trial began winding down toward summations and the Judge's instructions to the jury, I left Foley Square, gave up my status as "Mr. Ulysses," and returned to Broome Street and the filing cabinets. I no longer felt claustrophobic. The defendants were convicted as charged, by a jury made up of people from every economic class the defendants could ever have wanted to sit in judgment on their fate. What I saw taking place in Judge Medina's courtroom didn't turn my head in any particular political direction. I had a job to do and, as Lieutenant Crane commanded, I had to do it right, but I couldn't help feeling that if the defendants had been acquitted they would have put a gun to America's political head. Violent demonstrations would have been commonplace in the streets of every city in America. Yet, the world outside BOSSI's file room was full of conspirators and schemers, other than members of the Communist Party, who hunted for ways to grab the reins of power. The boys from the streets whom I knew as a kid could grow up to blow up their own playhouse and maybe even kill its builder.

Except for the maintenance of undercover personnel in the Communist Party, the end of the Second World War signaled the end of Special Squad I's undercover operations. The world I knew wanted a parade and a hug and a chance to heal and rebuild itself without the need for undercover investigations propping up its freedoms. The euphoria of victory over the Nazis and the Japanese seemed, at least for awhile, to be enough. In a flurry of good-will, the name of the ominous-sounding Bureau of Criminal Alien Investigations was changed to the Public Relations Squad. This gimmicky title lasted as long as the Neutrality Squad had during Wilson's time. On April 15, 1946, the Public Relations Squad became the Bureau of Special Service and Investigation. That was its name when I was sent there in February 1949. Sounded aloud, BOSSI, pronounced BOSS-EE, had a bravado ring to it. Regardless of any other name my squad has ever had, my designation as "a BOSSI man" or "that's a BOSSI matter" remains the label anyone connected with the squad recognizes as the name that says it all. Officially, Mayor LaGuardia let it be known that he didn't like the word "investigation" spelled out in public. But the word stayed in the squad's title until 1951 when BOSSI was put under a bigger bureaucratic umbrella called the Central Office of Bureaus and Squads. On August 1, 1955, the word "Investigation" was officially cut from BOSSI's legend. But not from those detectives, like me, who were working inside it.

THE decision to locate the headquarters of the United Nations in New York changed everybody's life in the Police Department. The United Nations Charter specifically designated the NYPD as the agency in charge of UN security. The Police Commissioner put BOSSI in charge of the personal security of the world leaders whenever they attended sessions of the General Assembly or of the Security Council. Protecting world leaders was nothing new to BOSSI. Under its various official titles, the squad had for many years been in charge of protecting global potentates whenever they came to New York.

With the arrival of the United Nations, however, BOSSI had to cope with the fact that many of the world's leaders would arrive in the city at the same time. By September 1949, when the United Nations first opened its temporary headquarters at Lake Success on Long Island, fifty-seven member nations were sending their representatives— including kings, queens, chancellors, and prime ministers—to attend its sessions. Security for every one of them and their staffs presented BOSSI with a logistical nightmare. Finally, we were told to concentrate our efforts on the big boss of each country; lower echelon diplomats were to be on their own. That created its own set of problems because the gift of diplomatic immunity to UN mission officials provided a perfect cover for espionage activities. The movements of these officials were tracked primarily by the FBI. When the leaders of the world gathered for a dinner in the Grand Ballroom of the Waldorf Astoria—what we in BOSSI called the Great Feast House—you could usually find me there below the chandeliers exchanging my kielbasi, pierogi, Coke, and bologna sandwiches for plates of Filet Mignon Chasseur, Nest of Beignet Potatoes, and Bibescot Glace New Waldorf. (I drove the chef nuts because I always wanted my steaks charred.)

BOSSI's Commanding Officer rotated our assignments escorting global big wigs. These assignments were variously governed by se-

43

niority, language requirements, a dignitary's special request for the same escort team, or simply by what team of detectives was available at the time. When the President of the United States came to town, security measures were coordinated with the Secret Service. In advance of the arrival of any foreign leader in New York, the State Department notified BOSSI headquarters. For each twenty-four hour stay in New York, a two-man team from BOSSI would remain with the dignitary until his departure. Every BOSSI escort team was required to prepare a preliminary report for the Mayor, the Police Commissioner, the Motorcycle Division, and appropriate precinct commanders as to the dignitary's itinerary. This report would cover the arrival and departure routes and all planned events scheduled to occur during the dignitary's stay. Every foreign delegation attending the United Nations had its own peculiar security requirements. BOSSI's escort team was required to check the presence and whereabouts of all individuals or groups who opposed— or supported—the government of any member nation. The intrigues and power struggles of South America, the tribal and racial rivalries of Africa, the hair-trigger hostility between countries in the Middle East, and the cold heat of Russia's paranoia all brewed together. (The United Nations was hardly united.) New York City became more than a melting pot; at times, it turned into a furnace. Demonstrations and threats of assassination were BOSSI's constant concern.

Royalty and heads of state also relied on BOSSI escort teams to insure both their safety and comfort. Preventing an assassin from ambushing a dictator might be blended with taking a queen for an ice cream soda or making sure a king had his toothbrush. We also guarded the wives and children of many a leader whose position of power in his own country was precarious at best. We followed princes and princesses on shopping sprees from the jewel palaces of Fifth Avenue to the hovels of discount bargains on New York's Lower East Side. We rated the treatment visiting dignitaries were to receive in BOSSI's escort book. At the top of our rating system was the mogul or hero who was to get a ticker-tape parade up Broadway, the roaring adulation of the crowd, the presentation of a ceremonial key to the city on the steps of City Hall, and then lunch at the Waldorf. As we put it, anyone getting that treatment got "the full enema." With all our escorts, we also had to learn the refinements of etiquette. We had to mind our manners, and we also had to learn what to call these leaders. Was it to be "Your Highness or Your Lordship?," "Mr. President or Mr. King?" Detective Aristedes Ramos, one of the men assigned to the Duke and Duchess of Windsor, kept referring to them as "you and the Mrs."

Sharing BOSSI's responsibility for all these tasks were a bunch of detectives who were drawn out of every immigrant mold New York City had ever produced. At BOSSI's Rack, poking in filing cabinets, listening to Lieutenant Crane, reading or typing reports, cutting out newspaper articles, or checking the escort book, you could find names like Theologes from Greece, Taraska and Wasylciow from the Ukraine, Graumann and Weidinger from Germany, Ramos and Lopez from Puerto Rico, O'Connell and Fitzpatrick from Ireland, Necas from Czechoslovakia, Horvath from Hungary, Bohman from Sweden, Isengaard from Norway, Carrington from Black America, Kerner from the heritage of the Jews, Bianco from Italy, and Gwozdo, Bystricky, and Ulasewicz, me, from Poland. We had some crew.

At times, anyone walking into BOSSI headquarters who was unfamiliar with our operations might have thought they were in a nut house, or a zoo, or anything but a Police Department intelligence squad. On some days we looked like we couldn't pass kindergarten. One of Lieutenant Crane's most irritating tasks was to verify for some thick-skulled precinct captain that one of his men was really a cop. Crane's prime candidate for a precinct rejection was detective Mario Fochi. Off duty, Mario ran a driver training business on Mulberry Street in Little Italy. He weighed so much he had to take the front seat out of his car in order to get in. He sat on a cushion, but he was so low in the car it looked like it was being driven on automatic pilot. On many occasions, when BOSSI wanted special infiltration or attendance at some gathering, it would send Mario—size 72 and growing. He would pay his dues or money at whatever place the meeting was held, then go in and sit down. He looked so disheveled and so enormous that nobody would go near him. Going into a precinct and identifying himself as a cop usually produced disbelief and the strongly voiced opinion that nobody in his right mind would have let Mario wear a badge. That's not what Lieutenant Crane wanted to hear from some precinct overlord. His appearance to the contrary, Fochi was one of the most effective detectives BOSSI ever had. After he retired from the squad, the last postcard he sent to us read: "Feeling good. Down to 400 pounds."

All calls coming into BOSSI's nerve center at The Rack were logged in a casebook. Teletype alarms from every precinct in the city were delivered to the Bureau every eight hours and read by each man covering The Rack. When the phone rang, the call could be anything—the State Department reporting the expected arrival of a foreign official or a report from a precinct that someone with a bomb was threatening to blow up Times Square. Whoever caught the call at The Rack had to follow it up; log it in the escort book or refer it to the Bomb Squad; and then keep track of the matter until the bomb threat was determined to be a hoax or the bomb itself was a dud, or, in fact, accomplished its mission causing loss of life and property.

Desks in BOSSI headquarters were not occupied solely by BOSSI personnel. The FBI also had a desk there for its liaison man, Gus Micek. Micek's job was to coordinate information on cases that both the FBI and BOSSI detectives were involved in and, more importantly, to make sure there was no screw up or interference in the investigation by other FBI agents who might stumble onto our work. Jealousy and competition are inherent in police work, but Gus had earned Lieutenant Crane's trust and respect. Jurisdictional lines between state and federal matters sometimes got blurred. To the extent possible, Micek tried to make things work smoothly between BOSSI and the FBI. J. Edgar Hoover and Gus once had a run-in over an accident Gus had in New York with his government-assigned car. To Hoover, having an accident that damaged government property was a mortal sin. As punishment Hoover sent him packing to an FBI office in the Midwest. Over and over Hoover acted as his own judge and jury for every agent. But when Hoover sentenced Gus he made a tactical mistake. In his rush to punish, he sent Gus back to his own hometown. To help him get back to BOSSI and New York, Lieutenant Crane and the rest of us decided not to cooperate with Gus's replacement. Nothing personal, just enough silence and isolation to let Hoover know BOSSI wasn't just some podunk outfit he could take for granted. As a result, Hoover didn't get the reports he wanted. He began blowing

his top at the New York FBI field office. To get what he wanted from
BOSSI, he had to agree to bring Gus back. And he did.

O NE of my first escorts to get the "full enema" was the Right
Honorable Sir Denys Lowson, Lord Mayor of London, who came
to New York for a visit in September 1951. For his ticker-tape parade the
Lord Mayor wore a maroon, ermine-trimmed robe that dropped all the
way to his ankles, and an oversized floppy hat that looked like a souffle
about to flow over his ears. He carried a wooden staff as a symbol of his
authority. At City Hall, Mayor Vincent Impelliteri presented Sir Denys
with a scroll paying tribute to his exceptional government service. The
Lord Mayor then went to the Waldorf for his lunch, after which he did
some sightseeing around Manhattan still wearing his parade dress.
When he was finished touring the city, my escort partner, Detective Ray
Clarke, and I drove him to the Plaza Hotel near Central Park. We got out
of the car and stood in front of the Plaza's famous fountain. "What do I
do now?" Sir Denys then asked with a puzzled look on his face.

"Go to your hotel room, I suppose," I answered, equally puzzled by
his question.

"Is this where I'm staying?" the Lord Mayor asked again.

"We were given orders to drive you here," I responded.

"Nobody told me," he replied, "where I was staying."

He was right. Nobody had. Not the Governor, not the Mayor, not the
State Department, or whoever had invited him to come to New York in
the first place. "Where are your bags?," I asked.

"I don't know," he answered. His day of glory was becoming a bust.

As the Lord Mayor stood by the fountain, some celebrating drunks
tried to hire him to drive them around Central Park in a horse and buggy.
As a small crowd began to gather to look at the guy in the floppy hat and
the robe, I ran into the hotel to check on the reservation. Finding out he
had none, I quickly made one. I also put out an SOS to find his luggage.
When I returned to the fountain, the Lord Mayor and Ray Clarke were
surrounded. When Clarke and I began escorting the Lord Mayor into the
hotel lobby, the crowd began howling that we were spoiling a harmless

old kook's fun. "Don't arrest him," they pleaded. "He didn't do anything. Let him alone."

It was pointless to explain to the crowd that this was the Lord Mayor
of London and that we were just trying to get the guy a place to sleep.
And the embarrassment didn't end there. Until we finally convinced the
hotel manager who was really registering, he refused to give the Lord
Mayor his room key until he could prove he could pay his bill.

OCCASIONALLY, such as during Haile Selassie's State visit to the
United States in 1954, an ugly American would suddenly emerge
from a crowd and threaten the dignitary or a member of his family. In
Selassie's case, it was two of his grandchildren who were put in jeopardy.
I had just taken them—two lovely black Princesses—to a holiday show
near Times Square when several white, drunk, bell-bottomed sailors
staggered out of a bar and began shouting. "Hey, white boy, what a' you
doin' with them black hens—pimping? Hey, boy, you stay right there.
Hey, you hear? Hey, come back here you!" I turned around, flashed my
shield, and told the loud mouths to back off. I didn't want to pull my
service revolver and create a disturbance that might end up in an
explosion. Ignoring my shield and my shouts, they charged and a fist
caught me on the shoulder. Before I lost my head and started swinging
back, I yanked both girls and made a dash for the escort car that was
supposed to be waiting for us around the corner. Thank God it was. By
the time I radioed for assistance the sailors had disappeared into the
crowd.

I thought that Selassie, despite all his imperial majesty and his track
record as an imposing, courageous world leader, couldn't really see
what was going on in his own country. My reason for saying this is that I
caught Selassie's Chief of Imperial and Military Security making a
clandestine visit to the Soviet Consulate in New York. Middle East and
African potentates always dressed to the nines. They wore whatever
uniform, insignia, turbans, or medals their countries bestowed on them
(or they bestowed on themselves) with great pride and dignity. You
could go blind looking at some of the jewelry they wore. Selassie's man,
however, wore a plain dark business suit and dark glasses when I

watched him being escorted inside the Soviet Consulate. Our information was that Selassie's imperial throne was being eaten away on the inside, but the word passed back to me from Washington, after I spread the news of the visit of his head of security to the Soviet Consulate, was that Selassie had no fears. At the time, Ethiopia was nowhere near the Soviet Union's ideological campground. It soon would be.

Haile Selassie had come to the United States in response to an invitation originally extended by President Roosevelt when they met in the Suez in 1944 and renewed by President Eisenhower in 1954.

In the early 1950s, I was also part of President Eisenhower's security detail. I sometimes rode along with him in his limousine when he came to New York. I was always in his motorcade either riding in the point car in the front or in the backup "hit" car that had the lookout detail watching for rocks, bottles, eggs, or other more serious missiles. The long limo had two flags sticking out of the right and left front fenders. One had the Presidential seal on it, and the other was the Stars and Stripes. Whenever the President's limo was parked for any length of time, a Secret Service agent removed the flags as a precaution against theft. One evening at the Waldorf, the agent forgot where he had put them. The dinner speeches were almost at an end when he realized he couldn't remember where they were. His first worry was that he was about to get fired. I asked him to retrace his steps. Where had he been standing? Did he leave the room? Where was the last place he saw them? He said he thought he had left them on the piano off to the side of the dais. We looked but they weren't there. Did you go to the bar? Have a drink? That triggered something. He remembered putting the flags down on the dais when somebody handed him a scotch. Where on the dais did you put them down? Over there, he pointed, right next to the American flag. I told him the flag had been rolled up to the ceiling and that I thought his flags were up there, too. "Oh, no!" he said. To check if I was right, I convinced the hotel management to roll down the squeaky apparatus during the last speaker's address. The President's flags were tucked inside the last fold of the Waldorf's Stars and Stripes. The Secret Service agent stuck the flags back in their slots on the fenders and retired for the night in peace.

It was at the Waldorf, too, that I first met Richard M. Nixon. He was then Vice-President. Although he was biding his time for the Presidency, he didn't reek of ambition. He simply struck me as a man who carefully thought out all his next moves. He was a public figure with very private thoughts; he played his cards close to his vest. He was cordial and seemed quite compatible with his President. They sat on the dais together and appeared to enjoy each other's company. Although many years later I would be hired by John Ehrlichman to be Nixon's own private investigator, I would not see Nixon again until 1977 when I visited with him at his home in San Clemente, California. By that time, he had not only won the Presidency twice, but he had also lost it by his forced resignation.

M Y partner in BOSSI for almost ten years was Irish Detective Eddie Fitzpatrick. Fitz joined the Police Department in 1938; soon after, he worked undercover with the Bureau of Criminal Alien Investigations, tracking the movements of suspected Nazi sympathizers. When I met him in 1949, Fitz had a reputation as being BOSSI's best dressed cop: he wore spats, a bowler hat, and always carried a cigar. He was trim and feisty; he was BOSSI's "Jiminy Cricket." During the 1948 Presidential election campaign, Fitz went on special assignment as Earl Warren's personal bodyguard when Warren ran for the Vice-Presidency on the Republican ticket with Governor Tom Dewey of New York. Secret Service personnel did not begin to guard Presidential candidates until years later. On my first escort detail with Fitz, we were to guard President Quirino of the Philippines. We were stationed on the floor of the President's suite at the Waldorf when one of the President's countrymen, who didn't share his views, managed to slip through security. He was already headed for the President's room when Fitz spotted him and decked him with one punch. Fitz actually broke his hand on the intruder's jaw. "You're on your own, kid," Fitz said to me as he disappeared down the elevator on his way to the hospital.

Before I became his full-time partner, Fitz occasionally shared escort assignments covering top Soviet leaders with BOSSI detective, Charlie Necas. If you could have crossbred Fitz with Mario Fochi, Charlie Necas would have been the result. There wasn't a wasted piece of flesh on

Charlie's bones. He had the size and strength of the Finnish sailor whom I had arrested as a rookie cop in Harlem. He tested the structural integrity of a new home he was buying by putting his fist through one of the walls. For more than fifteen years, Charlie Necas worked side by side with Artie Silk on New York's docks reporting on the political and criminal turmoil that surfaced every day in the Port of New York. After many years they became the trusted conduit for Union leaders' messages to City Hall to break a deadlock in labor negotiations and bring a crippling strike to an end. Necas and Silk became known as the "Silk Team."

At least one of the detectives on duty safeguarding Soviet leaders had to understand and speak some of their language. With Necas' Slovak background he was able to communicate with the Russians. From time to time, he would be pulled off the waterfront to help the Department understand what the Russians were talking about, what they wanted or where they were going. Sometimes the Russians wouldn't talk, but just stood and stared. After leaving the Soviet compound on Long Island late one afternoon, Fitz and Charlie picked up a couple of beers, drove to a remote beach, and fell asleep. While they slept the tide came in; in a desperate attempt to start the car and escape, Charlie pulled the choke and all its wires right out of the dashboard. They were lucky to get a tow truck to pull them out of the ocean before floating off to Europe.

When the United Nations first opened its doors, the Russians would have brought their own tanks to the streets of New York if they had thought they could have gotten away with it. At first, Soviet NKVD personnel carried machine guns under their raincoats. Until we convinced the Russians that the NYPD wasn't waiting on a side street with a howitzer, the Soviet NKVD security men carried their bulky weapons everywhere they went. We finally persuaded the Russians that Police Department security personnel carried hand guns—not cannons—as a sign of civilized diplomacy. Even when the Soviets finally switched their armaments to the holster-size variety, their diplomats acted as if they were under siege. They were trained to look grim. Their faces seemed poured in cement, and their suits were square and rigid as if stitched with steel thread.

In escorting the Russians, we found that what they cared about most

51

was that we get them to their destination with lightning speed. Pot holes, detours, flat tires, accidents—anything that slowed us down or held us up, even fog—were, to the Russians, all capitalist conspiracies. Late one evening when Fitz and I were bringing the Soviet leaders back to their Long Island compound, we found ourselves bogged down in traffic due to an accident on the Triborough Bridge. I was driving. As a status symbol to match the Russian Cadillacs, I was behind the wheel of the New York City Police Commissioner's Lincoln Continental. To get through the Triborough toll booths without stopping, Fitz opened the window and flashed the Commissioner's most prized possession—his porcelain embossed official metal emblem showing him to be New York's Number One Cop. It was the magic plate of the dashboard—the Commissioner's guarantee of a parking place where there was none. To bypass the congestion on the bridge, I gave a touch to the siren while Fitz stuck the Commissioner's plate out of his side window, waving it like a cheerleader's pom pom at the traffic. It was a windy night. Suddenly, FLU-EESH!—a burst of wind tugged the plate out of Fitz's hand and sent it flying like a frisbee over the tops of the cars behind. We would have been better off losing the Commissioner's car.

After saying good night to the Russians, we drove back to the bridge and searched every inch of it. The traffic had lightened up considerably because of the lateness of the hour. We went back and forth through the toll booths four times. We knew that if we reported that the Police Commissioner's treasured emblem was lost somewhere on a bridge, in the grit, we'd both be back in Harlem the next day wearing brass buttons and swinging a bat. Amazingly, Fitz spotted the plate resting up against the stone shoulder of the bridge. Venus was never caressed as much as this plate. But the episode wasn't over. The toll collector, having become suspicious watching us nod and grin as we showed our shields and repeated our journey, had reported us to Police Headquarters. The message passed on to Headquarters was that two cops in the Commissioner's car were engaged in some kind of wacky frolic. The next morning at 400 Broome Street, Crane handed Fitz and me a note. "You've got one hour to get your butts over to the Commissioner's office. You better make it good!" We went and were made to cool our heels for several hours sitting outside the Commissioner's office. Then we were told to come back at the same time the next day. We did and sat again. We got the message: "Don't let it happen again."

When I was security escort for the late Soviet Foreign Minister Andrei Vishinsky, the limousines in his motorcade drove from place to place like bank robbers fleeing a holdup. Fitzpatrick and I always rode in the car directly behind Vishinsky. Traveling in New York City posed no speed problems because we usually alerted the precincts we would pass through in time for them to crank up a motorcycle escort. We were safe until we crossed the East River and headed for Long Island. Once we reached Nassau County, the Nassau County Police Department gave us the required backup support to help us get the Russians safely back to their mansion in Glen Cove. But when we hit the boundary line of the Village of Glen Cove, we were in trouble, especially in the daytime, if Officer Timothy O'Neill of the Glen Cove Police Department was on duty. He had definite opinions on many things. For openers, he couldn't stand the idea that any Russian official was allowed to live on American soil. He also didn't like New York City detectives, like us, whom he said were a bunch of badge-carrying free loaders and "coopers"—in short, lazy bums—roaming his territory. Whenever Vishinsky's motorcade drove in or out of Glen Cove with the sun still shining, there would be Officer O'Neill in pursuit. He followed the Russian limousines everywhere they went, hiding behind trees, revving up his machine, waiting for the kill. We nicknamed him "Tim O'Schenko."

In September 1950 when Vishinsky was on his way to debate American Secretary of State Dean Acheson before the United Nations General Assembly over the armed conflict in Korea, Officer O'Neill-Schenko stopped Vishinsky's motorcade. Vishinsky was already late for his UN confrontation with Acheson, an event the world was anticipating. O'Neill told Vishinsky he was driving too fast, and this time he was getting a ticket. At first, Vishinsky wouldn't accept it. Having earned his fame in Russia as Joseph Stalin's chief prosecutor during Stalin's purge trials of the 1930s, he hardly cared about what a hyperanxious American cop on a motorcycle had to say about anything. Glen Cove's finest became a single-handed blockade of Russian progress. The Third World War was prevented when Vishinsky finally accepted the warning.

When the Russians first came to the United States to attend UN

53

sessions, they refused to eat any of the food prepared in the Waldorf's kitchen. They had their food cooked elsewhere, under Soviet security supervision, and then had it delivered to them. On one occasion, when the Foreign Ministers of France, England, the United States, and the Soviet Union met in the Waldorf Tower Suite of the United States Mission to the United Nations, the Russians had difficulty maneuvering their trunks of food through the hotel's revolving doors. They twisted and angled their odd luggage until the trunks were turned upside down. Their borscht soup began to leak onto the sidewalk and then spread inside the lobby, creating havoc as hotel guests tried, without success, to escape the purple tide.

Once, when Fitz and I were on call at the Soviet compound on Long Island, Fitz got tired of eating Chicken Kiev, Chicken Stalingrad, Chicken everywhere in Russia. One mealtime, he corralled the Russian cook and, through sign language and some pig Russian, tried to get the menu changed. The Russian cook flamboyantly agreed to give us some "hot duck" the next day. I decided not to translate for Fitz what the cook really meant. Fitz couldn't wait for the change.

The next day when we sat down for lunch, the Russian cook brought out a huge punch bowl filled with American hot dogs. "Hot duck," he said. No mustard, no relish, no hot dog rolls. Just a big bunch of goddam weenies. It was time for Fitz to go back to eating chicken. He didn't dare ask for a hamburger.

In contrast to the Russians' grim appearance and their paranoia about everything offered or proposed to them, the kings, sultans, and shahs of the Middle East and African countries couldn't wait to taste the food prepared by the Waldorf's master chefs. On one visit to New York by Saudia Arabia's late King Faisal, one of his staff members paid a visit to the FAO Schwarz toy store on Fifth Avenue and bought almost every train set in the place. The miniature trains, their tracks, and all the trappings that would thrill any kid at Christmas were delivered and set up in the Waldorf Astoria's Grand Ballroom. Ice sculptures, in the shape of mountains, with tunnels at their base, were then ordered from the Waldorf's kitchen and, when finished, placed on tables circling the ballroom. The trains' freight and coal cars carried hors-d'oeuvres and drinks around on the train tracks to the honored guests and other diplomats attending the affair. King Faisal and his court played like children while they nibbled at Pate de Foie Gras and Beluga caviar.

The Iranians nearly fired us one evening when Fitz and I played Alphonse and Gaston to the late Iranian Prime Minister Mohammed Mossadegh. When we were escorting him out of the Hotel Pierre on his way to the airport for his return flight to Iran, I first went outside the hotel to make sure the coast was clear. Fitz stayed inside to wait for my signal that everything was okay. When Mossadegh, a tall, somewhat bandy-legged man, entered the hotel's revolving door, Fitz and I both gave the door a shove at the same time, just to help the guy along. Mossadegh came flying out the door, wobbling and lurching head-long toward his limousine. If his chauffeur hadn't opened the rear door, Mossadegh would have hit it head on. Fitz and I looked on helplessly. Mossadegh made it half-way into his limousine, his head and shoulders sprawled on the back seat and his legs and feet never making it. He began yelling (I suspected cursing) as he tried to gain his composure and his balance. Looking around for his aides, he shot us a glance that said he would find a way to string us up. Fitz and I hurried inside the hotel to see what was holding up Mossadegh's staff. They were arguing with the hotel cashier over an item on the bill. It was almost $40,000. The size didn't bother the Iranians; they always had luxurious accommodations and the best room service money could buy. I know because I stayed on the same floor as Mossadegh. What bothered the Iranians was an item on their bill for sixteen dollars worth of liquor. The Iranians, like their other Muslim brothers, didn't drink. It was against their religion, but that didn't stop us from downing a scotch or two. The hotel's itemized bill had the word "Pinch" on it.

"Pinch. What is Pinch?," one of Mossadegh's staff asked the cashier.

"It's 'Pinch bottle,'" the cashier answered.

"We didn't pinch any bottles!" the Iranian responded, raising his voice. He looked insulted.

"No, no. It's Haig & Haig," the cashier said, trying to calm things down.

"Get them to pay, not us," the Iranian demanded.

"No, Haig & Haig is scotch."

"Scotch? So, we are Muslim. We don't drink. We don't pay this."

"Fitz," I called to my partner. "You got eight bucks? I'll split the tab with you. Let's get everybody out of here."

It seems that our escort relief, Detectives Ray Clarke and Gene O'Connell, had ordered a bottle of Haig & Haig pinch bottle of scotch the night before Fitz and I relieved them of duty. The bottle was in our room when the Iranians checked out. By agreement with all foreign delegations, all the costs for our room and board were picked up by the government whose top official we were assigned to guard. We stuck like glue to the official from the moment he arrived in New York until his departure. We stayed in the same hotel, usually on the same floor. When an official, and usually the members of his family as well, were secured for the night, it was time for us to lighten up and have a drink. Ordinarily, with the type of room service the official was receiving, a bar was set up in our room without our even asking for it. This was just an extension of the receptions and dinners we attended with the dignitaries who were under our protection. It wasn't that the Iranians were acting like cheapskates; they just wouldn't be able to explain to the folks back home what a charge for booze was doing on their bill.

A major reason why it was important that at least one BOSSI detective understand Russian was the introduction of the word "defection" into the language of the Cold War. On August 12, 1948, about six months before I joined BOSSI, Mrs. Oksana Stepanova Kosenkina, a Russian school teacher at the Soviet School in New York, in a desperate attempt to escape to freedom, jumped out of a third-floor window of the Soviet Consulate at 7 East Sixty-first Street. She landed in the courtyard of a building next door. Although she broke a lot of bones, she survived. Mrs. Kosenkina's leap to freedom was an extreme embarrassment to the Soviet Union (as well as a very risky way to defect). After being rushed to a hospital, Madame Kosenkina was placed under tight police security. Talking in her native language, she gave a statement to Edward Mullins, Deputy Chief Inspector of the Police Department. BOSSI detective Bill Taraska acted as her translator. Madame Kosenkina told Taraska that she didn't want to see anyone from the Russian Consulate. "I am afraid to see them," she was qouted as saying. "I fear them and I will not see them." Angry about his (and other Soviet officials') exclusion from Madame Kosenkina's hospital room, the first Vice Consul of the Soviet Consulate, Zot I. Chepurnykh, claimed that Kosenkina's message to Taraska had been lost in translation. Soviet Foreign Minister Molotov pressed the issue and filed a formal protest with the American Ambassador in Moscow charging that Kosenkina had been kidnapped and that the United States was in cahoots with whoever planned her leap to freedom. (The Soviets labeled them "White Russian" gangsters operating on the support beam of the Tolstoy Foundation. Countess Alexandra Tolstoy emphatically denied the accusation.) Tensions remained high as the Soviet Union tried, futilely, to have Mrs. Kosenkina returned to their control. The key to the outcome of this struggle was the accurate translation, and its transmission to State Department officials and the FBI, of exactly what Mrs. Kosenkina was saying. Her jump could have been a suicide attempt having nothing to do with an attempt to defect. In instances such as the Kosenkina affair, a BOSSI detective was, most often, first on the scene.

BOSSI detectives also translated letters from Europeans seeking help in finding a missing relative who might be living in New York. Most areas of New York began as ethnic neighborhoods where people kept close tabs on each other. BOSSI detectives were asked to tap into their network for help in finding a brother, a sister, a distant cousin, someone who might help the person who wrote the letter to come to America. At the time of Madame Kosenkina's jump to freedom, hundreds of thousands of displaced refugees from Eastern Europe, including thousands of orphaned children, were in search of resettlement following on the horrors of World War II. Many refugees from Communist-dominated countries refused to return to their homes after the war. They were afraid of prison or of being sent to their grave in Siberia.

On July 12, 1961—some twelve years after I joined BOSSI—a Polish sailor named Kosimers Sabolonski jumped ship into the waters of New York Harbor in an attempt to win political asylum in the United States. Sabolonski was pulled out of the water by the United States Coast Guard and taken to King's County Hospital in Brooklyn. When he gave a statement, I served as his translator. "Before God," Sabolonski said, "I want to stay in this country. I would rather die than leave this country."

Ironically, as a detective, I also had to deal with people who wanted to tear up our constitution in the name of the freedoms Sabolonski would have given his life to enjoy.

WHILE the establishment of the United Nations in New York served to expand the NYPD's operations, not until Soviet leaders arrived on our soil did BOSSI's major concentration shift to the activities of world leaders. Much like the FBI and the State Department, BOSSI established "desks" for the countries whose heads of state we guarded.

Foreign governments were well aware of our contacts with the FBI, CIA, and State Department in Washington, but generally brushed aside the significance of our contact as a risk of coming to New York for sessions of the United Nations General Assembly or its Security Council. BOSSI didn't operate on foreign territory or try to overthrow governments; we had only peripheral knowledge of foreign government activities except as they might involve the security of a head of state. If a legitimate request was made for what we had seen or heard, we shared the information. But we were nobody's stalking horse; we didn't turn over our files or answer questions just because somebody asked us to. We screened every request, and we made sure we weren't breaching a confidence, giving up one of our informants, or jeopardizing an ongoing investigation. BOSSI called its own shots.

The CIA started knocking on our doors soon after that organization was officially recognized by the National Security Act of 1947. In BOSSI, we nicknamed the CIA agents the "big brims" from Washington, because they walked around looking as if they carried bigger thoughts under their hats than anyone else. When the Russians moved into their Consulate at 68th Street and Park Avenue, the CIA asked for maps of the city's underground that would show the location of all manhole covers, sewer tunnels, and telephone lines running below the street near the Soviet Consulate so that they could place wire taps and other surveillance equipment as close to the Consulate as possible. Because of my escort duties for Soviet leaders, I had already made some drawings of the interior of the Soviet Consulate and had shipped them off to Washington. Under the National Security Act, the CIA was prohibited from operating on U.S. soil, but it was not prevented from vacuuming information gathered by other law enforcement agencies.

During the early stages of the Korean War, the Central Intelligence Agency called BOSSI with a request which it said was an "emergency." Tensions were heating up between the United States and the Soviet Union. If the two nations were going to come to blows, the CIA wanted to know the precise location of the Soviets' code room operation in their Consulate on Park Avenue. BOSSI assigned me to get the answer.

Generally speaking, Soviet security at the Consulate was pretty tight. The front door to the Consulate always remained locked. Only one BOSSI detective was allowed inside at any given time. The Consulate's vestibule was brightly lit. There was an ante-room off of it and a stairway leading upstairs to living quarters and Consulate offices. Leading back from the vestibule was a long corridor. At the end of it was a desk. There was an intercom on the wall and a buzzer that controlled the opening of the front door. As opposed to the vestibule, the corridor was dimly lit. It was difficult for anyone standing in the bright light of the vestibule to see as far as the desk or who might be stationed there. This setup was deliberate so that Soviet NKVD security personnel could remain strategically obscure while identifying and monitoring the movements of those who entered the Consulate. Whenever I was stationed inside, I remained at the desk with the NKVD agents (always two of them) or with the Soviet military personnel who sometimes covered the desk in their absence. In BOSSI, we were convinced that the Soviets had personal dossiers on every detective ever assigned to cover Soviet personnel. The dangers inherent in this code room assignment were obvious; the stability of all BOSSI intelligence operations was also at risk. Since I was not a member of the U.S. armed forces, what I did for the CIA inside the Soviet Consulate made me a spy. The Consulate was the territory of a foreign government. It was owned by the Soviet Union and was protected under international law. Once inside, I was subject to the laws of the Soviet Union, and if caught, I could have been prosecuted under them. The CIA would never acknowledge my assignment, nor could I reveal the source of my directive. It was a hairy time. If I was caught in the act and the Soviets then blew the whistle, they still had a serious problem. They would still need protection on the streets of New

York. The only replacement for BOSSI would be the feds, and the Russians wanted no part of any FBI or CIA escort service. The potential chemistry of Soviet and U.S. intelligence agents mixing together during episodes of escort protocol was out of the question.

The CIA thought the code room was located in the basement of the Consulate. So, I knew, was the men's room. Whenever I had to go to the john, I was always escorted. With my ability to speak and understand Russian, I gained the confidence of a Soviet agent who, on one occasion, didn't bother to follow me to the men's room. I didn't need a second invitation to turn left instead of right at the bottom of the stairs. At the end of the hall, I spotted a heavy curtain. When I touched it, it felt like lead. I pulled it open a few inches and saw filing cabinets and the coding machines which the CIA had told me to look for. At that moment the Soviet agent spotted me, a look of shock in his eyes. Before he had a chance to react, I excused myself in Russian for mistaking the location of the men's room and quickly walked upstairs. I never did go into the men's room, and I knew that the Soviet agent would figure out what I had been up to in a hurry. I was sure that I had just bought myself a one-way ticket to Siberia; just my being downstairs alone was a breach of Soviet security. But the agent in charge of consulate security apparently decided not to expose me, figuring that it was his mistake after all that allowed me to visit the men's room without a guide. To arouse the suspicions of his colleagues would have called attention to himself. Furthermore, I had become a fixture around the Consulate. If I were now to be denied access to the Consulate, he would have to answer too many uncomfortable questions. So I was able to inform the CIA of the location of the code room and at the same time remain at my post.

Only rarely did the CIA ever thank a BOSSI detective in person for a job well done. The success of the code room assignment, however, prompted the CIA to have a small get-together at a hotel near the Soviet Consulate shortly thereafter. I went to the hotel with BOSSI's Chieftain and had a few drinks with the "big brims." One of the CIA agents commented that they had had an easier time wiring the White House. "We've got everything covered there," he said. "Going in and coming out. We know everything that goes on in the Oval Office." Years later, when the brouhaha over Nixon's White House tapes erupted, I assumed that if one set of tapes had been destroyed, another set would have been available, courtesy of the CIA.

Protecting the outside of the Soviet Embassy was a major concern of the New York City Police. It was almost as important as finding out what was going on inside the Consulate. In November 1956, after Russia invaded Hungary, brutally ending the Hungarian Revolution, the Soviet Embassy in New York held its annual black tie anniversary celebration of the 1917 Bolshevik Revolution. Hungarian Freedom Fighters picketed the Embassy with signs, demonstrating with festering anger. Hungarian resentment of the Russian presence in New York was explosive. A phalanx of uniformed police, shaped like an inverted "v," guarded the entrance to the Embassy on Park Avenue. On the sidewalk, two rows of uniformed officers, standing back to back, prevented the pickets from interfering with the arrival of guests attending the evening's affair. All the pickets were restricted to an area on 68th Street.

Dressed in laborer's clothes, wearing a rumpled cap and a two-day-old beard, I infiltrated the picket line. I grumbled along with the other pickets who were bunched together, straddling the sidewalk on 68th Street, in groups of fours and fives. If I overheard or spotted any signal for action from the pickets, my assignment was to move in behind the head agitator. I was then to take off my cap, scratch my head, and put my cap back on. This would signal another BOSSI detective assigned to watch me to notify the uniformed commanding officer, then on duty, that trouble was coming. He, in turn, was to order his men to move into the picket line to clear out the potential troublemakers. As soon as I gave my signal, I was to move to another section of the picket line. Only my BOSSI partners and the uniformed commanding officer knew that I was among the pickets.

To keep the pickets contained, 68th Street was closed off to all vehicular and pedestrian traffic between Madison and Park Avenues. Barriers and policemen were placed at each end of the street. As I stood in my disguise, I spotted a lone figure walking toward me on the south side of 68th Street. He was dressed in a tuxedo and carried a bouquet of flowers. "Who the hell let this guy through?" I wondered. As he moved closer to the picket line, I said to myself, "Stay away." He began to cross the street and walked toward the Embassy. Those in the picket line quickly focused on the approaching figure; it was Johnny Ray, the torch singer, who was about to get the biggest surprise of his life, a gang beating from some mighty angry Hungarians. I heard one of the pickets yell, in Hungarian, "Let's get him." There was no time to take off my cap or scratch my head or change signals or yell I was a cop without creating a worse scene than the one already developing. I had to make a move. The uniformed cops on duty didn't know I was in the picket line. All I needed was to have some overanxious rookie cop start shooting once I broke from the picket line and headed for Johnny Ray. I had seen that happen once before during my days in Harlem, and it had cost the life of an innocent man. I took a chance and ran into the street shouting, "I'm a cop, I'm a cop, don't shoot!" I grabbed the startled singer and pulled him into the doorway of a building across the street. As soon as I settled him down, I left the area. I couldn't afford to have my face branded in the minds of the Hungarian pickets. The equally startled Hungarians were apparently numbed by the suddenness of the event. The red paint which we suspected some of the pickets had been carrying under their coats stayed in place. The Soviet Embassy, at least on this evening, suffered no damage. Before leaving Johnny Ray's side, he told me that he had been on his way to visit Dorothy Kilgallen, the noted columnist who was a regular participant on the television show, "What's My Line?" My line of work let Johnny Ray keep his date.

S OVIET officials, having learned a painful security lesson from the Kosenkina affair, were not about to let me or any other United States citizen mess with the bones of Andre Vishinsky when he died, supposedly of a heart attack in New York on the morning of November 22, 1954. Vishinsky's demotion from the rank of Soviet Foreign Minister after the death of Joseph Stalin in 1953 led some of us to regard him as a candidate for defection. He was an unlikely prospect, however. He was a living museum piece of just how caustic a Russian leader could be in his speeches against the United States, speeches that earned him the nicknames "Kremlin's Gremlin" and "master of the vitriolic word." But Vishinsky was also a cultured, scholarly man whose appearance as a Bolshevik bully was more staged than real. Because of his raging performances he was the most pointed-at diplomat in the General Assembly Hall of the United Nations. However, when we noted the discrepancies between his public outbursts and his private statements to Western diplomats, we began passing his remarks along to the State Department. Word came from Washington that we should be ready for a possible signal from Vishinsky that he wanted political asylum. After I was assigned as one of his detective escorts upon his arrival in New York, I listened all the more carefully to everything he had to say.

Vishinsky's death, whatever the cause, put Soviet officials into a head-to-head confrontation with the New York City Police Department and the city's Chief Medical Examiner, Dr. Milton Halpern. Although the Soviets properly notified the police of Vishinsky's death, they refused to allow his body to be moved out of the Consulate, citing diplomatic immunity (never before given to a corpse). More than that, they wouldn't even let his body out of their sight for a second. Soviet officials haggled with police brass over who would be permitted to verify the cause of death. The Soviet physician reported that Vishinsky had died of a heart attack but since he wasn't licensed to practice medicine in New York, technically he couldn't sign the death certificate. When the Soviet physician was denied permission, the Russians felt it was an affront to the dignity of their country. In retaliation, they refused to grant permission for an autopsy.

This stalemate lasted almost ten hours, during which Vishinsky lay fully dressed, unembalmed, on top of his bed. After a compromise was worked out, allowing Dr. Halpern to examine the body but not to conduct an autopsy, the Soviets then refused to let the body leave the Consulate for the embalming. The Soviets demanded that the morticians bring their equipment to Vishinsky's bedside. The whole affair was becoming gruesome. For their part the Soviets claimed that, since their Consulate was foreign territory, they held absolute sovereignty over Vishinsky's remains. The only way he was going to leave the Soviet Consulate, they maintained, was in a box, and the only place it would be permitted to go was to the Soviet Union. So Vishinsky was indeed embalmed in the Consulate and shipped off to Moscow, and upon his arrival there, he was cremated. His ashes were placed in an urn and then neatly tucked away in a slit in the Kremlin Wall. And so much for any autopsy.

Around midday on the morning of Vishinsky's death, I took a call at "The Rack" at BOSSI headquarters from the State Department. When asked what I knew about the details of Vishinsky's death, I replied "very little," nor did any other BOSSI detective on duty know very much. Technically, his death was a matter for the Nineteenth Precinct because the Soviet Consulate was located within its jurisdiction. Lieutenant John McCarthy, the precinct's Detective Squad Commander, was first notified of the death by the Soviet Consulate. McCarthy took charge of the Police Department's official response. BOSSI had no jurisdiction over dead bodies, but the State Department insisted that I go up to the Consulate and nose around.

When I arrived at the Soviet Consulate, I learned that I had just missed a Soviet spokesman's announcement of Vishinsky's death. A group of reporters, still gathered outside the Consulate, looked puzzled: While they had to report what they heard, their guts told them that what they were reporting wasn't the truth. When I entered the Consulate, the hostile atmosphere I felt there was unlike anything I had ever experienced since I had begun escorting Soviet leaders. The Soviet security personnel who greeted me at the door were strangers. Before his death, Vishinsky's demotion to the rank of First Deputy Minister for Foreign Affairs had denied him the more extensive escort protection he had had as Soviet Foreign Minister. At the time of his death he was in effect a prisoner. He couldn't make a move without a Soviet security escort, and he had become nothing but a figurehead with no say in Soviet policy decisions. The Soviets, exercising their rights under the UN charter, had used a demotion in rank to terminate BOSSI's relationship with Vishinsky. So when I showed up at the Consulate my role as his escort had already ended.

The new faces at the Consulate knew me but they were obviously unhappy about my unexpected presence. I decided not to ask too many questions because after all Vishinsky's death was a precinct affair and, as the Soviets well knew, did not involve BOSSI's escort or intelligence apparatus in any way. Careful to avoid appearing as a snoop, I simply asked about when other Police Department dignitaries would be able to pay their respects. The Soviets answered that they had already talked with Lieutenant McCarthy at the Nineteenth Precinct and that I should ask him, not them, about calling hours. The Soviets' chilly, condemming stares clearly signaled that Vishinsky's death was a matter they wanted left alone.

This whole episode reeked of coverup. When I asked some of the precinct boys who were stationed outside the Consulate about the events preceding the report of Vishinsky's death, they answered that Vishinsky had attended a dinner for French Premier Pierre Mendes-France that night, and when he arrived back at the Consulate, he quickly came out of the Consulate again and collapsed on the sidewalk. I assumed that Vishinsky must have come down the staircase and gone out the front door while the NKVD was back at its security post. The patrolman told me Vishinsky appeared to be in a hurry to get away. "Escape," I said under my breath. When he fell, he was apparently heading for his limousine. Soviet Consulate personnel immediately picked him off the ground and hustled him back inside the building.

The Consulate's formal statement reporting Vishinsky's death was a little different. Around 2:20 that morning, it claimed, Vishinsky complained of a heavy, tight feeling in his chest. After being given some nitroglycerine pills, he fell back to sleep. At 5:00 a.m. Consulate personnel, observing that he was resting comfortably, did not awaken him for further examination. The Consulate statement went on to say that after a light breakfast, Vishinsky had a stroke and died of a heart attack.

While no proof of foul play was ever unearthed, suspicion arose because in recent months Vishinsky had changed dramatically, in both attitude and style of dress. His suits had more rounded edges, and he had obviously mellowed during his years in the West. He encouraged the United States and the Soviet Union to "dig the tunnel of friendship from both sides." I noted that he talked more and more with Western diplomats in the UN Delegate Lounge. He also seemed to be a more reflective man, easing up on his public expressions of hostility against the West. First as Stalin's top prosecutor and then as Soviet Foreign Minister, he must have been under immense pressures, pressures unrelieved by family. (His wife and daughter were never permitted to be with him when he came to the United States or when he traveled to other Western nations. One or the other was always kept home in Russia.) Indeed, Vishinsky was a prisoner with a title.

The only Russian leader I ever escorted who went wherever he pleased whenever he wanted was Andrei Gromyko. I have always been suspicious that he was the one who called the shots (or the injections or the poisons) that eliminated men like Vishinsky from the scene. Gromyko was the eye of the big brother, the Soviet bear that growled orders for death or Siberian exile behind the scenes. Groymko was the most slippery, devious Soviet big shot I ever protected. It was always a struggle keeping up with him. Most of the time he never let us know in advance where he was going or when he was leaving. He didn't want any detective escort around him even though that was our job under the UN charter. One afternoon Gromyko skipped out a side door of the United Nations building and disappeared. I tracked him to a Middle East Consulate (not Israel's) and through my informants learned that he had gone there to firm up a Soviet border security deal. The purpose of his visit to this Consulate was none of my business, but the way Gromyko maneuvered to keep us out of his way was my concern. In my opinion Gromyko was the hatchetman, the Soviet godfather who ordered the hits, the exiles, and the hard labor imprisonments for anyone caught even dreaming that there might be another way of life besides a communist one.

While under BOSSI's protective wing, Vishinsky and I talked many times about life in America. We always spoke in Polish because Vishinsky loved to talk that language. Our favorite topics were the raising of children, American traditions, and the freely celebrated family holidays and traditions from the Old Country. The Americans' freedom to celebrate their immigrant heritage especially fascinated him. The Soviet Union, Vishinsky told me, only celebrated its revolution, which of course was a rejection of its own past. As I stood in the Consulate on the day of his death, the Soviets were busy ridding themselves of the memory of Vishinsky's existence. "Get out," I felt the Soviets were saying, "and don't ask any questions."

T HE contrast in temperament between the mellowing Vishinsky and the shoe-pounding Soviet Premier Nikita Khrushchev who came to the UN in 1960 couldn't have been greater. Khrushchev acted as if he had been picked for the part from a Hollywood casting lot. Unlike most

Russian public figures who were generally as grim as the American press made them out to be, Khrushchev had a genuine sense of humor. He had the instincts of a good comedian, if not those of a clown. He surrounded himself with straight men who smiled on cue. He was in a sense not unlike many of the kids I grew up with on the Lower East Side. Like my gang, the Meteors, he would have tested everything (and everyone) around him, pressed against the edge, and probably swum with me across the East River to Brooklyn. He was a streetwise exhibitionist, a scrapper and at times probably would have been a bully. Khrushchev would have been a strong, hustling player in our stick ball games and, I have no doubt, a good crap shooter; he knew how to play the odds. At the same time, he wouldn't have hesitated to blow up the playhouse or risk the survival of this planet if he thought he could have gotten away with it. He tried it once during the Cuban Missile Crisis in 1962. He backed away from nuclear war at the last instant, but the point to remember about Khrushchev, at least from my vantage point, is that he tried to stare down the United States at the risk of annihilation.

Khrushchev's visit to New York coincided with that of Cuba's Fidel Castro. The United Nations planning committee had originally reserved rooms for Castro's party at the Waldorf Astoria, but when Castro arrived there, he denounced its opulence as a symbol of American decadence. He used the occasion to praise the sacrifice of his fellow revolutionaries when they lived off the land while they fought for freedom and justice against Fulgencio Batista's corrupt regime. Castro declared that sleeping at the Waldorf would be like taking a siesta in the lair of the devil. A uniformed sergeant on duty at the Waldorf therefore suggested that Castro check in at the Hotel Theresa in Harlem. The Theresa was known as a roach ranch without room service, but to my knowledge, nobody bothered to tell Castro about that.

When Nikita Khrushchev decided he was going to pay Castro a visit, I went on a dry run to the hotel to double check on all the security arrangements that had been made so there would be no surprises when we finally got there. I hadn't been to the Hotel Theresa since I was a uniformed cop in Harlem. When I arrived there, I was greeted with a most unexpected sight: Large stainless steel pots were being carried up to Castro's floor, and chicken feathers were everywhere. It seemed that chickens were being plucked in the halls, on beds in the hotel rooms, in the bathrooms. Besides its army of cockroaches, the Hotel Theresa had now become a chicken house. When Khrushchev arrived at the Hotel and we got on the elevator, he looked at the ancient chain pulley mechanism that was going to haul him up and mockingly said, "So this is the great American technology?" As we got off a detective, who had lost a son in the Korean War, grumbled, "Here comes that bastard!" Khrushchev's Soviet security chief asked me what was said, and he turned red in the face after I told him. Khrushchev, with what I thought was a twinkle in his eye, asked him, "What did he say?" I listened while my Soviet counterpart groped his way through the definition of a bastard. "Me basTARD!, me basTARD!," Khrushchev walked around laughing and saying to anyone who would listen.

With the single exception of the cold shoulder treatment I had received at the Soviet Consulate after Vishinsky's death, my social relationship with Soviet security personnel was cordial, if not downright pleasant. I worked very hard cultivating that relationship, and it was clearly good for business. Khrushchev's visit changed all that. With him in charge, even with his comic antics, it was back to dealing with grim faces and steel-threaded suits. Khrushchev ordered Soviet Army officers to masquerade in civilian clothes so we wouldn't be able to distinguish who was part of the Soviet intelligence apparatus and who was just a soldier. The ruse didn't work, however, because his military men wore identification pins in their lapels that allowed other Soviet diplomats to recognize them for who and what they represented. We spotted the pins immediately but didn't let on we recognized the charade.

Khrushchev genuinely didn't seem to care about the consequences of many of his actions—like the time he took off his shoe during a session of the UN General Assembly and pounded it on the desk in front of him. I was in the UN delegates lounge at the time. Khrushchev, together with other members of the Soviet delegation, was seated in the General Assembly hall listening to the remarks of Lorenzo Sumulong, a member of the Philippine delegation. When Sumulong criticized the Soviet Union for what he called its ruthless domination of Eastern Europe, Khrushchev exploded. To the Assembly's dismay, he took off his shoe, shook it in defiance at Sumulong, and then began pounding it on the desk in front of him. A few days earlier, Khrushchev had pounded the same desk with his fists during the speeches of UN Secretary Dag Hammarskjold and Prime Minister Harold Macmillan of Great Britain.

Storming out of the UN General Assembly, Khrushchev, with the entire Soviet delegation in hot pursuit, rushed through the delegates' lounge where I had been waiting. When he first bolted through the doors, I jumped up from my chair. He had that prankster's twinkle in his eye again as he glanced over at me. He had a smile on his face and, with his look, seemed to be saying, "Catch me if you can, Antoni." Khrushchev, despite his weight, was extremely quick on his feet. I had to move just as quickly to make sure my car was in position to follow his limousine. Just as his car pulled away from the curb, I jumped in the car on the run and sped after him. We finally caught up to him just a short distance away from the Soviet Consulate. When we pulled up in front of its Park Avenue entrance, Khrushchev bounced out of his limousine like a rubber ball and went bounding up the Consulate steps. He stopped abruptly at the top step and like a Hollywood film director turned around to check the spectacle he had created. "Hey, Antoni," he called out to me. "Next time, I'll wear shoelaces so you'll have time to catch up." Khrushchev laughed and then walked off stage through the Consulate door.

Early one morning, when the streets were still quiet and New York's skyscrapers were silouetted against the dawn, Khrushchev came out onto a small balcony of the Soviet Consulate that overlooked Park Avenue. I had just come on duty and saw him standing above me. Looking down at me, he bragged, "Antoni, some day this will all be ours." Then he asked me, "What do you want, Antoni, when we have it all?"

"Well," I answered, "you know when we crossed that bridge and stopped and paid that toll the other day? I'd like to have one of those booths." Khrushchev laughed. "Antoni," he said in response, "I'll make you the Commissar of the whole line."

Police Commissioner Stephen Kennedy wasn't having any Commissars in his Department, and he was a little miffed when he heard that

Khrushchev had invited me, and not him, to go to Russia as his guest. I tried to convince him that Khruschev's invitation wasn't my idea, but he still wouldn't let me go.

A LTHOUGH I never got close to Fidel Castro when he and Khrushchev met at the Hotel Theresa, on the night Castro won his revolution in Cuba, I was guarding the children of his enemy, Fulgencio Batista, in the Presidential suite at the Waldorf Astoria while Batista was fleeing from the Presidential Palace in Havana.

It was New Year's Eve 1958. I watched as Manola Benitoa, caretaker of Batista's fortune, nervously paced the floor, visibly shaken by the news he was receiving from the Cuban Embassy in Washington and the Cuban Consulate in New York. Castro's rebel army was unstoppable; his revolution had now reached the confines of the Presidential Palace. Batista's time was running out, and so was Benitoa's. His polished manner had been worn thin by the anxiety of the last few days. He looked as if he hadn't slept for a week. Batista's two sons, Carlos Manuel, age 10 and Roberto Francisco, age 11, watched television in an adjoining bedroom while Benitoa paced the floor. The boys had arrived in New York on December 30, and I had met them at the airport. The official line Cuban authorities issued to the press was that Batista's kids were coming to New York as a present from their father. No one bought the story, of course. This trip, as everyone knew, was a move to protect their safety. They would not be returning to Cuba.

As the hour neared midnight, Benitoa called me into the living room of the hotel suite and told me to wait by the phone. A call was expected from Batista himself. After I checked to see that the boys were settled, I took up a post next to the telephone.

"El Presidente wants to talk with you, Tony," Benitoa said. "I think he's going to leave the palace."

"If that's the case," I responded, "I think we should begin to take precautions." I was concerned that pro-Castro hotel employees, reacting to reports coming over Spanish radio stations predicting Castro's triumph, might get cute and try to block off the floor we were on, preventing any attempt we might make to leave. Batista's sons were worth a King's ransom and so were prime targets to be held hostage.

BOSSI detective Ray Clarke was on duty with me as I waited for Batista's call. I asked him to go to another phone and call Gene O'Connell, another BOSSI detective who worked the Cuban desk but who had the night off, subject to being recalled if we needed him. I told Clarke to have O'Connell bring an unmarked car around to a side entrance of the hotel and be ready to move in a hurry. To avoid arousing suspicions that we might be moving Batista's sons to other quarters, I ordered food from room service for everybody to make it appear we were staying put for the night. As soon as the food arrived, we moved the boys out of the Waldorf. Clarke stopped at different floors on the way down and switched elevators several times. He then steered them out a side door and into Clarke's unmarked car. The boys were driven to another hotel and registered there under assumed names. Then, as planned, they were whisked out a side door of this hotel and driven to yet another hotel, registered under still different names, and then put to bed.

I stayed behind at the Waldorf to await Batista's phone call. At precisely midnight, the phone rang. After a few words in Spanish, Benitoa handed me the phone.

"Tony," Batista said, "I am leaving the Palace now. I want to know if my children are all right. Dr. Benitoa has assured me they are in good hands, but I want to know from you if there is anything I should be doing for them. Is there anyone I should call?"

In happier times, Batista could have called the President of the United States to talk about his kids; for the moment, I was all he had. I told him his sons were safe, and I advised him not to call anyone else because it might create more publicity and jeopardize the safety of his boys. I didn't tell Batista that I had already moved them out of the Waldorf. What he confirmed in his phone call was that the television and radio reports that said his troops and tanks were repelling Castro's rebel forces were false; the reports were simply designed to buy him time to secure his escape. Batista's call to the Waldorf was the last one he made before fleeing the Presidential Palace.

After Batista hung up, I called BOSSI headquarters to get an update

71

on what was happening on the streets in the Cuban sections of Manhattan, the Upper West side, and the South Bronx. I found out that violent clashes were erupting between pro- and anti-Castro supporters; panic was beginning to set in at the Cuban Consulate. "The Rack" was being flooded with calls, including some from the office of the Police Commissioner and the Chief of Detectives, as to what our intelligence reports showed was going to happen in New York when Castro took over. Who would we authorize to enter the Cuban Consulate in New York? How about Cuban delegate headquarters at the United Nations? Who would have access to the money in Cuban accounts in New York banks? How were the deposits in Cuban banks of American companies and businessmen going to be protected? At the time, nobody had any satisfactory answers. From the start of Castro's movement against Batista, new so-called "committees" and "clubs" such as the Directoria Revolucionario Club, were formed every day in New York. Leaflets, posters, subway graffiti, flags and pickets began appearing everywhere, especially in front of the United Nations and the Waldorf Astoria. Ironically, the battle cry for Castro's sympathizers was "Viva Cuba Libre" (Long Live Free Cuba).

Although Castro had telegraphed his revolutionary punches long before he seized Havana's Presidential Palace, BOSSI and the FBI had to continuously play catch-up ball to keep track of accelerating events in Cuba, most of which we felt the CIA was manipulating to insure Castro's success. The CIA was swimming so deep in Castro's revolutionary soup that we didn't trust the measly scraps of information that were being fed to us by CIA sources. As Benitoa stalked the floor while we waited for Batista's call, he repeated his anger and frustration at the U.S. for allowing Castro's takeover. "This wouldn't be happening," Benitoa said to me, "if your government let itself know the truth."

Before stepping down and heading for exile in Spain, Batista had been very careful to protect his money. He kept some of it in a Boston bank. I know he did because a few months before Castro took over I carried a suitcase full of Batista's dough, after I paid a visit to the Boston bank with his wife and Manola Benitoa. (Part of our escort duties required us to accompany members of a government's official family wherever they went, even out of state.) One morning we left for Boston in a chauffeured limousine and arrived at the bank shortly after noon. Benitoa removed two suitcases from the trunk of the limousine and carried them inside; I followed him and Senora Batista, both of whom headed for the bank's vault in the basement. Senior bank officials were there to greet them, prepared with withdrawal papers prepared for Benitoa's signature. Once he signed the papers, armed guards wheeled two carts, stacked with metal boxes, into the room. Each of the carts measured four feet long, four feet high and about two feet wide. The metal boxes on the carts were stacked on top of one another. Benitoa selected two of the boxes and had them moved to a conference table in a private room. I stood next to him while he opened one of them. It contained banded stacks of hundred dollar bills. Benitoa stuffed one of the suitcases full with the bills and partially filled the other suitcase with more cash.

By 1:00 p.m., we were on our way back to New York. Benitoa had me carry the fully loaded suitcase on my lap: It contained over a million dollars. The other suitcase, which contained the rest of the two million bucks Benitoa had removed from the bank, was placed in the trunk. When we reached New York, we got stuck in a traffic jam on the East River Drive. If we had had an accident, I wondered who would I save? Senora Batista, Benitoa, the chauffeur, or maybe just the suitcase? There was no accident and the contents of the suitcases eventually made their way into Batista's hands. If he was going to try and buy the right to keep his Presidency, it was too late. Castro's revolutionary juggernaut was knocking on his palace door.

Ironically, Castro's revolution gave law enforcement officials something to smack their lips about, and that was the forced return of high rolling mobsters to the United States. They had to flee Cuba or risk being locked up in a Cuban jail. Chief of Detectives Jim Leggett ordered his men to station themselves at all New York airports to check everyone suspected of having underworld connections or who might have had a warrant of arrest outstanding. A lot of investigations into unsolved crimes would be reopened. To help trace the tentacles of organized crime in the metropolitan area and identify all the members of its families, a new investigative unit of the New York City Police Department was formed called the Criminal Identification Bureau (CIB). Six BOSSI detectives were moved over to CIB to help staff the fledgling unit. Along with Leggett's troops and CIB detectives, FBI agents waited at New York's airports with open arms.

Castro hadn't been Batista's only enemy in the Caribbean; Batista also had had to be wary of his neighbor, Rafael Trujillo, Dictator of the Dominican Republic. Benitoa never stopped complaining to me about Trujillo, another head of state whose safety I helped guard. Trujillo resented Batista because Cubans openly treated Dominicans as second-class citizens. Cuban diplomats, in addition to Benitoa, regarded Trujillo as a tin-horn dictator with visions of grandeur, privately mocking him as the "Buddha with the belly." Sometimes I felt like a nursemaid when I had to listen to the leaders of the world complain about each other. They played with their power like it was a game; ruthless, but nevertheless a game and when they didn't like the outcome they took their ball home just like every other spoiled sport. When Batista was inaugurated as President of Cuba, Benitoa said Trujillo sent five Dominican hit men to assassinate him during the ceremonies. (From time to time I also escorted Nicaragua's President, Anastasio Samoza, who said he didn't want to have anything to do with either Batista or Trujillo.)

I got an earful from Benitoa when he said he was convinced the CIA was bankrolling Trujillo in order to insure their use of Dominican soil as a support base for rebel efforts to get rid of Batista. Backed by the CIA, Benitoa claimed small airplanes based in the Dominican Republic were being used to shuttle arms and ammunition to Cuban rebels, the planes landing at night on remote airstrips to avoid detection. To Benitoa, the money the CIA was pumping into rebel efforts was going to support a Communist takeover, not a democratic one, a prophecy that had now come true.

Benitoa claimed the U.S. government couldn't see the forest for the trees and had turned a deaf ear on the truth. Benitoa said he thought the CIA had promised Trujillo a big chunk of Cuba's gambling operations after Batista was overthrown. The tourist attraction of Havana's gambling casinos and its lush hotels had made Trujillo's mouth drip with envy. Benitoa told me he thought Trujillo had been riding piggyback on the United States plot to blacken Batista's image because of his ties to organized crime. When Batista finally fell, Trujillo waited with open arms for the high rollers and Mafia kingpins fleeing Cuba to head for sanctuary on his soil.

I knew Trujillo had a complex marriage contract with the CIA. CIA big brims used to bring suitcases full of cash to Trujillo's hotel suite and leave with other empty ones that were ready to be filled again with good old U.S. government greenbacks. I always assumed the money was either a payoff to keep Trujillo in line or his cut from business operations that were fronts for the CIA.

My duties as a BOSSI detective guarding Trujillo led me into investigating one of the most mysterious kidnapping and murder cases ever to confront intelligence operations in New York City. The efforts of J. Edgar Hoover and the FBI to solve the mystery and prosecute the guilty were monumental, continuing even until Hoover's death in 1972. The case? It was the disappearance of Jesus de Galindez, a Professor at Columbia University who wrote a book attacking Trujillo as nothing but an assassin and was never seen again after the night of March 12, 1956. The Justice Department together with the National Archives have placed this case on the list of those having permanent historical value.

Galindez

I was off duty when Galindez was first reported missing. That was four days after he was last seen by one of his students entering the 8th Avenue subway station at Columbus Circle, near 57th street, in Manhattan around 10:30 P.M. on March 12, 1956. It was Stanley Ross, owner and publisher of *El Diario de Nueva York,* New York's largest circulating Spanish newspaper who reported the disappearance. Galindez had been a contributing columnist to Ross's paper and, by March 16, his column was long overdue. Ross first reported Galindez missing to the desk sergeant at the Eighth Precinct because Galindez lived within that precinct's jurisdiction in an apartment house on Fifth Avenue near 10th Street. The desk sergeant told Ross to call the Bureau of Missing Persons which was located two floors down from BOSSI headquarters.

Interviewed later, Ross said that before he called Missing Persons, he called the FBI but got the cold shoulder. According to Ross, the FBI said that without evidence showing Galindez was the victim of a federal crime, they had no jurisdiction in the case. Ross said that when he did call the Missing Persons Bureau, he was told that only a relative could file a formal complaint. Ross wasn't a relative, and since he didn't have any proof that Galindez had been the victim of any criminal act, both the Police Department and the FBI had shut the door in his face. That wasn't any help to anybody given the fact that no one knew where Galindez was or what had happened to him. But Ross must have stirred somebody's memory because soon after one FBI agent gave Ross the brushoff, another agent called him back. Ross was asked if he knew of any threats that might have been made against Galindez; did Galindez ever tell him he feared for his life? Ross answered yes. Even with that answer, Ross said he was still told to go elsewhere with his report. He then went in person to the Missing Persons Bureau and demanded his right to file a formal complaint about Galindez's disappearance. He insisted that the police do something about the case. Within a few hours after he left Broome Street, a thirteen-state alarm sounded along the East Coast.

As soon as I returned to work, Inspector Robb called me into his office and told me that before Galindez was reported missing, Police Commissioner Stephen Kennedy, at the request of the CIA, had instructed him to go into Galindez's apartment, find his briefcase, empty it, and deliver its contents, with no questions asked, to the Commissioner's office. Since I had been off duty, Robb had sent BOSSI Detective Eli Kerner to do the job in my place. Whatever Kerner had taken out of Galindez's apartment was quickly routed to the Commissioner's office and then, Robb presumed, on to the CIA. Robb said he was handing me the Galindez investigation, but he had nothing to give me except his speculation that Galindez had been a CIA agent and that his briefcase contained highly sensitive classified documents. Robb did not know what Kerner found, or was supposed to find, nor did Kerner examine the contents of the briefcase before sending them on to the Commissioner's office. At CIA request, no reports were filed on Kerner's journey to Galindez's apartment. Robb said he had been told to keep his mouth shut. Commissioner Kennedy had told him only that the CIA request involved national security and affected the lives of hundreds of people, but he didn't give any specifics, nor did Robb think Kennedy had any details to give.

The motive behind Galindez's disappearance, however, was another matter. Robb told me it was my job to find out why he had vanished and who, if anyone, had ordered him cut from the scene. Robb said the CIA was out of it now, but too many questions were being asked to let this case remain at the precinct level or in the hands of the Bureau of Missing Persons. I didn't blame Robb or the Police Commissioner for not providing more details about what was involved, but I had a gut reaction that some mighty powerful people were maneuvering to make sure nobody found out what had really happened to Galindez or why.

The chain of command for the Galindez investigation was to have Police Commissioner Kennedy and the Chief of Detectives, Jim Leggett, handle the public and press demands for information on the case while I and my partner, Eddie Fitzpatrick, worked behind the scenes. The Eighth Precinct Detective Squad would remain on the investigation because Galindez lived in their jurisdiction. Detective Pete Heinz was assigned to head up the Eighth Precinct's investigation and would work under orders from Leggett's office. What that meant was that if I wanted something done, Leggett's office would issue the order. This procedure was set up to prevent any squabbles during the investigation as to who was supposed to do what. In turn, I was to let Leggett's office know what, if anything, my investigation turned up.

It was also necessary for me to get together with FBI agent Tom Spencer and Gus Micek, the FBI's liaison agent whose office was located inside BOSSI headquarters, in order to pool any information we had on the case. Spencer was in charge of the FBI's Dominican desk in the New York field office. We had known each other a long time. Whenever Trujillo came to town we were in constant touch with each other to make sure there were no sudden violent flareups between anti-Trujillo demonstrators and Trujillo supporters we hadn't prepared for. We had worked closely together in 1954 when a rumor was then being circulated that Trujillo had been put on an assassin's hit list by Dominican dissidents and that the next time Trujillo stepped on U.S. soil, he would be killed.

The Galindez case created an awkward situation because I was under orders not to tell Spencer or Micek about the CIA's request to the Police Commissioner to send one of BOSSI's men into Galindez's apartment before anyone else started snooping around. I felt uncomfortable about that because sooner or later Gus Micek was bound to figure out something wasn't kosher about this investigation. Furthermore, I knew that if Hoover learned that the CIA had been poking its nose into Galindez's records, before he had his chance to look them over, there was going to be one hell of a brawl down in Washington. BOSSI was going to find itself smack in the middle of an intelligence war. I could feel it coming.

I suspected that the CIA's request to get hold of Galindez's records was an effort to legitimize what they had probably done already, namely, gone into his apartment before Robb sent Eli Kerner there and taken out what they wanted, leaving us the scraps. A lot could have happened between the time Galindez was last seen and Ross's report to the Missing Persons Bureau. It was possible that the CIA notified BOSSI of its interest in Galindez's records, as an intelligence ploy, to give themselves permission to talk to us about the case; the CIA had no jurisdiction to investigate domestic disappearances. However, from the CIA's urgent move to get access to Galindez's papers, I assumed his disappearance had severed a link to a complex intelligence operation. That did not mean Galindez was a CIA agent or even that he knew how important he might have been to whatever concerned the CIA; nor did I expect the CIA to volunteer any information or to tell us the truth if we asked how Galindez fit in with their operations. I also had to consider the fact that whoever was responsible for Galindez's disappearance had the best chance to get inside his apartment the night he vanished and to set the stage for whoever showed up next. Common sense dictated that, if Galindez was kidnapped, he would have been carrying a key to his apartment.

In reconstructing the events the night Galindez disappeared and fixing the time when he was last seen, I learned that Galindez had taught an evening course at Columbia University on the night of March 12 and then stopped to have coffee with some of his students after the class was over. It was one of his students, Evelyn Lang, who then drove him to the subway station at Columbus Circle. That was the last time anyone ever saw him.

When I contacted Pete Heinz at the Eighth Precinct to talk about the case, I was surprised to learn that he, along with a couple of detectives from the Missing Persons Bureau, a lady friend of Galindez's named Lydia Miranda, and Stanley Ross, had already paid a visit to Galindez's apartment. Heinz told me that there was no evidence of a break-in or a struggle; everything was in order. Newspapers for Monday, March 12, were on Galindez's bed, his clothes were hanging in the closet, and his desk showed no signs of disruption. Burglary was ruled out because approximately $1,000 in cash had been left untouched. The Missing Persons bulletin stated that when last seen Galindez "was carrying a dark brown briefcase." Heinz said he saw a brown leather briefcase on a chair near Galindez's bed but that it was empty. Lydia Miranda told Heinz that Galindez carried this briefcase like it was another arm. Whatever it had contained was gone, but I couldn't tell Heinz that the CIA had its contents. For the moment, at least, my lips were sealed.

It wasn't just Robb's orders that restricted the information I gave to Heinz. The fact was that when Heinz asked me, "What have you got on Galindez, Tony?" BOSSI had nothing except what Robb had told me was the CIA's interest in the case. Galindez had never been reported to BOSSI as a threat or a bother to anyone. Fitz and I backtracked through BOSSI files to see if we had any record of any link between Galindez and the Dominican exiles opposed to Trujillo; we didn't. I was surprised about that because in late December 1955, a high-level associate and confidant of Trujillo's named Dr. German Ornes Coiscu held a press conference in the office of *The New York Times* to announce that he was breaking his ties with Trujillo. Because Ornes had stuck his neck in Trujillo's noose by going public with this announcement, detectives were assigned to protect Ornes's safety. If there was a direct link between Ornes and Galindez, in their opposition to Trujillo, I had yet to know about it. The column Galindez wrote for Ross's newspaper, *El Diario de Nueva York,* didn't establish that connection, even though Galindez stuck as many editorial barbs in Trujillo's dictatorial hide as he could.

Before Galindez disappeared, my other contacts in the Dominican dissident community never brought up his name. Galindez was an intellectual and, at least publicly, didn't travel in the circle of dissidents like Nicholas Silfa, Jose Espaillat, or Alberto Aybar who headed up anti-Trujillo organizations called the Dominican Revolutionary Party and the Casa Dominicana. During my years guarding Trujillo, I kept in constant touch with Silfa, Espaillat, and Aybar so that nobody was killed on my watch. But until Robb gave me the Galindez case, the BOSSI card indices had no spot for the name Jesus de Galindez, nor did we have any informants to question who could tell us what could have happened to him. For the time being, it was all guesswork. Galindez had simply vanished; there was no eyewitness to any abduction, no ransom demand, no evidence that he was taken across state lines, no massive bills stacked and unpaid, no unexplained bank withdrawals, no dramatic change in his lifestyle.

Knowing Trujillo, I had to assume that, for the time being, he was involved in the plot to have Galindez disappear. This wouldn't have been the first time Trujillo had had one of his enemies kidnapped, except that wasn't how he operated against his opponents on the streets of New York. Here, he usually had them gunned down, mob style. Back in 1935, Trujillo's son-in-law, Porfirio Rubirosa, whom I later came to know as Trujillo's shadow (and bodyguard), was the prime suspect in orchestrating the assassination of a Trujillo dissident named Sergio Benscome. I couldn't get it out of my head that, if Trujillo had made up his mind to get rid of Galindez, then why not just shoot the guy, get it over with, take the heat for awhile, and then get on with the business of being a dictator? Why create a mystery that was becoming more complex each day?

The unanswered questions were piling up. If Galindez was kidnapped, then how did the kidnappers happen to know the precise time he would enter the subway station at Columbus Circle or get off at his destination? Was he followed? Did he ever arrive at his apartment? If so, was he then coaxed out of it by someone he knew? Did he have a prearranged meeting with somebody? Was he then snagged like an animal in a trap? What did the CIA have to do with all this? Was it really the CIA or somebody using its credentials that got the Police Commissioner to have Robb send Kerner, as my replacement, into Galindez's apartment? What was in his briefcase that was so important? The only conclusion I could draw at the time was that the mission to get rid of Galindez had to have been carefully planned; there had to be more than one person involved.

Using newspapers, information about Galindez coming in to Police Headquarters over the teletype, and what I picked up from several talks with Tom Spencer, I began to put together a profile of Galindez. Of immediate interest was the book Galindez had written attacking Trujillo's rule that had been published as a doctoral thesis for Galindez's degree from Columbia University. Entitled *The Era of Trujillo*, the book charged that from the time he seized power in 1930, Trujillo and his death squads had been responsible for more than 140 assassinations. Before dealing with the present, however, I had to learn as much as I could about Galindez's past.

I learned that he was born in 1915 in the Basque Province of Spain, the son of a wealthy ophthalmologist. As a kid, he lived in Madrid where his father had his office. He had one brother, and his mother died when he was very young. Galindez graduated from the University of Madrid Law School in 1936. In 1937, he worked as the Legal Attache of the Basque Legation in Madrid. He served on the board of the Spanish Bureau of Prisons. He became a lieutenant in the Spanish Republican Army but eventually switched his allegiance during the Spanish Civil War to support Spanish Loyalists against Franco's Republican Army forces. That information moved me to check BOSSI files to see if Galindez's name ever appeared in the reports of undercover operators who had infiltrated communist-front organizations like the Veterans of the Abraham Lincoln Brigade. The Brigade had fought with the Loyalists against Franco during the Civil War and afterward made its headquarters in New York. Spanish Loyalists were supported, in part, by the international communist movement headquartered in Moscow, but that didn't make Galindez a communist, nor could I find any record of his name in BOSSI files. At the end of the Civil War, Galindez fled to France where he stayed until the fall of 1939.

After France was overrun by the Germans at the start of World War II, Galindez, together with other Basque exiles, left France for the Dominican Republic at Trujillo's invitation. Some Basques remained in France during the war and fought with the French underground which, in turn, worked closely with American OSS agents to help defeat the Germans. The OSS was a forerunner of the CIA. After the war, the Dominican Republic became the centerpiece for intelligence operations in the Caribbean Basin and in all of Latin America. Hoover stationed FBI agents, trained primarily in counterintelligence, in the American

Embassy in the Dominican Republic. Until the CIA came along, Hoover had complete control over Caribbean and Latin American intelligence operations. I had no doubt that somewhere along the line during the Galindez investigation the conflict developing between the FBI and the CIA over who would control foreign intelligence was bound to surface. The FBI and the CIA were on a collision course. I assumed that when Galindez left France, he didn't leave his connections to the Basque underground behind and might have been recruited for a U.S. intelligence mission. But for which agency? I didn't know, and at the time neither the FBI nor the CIA was owning up to anything. I felt like I was heading blindfolded into a swamp.

Galindez lived in the Dominican Republic from 1939 to 1946. Trujillo granted sanctuary to a lot of Basque refugees like Galindez to come and live in the Dominican Republic. The Basques were good fighters and smart people, and Galindez was no exception. While living in the Dominican Republic, Trujillo took a shine to Galindez and appointed him to various government positions. Galindez worked as a legal adviser to the country's Department of Labor. He also taught at the Diplomatic School attached to the Foreign Office of the Dominican Republic government. He became Secretary of the Minimum Wage Commission, but got fired in 1946 for promoting the settlement of a sugar workers' strike that cost Mauricio Baez, the strike's leader, his life.

Fearing retaliation, Galindez fled the Dominican Republic and settled in New York. Once in the United States, he registered as a foreign agent with the Justice Department in Washington representing the exiled Basque government. When Galindez moved to New York, the Basque government-in-exile's President, Jose Antonio Aguirre, moved the world headquarters to Paris. Galindez's registration statement described most of his duties as involving the receipt and distribution of money contributions to the Basque cause, to Basque exiles in need of financial support. The annual financial statements Galindez was required to file with the Justice Department disclosed that, from 1950 until his disappearance, Galindez had collected and distributed over $1 million. This activity had raised no eyebrows because Galindez's efforts on behalf of Basque exiles had been primarily charitable. Exiles often banded together to form political alliances, reaching out to help one another through parent organizations like a government-in-exile. What Galindez was doing was in no way unusual, especially since he registered with the Justice Department as a foreign agent and filed financial reports to show where the money went. After he vanished, however, the CIA's interest in Galindez created the suspicion that Galindez was a paymaster for CIA agents, buried within the Basque movement, who were operating under deep cover in Europe and South and Central America.

In tracing the distribution of some of the money Galindez collected, it was established that he maintained two numbered Swiss bank accounts in Geneva. Instructions were on deposit with the bank to credit the money to the accounts of various individuals. It didn't take much brains to assume that these names were of vital concern to the CIA. While the maintenance of these accounts didn't prove any direct connection between Galindez and the CIA, it did show, as far as I was concerned, that his activities were linked to something much bigger than Galindez's singular fight with Trujillo. I had a hunch that whatever was in Galindez's briefcase had more to do with his role as an intelligence agent than anything else.

The fear Galindez told Stanley Ross he had for his life centered on the movements of a man he knew as Felix Hernandez Marquez. In November 1955 Hernandez had unexpectedly stopped Galindez in the lobby of his apartment house and had tried to tell him about a plot to kill Trujillo. In his debriefing of the events surrounding Galindez's disappearance, Ross said that Hernandez had pressed Galindez to let him come up to his apartment to spread out the details of the plot but that Galindez had refused. Galindez told Ross he was convinced Hernandez had been involved in the murder of Mauricio Baez, the labor leader Galindez had tried to help in the settlement of the strike against Trujillo in 1946. Baez fled to Cuba, but Trujillo's death squad, with Hernandez right in the middle of it, caught up with him and killed him. Galindez, in turn, had fled to the United States.

I found Galindez to have lived an ordered, frugal, almost ascetic existence, even though he lived just steps away from fashionable Fifth Avenue. His reported earnings were very modest. In the year before he disappeared, his income was a mere $3,600, hardly enough for him to start a career as a bon vivant. The Basque government-in-exile paid his rent and his utilities out of the contributions he collected. I also found out that Galindez liked the ladies, but none of his relationships provided any material for a scandal. His major weakness appeared to be what Juan Onatibia, Galindez's successor as Basque delegate in the United States after Galindez disappeared, said was Galindez's "almost child-like desire to engage in political intrigue." In Paris, Jose de Aguirre said that, even though some of Galindez's attacks on Trujillo were an embarrassment to the Basque movement, Basque exiles would not have cut him off as one of their leaders.

At Columbia University, Galindez taught a variety of classes in Latin American history, politics, and government. When word broke that Galindez's book attacking Trujillo was starting to circulate in the Dominican Republic, Trujillo struck back at Galindez with the accusation that Galindez was just a pawn for communist elements in the labor force. That was always Trujillo's first offensive against an enemy before killing him: label him a communist sympathizer and, if that wasn't strong enough to discredit an opponent, then call him a pervert. Whenever I guarded Trujillo, he thought communists were everywhere, like germs; he had me and Eddie cover him like a blanket. He was paranoid about assassination attempts and was convinced that whoever tried to kill him would have to be a communist. In writing his book, Galindez had struck back at the hand that fed him.

During Pete Heinz's search of Galindez's apartment, he found an envelope that was addressed to the New York City Police Department. The envelope was marked with the instruction that it was to be opened in the event of Galindez's death or disappearance. Inside the envelope was Galindez's signed statement to the effect that said, if anything happened to him, the police were to look for his enemies in the Dominican Republic. He wrote that Trujillo would be to blame and that Felix Bernardino would have carried out Trujillo's orders. (Bernardino, Consul General of the Dominican Republic from 1951 to 1953, was suspected of masterminding the assassination of Andreas Requena, another Trujillo opponent, who was gunned down on the streets of New York in 1952.) The search of Galindez's apartment also turned up a will he had written that left all his possessions, including his writings, to any publisher who wanted them. Among Galindez's unpublished writings was an unfinished novel that was to be based on the lives of members of Trujillo's family, especially Trujillo's adopted son, Ramfis. The novel was intended to be an expose of Ramfis' corrupt lifestyle. Ramfis, whom I met when Trujillo's bodyguard Porfirio Rubirosa married the American heiress Barbara Hutton, lived fast and loose and had become something of an embarrassment to American authorities with his playboy antics and carousing with the fast-track Hollywood crowd.

Even though Galindez was a known Trujillo opponent, I quickly eliminated the CIA as being responsible for his fate. There would have been no trace of the CIA if they had wanted Galindez eliminated, nor would they have involved the New York City Police Department to get the contents of his briefcase. The CIA would never deliberately put itself in the intelligence spotlight if it had also ordered Galindez terminated. A possibility did remain, however, that his removal was a rogue intelligence operation that hadn't been cleared by CIA headquarters. If the Galindez caper was a maverick, unauthorized operation, I doubted at the time that anyone would ever find or identify those responsible.

When I guarded Trujillo, I found it interesting that, even though he consented to placing CIA operatives in his own country, he didn't want the FBI or the CIA checking on his activities when he was in New York. He didn't trust them. Trujillo told me on more than one occasion that he thought the CIA and U.S. business interests in the Dominican Republic would sell him out if he didn't play ball exactly as they wanted, and, if he didn't, they wouldn't hesitate to plot his own assassination. Trujillo, however ruthless he was, told me that at times he felt imprisoned by his own power—even though I had no illusions that he would use that same power to stop his opponents dead in their tracks.

Behind the scenes, I knew that members of the Dominican Republic's delegation to the United Nations let it be known that they were sympathetic to the goals of the Dominican Revolutionary Party and the Casa Dominicana. Without the backing of the Dominican military command, however, they didn't stand a chance of freeing their country from Trujillo's domination. Short of killing him, the Dominican Revolutionary Party and the Casa Dominicana had a perfect right to try and topple Trujillo. But an open break with Trujillo, without a lot of muscle behind it, was a self-imposed death sentence. Trujillo's secret police conducted round-the-clock manhunts for his enemies and it didn't matter what country they were in. His agents tracked, killed, and sometimes kidnapped his opponents from locations all over the Caribbean and as far north as the streets of New York. Silfa, Espaillat, and Aybar were afraid that Trujillo agents had already infiltrated their organizations. To protect their identity, Silfa had his supporters wear black executioner's hoods whenever he held a meeting. In exchange for my promise of no leaks, Silfa, Espaillat, and Aybar gave me the names of the members of their organizations in case any of them had to reach me or my partner, Eddie Fitzpatrick. Once in my possession, these names were kept in specially coded files in BOSSI headquarters. Access to these files was restricted to Inspector Francis, J. M. Robb, then BOSSI's commanding officer, Lieutenant Tom Crane, myself, and Eddie.

My other contacts in the United Nations made it clear that in its investigation of the case, the United States government had better show that America was still a safe place for exiles, dissidents, and emigres to protest wrongs in their native lands. Uruguay's Mission to the UN charged that whoever plotted Galindez' disappearance had violated the UN Charter. Galindez, if he hadn't already become a world figure in political circles championing the rights of people against dictators like Trujillo, became one overnight.

On March 30, *The New York Times* published another interview with Dr. German Ornes Coiscu. Coiscu blamed Trujillo agents for kidnapping and then murdering Galindez. Ornes said he was now in extreme fear for his own life. Police protection of Ornes had continued ever since he publicly broke his ties with Trujillo in December 1955. We intensified our surveillance to see if he or any members of his family were being followed by Trujillo agents. If so, we were hopeful of getting a lead on Galindez. Hispanic American groups gathered in public to demonstrate against what they claimed was another example of Trujillo's monstrous behavior. I watched and listened to most of the speeches.

Nicholas Silfa of the Dominican Revolutionary Party had his own theory about how Galindez disappeared, and that caused Chief of Detectives, Jim Leggett and his crew, nothing but grief. Silfa told a group of reporters that Galindez had been kidnapped and then thrown alive into a ship's boiler on the S.S. *Fundacion*, a freighter owned by the

Dominican Steamship Line which, in turn, was controlled by Trujillo. Silfa's allegation triggered a flood of phone calls to Police Headquarters. On orders from the Police Commissioner, Leggett had to organize a team of detectives to interview every crew member of the S.S. *Fundacion*. BOSSI was never to be exposed as leading the Galindez investigation. Leggett didn't like this assignment one bit. He had to conduct his investigation in a fishbowl. The detectives he assigned to investigate Silfa's allegations were followed by reporters wherever they went. All the churning stirred up by Silfa's charges finally stopped when it was proven that Galindez's body would never have fit through the door of the ship's boiler. I told Silfa to keep his theories to himself and his mouth shut.

The Galindez investigation started expanding into New York's Harbor, however, when BOSSI detectives Artie Silk and Charlie Necas, BOSSI's waterfront experts, were sent to the docks to sound out longshoremen, union stewards, and steamship owners to see if they might know anything about the case. At that time, the Port of New York, especially north of the city on the Hudson River near Yonkers, was a major depot for unloading sugar imports from Cuba and the Dominican Republic. Sugar from the Dominican Republic was arriving at a far more rapid pace than sugar steaming in from Cuba. The competition between the two countries over sugar dollars amounted to high-stakes poker. The docks and harbors of the United States, like the gambling casinos in Cuba and Las Vegas, were also targets of control by organized crime. One reason why Trujillo was so upset over labor strikes in his country was that these strikes undercut his main advantage over Cuba, namely, cheap labor. Cheaper sugar prices from the Dominican Republic meant that refineries would begin stockpiling Dominican sugar rather than the more expensive Cuban variety.

I had to consider whether Galindez's disappearance was related to this sugar battle, even though Galindez himself was not connected with either sugar market. The point to be made was that any attempt to discredit Trujillo had to hurt him in his pocketbook. Galindez had discredited Trujillo in his book, and it was being published in South America and circulated throughout the Caribbean. As a result, the dissident jungles were rumbling. Those opposed to Trujillo were beginning to feel their oats. Although Trujillo couldn't kill everybody, the question remained as to whether it was Trujillo who had stopped Galindez in his tracks. The docks in New York Harbor failed to provide us with any clues.

Stanley Ross was openly criticized for waiting too long to report Galindez missing. Silfa told me that he had become suspicious of Ross when he learned that Ross had checked with the superintendent of Galindez's apartment building soon after Galindez disappeared but then waited four days before notifying the police. Why Ross insisted on being present in Galindez's apartment together with Pete Heinz and Lydia Miranda came into question because before the disappearance, Ross had never been inside his apartment. Miranda reported that Galindez had also been suspicious of Ross. Miranda claimed Ross knew all about the novel Galindez was writing about members of Trujillo's family. Miranda said Ross was sending Trujillo advance copy of Galindez's work through the Dominican Consulate in New York. She also revealed that in January 1956 Galindez received a letter from Ross telling him he would no longer be paid for his column. Galindez, Miranda said, had become convinced that Ross was acting under orders from Trujillo to cut off the purse strings.

When a Dominican informant confirmed that Ross was, in fact, reporting all of Galindez's activities to Trujillo's Consul General in New York City, I became suspicious that Ross might have been involved in the disappearance. The Galindez to Ross to Trujillo connection was the first clue to help prove Ornes's argument correct, as well as to help verify the truth of Galindez's statement, that Trujillo was responsible for his disappearance. Ornes claimed that Ross was working as a Trujillo intelligence agent at the time Galindez disappeared.

While sorting out all these accusations, my memory bank kept reminding me that Ornes had been a target of suspicion for an ex-FBI agent named John Frank whom I had met at BOSSI headquarters in January 1956; that was two months before Galindez disappeared. I wondered what Frank might have known about Galindez even though his name never came up during our meeting. On January 17, shortly after Ornes put his life on the line by breaking with Trujillo, Eddie Fitzpatrick received a telephone call from Frank at BOSSI headquarters asking him if he was going to be around the next morning. Frank told Fitz he had something very important he wanted to discuss with him. Fitz called to tell me about Frank's call and asked me to make sure I'd be around the next day to find out what it was all about.

As scheduled, Frank showed up at BOSSI headquarters the next day to meet with Fitz. When he arrived, Frank was accompanied by Detective Lieutenant Arthur Schultheiss who was then head of a precinct detective squad. He had once been assigned to the Bureau of Criminal Alien Investigations, one of BOSSI's forefathers. Inspector Robb, BOSSI's commanding officer, handled the introductions. (Lieutenant Tom Crane was still in charge of BOSSI's daily operations, but in the increasingly political structure of the Police Department, an Inspector—in this case Robb—had been named BOSSI'S chief. He carried the spear, but behind the scenes, Lieutenant Crane still ran the show. Robb acted as the liaison between BOSSI and other branches of the Police Department, the District Attorney's Office, the Justice and State Departments in Washington, and top-level command posts in the FBI and the CIA).

Robb said that Frank and Schultheiss were old buddies; he had known both of them since World War II. Frank was then working for the FBI and had also worked for the CIA. He and Schultheiss had gotten to know each other when Schultheiss was assigned to the Bureau of Criminal Alien Investigations. In the early years of the war, Frank and Schultheiss had worked together as a team executing presidential search warrants against the homes of German and Japanese nationals as part of a nationwide effort to uncover spies and saboteurs. Fitz knew Schultheiss from those years but had never met Frank before this day.

Frank explained to us that he was representing, as a private attorney, some Dominican companies and had some information about the activities of Dr. German Ornes Coiscu which he thought we might want to investigate. My ears perked up because, just a few weeks earlier, Ornes had publicly ended his ties with Trujillo. Frank said he was convinced that Ornes had skimmed money from the bank accounts of a Dominican printing company and had illegally wired this money to a bank account he had opened for himself in the First National City Bank in New York. Frank claimed approximately $80,000 was missing from the till. I sensed, however, that this story was a smokescreen to disguise what Frank was really after, and that was information about anyone we knew to be an anti-Trujillo dissident. BOSSI had no jurisdiction over embezzlement cases, nor did BOSSI detectives formally charge people with crimes or make arrests. BOSSI was an intelligence operation. Even if Ornes was guilty of embezzlement, his activities posed no threat to the people or property of the city of New York. He might have been a threat to somebody's pocketbook but not, as far as I was concerned, to the security of New York. I waited for the real story to surface.

After the preliminaries, Frank finally leveled a broadside against Ornes and accused him of using the money he stole to help support communist guerrilla activities in Cuba and Guatemala. He claimed that Ornes was going to tie in with anti-Trujillo forces and that they were going to help him funnel the money into communist rebel hands. As soon as I heard this charge, I knew it had to come from Trujillo. Frank went on to describe his knowledge of the activities of the Dominican Revolutionary Party and the Casa Dominicana. He also claimed to know all about the alleged assassination plot to kill Trujillo that Spencer and I had checked out in 1954. I wondered whether Spencer had tipped off Frank about the plot. Frank had worked out of the New York field office when he was in Hoover's stable, and I assumed he had kept up his contacts there. Frank's role as an attorney for private interests didn't cut him off from those contacts, especially since Frank was beating the drums for us to help him gather more information about Trujillo's opponents so that he and his clients could stop them from supporting communist insurrections in Latin America.

After meeting Frank and Schultheiss, I learned that before we met, the Justice Department had already refused to act on Frank's complaint against Ornes. Frank apparently didn't have as much muscle with the U.S. government as he thought he had. On January 9, 1956, Frank had gone to the office of Myles J. Ambrose, then Administrative Assistant to the United States Attorney for the Southern District of New York. According to Ambrose, Frank said he figured that since Ornes had used cablegrams to wire the embezzled loot to New York, he had probably violated some federal law. However, between Frank's meeting with Ambrose and our meeting in BOSSI headquarters, the Justice Department begged off the case and told Frank they were not going to file any charges against Ornes. The money, if in fact it was wired to a bank in New York as Frank claimed, passed through international channels, not through interstate connections. So, I asked myself, why did Frank then come to us? He said that he had a lot of connections inside the halls of government, but so what? His connections weren't going to change BOSSI's stripes and make it a prosecutor instead of an investigator. Frank was only a private citizen and had no authority to see BOSSI files, if that was what he was after. His friend Schultheiss had to know that no BOSSI detective could recommend prosecution for a crime over which it had no jurisdiction or permit a private citizen access to our records. Neither Schultheiss nor his squad had any jurisdiction over the Ornes matter, the activities of the Dominican Revolutionary Party, or any other anti-Trujillo faction. If a private citizen, no matter what his past intelligence connections were, had free access to our records, then the integrity of BOSSI's entire apparatus was at stake. Reluctantly, I had to ask myself whether Frank had already received his information about Dominican dissident activity in New York from both Spencer *and* Schultheiss who, in turn, was getting it from his old friend and my boss, Inspector Robb.

The New York City Police Department's inner circle of power was just as chummy and restricted as any other exclusive men's club in the country. The only difference was that, instead of suits and ties, its members wore uniforms and badges. Schultheiss and Robb belonged to this club. By 1956, the year Galindez disappeared, members of this inner sanctum had a lot of stories to share. Most of NYPD's brass came up through the ranks in the late 1930s and 1940s. They saw the coming of the United Nations to New York and watched the world become showcased within its boundaries. They became part of the big parade. They met for coffee and for lunch, they occasionally attended formal affairs as the guests of foreign governments—including that of Rafael Trujillo's Dominican Republic—and they enjoyed the perks that go with their rank. In the hierarchy of power in the Police Department, rank kept company with rank. But the disappearance of Jesus de Galindez and the sinister overtones of this mystery stripped this hierarchy of its insulation. No matter how hard men like Frank, Schultheiss or Robb tried, they weren't going to be able to keep the lid on this investigation. Ornes's defection from Trujillo and the disappearance of Galindez following so shortly thereafter put a spotlight on everyone interested in their fate.

While my efforts to put the lid on Silfa's public outcries appeared to be working, privately he persisted in his accusations of Ornes as a Trujillo double-agent. Silfa maintained that Ornes had once been a Trujillo fat cat; cutting his ties with Trujillo meant giving up access to a big chunk of money. Ornes had been, according to Silfa, an extremely vocal supporter of his chief until he suddenly split with him in 1955. Trujillo had let Ornes become president of El Caribe as well as its majority stockholder. Ornes was an attorney with powerful connections and was retained as local counsel by several American companies doing business with the Dominican Republic. Silfa asked why Ornes would leave Trujillo's fold if he had all that going for him? Why was his severance with Trujillo so sudden?

My answer to these questions was a simple one. Ornes, I learned, had divorced his wife, and that had caused something of a scandal in the Dominican Republic. They were being ostracized from Dominican society. Ornes's new wife was not Catholic, which amounted to heresy in the Dominican Catholic society of that day. When I interviewed Ornes, he said he felt Trujillo's time was running out and that the book Galindez had written was rapidly undermining whatever power Trujillo had left. It was time, Ornes had convinced himself, to get out of the Dominican Republic as fast as he could and start a new life. I didn't tell Silfa that Frank wanted Ornes prosecuted for embezzling money from one of Trujillo's companies. I told Silfa he was still barking up the wrong tree.

Questions arose about Silfa himself after Dominican Consul Arturo Espaillat called me late in the summer of 1956 to tell me that Silfa had disappeared and had probably hooked up with Galindez somewhere in Europe to divide up the money Galindez had stolen from a bank account he was handling as a representative of the Basque government-in-exile. I didn't believe anything Espaillat had to say. He had a diplomatic title, but he was actually the head of Dominican intelligence operations and Trujillo's secret police. He was as ruthless as they come. (Espaillat was also a graduate of the United States Military Academy at West Point.) Espaillat's allegation was the first sign that Trujillo was trying to launch a campaign of disinformation in order to distance himself from any crime involving Galindez. As it turned out, Espaillat's information was totally false. Silfa had told the FBI he was going to Paris to attend an international labor conference as the official representative of the Confederation of the Organized Democratic Dominicans in Exile. Tom Spencer told me that Silfa's trip was approved and that, for his protection, his movements were being monitored by FBI agents in Europe. Espaillat's phone call to me verified that Trujillo agents were also tracking Silfa's every move.

While Fitz and I were looking into Silfa's accusation of Ornes's possible role as a Trujillo double-agent as well as Espaillat's red flag rumor about Silfa, a curious event took place that added even more mystery and suspicion to the Galindez investigation. After Ornes held his news conference at the office of *The New York Times* in December 1955, he, like Silfa, demanded police protection. Although Silfa publicly refused police protection, he had no objection to our keeping him under constant surveillance. Ornes expressed doubts about the real intentions of the Police Department because, he said, a man who represented himself as a police lieutenant had knocked at his apartment and claimed the Police Commissioner had sent him to pick up his passport. Ornes said he found that request very strange. This lieutenant then showed him a letter from the Dominican Ambassador to Police Commissioner Stephen Kennedy asking Kennedy, on his behalf, to pick up his passport. When asked for the passport, Ornes refused to turn it over. The lieutenant—or whoever he was—left empty-handed and never returned. As Ornes well knew, the Police Department has no jurisdiction to collect passports or to revoke visas; that's the exclusive territory of the State Department and the Immigration and Naturalization Service. Neither the State Department nor any Immigration official ever notified Ornes that his diplomatic passport or his right to be in the United States was in jeopardy.

When I heard about Ornes's encounter with the lieutenant, I immediately assumed it was part of a plan to make sure he didn't leave the country; that whoever wanted him to stay put was placing him in the same target zone Galindez had been in on the night he disappeared. After Ornes reported this unauthorized request, Inspector Robb told me that he had never seen the letter supposedly sent to Commissioner Kennedy by the Dominican Ambassador and knew nothing about it. If Kennedy had, in fact, received the letter, he would have told Robb about it—and he didn't. Robb looked dumbfounded. The only lieutenant remotely connected to Ornes was Frank's Police Department buddy, Lieutenant Schultheiss.

On September 19, 1956, Frank unexpectedly called me at my home to tell me that Ornes and Silfa were friends and that he knew about Silfa's trip to Paris to attend a labor conference. Someone had given Frank my phone number. Frank's call again raised the suspicion that he was trying to use the Police Department to gather information about Dominican dissidents and their movements. At least on the phone, Frank was trying to push his way past BOSSI's Rack and get inside our files. I told Frank I already knew about the connection between Ornes and Silfa and let the conversation end right there. I didn't trust him. If I had let him go on, there was a good chance that someday he might try to involve me in whatever he was up to simply by telling someone else that he had told me his concerns, thereby creating the impression that I shared in those concerns and had become part of his plan. Sometimes in intelligence work it's necessary to avoid knowing too much about what someone else knows, especially if your instincts tell you to be on guard. My guard was up with John Frank.

Right around the time Frank called my home, something else began bothering me about the Galindez investigation. The FBI was pulling back on its cooperation on the case. Never before had I felt that the FBI was holding out on a case in which we were both heavily involved. My long and close relationship with Spencer, who was still in charge of the FBI's Dominican desk, had now grown distant and awkward. My phone calls to him were not returned and he even stopped providing me with progress reports on leads we were both working on, such as the possible involvement of Felix Hernandez Marquez, the man who had stopped Galindez in the lobby of his apartment house the previous November. I began to wonder whose cards Spencer was playing in the investigation. Not only had everything been hushed up right after Galindez disappeared, courtesy of the CIA, but now I felt a second coverup was underway and that Spencer, at least, was part of it.

Both Fitz and I felt left out, that somehow we weren't playing by the rules of the game. But whose game? Publicly, the FBI insisted that no evidence had yet turned up to show that Galindez was the victim of a crime. Behind the scenes, however, it was all over the case. The FBI had been doing a dance trying to stay out of the public spotlight on the case, but, like it or not, they were being forced into it. The Galindez case wasn't some interstate hijacking or bank robbery the FBI could keep to itself. This was a loaded, menacing, explosive kidnapping, and possibly murder, case with international implications. It's one thing to have separate investigations going on without sharing results; that's commonplace given the competition that exists between city, state, and federal law enforcement agencies. But it's another matter entirely to have a joint investigation go bust because one side—the FBI in the Galindez case— suddenly decides it's time to stop trusting the other side with information. Jealousy never helped solve a crime. I wanted to know what Spencer and/or the FBI was afraid of disclosing. I wanted to know who in the Police Department Hoover didn't trust.

After six months, I was still at square one in my investigation of why Galindez suddenly vanished and who was it that pulled the strings to cause his disappearance. The one solid lead that I thought I had went up in smoke. Even with Spencer's reluctance to continue opening up his file, I had put together a pretty thorough picture of the character who had put fear in the mind of Galindez in November 1955—Felix Hernandez Marquez. That wasn't his real name. It was Francisco Jesus Martinez Jara. Our files in BOSSI headquarters listed him as having at least twenty aliases. He was nicknamed "El Cojo" (the lame one) because he limped and walked with a cane. El Cojo used his aliases as a cover for various criminal enterprises such as forgery, drug smuggling, and securities fraud and as a hit man for Trujillo. Shortly after Galindez disappeared, an article appeared in the Cuban newspaper, Tiempo, that was headlined: "The Same Man Who Kidnapped Jesus Galindez Planned the Murder of Pipi Hernandez." Hernandez was a Dominican exile, living in Cuba. The article's subheading read: "Revelations in the Case of the Kidnapping of Professor Galindez." El Cojo was named in the article as the mastermind of the plot to abduct and then murder Galindez. On May 23, 1956, a dispatch from Havana over the wire services reported that a Rafael Soler Puig, alias "El Morte" (the corpse), had told Havana police that he had turned down an offer of $100,000 to murder Galindez. Puig claimed that El Cojo was the one who had made the offer. The FBI had tracked El Cojo to Miami, Florida, where he supposedly told a man named Orestes Portales that Trujillo had sent him on a mission to find two assassins to kill Venezuelan President Romulo Betancourt and Jesus de Galindez at a price of $35,000 a hit. El Cojo also told Portales that he had traveled to Detroit and then to New York to recruit a couple of hit men but had found no takers. After meeting with Portales, El Cojo fled the United States and was never heard from again. His girlfriend, Ana Gloria Viera, was found dead in the wreck of a car in the Dominican Republic. She had been El Cojo's bait to lure Dominican exiles into compromising situations. She was the only passenger in the car and she didn't drive. She was clearly murdered.

What made no sense to me at all was Trujillo's position in all of this. Why, I asked myself, would Trujillo hire a big-mouth con man like El Cojo to say he was sent to hire a couple of hit men to knock off Betancourt and Galindez? Trujillo was too smart to expose himself so easily. I felt that El Cojo was either intentionally, or maybe even unintentionally, screwing up some other plan to get rid of Galindez. Ironically, El Cojo was providing more fuel for Trujillo's opponents by broadcasting his assignment. There was also a third possibility: that El Cojo was deliberately being used as a cover for the real plan to kidnap and then kill Galindez. If so, then who, if it wasn't Trujillo, was behind that scenario? El Cojo was never allowed to answer that question.

O N December 3, 1956, the lid on the Galindez investigation blew sky high. An abandoned car was found next to a cliff near a slaughterhouse in a remote section of the Dominican Republic. The car belonged to an American journeyman flier named Gerald Lester Murphy. Hordes of sharks swam in the waters below the cliff, feeding primarily on the offal dumped by the slaughterhouse. Murphy's body was never found, and at the time, it was presumed that he had become another meal for the sharks. Later, however, it was established that he had been killed in a backroom of the Police Station in Ciudad Trujillo and that his body had then been dumped in an unmarked grave. Before Murphy disappeared, he told some friends that he had been hired to fly a "wealthy invalid"—someone with cancer—from Zahn's Airport in Amityville, Long Island, to an airfield in the Dominican Republic. When a picture of Galindez appeared in a newspaper and Murphy apparently saw it and realized the true identity of the person he piloted out of New York, he started talking about it to his friends. That was a fatal mistake. Murphy blabbed that, while he was waiting for his passenger to arrive for the flight, an ambulance—or what looked like one—drove onto the tarmac and a man, comatose or drugged, was carried onto the plane and placed on a stretcher specially fitted inside the seating compartment. Murphy took off for the Dominican Republic the night of March 12, 1956—the night Galindez disappeared. Murphy talked about his mission, committing the most lethal of mistakes in the process, and got himself killed.

A few weeks after Murphy's car was discovered abandoned near the Dominican cliff, the body of Octavio Antonio de la Maza was found hanging from a broken shower pipe in a jail cell in Ciudad Trujillo. Dominican officials reported that de la Maza had left a suicide note in his cell claiming responsibility for Murphy's death. The suicide note, the Dominicans stated, was de la Maza's confession. The note said that Murphy made sexual advances to him, they then had a fight, and in the struggle, Murphy had fallen over the cliff and joined the sharks. De la Maza had been Murphy's co-pilot on a leg of the flight from Zahn's Airport to the Dominican Republic. He had joined Murphy at Lantana Airport in West Palm Beach, Florida, during a refueling stop. The airport maintenance man, Donald Jackson, who refueled the plane at Lantana, told FBI agents in Miami that when he went inside the plane to fill the extra gas tanks, he saw a man lying motionless on a stretcher. Mixing with some leaking gas fumes was a peculiar stench. Something medicinal, Jackson said, like anesthesia.

Despite the attempt to make it look like suicide, it was clear that de la Maza was murdered. His suicide note was simply a forgery. Before he could escape from the Dominican Republic, a squad from Trujillo's secret police picked him up and killed him. A man with a varied career, de la Maza had killed Felix Bernardino's brother in a gun battle on a

London street in 1954. Even though Bernardino was a Trujillo hatchet man and de la Maza appeared to have been on a mission sanctioned by Trujillo, de la Maza's death was regarded as Bernardino's revenge for the murder of his brother. The bodies were beginning to pile up. No one seemed to doubt that Galindez himself had also been murdered.

Shortly after Murphy's car was discovered and de la Maza found hanging in his cell, a heavy-duty skull session was held at BOSSI headquarters to try to sort out the case. Those attending were Inspector Robb, myself, Fitz, Spencer from the FBI, Lieutenant Crane, and two "big brims" from the CIA. This meeting had the flavor of an intelligence agency grudge match as if we had all been competitors in a game. The atmosphere was brimful of mistrust, and we all knew that if we let that mistrust overtake our judgment we'd be playing right into the conspirators' hands. Suddenly, the big brims from the CIA began sniping away at Robb as to why he was letting Schultheiss get BOSSI's reports of our investigation of the case. I hadn't known he was. I was stunned at the disclosure because, as far as I was concerned, Schultheiss had no reason to be poking his nose into the investigation. The tension in the room grew as the CIA men, with their questions, pushed Robb against the wall. Robb's answer to the CIA was that he thought Schultheiss could keep him informed about Frank's activities. In unison, the CIA team exploded.

"What activities?"

"They've been friends for a long time," Robb answered.

"So what?"

"We worked together back in the war years," Robb responded, "when Roosevelt ordered the homes of Krauts and Japs searched."

"What's that got to do with the Galindez case?" the CIA pressed. "What did Frank tell Schultheiss he was up to? What does Schultheiss know about Galindez?"

The CIA obviously had some damaging information they were using, without disclosing it, to trap Robb. As they waited for Robb to answer again, there was dead silence in the room. The flustered Robb turned red in the face while I sat still and listened. Throwing Schultheiss's name into the soup, along with Frank's, meant that the CIA had already concluded that they were connected in some way to Galindez's disap-

100

pearance. I only knew Schultheiss through Robb, but still I found it impossible to believe that he or any cop in his position of command would become involved in a kidnapping and murder case and expose the whole New York City Police Department to a massive scandal in the process. I figured it was the CIA, and not Spencer, who raised the spectre that Frank and Schultheiss might have some fresh skeletons in their closets because Spencer was an old friend of Frank's. Frank was FBI, ex or otherwise, and if he was somehow connected with this whole mess, Hoover would be pressing every available agent into the investigation. But Spencer kept his mouth shut. My hunch was that he had more than a passing acquaintance with Frank and Schultheiss and that, for the time being, he preferred keeping the connection to himself.

"Don't throw it all on my shoulders," Robb shouted back at the CIA. "You're not telling us anything, except to point your fingers."

"That's right," the CIA responded, "that's exactly what we're doing."

The meeting ended abruptly with the CIA men getting up and stalking out of the room, leaving Robb sitting in his chair drowning in a pool of doubt. After everyone else had gone and just Fitz and I were left with him, Robb looked at us and asked: "What the hell is going on? Can you figure it out? This case is bigger than the FBI and the CIA put together. I'm the guy who's supposed to be on top of it all and the more I'm on top the more I feel I'm covered by a stinking mess." He was right. Robb said he felt like he'd been sucked in by Frank and Schultheiss and that Hoover and the CIA were on his back to explain what the hell he was doing hanging around with them. "I had nothing to do with Galindez," Robb said, and the way he looked, haggard and worn out by the tension that had been brought to his brow, I believed him. He had to hope Hoover would too.

None of us knew it at the time, but we soon learned that among Murphy's papers that were found in his apartment in Ciudad Trujillo was a notebook with the name Horace Schmahl, c/o the District Attorney's office in New York, scrawled inside. Schmahl ran a private detective agency in Manhattan. The discovery of the notebook moved Hoover into high gear. It was a map into the nest of conspirators who had plotted to kidnap Galindez. It was the big break Hoover had been looking for, but with Murphy and de la Maza (as well as El Cojo) now out of the way, the case was still in danger of ending up in a circumstantial graveyard.

Robb, Fitz and I had to think hard and fast about where this case was leading because moonlighting for Schmahl had been Lieutenant Artie Schultheiss. Schmahl's agency had apparently been handling assignments in New York for Maheu Associates, a private detective agency based in Washington, D.C., headed by Robert Maheu, an ex-CIA agent, and Schultheiss was getting a piece of that action as a result of his connection to Frank. (Maheu later became Howard Hughes' right-hand man and ran the Hughes empire from a suite in one of Hughes' Las Vegas hotels.) The FBI had traced telephone calls Frank had made to Schultheiss right before Galindez disappeared. Frank was working out of Schmahl's office at the time Galindez vanished. Frank made most of his phone calls to Schultheiss from a suite Maheu kept at the National Republican Club on West 40th Street. This was more than a pandora's box being opened. There were now a lot of coffins in the ground. I realized I was going to have to be involved in the intelligence equivalent of an autopsy to be performed on the careers of a high-ranking officer of the New York Police Department and an ex-FBI agent. I understood immediately why Spencer had clammed up. He had to have known about the Frank/Schultheiss connection long before Murphy's notebook was found, obviously before Murphy was killed. I also suspected that Inspector Robb was under Hoover's searchlight and was trying to find a way to extricate himself from the close ties he obviously had had with both Frank and Schultheiss.

As we tried to catch our breath over the implications of the evidence we had now come face to face with, other facts began to surface that not only filled in pieces of the puzzle but also moved the intrigue of the case up another notch. A rumor began circulating (and I hate rumors) that one of the reasons Murphy was knocked off was because he was double-crossing Trujillo by offering to sell information (documents) to Batista about how Cuban rebels, along with guns and ammunition, were being flown from the Dominican Republic to secret landing zones outside of Havana. That sounded like a story I had heard from Manola Benitoa, Batista's confidante, when I first began guarding Batista's wife and kids when they came to New York. If true, and if Murphy was also one of the pilots who ferried the rebels and their cargo to Cuba, then his murder was designed to silence much more than his airborne escort of Galindez. Murphy was only 23 years old when he died. On November 17, 1956 he wrote a note to his employer resigning from the job Trujillo had arranged for him. "I feel that this course of action is definitely best for all concerned." The rumor had it that Murphy was picked up by Trujillo's secret police before he had a chance to get out of town, knocked silly by a blow to the head and then choked to death with a rope Trujillo henchmen used as if they were hog tying a steer. The rumor about Murphy's possible double dealing also raised the spectre that Galindez was somehow interfering with the rebels' mission to overthrow Batista.

Murphy was a kid born in North Dakota who had dreams of adventure in his head. He fulfilled one dream when he became a charter pilot for an air charter service in Miami, Florida. On March 4, 1956, eight days before Galindez vanished, he took a leave of absence and headed north for Linden Airport in Linden, New Jersey. The previous week, on February 27, 1956, he had called the Trade-Ayer Charter Service at Linden Airport and had asked the manager there whether he had any twin engine military surplus planes available to rent. Murphy said he would need the plane for about a month. When the manager answered yes, Murphy started heading north. On his way to New Jersey, he made a stop in Washington, D.C., to pick up an old friend of his, Harold French, whom Murphy knew from his flying days in Seattle. French was an experienced airplane mechanic who was then on leave from the United States Air Force. He held the rank of sergeant. On March 5, Murphy and French left Washington by train for Linden Airport. They got off in Elizabeth, New Jersey, and checked in at the Rahway Tourist Motel for a night's sleep. The next day they went to Linden Airport to check on arrangements for the plane. After meeting the manager of the charter service and going over the plane, Murphy plunked down a $1,500 cash deposit for the month's rental of a twin engine green-striped yellow Beechcraft. Murphy told the manager to make out the receipt to a "John Kane." That was an alias for John Frank.

The telephone call Murphy made from Miami to the charter service in New Jersey followed a meeting that he had had in Miami with "Kane" and Brigadier General Arturo Espaillat, then Consul General for the

103

Dominican Republic. When Murphy went to the airport to rent the twin engine Beechcraft, he was met there by "Kane," Espaillat, and Felix Bernardino, Espaillat's predecessor as Dominican Consul General. (Bernardino was the man Galindez said would be primarily responsible if anything happened to him.) After rental arrangements for the plane were completed, all of them went and stood in front of the plane and had their picture taken. Espaillat later denied that he was in the United States at the time. He claimed he didn't arrive in the United States until May 1956, which was two months after Galindez disappeared. That's what his passport showed, Espaillat said. But I knew that Espaillat had more than one passport; he had boasted to me, more than once, that he had more than one undetectable way to enter the United States.

On March 8, Murphy, French, and "Kane" met again at Penn Station in New York. The next day Murphy and French purchased four steel drums that, according to French, were to be used to store extra gasoline. They also bought some blankets and pillows, some clothesline to tie and secure the auxiliary tanks, and emergency flares that were normally used for flights over long stretches of water. On March 10, Murphy and French took the rental plane on a short side trip to Staten Island where its rear seats were removed. This was done so that the plane could carry a passenger laid out on a stretcher. Outfitted for its journey, the plane was taken on a test run to Newark Airport. On March 12, the plane was flown to Zahn's Airport on Long Island. It was now ready for its mission. Before leaving that airport, Murphy filed a flight plan: The last stop was Montecristo Airport in the Dominican Republic.

After Murphy completed his mission and delivered his human cargo to the Dominican Republic, Trujillo rewarded Murphy with a job as a co-pilot with Compania Dominicana, a small Dominican airline that hauled cargo and mail, and ran charter flights around the Caribbean. Murphy then rented an apartment, bought a car, fell in love with a Pan Am stewardess named Sally Caire, and wrote home to his parents that all was right in his world. One of Murphy's confidants had been the Chief of Police in Ciudad Trujillo. Just before Murphy's car was found, someone who didn't like the Chief, or what Murphy might have told him about his flight, walked into the Chief's office and shot him to death. "Good God," Murphy reportedly said to his fiance when he heard of the Chief's murder. "What am I going to do now? They've killed the only protection I had." Murphy never had a chance to tell anyone who the "they" were. After Murphy disappeared, Sally Caire said that he had felt uneasy and suspicious about his mission to fly the so-called wealthy invalid to the Dominican Republic. He had been sold a bill of goods that his would be a mission of mercy to fly a dying man to see his mother one more time. I doubted the conspirators told Murphy, "Hey, kid, want to make a few bucks flying someone we're about to kidnap to the Dominican Republic?" Murphy told Caire that he secretly stored a tape recorder in the cockpit of the plane and recorded everything that was said during the flight. After finishing his mission, he said he mailed the tape to his friend "Johnny" in Washington. According to Caire, the tape was to be used if anything happened to him. The tape was never found.

In early Spring 1957, Robb was notified that the Internal Security Division of the Justice Department was starting a Grand Jury investigation into the Galindez case and wanted to pay him a visit. The Horace Schmahl/John Frank/Artie Schultheiss connection led right to BOSSI's doorstep because Schultheiss had once been assigned to BOSSI's forefather, the Bureau of Criminal Alien Investigations, and had worked side by side with Frank when he was with the FBI. Robb called me into his office to tell me that a couple of government lawyers wanted to interview both me and Eddie Fitzpatrick about the meeting we had had with Frank and Schultheiss in January 1956. Robb said he had already confirmed that Frank had come to BOSSI after trying unsuccessfully to get Myles Ambrose at the U.S. Attorney's office in New York to prosecute Dr. German Ornes Coiscu. Robb said that to crack open the Galindez case, Frank was going to be charged with failing to register as a foreign agent and I, and probably Fitz, would be called to testify against him. At the time, Robb said nothing about Schultheiss and I didn't ask what the Justice Department was going to do about him. That was obviously a hot potato and unless pressed to do it, I wasn't going to stick my nose in the oven to find out. Robb said Internal Security had concluded that when Frank came to BOSSI headquarters posturing as an attorney for some Dominican companies to complain about Ornes, he was actually in charge of Trujillo's overseas intelligence operations. Hoover and the Justice Department wanted to know what we knew about Frank's activities tracking the movements of Dominican dissidents. Robb said Frank had been targeted by Hoover as the mastermind of the Galindez kidnapping. It was now up to Justice Department lawyers to break Frank apart. If I knew anything about Hoover, he wouldn't stop until he had ground his former agent into dust—and for good reason.

The FBI had mounds of reports on Galindez, many from Galindez himself, because, as I came to learn from FBI contacts other than Spencer, Galindez, code name "Rojas," had served as one of Hoover's paid confidential informants from June 1944 until he disappeared. Before officially going on Hoover's payroll, Galindez had been secretly employed by U.S. Military Intelligence at the same time he was serving as an official of the Trujillo government. Under the code name DR-10, he had been an informant for the Office of the Legal Attache before fleeing the Dominican Republic for the United States. Galindez had developed his own string of informants from inside the Dominican Republic National Army, the Grenada Company, a subsidiary of the United Fruit conglomerate, and other companies scattered throughout the Dominican countryside. Most of the information Galindez provided centered on the activities of those Spaniards who migrated to the Dominican Republic after the Spanish Civil War. Galindez spied on his own people to determine their communist sympathies or their allegiance to Nazi interests that began flourishing in Latin America both before and after the Second World War.

Once he started operating in the United States and until his disappearance, Galindez supplied hundreds of written reports to the FBI that covered alleged communist activities within the Spanish-speaking community in New York City. He attended rallies, published articles in many Spanish-language publications, and steadily rose in stature within New York's Latin American community. Galindez regularly reported to the FBI on the actions of the Nationalist Party of Puerto Rico, the Committee for Latin American Unity, and the Veterans of the Abraham Lincoln Brigade, all suspected of being communist-front organizations. He also supplied information to the FBI about Argentine, Cuban, Dominican, Mexican, Venezuelan, and other Spanish nationals "and the groups to which they belong." The FBI summarized some of Galindez's reports, "such as fund-raising dances held by a group of Cubans, led by Fidel

Castro, who are reportedly planning to overthrow the present government of Cuba." Galindez had warned Hoover about Castro years before Castro's rebel forces gained enough momentum to overthrow Batista.

Whoever Galindez's contacts were, they provided invaluable information on communist movements in Latin America. He also kept tabs on the network of some of the Basque nationals who had stayed underground in Europe and secretly returned to Spain long after the end of World War II. Galindez once advised the FBI "that the underground operated by the Basque Government is so secretive, that not all members of the Basque Government-in-exile are aware of its existence." On March 7, 1956, five days before Galindez disappeared, the FBI field office in New York recommended to Hoover "that the Bureau authorize continued contact with this informant with payments at the rate of up to $125 per month, plus reimbursement of expenses actually incurred not to exceed $30 monthly for a three-month period effective April 1, 1956." Galindez made his last report to the FBI on March 9, 1956, three days before he vanished.

The fact that I hadn't initially known that Galindez was an FBI informant didn't really make any difference in my investigation. Had I known about it, I might have guessed why Galindez was eliminated, but I still wouldn't have known exactly who was behind it. Public disclosure of Galindez's intelligence role would have provided an even deeper cover for the culprits, especially if his disappearance had nothing to do with his connection to the FBI. It was also obvious from the very beginning of my investigation that Galindez was connected to an intelligence operation. What now made a difference to everyone connected to the investigation was that one of Hoover's own former agents was the prime suspect in the kidnapping and murder of one of Hoover's informants. To make matters worse, it was a batch of ex-FBI agents and one of Hoover's top aides who had originally suggested John Frank to Trujillo's recruiter, Pedro Blandino.

The Justice Department's campaign to label Frank a Trujillo agent and to tie him with the plot to kidnap Galindez was creating all sorts of bad publicity for Trujillo. Newspaper editorials all over the world were condemning him, and tourists began to stay away in droves. With so many people shaky about going down there his World Trade Fair was turning into a big financial bust and with it his plan to capture Cuba's gambling empire was going down the tubes. In going after Frank, Hoover didn't give a damn about Trujillo's headaches. At whatever cost, his aim was to crucify Frank, and if that effort also brought down Trujillo, so be it.

When Robb, Fitz and I met with the lawyers from Internal Security, I had the feeling that somebody was trying to tie me and Fitz into the Galindez conspiracy because of the way certain questions were being asked—the "when did you stop beating your wife" variety. An example occurred when I was casually asked about visits to Frank's Washington law office that I never made. When those questions were asked, I assumed that my picture was being shown around as a check on my story. Either efforts were underway to disprove it, or there was a legitimate need to eliminate me as one of the conspirators if I was going to testify against Frank. I accepted the latter as the reason and just rolled with the punches. When all the questioning was completed, the Justice Department attorneys asked Robb to take statements from me and Fitz. They added Schultheiss's name to the list. He was then the Commanding Officer of the Fourteenth Precinct Detective Squad.

The statements, which were directed to be completed in question and answer form, were to cover the number of times we met or talked with Frank and the substance of the conversations we had with him. Schultheiss's statement was taken on April 10, 1957, in Robb's office, with Robb conducting the questioning. My own and my partner's statements were scheduled to be taken on April 12. All the statements were to be transcribed and sent to both Hoover and the Assistant United States Attorneys who were conducting the Grand Jury investigation into Frank's activities. I was given copies of everyone's statements and I took them home to read. Schultheiss admitted that Frank had made several phone calls to him during the critical planning stages just before Galindez disappeared. Schultheiss also gave the history of his relationship with Frank, going back to the Second World War when they worked together. He denied any knowledge of Frank's involvement with Dominican companies. He insisted their relationship was strictly social, but the dates of the phone calls seemed to be saying something else. They were too coincidental. The first call traced to Frank came on January 17,

1956, the same day he called Eddie to see if Fitz would be in BOSSI headquarters the next day. That was when I first met Frank. Schultheiss had come with Frank to the meeting at BOSSI's offices; he was present when Frank made his pitch about Ornes embezzling money from a Dominican printing company. Frank's other phone calls to Schultheiss came on March 5, 7, and 8, days on which Frank met with Gerry Murphy about renting the plane. Schultheiss wasn't asked about his moonlighting for Horace Schmahl's private detective agency or what he knew about how Gerry Murphy happened to have Schmahl's name, c/o the District Attorney's office in New York, in his address book. I figured Robb was going to leave those questions, and a lot more, to the Justice Department.

The next time Fitz and I met with Inspector Robb in his office to discuss the case, he had several troubling items on his agenda. One of them seemed to make no sense at all: our income tax returns! Robb said he had received a tip that after Fitz and I became Trujillo's detective escorts, we were added to Arturo Espaillat's under-the-table payroll. (Espaillat was head of Trujillo's secret police and was then serving as Dominican Consul General.) Before we had a chance to blow our tops, Robb said he didn't think the story was true—but if it was, we were in big trouble. Robb assured us that we weren't targets of an investigation but that if we were going to testify against Frank in whatever case Justice Department attorneys were putting together, our credibility had been put at stake by this tip and we'd better be clean or our careers were out the window. As far as Fitz and I were concerned, this accusation meant somebody wanted us off the case. Robb said the Justice Department wanted a complete record of all banking transactions Fitz and I had made during the last year, as well as a copy of our income tax returns and a sworn statement of our assets and liabilities. "We're sorry to put you guys through this," Robb said, "but Internal Security wants another check done on both of you before you and Fitz go to Washington to testify. If you don't cooperate, the feds will get the records anyway."

If I was going to be on anybody's payroll, it would have been Trujillo's, not Espaillat's. I guarded Trujillo, not Espaillat, and I had every opportunity imaginable to grab a little loot on the side from Trujillo if I so much as winked for it. (He kept so much cash around I once watched him lay out enough greenbacks to buy a limousine to take him to the World Series when he couldn't rent one. While he was at it, he also bought—for cash—a fleet of cars for his Consulate staff.) I knew that Trujillo would do anything to show he wasn't linked to Galindez's kidnapping, but I also knew he wouldn't have pointed to me as being on Espaillat's payroll because that would have wrecked his relationship with the New York City Police Department. Whoever wanted to discredit me, and I assumed it was John Frank, wanted to tie me to Espaillat's intelligence operations. If Frank could prove that, then he could prove that whatever he was doing for Trujillo's government at least had the support of the NYPD; that support would have meant double-crossing the Dominican Revolutionary Party and the Casa Dominicana. Frank could also have been laying the groundwork to prove he had the support of the CIA or someone in that agency who had sanctioned the operation to get rid of Galindez. I got my bank statements and tax returns together and, in disgust, almost threw them on Robb's desk.

As soon as our financial records passed muster, Robb told us to pack our bags for Washington. Other than the Chief of Detectives and the Police Commissioner, the only persons who knew where Fitz and I were headed and the time of our departure were BOSSI Lieutenant Tom Crane and Inspector Robb. Greeting us with a nonchalant, "isn't this a coincidence," at Penn Station just as we were to board our train was Lieutenant Schultheiss. He said he wanted us to know that Frank—the man we were traveling to testify against—wasn't really a bad fellow after all. "No, not bad, just evil," I thought. Schultheiss was playing with a time bomb.

Shortly after we arrived in Washington, checked into our hotel, and unpacked, someone slipped a note under our door. "What the hell is this?" Fitz asked when he saw the paper on the floor. He read it and handed it to me. The unsigned note told us to come down to the hotel lobby and wait near a trophy case behind a lobby cloak room until someone contacted us. "Like Hell!," Fitz said. We ignored the note, but not the fact that we had been tailed to the hotel. We decided to get out of our room for a while and take a walk. "I'm almost twenty years on the job, Tony," Fitz said as we got on the elevator. "This is the first time I've ever felt the smell of a case. Something isn't rotten in Denmark, it's rotten right here." After we returned to our room, we found another note had been slipped under our door. "Come down to the lobby as requested. It's important!" the note said. Whoever wrote it was damn anxious to get us downstairs to the lobby and probably into a conspiracy to obstruct justice. The only place we were going to outside of our hotel room was to the Federal District Courthouse.

When I arrived at the courthouse and before I went in to testify before the Grand Jury, one of the Justice Department attorneys showed me a photograph of Frank, Murphy, Bernardino, and Espaillat as they stood lined up against the twin engine Beechcraft at the Linden Airport in New Jersey. In the photo they hardly looked like conspirators; actually, they looked more like old time flying heroes standing ready to destroy the enemy and save the peace. The first question that came into my head was why these men would let their picture be taken when so much secrecy and planning were involved in the abduction of Galindez. Espaillat had denied he was in the United States at the time Galindez disappeared; he claimed he didn't arrive in the States until May 1956. But nobody believed him, and it didn't matter what his passport said; the photograph didn't lie.

During my questioning, federal prosecutors asked how I thought Galindez was taken from Manhattan to Zahn's Airport. On March 11, 1956, the day before Galindez disappeared, Harold French, Murphy's sidekick, was asked to time how long it would take to drive to the airport from downtown Manhattan. He told the FBI that he had timed the trip as taking an hour and forty minutes. I had been hard pressed to answer what route I thought the kidnappers might have taken when I met with FBI agents and Justice Department attorneys in New York before heading for Washington. My credibility was still being tested. In view of the unfounded allegation that I was on Espaillat's payroll, I had to remain on the testing block as the FBI and the Justice Department tried to sort out the reliability of its own witnesses. If I had known the exact route to take or the time needed to drive to Zahn's Airport, then that would have been evidence that I had participated in the conspiracy. I had never been to Zahn's Airport. I only knew that the fastest and surest way to bypass traffic and get out of New York City was to have a red light or a siren or both in your car or to be driving an ambulance. Nobody stops a flashing light or the blaring sound of an emergency. The vehicle used, however, was, up to this point, apparently untraceable.

Playing a hunch that an ambulance might have been used to transport Galindez to Zahn's Airport, Fitz and I checked on every public and private ambulance service in the city. We didn't rule out the rental or purchase of a hearse either, or the use of a station wagon. Our first stop was Bellevue Hospital. They had two old war horse ambulances with the clanging bell on the side that were kept in a kind of graveyard garage. The engines of these relics were shot; they hadn't seen a road or a patient, dead or alive, in years. We checked private ambulance services all over the metropolitan area. We struck out, mostly because none of these services kept any decent records that might have helped us identify anyone who rented an ambulance for the period covering Galindez's disappearance. The hearse rental business in New York was just about nonexistent. BOSSI informants, with connections in the Mafia, came up empty-handed when they checked out the possibility that, for a price, the mob had provided the kidnappers with a hearse from a friendly funeral home. Although we also came up empty-handed, Fitz and I did reach two conclusions. The first was that whoever obtained the vehicle that brought Galindez to Zahn's Airport made sure it couldn't be traced. Second, the route taken to the airport had to be carefully plotted and timed; that effort required first-hand knowledge of the streets, bridges, tunnels, and highways that lead in and out of the city. Trujillo agents—his hit squad—couldn't have been the only ones involved. The mastermind who planned Galindez's abduction had put together a stopwatch operation. When Galindez was taken out of whatever vehicle brought him onto the tarmac, Murphy had the engines of the airplane already warmed up and ready to fly.

My Grand Jury testimony centered on the time and place I first met Frank in January 1956 and what he had said about representing Dominican companies in the United States and his interest in the activities of Dominican dissidents like Dr.German Ornes Coiscu. I was also asked about the phone calls Frank had made to BOSSI headquarters after that meeting as well as before and after Galindez disappeared. Frank's phone calls centered on the information he had been gathering on Ornes's activities and his conviction that Ornes was up to no good in hooking up with anti-Trujillo groups led by Nicholas Silfa, Alberto Aybar, and Jose Espaillat. The questions I was asked in the Grand Jury were designed to produce answers that would strip the shield Frank was using that he was only an attorney representing the interests of his clients and that one of them had been stiffed by Ornes out of a lot of money. If necessary, Fitz was going to be used at the time of trial to corroborate my testimony.

Fitz and I returned to New York the same way we had come—by train. Sitting in the bar car nursing a scotch and soda, I suddenly spotted Schultheiss coming toward us. My antennae shot to attention as he approached. Schultheiss started talking about old times, about how the police force had changed after the Second World War, about how men didn't really stick together anymore. He talked about loyalty, about the badge of a cop, about how it could help you get things done. It could also help bury you, I thought, if you reached too far into the cookie jar. There was always another hand in there waiting to pull you inside and drown you in the crumbs. Fitz and I listened and drank our scotch. We didn't say a thing.

When I reported back to Robb in New York I not only summarized my testimony, but I also mentioned our "coincidental" meeting with Schultheiss both on the Penn Station platform and in the train's bar car on our way back from Washington. Robb looked stunned. He paused for a long time and then told me that Commissioner Kennedy had just called his office and that the call was about Schultheiss. I wasn't sure I wanted to hear what Robb was going to say: it seemed that Schultheiss had become a target in Hoover's investigation of the Galindez case. Hoover wasn't satisfied that Schultheiss's relationship with Frank was "strictly social."

O N May 13, 1957, John Joseph Frank, alias "John Kane," was arrested by special agents of the FBI while he stood on a street corner in Washington, D.C. A few moments before his arrest, an indictment charging him with violation of the Foreign Agents Registration Act of 1938 was unsealed in Washington's Federal District Courthouse. FBI agents tailed him until they received confirmation that the indictment was out in the open. Then they moved against him. The indictment charged that starting in 1954, Frank, acting as "John Kane," had worked for the Dominican Republic without registering as a foreign agent with the United States Attorney General. Two weeks before his arrest, the State Department formally advised the Dominican Ambassador that it had established Murphy's connection with Galindez's disappearance. The State Department also claimed it had evidence linking Murphy to Frank.

On November 25, 1957, I was back in Washington, this time to testify at John Frank's trial. As expected, I was called as a witness to verify Frank's contact with BOSSI in January 1956 and about Frank's interest in the activities of anti-Trujillo dissidents. I and one other witness were the links to establishing Frank's true status as an unregistered foreign agent acting on behalf of Trujillo. His role as an attorney was nothing but a smokescreen. The other key witness at Frank's trial was Mrs. Sarah T. Newcomer, a former U.S. government secretary. She testified that in January 1955 Frank had hired her to do some typing. She said that Frank told her he was hired to investigate a plot to assassinate Trujillo and that Dominicans living in New York were the ones behind the plot. She said she typed Frank's reports, which she sent along to Trujillo along with bills for her boss's services and reimbursement for his expenses. One of these reports was entitled: "Investigation of a Plot to Assassinate Generalissimo Rafael Trujillo by Jesus Maria de Galindez and Nicholas Silfa." Frank's attorney argued that this report shouldn't have been shown to the jury inasmuch as it was confidential and was made in Frank's capacity as an attorney for Dominican interests, not as a foreign agent for Trujillo's government. Frank's report to Trujillo, over objection, was received as evidence. It also contained a recommendation for Trujillo's approval that an investigation be conducted on Galindez and Nicholas Silfa "along the lines of extensive surveillance and a technical surveillance," that is, using wiretaps. Frank wrote that "under suitable pretext the writer personally conducted certain additional investigations and surveillances in connection with this matter in New York City."

My contact during Frank's trial with the government's chief prosecutor, William G. Hundley and his assistant, Plato Cacheris, was a brush stroke on the canvas of my future. Almost seventeen years to the day after I testified in Washington, I would again testify in that same courtroom looking at Hundley and Cacheris as they huddled as defense, not government, attorneys. They were talking with their client, former Attorney General of the United States John J. Mitchell during the Watergate trial for obstruction of justice.

On December 9, 1957, John Frank's jury convicted him as charged. He was sentenced to eight months to two years in jail, but he never saw the inside of a jail cell. After his conviction he filed an appeal and stayed free on bail during the appellate process. The Federal Circuit Court of Appeals for the District of Columbia reversed his conviction and ordered a new trial. The court said that Hundley went too far during the trial when he attempted to link Frank's failure to register as a foreign agent with Galindez's disappearance. In his summation to the jury, Hundley talked about Frank "fixing up that plane for that strange mission" and being "involved with . . . Murphy and these mysterious deals." The court decided that Frank didn't get a fair trial because of the "prosecutor's attempt to connect him in the jury's minds with the Galindez-Murphy affair."

Frank's second trial was scheduled to start on March 5, 1959. I was told to pack my bags and get ready to testify again. I would be traveling alone because Fitz had retired from the Police Department after twenty years on the job. He also didn't want to be involved in another case like the Galindez one ever again. Before I headed back to Washington, however, Hoover called for a meeting in New York with federal and New York City law enforcement officials, to discuss Frank's prosecution and the stymied Galindez investigation. I was invited to attend the meeting along with Inspector Robb. Robb told me that Hoover was furious over the reversal of Frank's conviction.

The meeting was held in the tower suite of the Waldorf Astoria. This part of the hotel served as the official residence of the United States representative to the United Nations, and it was also where Hoover stayed whenever he came to New York. When I entered the meeting room, I was greeted by an anxious, frustrated group of law enforcement officials. It looked like a wake without the flowers. The Galindez case, almost three years old, was slipping out of Hoover's hands; the investigation, not Frank, was turning to dust. With the disclosure of the government's case during the first trial, the U.S. prosecutors expected new defense tactics to get Frank off the hook, new shots at Frank's own

115

government to keep him from serving even a day behind bars. The FBI hadn't yet been able to put enough evidence together to prosecute anybody for what happened to Galindez. Murphy and his co-pilot Octavio de la Maza had been murdered, El Cojo had vanished, his girl friend Ana Gloria Viera was killed (the FBI suspected she was also on board the plane and kept Galindez drugged during the long flight). Both the night watchman at Zahn's Airport and the mechanic who serviced and refueled the plane in Florida had died, the watchman from natural causes and the mechanic in an airplane crash. Dr. Miguel Rivera, a Dominican physician living and working in New York, committed suicide shortly before he was to be married. The FBI suspected that, for the sake of saving the lives of relatives in the Dominican Republic, Rivera had been the one who had drugged Galindez before he was put on the plane. Horace Schmahl, the private detective whose name was found in Murphy's address book, took the Fifth Amendment.

Hoover had more than an ordinary problem dealing with Lieutenant Schultheiss's alleged involvement in the case. Hoover was a great supporter of the NYPD, and he needed us more than we needed him. If he tried to bring down Schultheiss along with Frank, he was going to destroy his relationship with the Department and perhaps the credibility of the Department itself. He couldn't afford to do that unless he had positive proof. For the time being, Hoover had to accept Schultheiss's position that his relationship with Frank was "strictly social."

At the Waldorf meeting relations between Hoover and his CIA counterparts were clearly icy. The FBI, though in charge of Western Hemisphere security, had no control over CIA operations. The CIA hadn't been put under any public scrutiny over its handling of the Galindez case. Its records weren't available for review, and it didn't have to gather evidence to prosecute people. It went one better: It periodically arranged their elimination. But Gerry Murphy was an American citizen, and Jesus de Galindez was a valuable FBI informant. Hoover wanted Frank and the CIA to pay for their deaths. But the CIA wasn't a law enforcement agency and could basically thumb its nose at Hoover.

All the same, the CIA's public image had been badly stained and its problems severely magnified now that Castro and his rebels had won the revolution in Cuba. The CIA had backed the wrong man in Castro.

Galindez had warned the FBI about Castro several years before the Cuban Revolution got rolling. The Galindez case had become a major embarrassment to the CIA because it let a rogue operation get out of hand. It was now trying to figure out how to undo the damage. But the CIA, like a giant holding company, doesn't always know what some sections of the company are up to; most of the time that's a deliberate intelligence policy in order to insure that the least number of people know what's going on. This policy can create monumental problems in the field precisely because the right hand isn't told what the left is doing. The Galindez kidnapping, with Frank at the helm, was a fallout of that policy. The lives of Murphy and Galindez fell through the cracks.

From start to finish, the meeting with Hoover at the Waldorf was filled with acrimony over the reversal of Frank's conviction and the FBI's and the Police Department's failure to marshall enough evidence to indict Galindez's kidnappers. Just before I left the meeting, Hoover stood up, pounded his fist on a table, and vowed to "get John Frank if it's the last thing I ever do."

Also becoming a thorn in Hoover's side was Morris Ernst, the then famous civil rights lawyer who had been hired after Frank was arrested to represent Trujillo. Ernst was hired through the recommendation of a public relations firm to check (whitewash) the connection between Trujillo's murderous dictatorship and Galindez's disappearance. Trujillo had retained a public relations firm in New York to find him a good lawyer. Once he put Trujillo's money in his pocket, Ernst said that his investigation would be completely independent and that he would publish a report on all the facts. Ernst offered his cooperation to Attorney General Herbert Brownell, Allen Dulles of the CIA, and even President Eisenhower in exchange for information Hoover had on the Galindez case. I knew Hoover had no use for Ernst ever since Ernst sided with Alger Hiss (the alleged communist mole inside the U.S. State Department) during Hiss's prosecution for perjury. Hoover ordered his agents not to cooperate with Ernst.

Once Ernst was in the picture, Trujillo began issuing press releases calling Galindez a "swindler or a paymaster for communist secret operations." He claimed that, instead of protecting the assets of the Basque exiles, Galindez had siphoned off half a million bucks for himself and was killed for his betrayal. Trujillo said he had nothing to gain by killing Galindez. His press releases claimed that Galindez was worth more to the communists as a dead martyr than as a live enemy of the Trujillo government.

While Trujillo magnified his own publicity campaign to discredit Galindez—ridiculing, in the process, Hoover's efforts to link Trujillo to Galindez's death—Trujillo had cleverly orchestrated the use of Dominican diplomatic immunity to protect alleged conspirators like Arturo Espaillat and Felix Bernardino whom Hoover was convinced were part of the conspiracy to get rid of Galindez. Trujillo's agents fed rumors into foreign wire services claiming that Galindez had been sighted in Budapest, Mexico, and Venezuela and was running with a pack of communist rebels. Trujillo was pulling out all the stops to rub out the stain the Galindez case was spreading over his dictatorship. In New York, a rumor was planted that Galindez was a member of a tight-ringed communist cell headquartered at Columbia University. I checked it out and dismissed it, but if Galindez had ever been present at a communist cell meeting, I assumed that he reported what occurred to his FBI contacts.

A T the beginning of Frank's second trial, his lawyer claimed that his client was actually an informer for the U.S. government. What a twist of the truth! Frank was now trying to match cards against Galindez's status as an FBI informant. In a series of legal motions designed to block his trial from ever starting, Frank said he was entitled to a "qualified informer's privilege." His attorney, Edmund L. Carey, filed these motions as an attempt to block my testimony as well as that of Myles J. Ambrose, the Assistant United States Attorney Frank had complained to about Dr. German Ornes Coiscu in January 1956, and Sarah Newcomer, Frank's secretary. Without our testimony, Carey argued, the government had no case. That put me, along with Ambrose and Newcomer, on center stage.

Carey submitted three reasons why I shouldn't be allowed to testify. First, Frank's privilege as an informer (if he had one when he talked to me) could only be waived by the Mayor of the city or by the Governor of the State of New York, respectively. I was only a subordinate cop, Carey argued. He said I couldn't act for the government and waive Frank's privilege. Somebody much higher than me had to do it. Second, Carey argued, Frank himself had to waive his side of the privilege before I could testify and he hadn't. Third, and Frank's attorney said this was "the most fundamental" of his reasons, Frank's constitutional rights would be violated if his client wasn't free to come forth as an honest citizen to report evidence of criminal activity as when he came to BOSSI in January 1956 complaining about Ornes's alleged embezzlement. That argument gave the Justice Department fits. Carey also claimed that his client's "informer's privilege" made him a client of the Justice Department when he first went to see Ambrose in the United States Attorney's Office to snitch on Ornes. Carey said that only Frank could waive the attorney-client privilege. Frank was the client, and Ambrose was the attorney.

Frank's defense also argued that Frank was a victim of entrapment. He was set up, his attorney argued, when Robert Cartwright of the State Department, a former Special Agent of the FBI, first suggested that Frank might want to go to work for Rafael Trujillo in 1954. Frank wanted to prove that Hoover was then hatching a plot to discredit him simply because he had left Hoover's stable to make his own score outside the restrictions of government service. Sarah Newcomer shouldn't testify, Frank's attorney continued, because she was hired to work for Frank as a secretary when he was serving as an attorney for Dominican interests. Any reports she prepared for him fell within the category of the attorney-client privilege—only this time Frank was the attorney and Trujillo-controlled companies were the client. To the government prosecutors, Frank's arguments were nothing but legal witchcraft—the hocus-pocus of a crafty, clever man.

Before the trial began, a hearing was held on Frank's attempt to block the trial from ever starting. Without the jury listening, Frank testified that when he met with Cartwright at the State Department in 1954, he told Cartwright that "he would be quite willing to furnish the Bureau (FBI), on a strictly confidential basis, any information coming to his attention" concerning communist activity that might pose a threat to this country or to his new boss, Rafael Trujillo. Basically, Frank was claiming that the U.S. government accepted his offer to serve as a double agent when he went to work for Trujillo. As evidence of this agreement, Frank's lawyer tried to prove that when Frank was in Spain on Trujillo's business, a CIA agent asked him to provide information on a notorious French Communist who was posing as an artist and traveling in Central America. Although the government's objection to this evidence was sustained by the court as being outside the scope of the issues of the trial, Frank had made his point.

To support his position that I couldn't testify against him because he had a "qualified informer's privilege," Frank testified that, in exchange for the information about Dominican dissidents he gave to BOSSI, Inspector Robb had let him look at confidential BOSSI files on these dissidents in December 1954 and was allowed to copy our reports on condition that he not disclose the names that were mentioned. 1954 was the year Frank went to work for Trujillo. Frank testified that he covered his use of the information he obtained from BOSSI records with the clause, "under suitable pretext the writer personally conducted certain additional investigations and surveillances in connection with this matter in New York City." What Frank didn't explain was how Galindez's name happened to appear in the report he sent to Trujillo concerning "The Alleged Plot to Assassinate Rafael Trujillo by Nicholas Silfa and Jesus de Galindez." Galindez's name came neither from Police Department files nor from the FBI. Galindez, code name "Rojas," had the highest covered security clearance available. The FBI carefully protected his identity and wasn't about to offer him up as a sacrifice to Frank in exchange for Frank's offer to be an informant while he bodyguarded Trujillo.

I took the stand again on March 9, 1959. My testimony, unlike my testimony in the first trial, was anything but short. In the first trial, Frank's attorney tried to show that Frank volunteered information to me at BOSSI headquarters about anti-Trujillo dissidents who might have been a threat to the business interests of his Dominican clients. But nothing Frank volunteered to BOSSI was anything we didn't already know. In my second go around as a witness, Frank's attorney shifted strategy, taking me by surprise with a series of questions challenging me on whether Frank had ever asked me to divulge information to him about Trujillo dissidents and whether I had complied with his request. Carey began his cross examination in a light, casually deceptive manner, but then went on the attack with the question of whether I furnished information to Frank that came from confidential BOSSI files. I smelled a rat. "Did you at any time provide Mr. Frank," Carey began his assault on my testimony, "with information about the activities of certain Dominicans of the City of New York who were plotting to kill Trujillo, when he next came to New York City?"

"I did not, no, I did not," I answered.

"Did you ever furnish him with a list of names of these Dominicans who were plotting to kill Trujillo?"

"No."

Carey then began reading me a list of names. My mind began to race. Carey was reading off an accurate list of the names BOSSI had in its files concerning the activities of anti-Trujillo dissidents in New York City. I had no time on the witness stand to figure out where he might have obtained this information. Robb never told me he had given Frank access to BOSSI files, nor did I know at the time what Frank had said in his pretrial testimony about Robb's invitation to see them. After Carey finished reading off the names, he asked me whether these names appeared in the records of the New York City Department; they did and I answered "yes." Carey asked me whether I knew if Frank ever met with Inspector Robb in 1954. "I don't know," I answered.

The knowledge that Frank had been given complete access to Police Department files was being delivered to me in the form of a gut-wrenching cross examination. With firm voice I testified that I had never given Frank a peek at BOSSI records, but I know my denials must have sounded hollow, for they were contradictory to the exactitude with which Frank's lawyer was reading off the names Silfa, Aybar, Espaillat, Blanco, and others; those whom Silfa told to wear hoods to cover their faces at the meetings he held for his Dominican Revolutionary Party; those whose trust and confidence Fitz and I had nurtured and received and who would have been shattered if they thought their names were turned over to Frank. They had been double-crossed, but it wasn't my doing.

For an instant, as I sat on the witness stand, I wasn't sure whose side I was on. I had worked on the Galindez investigation as part of a team. A detective works on a case like a runner in a relay race. We hand the

121

baton, the results of our work, to the next guy and hope he runs like hell. Sometimes it's impossible to tell what's happening on the track. On the witness stand, I wondered who was chasing who. The Galindez case had become a chase between J. Edgar Hoover and John Frank. If Frank's lawyer could get to me, he would be getting back at Hoover. If he could show BOSSI was his partner, he would walk out of the courtroom a free man. No one had been charged with any direct crime concerning Galindez, and I didn't know if anyone ever would be, but instead of being back in the field trying to get some answers, I was sitting on a witness stand in Washington under a zoom lens of cross examination by someone trying to make me out to be a liar.

It was all too clear to me now that Frank's efforts in first coming to BOSSI, his talk about Ornes and assassination plots, and his pretense of concern about imposing criminal and civil penalties on Dominican exiles were all part of his scheme to protect his intelligence role for Trujillo. I also thought Frank had been part of the Trujillo big tease, keeping El Jefe happy by making him believe he would pick up the pieces of Batista's gambling empire once he was overthrown, in exchange for letting the United States use the Dominican Republic as a CIA training ground. Feed Trujillo greenbacks and let him kill his enemies; always keep the sharks at bay.

In his questioning, Carey started to get personal.

"Didn't you talk with me?"

"No," I answered.

"Didn't you?"

"No, well, somebody got on the phone," I answered, "and said he had an attorney who wanted to speak to me regarding the case. I said that in order for such permission to be granted it would have to come through my Department." This phone call had come in to BOSSI headquarters before my original testimony before the Grand Jury in the spring of 1957.

I wanted to climb off the stand and ask Frank's lawyer a couple of questions of my own. "Who slipped the notes under our hotel room door when Fitz and I came to Washington for our Grand Jury appearance? Who made the mystery calls to Broome Street and wouldn't leave their names? Whose surveillance were we under, Mr. Carey? Yours? Your client's?"

If it was Carey who tried to contact me at BOSSI headquarters before my Grand Jury testimony, he now acted as if he had been given permission to talk to me. No one had asked for my permission, and I wasn't about to give it to anybody. Carey, however, apparently thought otherwise. He kept up the challenge.

"Where was this call made?" Carey then asked.

"The call was made to me," I answered. "Lieutenant Schultheiss of my department said he had someone on an assignment I had who wanted to speak to me on the telephone."

As soon as I mentioned the name Schultheiss, I heard chairs move and scrape the floor. Papers were shuffled, like a sudden breeze had come to blow them away. During my telephone conversation with him Schultheiss never told me that Frank's attorney would be the one making the call. At this point, Judge Youngdahl jumped in and told Carey he was skating on some pretty thin ice. Carey was making himself a witness in the case without taking the stand, and, as a result, trying to make me out to be a liar just by the way he was asking me these questions. I also assumed that the Judge already knew about the Frank/Schultheiss connection and that if he let Carey continue coming at me with this line of questioning, I was going to tie Schultheiss around Frank's neck and blow this case wide open. Carey backed down and ended his cross examination by repeating, in a slightly different form, some of the questions he had already asked.

"You at no time furnished information from the confidential files of the New York City Police Department in connection with the alleged plot to kill Trujillo to John Frank?" he asked.

"No," I answered.

"Did someone else?" Carey probed.

"Not to my knowledge," I told him.

"Did Inspector Robb furnish such information?" Carey asked.

"I don't know," I answered.

"Did you give this information to anyone?" Carey asked.

"In December of 1954," I answered. "Lieutenant Crane, Edward

123

Fitzpatrick and I met with the Consulate General of the Dominican Republic. The source was not given but the existence of a possible group with plans for an attempted assassination of General Trujillo was discovered."

At this point, I was excused from the witness stand. Staying in the courtroom to hear the proceedings, I listened as Carey tried to attack the subject of BOSSI's records in a different way. He had subpoened these records and wanted to examine them to prove his theory that his client and BOSSI had been buddy buddy investigating threats against Trujillo. The records were brought to Washington from New York by Lieutenant Francis Sullivan, then BOSSI's new commanding officer. Carey argued for their release by saying the case against Frank was going to pivot on my testimony and on that of Sarah Newcomer. He wanted to match BOSSI's records against the names he had thrown at me during his cross examination. If he could get away with that, he'd then be able to convince the jury that Frank could only have obtained those names from our records. "I think it is powerful jury argument, Carey said, "for me to be able to say that Detective Ulasewicz says these reports are confidential and they were never given to John Frank." Judge Youngdahl stopped Carey in his tracks. "Examination of these records," the Judge said, "does not indicate that they were given to John Frank." My testimony stood its ground.

After Carey lost this skirmish, he leveled a final broadside against the U.S. government for prosecuting his client. He charged that the government had set Frank up for a fall from the very beginning. "I would doubt that," the Judge said. "I deny it, Mr. Carey," the prosecutor chimed in. "I don't care what you deny," Carey shot back. Judge Youngdahl did agree with Carey that the government was probably cooperating with Frank and "trying to give his friend Trujillo the red carpet treatment when he came over here." The Judge also said that the government was "fully aware" of what Frank was doing. My ears shot to attention when I heard that. Frank simply didn't register as a foreign agent, the Judge concluded, and he was getting burned for not doing so.

As I listened, I couldn't help wondering what the government really knew about Frank's ties to the Galindez case: who sponsored the connection? Was it Frank's clients, beside Trujillo, who paid him to use his contacts to get of rid of Galindez because he was a threat to their Dominican businesses? How much was the U.S. government relying on ex-FBI and CIA agents like Frank and Maheu to do its dirty work through private agencies like Maheu Associates? How much was paid to get the job done and who paid it? When and by whom was it decided that Galindez was a target for elimination? No wonder Hoover was angry. The warnings his agents gave Galindez right up to a few days before he disappeared had meant nothing. Another powerful section of Hoover's own government hadn't told him what was going on. He was furious at his exclusion and his isolation, as was so clear when we met in the Waldorf Astoria. If Galindez was kidnapped for no other reason than to please Trujillo, Hoover wouldn't have made all this fuss. Not because the loss of Galindez was unimportant, but because if Galindez had made himself expendable by ignoring the warnings of Hoover's own agents, why would Hoover beat Justice Department's war drums to prosecute Frank unless Hoover desperately wanted to teach somebody or some other arm of the government a lesson? Who was Hoover going up against? I thought again of his angry proclamation in the Waldorf that he would get Frank if it was the last thing he ever did. Galindez had set up a strategic chain of information. His disappearance wrecked a carefully wrought intelligence network, and it could never be put back together again. If the U.S. government knew everything that Frank was doing, as Judge Youngdahl implied, then the kidnapping was a carefully planned sanctioned intelligence operation.

Carey's last line of attack fell short. He even tried to impress the judge with his knowledge of clandestine operations by telling him that he knew that my next assignment was going to be guarding the children of Fulgencio Batista—a not so subtle hint that he and his client had up-to-date inside information on BOSSI operations. Actually, Carey was three months late with his news. If he had bothered to read the December 31, 1958, edition of the *New York Mirror*, my picture, along with Batista's two kids, was on the front page. Judge Youngdahl listened to everything Carey had to say and then denied his request to examine BOSSI records as well as his motion to dismiss the indictment. Before the jury heard summations in the case, however, Frank decided to plead no contest to the first and third counts of the indictment. In so doing he was admitting, without having to plead guilty, that he worked for Trujillo as a foreign agent and used the name John Kane, the name on the receipt for the rental of the plane that carried Galindez to his ultimate death. This plea was made in court on March 12, 1959, exactly three years to the day after Galindez disappeared. For his trouble, Frank paid a fine of $500 and walked free.

THERE was always a lot of speculation about how Galindez actually met his fate. The most reliable information came from Dominican dissidents who had pieced together the rumors that began circulating shortly after Galindez disappeared. On September 5, 1957, a press conference was held at the Socialist Party headquarters of Norman Thomas who had tried to get the FBI involved in the Galindez case right after Galindez disappeared. At this conference, Frances R. Grant, Secretary General of the Inter-American Association for Democracy and Freedom, revealed that Dominican exiles, whom she refused to identify, claimed that Galindez had been lured from his apartment by someone he knew or trusted. He was then drugged and driven to a plane on Long Island which took him to the Dominican Republic. Once there, he was put aboard another plane and flown to the "Hacienda Fundacion," a cattle ranch owned by Trujillo. There, Grant said, Trujillo told Galindez his life wasn't worth the price of a blank page in his book, struck him, and then turned him over to unidentified army personnel who slowly tortured Galindez to death. Trujillo's son, Ramfis, stood by and watched. One source reported that Ramfis wanted to make sure Galindez paid with his life for daring to write a novel condemning his lifestyle. In torturing Galindez, Trujillo's henchmen reportedly gouged out his eyes, cut out his tongue, pulled out all his fingernails one by one, and smashed every bone in his body with a sledge hammer. Afterward, his mutilated body was put aboard a Dominican Navy destroyer and burned in the ship's furnace. (The door was probably bigger than the one on the boiler of the S.S. *Funducion*.) Galindez's ashes and charred bones were taken out to sea by four sailors in a fishing boat. Once his remains were tossed overboard, the destroyer turned its guns on the fishing boat and blew the sailors to kingdom come. While Grant was holding her press conference, Ramfis was attending the Army Command and General Staff College at Fort Leavenworth, Kansas, as a guest of the United States government.

Until the death of J. Edgar Hoover in May 1972, he kept his agents busy investigating the case. Frank finally went to jail, but not because of Galindez. He caught the disease of greed and was convicted in a securities fraud prosecution. Hoover's death came more than a decade after Trujillo was assassinated by bullets fired from machine guns manned by soldiers from his own army. Hoover's death followed that of Trujillo's son, Ramfis, who, after his father's bloody end, blamed the United States for plotting his assassination. Ramfis threatened to support the Dominican communist movement in its effort to take over his father's country. Hoover's death also followed that of Arturo Espaillat, head of Trujillo's secret intelligence operations whom Ramfis accused of being part of the plot to rub out his father. Before he died, Espaillat wrote a book called *Trujillo: The Last Caesar*. (Trujillo would have liked the title.) In it, Espaillat claimed that his only connection with the Galindez case was his ability "to state with some authority" that the kidnapping of Galindez "was a factor in permitting the Communist capture of Cuba." Galindez had warned his FBI contacts about Castro's Moscow connections. As a result of his kidnapping and murder, Galindez became the missing link to information about the plans and tactics of revolutionaries all over Latin America. His ties to the Basque underground in Europe were also severed. An ex-FBI agent named John Joseph Frank had left J. Edgar Hoover holding an empty bag.

Notwithstanding the permanent historical value the Justice Department and the National Archives have placed on the Galindez case (in the same classification as the Lindbergh kidnapping), many of the records of the FBI and the CIA remain classified. Morris Ernst, Trujillo's lawyer who was hired to exonerate him and distort Galindez's significance, turned his entire file on the case over to the National Archives. He may have been motivated solely by frustration over never having solved the mystery of who Galindez really was. Or perhaps he did it to regain some historical respect, or perhaps he wanted to open the door for an inquisitive scholar to figure it out in the future. In a letter Ernst wrote to the public relations firm that recommended him to Trujillo, Ernst said he thought he had been "treated like a leper." For a time, Ernst wrote, "I felt like a little boy who peeked through the keyhole and saw some things he regretted having seen." After his short flirtation with Latin American intrigue, he wanted to return to practicing law in a world that was "less full of cloaks, daggers and filthy human beings." He concluded that the U.S. government, "on a risk for risk basis," figured it was better to let Trujillo die on the vine (or get assassinated) "rather than divulge an operation which might, in historic terms, be an element in the maintenance of freedom from Communism in Europe."

In the files of the New York City Police Department, Galindez is still listed as a missing person: Male, white, age now 75, approximate height 6'1", previous known weight, 160 lbs., fair complexion, light brown hair (slightly bald in front), brown eyes, good teeth; may be wearing a dark grey overcoat with belt in back and grey green fedora and carrying a dark brown briefcase. Subject is lecturer on International Law and Spanish at Columbia University, New York, N.Y. Special attention to all hospitals. Any information, call Missing Persons Bureau Canal 6-2000.

Rockwell—

The American Nazi

WHEN John Frank's attorney, Ed Carey, told Judge Luther Young-dahl that my next assignment was going to be guarding Batista's children, Batista was already long gone from Havana's Presidential Palace, and we had long before stopped hauling them around from hotel to hotel in New York. Castro's revolution was in full bloom, and his victory was a catalyst for the rebirth of radical and guerrilla movements all over the world. Revolutions, like Mao Tse Tung's in China, were no longer isolated events that Western intelligence agencies could confidently prepare against; revolutions could be exported just like shoes and rice. Castro's takeover of Cuba, with Soviet backing, began a new era of target politics in the world. On New York's street corners pamphlets began to appear, especially in Harlem, that advocated armed revolt. The city began to recycle itself back to the early 1900s when my old Lower East Side neighborhood had been the stomping ground for pamphleteers and anarchists who wanted our government overthrown. BOSSI's filing cabinets had to be cleared out to make room for new files on violent organizations that were forming on the wave of Castro's success like the

Revolutionary Action Movement (RAM) or the Progressive Labor Movement (PLM).

Castro won his revolution with guns and ammunition, and the pamphlets I began reading talked about rising up and striking back at American society with the same weapons. Striking specifically at the Jewish and black populations of America was a faction creeping along the right wing's radical fringe, and that was George Lincoln Rockwell and his American Nazi Party. Neo-Nazi groups and their supporters were nothing new to New York, but Rockwell was a completely different breed of cat. He looked like a Wall Street stockbroker with a briefcase in one hand but in the other he flaunted a swastika. While he consistently produced only anger and hostility wherever he appeared in public, behind the scenes his message of hate the Jews and the blacks seemed to charm people's money right out of their pockets. In the Fall of 1958, as Castro moved closer to the Presidential Palace in Havana, Rockwell, a former U.S. Navy fighter pilot in World War II, exchanged his salute to America's Old Glory for a stiff-armed Nazi Heil Hitler. He devoted all his energies to the business of hate. His effort to resurrect Nazism in the United States was the first large-scale attempt since Fritz Kuhn's German American Bund had flourished here in the 1930s and 1940s. Unlike Rockwell's wild-eyed, screaming street-corner predecessors like James H. Madole, James MacWilliams, Ralph Grandinetti, or the Dommer family of Staten Island, however, Rockwell played his racist demagoguery by the book. His goal was to march down the streets of the biggest American cities he could find and, with a constitutional permit, shove his message down the Jews' throats.

In the Spring of 1960, Rockwell filed an application with New York City Parks Commissioner Newbold Morris for a permit to hold a Nazi rally in Union Square on the Fourth of July. His application was met with a counterpunch by some fifty organizations that joined forces to stop him with a court order that would bar Commissioner Morris from issuing the permit. A hearing on the matter was scheduled for June 22 at the New York County Courthouse in Foley Square. (This was the same day the United Nations Security Council had scheduled the debate on Argentina's complaint that Israel had illegally pirated Nazi SS Commandant Adolf Eichmann away from Argentine territory.)

When Rockwell first went public with his plans to hold his rally, a strategy meeting was held at Police Headquarters attended by administrative heads of the leading Jewish organizations in New York, members of the Police Department's Legal Bureau, Deputy Chief Inspector Robb, and myself. When I was first assigned to BOSSI, my work at the filing cabinets included reading the publications of neo-Nazi groups and the arrest records of those who had been charged with defacing Jewish cemetery markers or with painting swastikas on public buildings. BOSSI kept detailed records on every troublesome anti-Semite in New York City. Dealing with the effects of prejudice and racism on a broad scale could not be resolved on a precinct level no matter how close precinct commanders were to a given situation. Any racial defilement of any gravestone or the defacement of any building, no matter where it happened in the entire city, had to be reported to BOSSI. We would do the leg work to find out who did it, and then precinct detectives would arrest those responsible after our investigation was completed. Defilement or defacement was never considered a prank. There was no age category in which racial or ethnic prejudice flourished best; sometimes kids unthinkingly echoed their parents' sentiments and acted them out when they thought no one was looking. Legal experts attending the meeting at Police Headquarters conceded that the courts—however high up the case might have to go—would someday allow Rockwell to hold his rally. The experts also argued, however, that he should find a path to that courthouse on his own; he shouldn't be given a map. Members of New York's Jewish intellectual community expressed broader concerns. They felt that Rockwell's American Nazi movement would feed off— and probably be financed by—Middle East extremists anxious to find another place in the world to roost their anti-Israeli hens. On a national scale, Jewish organizations were convinced that Rockwell was going to attempt to create a coalition between his neo-Nazi group and Ku Klux Klan units in the South. Klan leaders were known to be heavily entrenched in local Southern governments. The Jews believed that, together, Rockwell and the Klan would form a powerful union of prejudice and hate.

Everyone who attended the meeting agreed that if Rockwell was eventually given permission to hold a rally in New York, a police officer would have to be stationed on every roof top and check every window that faced onto Union Square. The area around Union Square was Jewish territory, serving as both home and workshop. At the meeting Jewish leaders emphasized that in no way could quotes from the Bill of Rights supporting Rockwell's right to hold a rally mollify New York's Jewish population. Rockwell's message, like Hitler's before him, was the extermination of the Jews and the confiscation of their property. Rockwell also preached the need to clear out the black man from America, like a forest of bad trees, and to ship them all back to Africa. If he was given a chance to open his mouth in Union Square, Jewish leaders said, there would be no holding back the crowds that would surge into the streets. Racial venom would mix with ethnic blood, and Rockwell himself, everyone agreed, stood a good chance of being torn to shreds. It was also agreed that someone from the Police Department should be in constant contact with Rockwell so that he wouldn't try for a quick burst of publicity by showing up unannounced in Union Square with his sound truck and his swastikas. Inspector Robb assigned me to cover his every move.

We discussed several plans to deal with the situation. Plan A mandated that, if he was to get his permit, Rockwell was to be conned into accepting an alternative site for his rally such as Madison Square Garden or a pier in the Hudson River. Madison Square Garden had a number of advantages. First it had turnstiles, aisles, and seats. Second, the number of attendees could be controlled, and the police would know what it had on its hands. The Garden might turn out to be a very angry bee hive, but the number of stings could be limited. A pier in one of New York's big rivers was even better. Rockwell and his troops would then be surrounded on three sides by water and on one side by cops, fire trucks, and barricades. Someone sardonically suggested that the rally be scheduled at a time when the tide was going out and that maybe the tide could take Rockwell along with it. The key to preventing bloodshed was to control the use of the space given for his rally. Union Square offered too many ways to get there and too many windows and roof tops surrounding it. But Rockwell was too smart to be conned into such restrictions: He wanted his words echoing in the air, rattling windows, chilling bones.

I first met Rockwell in the late spring of 1960 in Yorkville, the

German settlement on the Upper East Side. Earlier that spring, Rockwell had come north from his headquarters in Arlington, Virginia, to check out the street-corner rallies run by James Madole on behalf of his self-styled neo-Nazi National Renaissance Party. Every Friday night, Madole would show up on a Yorkville street corner. Each week, he would call BOSSI to find out which corner he should go to so he would be assured police protection. Knowing we couldn't altogether stop him from making street-corner speeches, we developed a plan to keep him guessing, until the last minute, before we told him where he'd be safe for the night. The idea was to wait long enough that he wouldn't have enough time to advertise his racist smoke. We couldn't have denied him police protection because that would have meant a riot. We moved him around like a chess piece and hoped for the best. The size of the crowds increased or decreased each week, depending on how heated things had been for Madole the week before. If he got a tomato or a rotten egg thrown in his puss, more people would show up the following week just to see the show. The more Madole got his clothes or his face messed up, the better he liked it.

I, or BOSSI detectives Bob Bystricky or Walter Karpowich, went to every one of his rallies. Backing us up was at least one uniformed patrolman, supported by a sergeant who would wait nearby to call in support if needed. Also watching Madole's street corner antics was Abe Schoenfeld, a full-time private investigator who worked for Jewish organizations. Madole, regarded as a nasty anti-Semitic nut, didn't have any visible broad-based support. He was a pest, a racist peddler who lived with his mother. He brought her to his assigned street corner every week and then, in his knickers and his high boots, screamed about the Jews, rolling his eyes back in his head while he let loose his venom. In between these performances, Madole worked as a pamphleteer for a closet neo-Nazi organization. Many of his followers kept post office boxes in Grand Central Station or at the main post office branch on 34th Street perhaps so that the missus and the kiddies at home wouldn't see the Nazi swastika on the envelope. I kept a post office box at the same station so that, for the benefit of BOSSI's intelligence records, I could receive a copy of every racist publication in the nation.

One of the regulars attending Madole's rallies was John C. Patler, a

133

young, rabid believer in Nazism who was actually a scavenger of any prejudice he could find. Hate was his hobby. What appeared to attract him most was the passion of Madole's hysterics. Patler stated that he saw a chance to resurrect Hitler's Youth Movement right on the streets of New York, but, Rockwell, and not Madole, would give him the best chance to get that going. In speeches made in other parts of the country, Rockwell had spoken about the value of discipline and about his goal of creating a corps of elite "storm troopers" and a semimilitary academy on the grounds of his Virginia headquarters. He claimed that his followers would march into the cities of America, recruit the young to his gospel, and free the nation from the trap of mixed races. It was Patler who introduced me to Rockwell at one of Madole's maniacal rallies.

When we met, I had already completed a womb-to-tomb profile on Rockwell. He was born in Bloomington, Illinois, on March 9, 1918. His parents were traveling actors, his father being a vaudeville comedian who called himself "Old Doc Rockwell." After his parents divorced, Rockwell was sent to a variety of private schools. He graduated from Hebron Academy in Maine and then entered Brown University. In 1940, his junior year, he left college to join the Navy. He flew combat missions from the flight deck of the carrier Wasp in the Pacific during World War II. Honorably discharged as a Naval Commander, Rockwell studied art at Pratt Institute in Brooklyn. He was recalled to active duty during the Korean War, serving in California and Iceland. Following his return to civilian life, he began publishing a magazine for servicemen's wives called *U.S. Lady*. Supposedly robbed of his profits by what he branded a band of bruising opportunists, Rockwell began his dip into the market of anti-Semitic literature. Rockwell was divorced several times, leaving unpaid alimony and child support obligations scattered around the country like his leaflets. In 1958 through an unidentified benefactor, he bought a house and some acreage in Arlington, Virginia, and began his evangelism for his American Nazi Party. Rockwell never flinched from his positions. When he spoke in public, he put on a stark, harrowing exhibition of racial hatred; he was determined to push the Constitution to its limits to prove he had a right to speak his piece in public. He wasn't going to be conned, stroked, or cajoled into leaving New York alone.

I had several meetings with Rockwell and followup conversations with him by phone, after which he finally promised he would let me know whenever he was planning a trip to the city. Sometimes he would come alone to meet with some of his backers. I warned him not to pull any surprises. If an incident were to occur while Rockwell was in the city minding his own business, at least the Police Department would know he wasn't there to stir up trouble. If he were to try to double-cross me, it would mean chaos in the streets. Without giving me advance warning that he was on his way, or if he tried to get cute and sneak into town for a quick burst of publicity, neither Rockwell nor innocent bystanders might survive the riot that was sure to follow.

For Rockwell's permit hearing on June 22, 1960, I told him to take the train and to keep his trip to the courthouse as low-key as possible. There wasn't going to be any police escort. We would have enough trouble dealing with expected protests and demonstrations without dramatizing his appearance by having him step out of a police car with a Heil Hitler on his lips. Once at the courthouse, my job was to get him in and out as fast as I could.

On his arrival at the courthouse, Rockwell was greeted by an angry mob. Many of the demonstrators wore the caps and insignias of World War II veterans or carried the scars and brands of the Nazi death camps from which they had escaped or were liberated.

When Supreme Court Justice Vincent A. Lupiano recessed the hearing shortly before noon, Rockwell walked into the rotunda of the courthouse where television cameras and a score of reporters stood waiting for him to open his mouth. It was exactly the scene he had hoped for. Walking up to the microphones, he shouted: "Eighty percent of the American Jews are traitors and should be exterminated!" The crowd went berserk lunging at him and punching at anything that stood between them and him. Umbrellas were used as swords to move people out of the way. Acting swiftly, arm-locked courthouse guards formed a ring around Rockwell and moved him back inside the courtroom. I shouted over to a lieutenant standing nearby to get me a taxi. After a short wait, I grabbed Rockwell's arm and took him from the courtroom and out a side door into the street. Police reinforcements, with sirens blaring, roared into Foley Square. As I neared the taxi commandeered by the lieutenant to get us out of the area, the crowd started punching at me and tearing at my clothes, apparently thinking I was one of Rockwell's buddies. Just before shoving Rockwell into a cab, a big glob of spit hit my face. As I wiped it off, I ordered the cab driver to head for LaGuardia Airport. I decided to put Rockwell on the first plane that was leaving, and I didn't care what its destination was. A horde of reporters chased after us. When we arrived at the airport, Rockwell told me he didn't have any money for a plane ticket. I looked at him in disbelief and told him to empty his pockets or I'd undress him on the runway. What little money he did have wasn't enough, of course, so I had to make up the difference for the ticket. I told him I'd collect it later. As Rockwell walked toward his plane, he suddenly thanked me for saving his life and invited me to come down for a visit to his headquarters in Virginia. I had already made up my mind to check him out on his home turf, but I had no intention of telling him that just yet. I wanted to surprise him, catch him off guard so that I'd get an accurate picture of what he was touting as the setting for his Nazi academy.

Within forty-eight hours after Rockwell left New York City, another high-level meeting was held in Inspector Robb's office. Bloodshed had been prevented, but the problem of dealing with Rockwell still remained; nothing had changed. We all felt certain that the demonstration at the courthouse was only a rehearsal for what would happen if he showed up in Union Square with his storm troopers and his sound trucks. It didn't matter that Mayor Wagner on his own initiative had denied Rockwell's permit application, calling him a "half-penny Hitler" in the process. Rockwell was going to appeal the denial, and it was only a matter of time before he got his permit. A way had to be found to neutralize his impact on New York's Jewish population which, for all practical purposes, was just waiting for the chance to tear him apart. Arnold Forster, President of the American Jewish Congress, was also concerned about picketing by the younger, more militant Jews; they were obviously becoming restless, and, anxious to prove their worth, they tended to more violent demonstrations to protect their Jewish heritage. Forster was also convinced that Rockwell would succeed in forging a coalition with the Ku Klux Klan. The Police Department couldn't affirm or deny Forster's contention. Except for Rockwell's promise that he would keep me informed of his movements, we had no way to measure his strength in other parts of the country. But it certainly wasn't going to take much for him to inflame New York's Jewish and black population.

That fall I sat down with the new Commanding Officer of BOSSI, Sanford Garelik, to discuss our options in keeping track of Rockwell's movements and to prepare for his inevitable rally in Union Square. We agreed that infiltration of the American Nazi Party was essential. At this time Rockwell began to break his promise to let me know his movements. Through my UN contacts I learned that Rockwell was taking clandestine trips to New York and that he had seen certain Middle Eastern representatives at the United Nations. The risk was growing that Rockwell might try to bypass the courts and that he might even try to stage a "spontaneous" noon rally in the United Nations Plaza which would trigger free worldwide publicity. He had already attracted some notable international attention. Gamal Abdel Nasser, President of Egypt, had publicly praised Rockwell for his anti-Zionist campaign.

Infiltrating the American Nazi Party was to be like no other undercover operation in the history of the Department. The reason was that no cover for the operator was really needed. Unlike the Communist Party, whose members had to undergo an intense background check, a neo-Nazi could be as secretive about himself as he wanted. From Fritz Kuhn on down, it was understood that men or women who joined the Nazi movement would still be welcome if they kept their mouths shut about their jobs and/or their families. Membership in a neo-Nazi organization was meant to be kept secret; exposure of that membership was a sure-bet reason to get a person fired. Neo-Nazi organizations also knew that Jewish organizations watched them carefully. If Abe Schoenfeld could identify a new member or one of the street-corner sympathizers at a neo-Nazi rally and then trace his employment, the boss would get an anonymous phone call the next day. To fit into the role of a neo-Nazi, I took a new police recruit who had just been assigned to BOSSI and began to train him for his new assignment.

My first task was to get my pupil a post office box at the main post office branch on 34th Street on the West Side. On his behalf, I wrote a letter in childlike script on school-lined paper to every anti-Semitic group in the country requesting their leaflets. I identified the writer as a collector of Nazi memorabilia and a secret admirer of Hitler's teachings. I then had my student, whom I called "J.B.," read every anti-Semitic file in BOSSI headquarters. J.B. also studied the pamphlets I regularly received at my own BOSSI post office box. Then on my instructions, he began appearing at Madole's street-corner rallies.

J.B. looked older than his years. He had the appearance of a teacher, an engineer, or at least a deep thinker. Adopting a cautious, somewhat reticent manner was attractive to neo-Nazi leaders. Madole, anxious for new recruits, invited J.B. to come to his home after one of his rallies. For the first few meetings with Madole, I instructed J.B. that he should just listen to what Madole had to say and not say too much in return. "Don't get too dressed up, look uncomfortable, uneasy," I told J.B. "When Madole begins cutting loose about the Jews, say you've got to leave. Keep him off balance. Tell him you've got an appointment. Tell him it's none of his business if he asks. If he ever grills you with: 'How do we know you're not a rat for the Jews?' get up and tell him you're going to leave; tell him you can't be bothered with him if he's going to act like that. Give him a buck for his troubles. Tell him not to bother you anymore and that you won't be back." I told J.B. that Madole would jump at anything to keep him in the fold.

Periodically, I had J.B. deliberately miss a meeting with Madole. I told him not to show up every Friday night to hear him screech and not to give any reasons for his absence or to reveal anything about his personal life. I had J.B. dress like an executive, like someone in authority. By playing coy and secretive, he was able to convince Madole that he held a responsible position in an important industry. As a result, Madole passed the word to Rockwell that J.B. was a prototype of exactly what Rockwell was looking for—an educated, potentially influential citizen who could draw others into the party. Madole was a station stop on the way to Rockwell: J.B. had passed Go.

In the months that followed, I had to decide how deeply I wanted J.B. to infiltrate Rockwell's party. Reports in the press quoted Rockwell as saying he was well on his way to establishing his proposed storm trooper academy. He claimed he now had a library, a conference center, separate living quarters for the brides of new recruits, starched uniforms, and a fresh sense of growing power every day. He also reported that he now had thirty full-time "troopers." At least in the press, Rockwell was being portrayed as a real threat to the stability of America's Jewish and black communities. Both to make up my mind about J.B.'s future undercover role and to find the truth about Rockwell's claims, I decided to take Rockwell up on his invitation and pay him a visit. I had no intention, however, of warning him I was coming; that would only give him time to put on an exhibition. I wanted to see his operation in the raw.

After receiving Sandy Garelik's blessing to travel out of state to visit Rockwell's headquarters, I made several anonymous phone calls just to make sure Rockwell was going to be there when I knocked on his door. It was a late Friday morning in the winter of 1961 when I turned my car into Rockwell's driveway in Arlington, Virginia. Off to the side of the driveway, I noted a sign that read: "Hatemongers Hill." I knocked on the front door, and the only response I received was a snarling, menacing growl. Finally, one of Rockwell's storm troopers opened the door. He was half-dressed and obviously not expecting anyone. "Does Rockwell know you're coming?," the trooper asked me after I told him who I was. "No," I answered, "but tell him I'm here to collect the money I loaned him for his plane ticket."

"What?"

"Just tell him Tony's here."

As I said this, the source of the growl and the snarl appeared and began to show its teeth. They belonged to a large, menacing German shepherd. The dog drew back his lips and dropped into a half crouch, ready to attack. "Auschwitz, be quiet," Rockwell's trooper ordered the dog. "Tell Auschwitz I'll put a hole in him and then one in you if you don't get that dog out of here," I commanded in return.

When I finally moved inside, what greeted me was a grubby haunted house rather than an academy. Clearly, this was no showpiece that would attract membership into Rockwell's party. His glowing, published accounts of his party's progress had been nothing more than a pack of lies. As I looked around, I noticed that bullet holes punctured all the walls of his house. Had his "academy" been used for target practice? I also saw a stack of unpaid bills piled high on a table. Rockwell's electricity had been turned off, and he used kerosene lamps to light the place. In a room off to the side of the entrance, an oil lamp lit up a large red Nazi banner

139

that was hanging over what appeared to be an altar. Whatever Hitler's ghost had promised Rockwell, it hadn't yet arrived.

Meeting Rockwell on his home ground was enough to convince me that I had no need for an undercover operator. His organization was virtually nonexistent. Instead of thirty storm troopers in residence as he had claimed, I saw only three. He admitted that he hired some of his storm troopers to appear for special occasions. Nor did I see any brides' quarters or library or paneled conference rooms. I saw nothing but a lot of dirt and debris. Yet, Rockwell's barnyard operation was getting national exposure in the media. He had been successful in getting public notice because he owned the key asset of a demagogue: his mouth, and he wasn't afraid to open it to preach against the Jews and the blacks.

North and South, our country is afflicted by prejudice, and Rockwell knew how to play on it. He was convinced that if he could hold his rally in New York, bags of mail containing hundreds of dollar bills would flood his headquarters, and he would then have enough money to barnstorm across America. Circuses marched into town, he said, so why couldn't he? He explained his method. First, he would send his pamphlets out; then newspapers and local television stations would help him drum up business by condemning what he was trying to do. Rockwell expressed a great deal of contempt for the press, stating he could manipulate it in any way he wanted. He also said he intended to launch a Presidential primary campaign and wreak havoc on the American political system which he said was full of hypocritical holes. He claimed that he didn't care how many people came to hear him speak; all he wanted was the advance publicity announcing his appearance. (In November 1963 Rockwell announced he was going to run in the '64 Republican presidential primary in New Hampshire. He said "I want to prove the people believe in the same thing that I believe in" and got the backing of the *Union Leader*, Manchester, New Hampshire's arch-conservative newspaper owned by William Loeb. I went to see Loeb to ask him if he knew what he was stirring up and whether he would please tone down the rhetoric. I was basically told to mind my own business.)

While Rockwell and I were talking, his understudy, John Patler, came into the room. My unannounced visit had surprised Rockwell, but it absolutely startled Patler. He also appeared irritated with Rockwell. As I already knew, Patler had been annoyed at Rockwell for some time. On one of his trips to New York, he confided that he had grown impatient with Rockwell. Patler preferred more action; he also wanted marches and parades. Like a child, he sought instant gratification; he wanted everything now. Not surprisingly, Patler didn't care to play by the rules and apply for permits which he said Rockwell had no chance of getting without a long court fight. Patler said that the goals of the American Nazi Party were being gobbled up by time, his time. He didn't care about election ballots or about giving speeches on college campuses. While these differences weren't aired that night, I sensed that the rift between them had become too wide to patch up. When Patler first came in the room, Rockwell stopped talking to me. Patler may have assumed that Rockwell knew I had planned this visit and chose not to tell him. At any rate, Patler appeared to be very unhappy, and he left the room without saying a word.

After Patler left, Rockwell asked me if I'd like to take a tour of the grounds. Even though it was snowing, Rockwell said he wanted to walk and talk. Naturally, I was all ears. As we walked, he revealed his plans for the future as well as his fears for his life. He thought he might be killed by one of the vigilante groups that almost nightly threw Molotov cocktails on his doorstep and fired rifle shots into his walls. I disagreed that he would be killed by any vigilante. "You'll get it from inside your organization," I said. "From someone like Patler. He's not your partner anymore. He's your enemy." Next, I tried to con Rockwell into telling me whether he was going to link up with the Ku Klux Klan. "You're not going to start wearing a hood, are you?," I asked him kiddingly. "You'll look a little silly wearing a white sheet over your goose boots." "No," was Rockwell's only response. I pressed him because the Klan could have provided him with the grass-roots connections he needed for the growth of his party. The Klan had kept the prejudice market fueled and profitable for almost a century. There was enough hate to go around for both the Klan and Rockwell. But Rockwell wouldn't take my bait. All he wanted to talk about was his frustration in not being able to buy customer lists from the telephone company or from credit companies so that he could add their names to his mailing list. The phone company wouldn't sell him anything, and the credit companies wouldn't return his calls. Unless he could hold his rally in New York, Rockwell said, he wouldn't have enough money to keep sending his pamphlets around the country, with or without new customer lists.

To get around some of his financial difficulties, Rockwell described how he randomly picked targets for his rallies. Once he publicly announced that he was coming, the public's fur, as he put it, would stand on end. Local newspapers, radio, and television would give him just enough publicity to guarantee the delivery of four or five sacks of mail to his doorstep. In between written threats against his life, Rockwell said he received a lot of "atta boy, George" letters with dollar bills folded up inside the envelope. He said that just the threat of his coming was good for a couple of grand. But at the time of my visit to Rockwell's headquarters, his cupboard was bare. He invited me to stay for dinner, but all he had, he admitted with some embarrassment, were some cans of tuna fish. I thanked him for the invitation but declined the offer and headed back home for some of my wife's good Polish cooking.

Still unanswered when I returned to New York was the question of whether Rockwell had established a working relationship with the Ku Klux Klan. For that answer, I had J.B. respond to Klan advertisements in radical right-wing magazines to which I subscribed for BOSSI intelligence records. J.B. became a pen pal of the Klan. He learned that the Klan was openly seeking recruits, just as much as Rockwell was. In one magazine, J.B. read an announcement that a big Klan rally was going to be held in Delaware. I told him that we were going there and that his assignment was going to be to make contact with a Klan organizer. "When you find him, tell him you've come all the way from New York," I instructed J.B. "Find out if there are any Klan contacts you could make back in New York. Offer to put a cell together. Get a name." When we headed south to Delaware, orders from our BOSSI commanding officer, Sanford Garelik, were in the "God is with you" category. None of us really knew what to expect. We didn't dare notify local or state police agencies about our coming for fear of a leak. We couldn't trust anyone. With so many swamps located around the site of the rally, I didn't want to get thrown into one or to have to go looking for J.B. if he disappeared.

We arrived at the Klan rally in a rented car with Delaware plates. I kept my distance, circling the eerie gathering while keeping an eye on

142

J.B. I watched the ritual burning of a cross. But other than smelling the drifting smoke from the fire, J.B. couldn't pick up any scent that suggested that the Klan's organization was heading north to New York or that the Klan might be planning to tie up with Rockwell. No news was good news. But I still had J.B. keep up his correspondence with Klan outlets until he was finally asked to start up a Klan cell in New York. But J.B. never responded to the request. We had our answer: There was no plan to hook up with Rockwell. In New York City, Rockwell was plotting to push against the Jews and the blacks all by himself.

One day, while Rockwell was still awaiting word on his appeal from the denial of his permit application, he phoned me, informing me that he was no longer waiting for the courts to approve his Union Square appearance. He was coming within the week, and he was going to march right across the George Washington Bridge. "You'll be arrested when you cross into New York," I warned him a few days later after he called to say he was on his way. I spoke to him over a field telephone from a command post we had set up at the base of the bridge. "We're coming, Tony," Rockwell said from a phone booth at the New Jersey end of the bridge. "The publicity will be worth it."

"There won't be any publicity, George," I told him. "If the papers know it—and we didn't tell them—they're not here. They know what you're up to. Nobody wants any part of it. You'll be arrested for conspiracy to incite a riot. I can't help you if you start across the bridge." There was a long pause on the phone after I finished talking.

"I'll call you back, Tony," Rockwell said. "I'm going to have it out with Patler. This is mostly his idea. I'll get back to you in ten minutes."

Waiting on the bridge near the marked boundary between New Jersey and New York were several unmarked cars loaded with plainclothes detectives. Reinforcements waited to block off the bridge if Rockwell started across. Once he made a move toward New York, his arrest would be in the hands of other detectives. When Rockwell first told me he was coming, I notified Inspector Garelik who, in turn, notified the Police Commissioner who then passed the word of the Rockwell threat along to the Mayor. My orders were simple: stop him!

At the end of ten minutes exactly, Rockwell called back just as he had promised. He was patched into me through the emergency phone network we had set up at our command post. "We're not coming, Tony," Rockwell said. The line then went dead. There wasn't anything more to say. His attempt to bludgeon the Jews and the blacks in New York was over.

Six years later, on August 24, 1967, John Patler shot and killed George Lincoln Rockwell from a sniper's stance atop the roof of a laundromat in Arlington, Virginia. Five months before his death, Rockwell had booted Patler out of his party. After the turnabout at the George Washington Bridge, Rockwell devoted the last years of his life to building that grass-roots support he said he needed in order to make his party a strong national force.

I saw him for the last time during a trip he made alone into New York. On that occasion he didn't carry or wear any arm bands, goose boots or swastikas—just a briefcase and some pamphlets. He boasted that his active contributors included lawyers, doctors, judges, government officials, corporate executives, and a lot of other people in the right places. He was getting their money in exchange for anonymity, just as he had been given the house and land for his headquarters in Virginia. People, Rockwell acknowledged, were ready to pay good money to keep their prejudices alive. In the last years of his life, he was invited to visit and speak in foreign countries as well as on college campuses across the United States. When he spoke at New York's Hofstra University on Long Island, I was there as a precaution. It was my job to keep track of everything he did. Rockwell finally won his court battle for the right to hold a rally in Union Square, but he never came. He decided it wasn't worth the risk.

Going Deep

Ⅰ n December 1962, another change of command took place at BOSSI headquarters. Sandy Garelik moved up from Commanding Officer to Chief Inspector of the New York City Police Department, replacing Robb. Moving into BOSSI to take over for Garelik was a tough field commander from Brooklyn named John Kinsella, an old-line cop who had come up through the ranks. Successively, he had been a patrolman, a detective, a squad commander, a division captain, and now, upon his promotion to BOSSI, a Deputy Chief Inspector of the Police Department. He was fiercely loyal to the chain of command. Underneath his big wide-brimmed hat, the tall, athletic Kinsella had a head of thick graying hair and a ruddy complexion. Inside his head was the mind of a vigorous, thorough investigator. As an administrator, Kinsella never tolerated excuses. For this reason he was sometimes accused of lacking compassion for his men. Those who defended him said that he showed his feelings only about things that counted, and for Kinsella two qualities counted the most: dedication and skill. If a cop didn't measure up to his standards, his steel blue eyes would search for the nearest pen to scratch him out of his life.

One of Kinsella's first moves when he took command of BOSSI operations was to find out how Police Department undercover units had operated in the 1930s, 1940s, and early 1950s. He was under orders from the Police Commissioner to evaluate and then recommend whether or not units like that could operate the same way in the 1960s. But these were quite different times. No Germans or Japs threatened to bomb or torpedo our shores. The Korean conflict was behind us, and except for a trickle of protest at the ballot box, the Communist Party, at least in this country, was history. (It's now history most everywhere.) America was living on the appearance that all was right with the world; it wasn't. The 1960s, when protest replaced patriotism, changed all that. Nothing's wrong with protest except when bombs and bullets are used as its symbols and innocent people are killed or maimed as a result. We had made it through as a nation in the 1940s and 1950s, but that wasn't good enough for the 1960s. America went to war with itself.

The words "Death to the Pigs" began appearing on walls and in subway stations all over the city and were directed at every police officer in the city. When a cop from a Harlem precinct, in response to an anonymous call for help, stood outside the Temple of Islam at 116th Street and Lenox Avenue and was told that "no pig cop was allowed inside," the gauntlet was thrown. Being called a pig was a slap in the face of every veteran cop who had ever served in Harlem. The cop decided not to enter the Mosque to find out why he was called. If he had, the result would have been mayhem. What is more, there would have been adverse publicity and charges of police brutality would have been leveled against the Department. The whole incident would have been blown out of proportion. Of course, there were many second guessers. Should the cop have called for help? Busted the doors down? Locked everybody up because somebody called him a pig? Gone back for a search warrant? For what? Was being called a pig now part of the price for wearing a shield? Was the cop supposed to hope it would all go away? He was kidding himself if he thought it would.

In Harlem and elsewhere in America, demonstrators weren't just marching, busing, sitting in, or going limp; they were also arming themselves. Pamphlets circulating on the streets of Harlem had one simple message for the black man: "Get off your knees, arm yourselves and fight." Militant sects like the Progressive Labor Movement (PLM) and the Revolutionary Action Movement (RAM) preached a gospel that called for "death to the police," "smashing the state," "organizing a people's militia," establishing armed camps in the ghetto, conducting guerrilla warfare in the slums, and posting a hit list for Uncle Tom leaders, black and white.

The most charismatic advocate of violence among the blacks was Malcolm X. Years earlier he had split off from Elijah Muhammad's nonviolent Black Muslims to form a group known as the Organization for Afro-American Unity. Malcolm X's message was that nonviolence was choking the black man to death. Blacks should have the freedom to arm so that they could achieve the goal of getting "whitey" off their backs. His headquarters were in the Hotel Theresa where I had taken Nikita Khrushchev to meet Fidel Castro. Malcolm X represented the flip side of George Lincoln Rockwell. Malcolm X's stated goal was to cut down the white man's forest, move in on his land, and send him packing. He vowed that he would execute anyone "on the spot" who abused a member of his race. He had plenty of reasons to hate whites. When he was four years old, his home was burned to the ground, reputedly by white racists. Later, his father died under the wheels of a street car. Malcolm X said he was pushed there and died as a result of "whitey's hate." Malcolm X had a varied career as pimp, drug dealer, and convicted felon for armed robbery before taking up what he defined as the goals for his race. He got his jail house seasoning, finished his sentence, and came out smoking.

The only thing Rockwell and militant blacks had in common was their use of pamphlets and circulars to drum up support for their cause. The potential violence that followed Rockwell around would have been in reaction to what he said or did. Militant blacks said violence was their only means of getting what they wanted. As their textbooks, they used the revolutionary manuals of Mao Tse Tung and Fidel Castro. At this time, in addition to the blacks, other violence-prone radical groups were also going underground to plan their bombings. As the threat to the safety of the city became more pronounced, we were compelled to know

147

more about their plans and especially to learn who their targets (besides cops) were. Our best, and really only, approach was to get inside these organizations, to go undercover, to go deep.

Kinsella began picking our brains about the earlier years of BOSSI undercover operations. My own work with the Department had not directly involved undercover operations except for recruiting and training "J.B." for placement within the American Nazi Party, but I had my opinions, and that was what Kinsella was after. First, he brought up the idea of using informants in place of new undercover units. He thought that too often undercover units simply allowed the wrong people to jump on board and to use the chance to go undercover as a ladder to promotion or as a way to work in the field without supervision. Kinsella asked me whether informants couldn't accomplish the same task at a cheaper cost. Unlike Garelik, Kinsella was under no budgetary restraints. He had been given a free hand, but he wanted to make sure that the funding of new undercover units wasn't going to be a waste of money. "Why not use informants, Tony,?" Kinsella asked me. "It sure would be a hell of a lot cheaper."

My response was that the trouble with the use of informants was that they knew what you wanted before you asked for it and then held back on what you were looking for until they controlled the situation. The innocent citizen volunteer of information or the dedicated confidential informant like Galindez is a rarity. Informants are useful in ordinary street crimes, but not in the bullring with violent radicals. If your goal is to start a revolution, then you have to be willing to kill in order to succeed; there is no middle ground. Sometimes if you arrest someone and he wants to cut a deal because you've got so many other things on him, then you have to use their information to make a greater score. Informants can be valuable if they're scared to death of getting iced or spending the rest of their lives in jail, but relying totally on informants this way is an undependable, inefficient method of running an intelligence operation. As an informant, the only consistently credible source you can push against is a cop, one who is trained from the beginning in how to gather information without extracting a price for its delivery.

Being an undercover agent is one of the toughest jobs in the world, and not just because of the risks and dangers it poses. Even more difficult is its requirement of staying power for the job. The undercover cop is much like an actor in a play. The tension in the drama can be enormous, and being someone you're not can get to you after awhile, especially if mentally you have to make a distinction between a commitment to your job and a pretense to a commitment to the cause you're assigned to track. Frank Hlvasa, the undercover agent I met when I first joined BOSSI, had staying power, but he surfaced before I replaced him during the Communist conspiracy trial in Judge Medina's courtroom because, in part, he was burned out. For nearly a decade, he had lived a lie about himself in order to tell the truth about the Communist effort to overthrow our government. The time finally came when he couldn't take it anymore.

In the case of Millie Blauvelt, she lasted inside the Communist Party for two sessions, the last one for nine years. Before Kinsella brought me into his office, he interviewed Millie about how her squad operated. She was about to retire, and her past experiences were invaluable. One problem in the past, she had told Kinsella, was that the old undercover command operation had been headquartered at Broome Street with the rest of BOSSI operations. Undercover agents showed up at the office at regular intervals to collect their paychecks. Groups suspecting they had been infiltrated would hang around outside 400 Broome Street taking pictures of anyone entering the building. The pictures would then be matched against the faces of those who appeared at the meetings of radical organizations. Sometimes agents swapped stories at BOSSI headquarters which became invitations to a leak. Identifying undercover agents became a game. But there were no games to be played in the 1960s.

To Kinsella's question as to how I would set up the Department's undercover operations, I answered that they had to be commanded from outside BOSSI headquarters. Sooner or later, undercover operatives reporting directly to BOSSI's office would be spotted, and when that happened, their work—maybe even their lives-would be wasted. There had to be complete physical isolation from Broome Street and from the security that even a precinct might provide, even in an emergency. There couldn't be any camaraderie, undercover partnerships, tether lines to the uniform, or any evidence of a cop's identity. Aliases had to be provided, new social security numbers obtained, and offices rented in different parts of the city with no doorman or elevator operator. Just minimal janitorial services would be permissible. The building also had to be in a secure neighborhood, easily reached by public transportation.

The more Kinsella drew out my opinions, the more I felt he was targeting me for some assignment, and I wasn't sure I wanted one. Including my wartime service in the Navy, I had already logged in twenty years as a cop, and I had lately begun thinking seriously of retiring and setting up my own private detective agency. My escort work had given me carte blanche access to the palaces of kings. If I chose to use my contacts and sources of information, my opportunities in private enterprise could be limitless. "I'm not just going to sit here and pick your brain, Tony," Kinsella finally said. "I want you to set it up. I'll get the money for it. That's not your concern. But I better see results. And," he added as he stared at me with his baby blues, "you better keep damn good records."

I didn't relish this assignment. Regardless of my professional feelings about the need for an effective undercover operation, this job would mean no more trips to Broome Street, no more escorts, no more parades or lunches or fancy dinners at the Waldorf. On the job it would be back to Coke and bologna sandwiches. At first, I felt Kinsella's directive was the ticket to oblivion which I had feared when I was first assigned to BOSSI. While I never brought my job home with me, I also had to consider the effect this assignment would have on my family. I now had five children and I didn't want to be a mystery man to any of them. There were practical considerations too. My two teenage daughters were monopolizing our home telephone. I'd have to put a lid on its use and keep the line open when I was home because I'd have to be available in case an undercover operator had to make contact. I'd also have to put a cap on saying anything about the particulars of any investigation. My wife and children had seen my picture in the newspapers many times as I escorted world leaders around New York. Through me, my family felt that in some small way they had been a part of history. Now I'd be operating in the dark, and I would have to keep my tasks to myself. But even with all these reasons, Kinsella didn't allow me to say no to the assignment.

Setting up a BOSSI undercover operation wasn't going to be a job for one man. I needed help, but I wanted a free hand in picking my partners. I needed men with a truckload of patience; men who were good students of police work and who could skillfully handle other personnel; men who could be both demanding task masters and supportive when the tension of the job might bring one of our operators to a breaking point. We had to be able to work together, to instinctively know how to advise one of our operators if trouble erupted.

Lieutenant Barney Mulligan and Detective Teddy Theologes were chosen to work as my partners. Mulligan had a keen, almost scholarly mind, well suited for evaluating a case or directing an investigation. He would act as liaison with Kinsella and would report the results of on-going investigations on up the chain of command. Mulligan's job was to filter our operators' reports; file them in BOSSI headquarters, or alert Kinsella that action had to be taken to prevent violence or death. Theologes would act as a cross between a drill sergeant and a priest. He would be the taskmaster in the training and supervision of recruits, especially on how to prepare a report and how to follow through on an assignment. He would also have to listen and counsel recruits as they struggled with their roles. My job would be in the field. Our identities were never to be linked to the report of any operator that was passed up the line. If our names ever appeared in a report and we were called to testify in court, it could jeopardize an entire undercover operation. That was to be avoided at all costs.

To set my new assignment in motion, we had to take certain key clerical personnel into our confidence. The first was Louis Stuttman, Chief Clerk of the Department and a civilian in charge of departmental personnel records. We wanted the records and applications of new recruits scrutinized, noting in particular those who had passed the police exam with flying colors but who were still waiting for their appointment to the Police Academy. The organizational phase of this undertaking required the adoption of a careful screening process for potential candidates. My records and those of Mulligan and Theologes were also to be pulled from the official file drawer and kept in Stuttman's safe. If a recruit was selected to work as an undercover agent, he would not enter the Police Academy until he had completed his assignment.

Academy personnel were not to know what happened to the recruit, and the recruit's name would not appear in official Police Department files until he or she surfaced. Screening the applications of these recruits was tedious work, involving interviews of hundreds of new recruits in order to get three worthy prospects. We wanted fresh raw goods, those who hadn't yet learned the jargon of a cop.

First, we developed a list of prospective candidates, primarily those with the highest grades on the police exam. Then we called them in one by one and told them that the Department was conducting a survey to determine the type of young person attracted to police work, what they felt they could offer in the way of service to the Department, and how the Department could make the best use of their talents and special abilities. We met in the old Police Academy that was once housed in a school on the Lower West Side of Manhattan. If I ever scheduled a meeting at the new Police Academy on 20th Street, it was always at night, when the Academy would be closed and when we could have the place to ourselves. Wherever we met, the prospective candidate would be told that his or her answers would be used for statistical purposes and would be kept confidential. In turn, the recruit was advised that the interview was to be treated as confidential and that untimely or un-guarded discussion could jeopardize his or her career as a police officer. When the formalities of the interview were completed, we dropped some loaded questions on the recruits. "Do you have any feelings about how we should deal with Cuba, with Russia? What's your feeling about the demonstrations building up in our country? Do you know about the Black Muslims? How do you feel about the Black Power movement, Malcolm X, the civil rights movement? Have you ever studied commu-nism or socialism? What do you think about the American Nazi Party? Do you have any opinion about government agencies investigating radical groups?

How they handled themselves in responding to the questions was more important than the answer they gave. We didn't want people who mouthed answers they thought we wanted, or who were trying to mirror our thoughts or those of someone in their family. The last person we wanted was someone with a relative in the Department because it would ultimately be impossible to protect his or her cover. There would be too much pressure at home to disclose what he or she was doing for the Department. We wanted the men and women we interviewed to show their feelings. We weren't looking for rigid allegiance to a particular social, political, or ethical code. Yes, we wanted Americans, but we had no opposition to anyone who wanted to change the way things were. What mattered to us was how these recruits saw themselves. They also had to be people who could adapt to risk, who were comfortable with themselves and who understood that what they would be doing was important for the safety and security of the City of New York.

In addition to the screening, training and selection process, we had to establish which organizations these undercover agents would be asked to infiltrate. These organizations had to be clearly subversive or pose a threat to life and property. Undercover operators were instructed that they would be pulled from this assignment if a criminal act was the only way they thought they could remain inside the organization. Nor did we ever want an operator to assume a leadership role within an organization. Unlike undercover squads of the past, no undercover operator was ever to know the identity of any other. No operator would be told that a backup was being placed inside the same organization. This system would provide an additional cross-check on the accuracy of the information we were receiving and would protect against the emergence of a double agent. If we discovered a turncoat, that person wouldn't know that a replacement was already within the same organization ready to take over.

Each operator infiltrating the same organization would likely establish different degrees of status and credibility. We would have operators on the same assignment or covering the same group report to different offices, on different days of the week, in different parts of the city. The offices I rented were to be used for meeting with my operators at preappointed times in order to scrutinize their reports and to provide cover for their employment. These offices were to be just large enough to hold a desk, a table and chairs, a typewriter, and some office supplies kept in a filing cabinet. To fill our needs we bought used furniture on Canal Street. No BOSSI files were to be kept there. We'd be sure to empty the wastebaskets every day. In the event of a threat that the operator's cover was about to be blown, the office could be cleaned out in a matter of minutes. We'd leave the furniture. My plan was to rent these offices in the names of fictitious tenants, with a few months' extra rent left in an envelope on the table if it became necessary to move out in a hurry.

Adopting various identities, I became the butcher, the baker, the candlestick maker as I signed leases, established employment covers, opened up bank accounts, and obtained the cooperation of the Social Security Administration in issuing new social security numbers to my flock that couldn't be traced back to the Police Department. I had to forget I was a cop as I traveled around New York. I couldn't flash my shield in a subway station and pass through the exit gate without paying. I couldn't let my jacket flop open to reveal my gun or sit at a desk in an office with my holster showing. For my record of expenses, I had to keep tabs on subway token costs, cab fares, bank deposits, and payroll records. In the beginning, I had to count out the exact pay for each of my sheep before I could trust a bank official to make up payroll envelopes. Directed by Kinsella to reestablish BOSSI undercover operations for the New York City Police Department, I realized I hadn't been sent into the oblivion I once feared when I first joined BOSSI. I was being sent back to my home in the streets. I was in the field with my flock, and that was just where I belonged.

M Y first recruit was a husky former high school football player from Chester, South Carolina, named Raymond Adolphus Wood. Mulligan, Theologes, and I gave him the alias Ray Woodall. When Wood's father died in 1951, Ray had to drop out of high school because his father had been the sole means of support for the family. He joined the Air Force and within four years earned a classification as a communications specialist. While in the service, he received his high school equivalency degree. After his discharge, he headed north to New York. During the day he worked as a teletype operator, and at night he attended classes to earn a college degree in business administration. He also took the New York City Police exam and passed it with flying colors. In April 1964 we tapped him for inclusion in the interview process. After our first meeting, Mulligan and Theologes complained that Wood looked so much like a cop he was too obvious for the job. I said that was the very reason he was the man we needed. If you put a big-brimmed hat on his head and a diamond on his pinky and stuck him up in Harlem, I argued, he could appear to be all things to all people. He could talk the talk, take care of business, act like a numbers man, a pimp, a big drug connection, an after-hours craps dealer, or a successful businessman tired of the white man's jive. If he talked like that, I figured no one would guess he could possibly be a cop. Wood moved around like he carried glory dust in his pockets. I knew we'd have to sit on him once in awhile if he got too cocky, but without doubt he was the man for the job.

While Wood was meeting with us to learn his trade and how to make out his reports, a jurisdictional dispute had to be resolved between BOSSI and the Central Investigations Bureau (CIB) before we could send him into the field. The Police Department had set up CIB in order to track organized crime which stretched beyond the territorial limits of any one precinct in the city. CIB sent one of its undercover agents into Harlem to pinpoint who controlled the drug, gambling, prostitution, and loan sharking rackets. He began to drift into radical political circles, and for awhile, CIB and BOSSI clashed over who was the boss of citywide intelligence operations dealing with radical plots for violence. BOSSI was designated to remain in charge of those investigations.

When we sent Wood out on his own, he was instructed to rent an apartment and to get a job performing menial tasks, like cleaning up someone else's mess. We told him to roam the streets in his off hours and hang around the headquarters of the Congress of Racial Equality (CORE) located on 125th Street. CORE's charter called for strictly nonviolent action, but at the time Wood started showing up outside its office doors, CORE was vigorously picketing the White Castle chain's branches around Harlem and the Bronx. CORE's picketing was designed to change White Castle's alleged discriminatory hiring policies and at the same time to pacify more militant activists who would have preferred to blow up the castle. Some of these militants, especially the members of the Progressive Labor Movement (PLM) or the Revolutionary Action Movement (RAM), attached themselves to CORE in order to monitor its direction and hopefully benefit from its failure. CORE was becoming successful in raising money. It was busy renting storefronts,

155

distributing leaflets, making speeches, capturing media attention, and trying to recruit new members. In contrast, the PLM and RAM weren't getting that kind of attention or money, and they were jealous.

CORE's leaflets preaching nonviolence began competing with pro-Chinese Communist publications that were surfacing on the same street corners which CORE's people were trying to control. A pro-Chinese Communist newsletter called *The Hammer and Steel* proclaimed that the manifesto for all blacks should be: "Arm Yourselves!" While circulating among these wolf packs that were waiting for CORE to fail, Wood made contact with a few members of RAM. He reported that there was so much infighting among RAM members that they were not considered a viable organized threat. Their time would come.

To save itself in the storm and keep its supporters in tow, CORE's chairman in Harlem, Herbert Callender, announced he was going to march on City Hall. Callender charged that Mayor Wagner and the city government were discriminating against blacks and misappropriating public monies on city-financed construction projects. He claimed that, because of his color, the black man was being denied a chance to work on union-controlled construction projects paid for with taxpayers' money. In retaliation—and in a clear play for publicity—Callender planned to make a citizen's arrest of Mayor Wagner for violating the blacks' civil rights.

When Wood reported Callender's plan, we told him to tag along. See what happens, we told him. While Callender's efforts were going to be mostly symbolic, regardless of how much noise and publicity he created, Wood's participation in this protest would give him instant recognition as a militant. Instead of just drifting and listening to the voices of Harlem and reporting to us what he heard, Wood suddenly found himself under arrest, along with Callender, for breach of the peace. Wood was arrested in front of City Hall, and his picture showing him being led off to jail appeared in all the city's newspapers. The revolutionary world had to see it all. Before he went to City Hall with Callender, I told Wood not to do anything that would invite a smack in the mouth. I didn't want him charged with resisting arrest or assault in addition to his bust for disorderly conduct. "Just don't aggravate the situation," I told

him. It would have been very awkward for us to get him out of jail
without creating suspicions.

On the same day Woods' picture appeared in the papers, a black
teenager named James Powell was shot and killed by a white cop. The
shooting took place across the street from the Robert F. Wagner Junior
High School in Yorkville, south of Harlem, on the Upper East Side.
Neither the boy nor the cop lived or worked in Harlem, but that didn't
matter. On the night of July 18, 1964, a demonstration was organized to
protest the killing. A rally at 125th Street and Seventh Avenue was held
in advance of the demonstration that was to follow in front of the 28th
Precinct on West 123rd. At the rally, speaker after speaker condemned
the shooting as another tragic example of police brutality. William
Epton, the firebrand of the Progressive Labor Movement, led the
charge. All the necessary embers were being stoked for a riot. When the
police barred the entrance to the 28th Precinct with arm-locked patrolmen and cleared 123rd Street between Seventh and Eighth Avenues,
angry blacks bellowed their frustrations. It was white on black, William
Epton had shouted, and that's all it took for Harlem's streets to burn once
again. The riot that followed provided a perfect opportunity for the
PLM, RAM, Malcolm X, and the Black Muslims to recruit new members.

Among black militants, Wood's arrest was proof of his willingness to
put his butt on the line, even though Callender's attempted arrest of the
Mayor was regarded as a joke and an embarrassment by angry blacks
who wanted real action from CORE, not just symbolic action doomed to
failure. Wood's conviction for disorderly conduct gave him solid credentials as a militant. Callender himself was sent off to Bellevue Hospital
for observation. A judge was discreetly asked not to impose a jail term
on Wood as a first offender, and he was released. When Wood was
offered the job as Callender's replacement as head of CORE in Harlem,
we told him to decline. He soon joined up with Robert Collier, Walter
Augustus Bowe, and Khaleen Sultarn Sayyed, three other former members of CORE who had tired of its nonviolent stance. Collier, Bowe, and
Sayyed were also the founders of the Black Liberation Front (BLF).
Collier, head of BLF, was a bright, young, angry black man who worked

157

as a clerk at the New York Public Library. In his free time he studied the manuals of guerrilla warfare.

As soon as I learned about Wood's contact with Collier, Mulligan went to work developing a profile on Collier. By this time, with Kinsella's help, a support team for BOSSI undercover field operations had been established in BOSSI headquarters. A stationary backup team was needed to check out leads, profile radical agitators, obtain orders for wiretaps, listen to the results, establish contact with detectives assigned to the District Attorney's Office, and shepherd undercover agents if they had to surface when an investigation was breaking. Our FBI, State Department, and CIA contacts had to be given the impression that our request for information on Collier was routine. Knowledge of BOSSI's resurrected undercover operations was off limits to every one except Kinsella, the Police Commissioner, and the detectives assigned to support us and our men in the field. Despite our precautions, I knew that at least the FBI's Gus Micek was aware something was brewing. For one thing, I was no longer around BOSSI headquarters to say hello. Second, with new, color-coded files being placed under restricted access, I had no doubt that Gus guessed what was going on. Gus was discreet, however, and would bide his time until BOSSI decided to verify his guess.

Combining a review of BOSSI, FBI, State Department, and military service records, we learned that Collier was married and the father of a young child and that he first went to work for the New York Public Library in December 1964. He lived in an apartment at 211 Eldridge Street in lower Manhattan. For one semester between September 1962 and January 1963, he studied electrical engineering at Lowell Institute in Massachusetts, after which he left school and moved to New York. His first brush with the law occurred during his stint with the United States Air Force when he was convicted of knifing a man during a fight while he was stationed in London.

In addition to joining CORE, Collier attached himself to a group called the Student Committee for Travel to Cuba, the same committee that later announced the formation of the Black Liberation Front. In the Spring of 1964, he and eleven fellow Committee members traveled to Cuba, even though the trip violated a State Department ban on travel to that country. While in Cuba, Collier was granted an audience with Che Guevara from whom he sought to learn ways to establish and train hit-and-run demolition teams. Collier's plan was to start similar training sessions in the United States. His other motive for seeing Guevara was to ask him how to get arms and ammunition through his black market sources. Collier was advised to try and get his explosives through the terrorist wing of the French-Canadian Separatist Movement.

In the late Fall of 1964, Guevara came to New York to make a speech before the United Nations General Assembly. It was at this time that a group of anti-Castro belligerents, protesting Guevara's presence at the UN, attempted to fire a bazooka from Long Island City across the East River into UN headquarters. The bazooka shell fizzled and fell harmlessly into the river. Detectives assigned to BOSSI's "Cuban Desk" broke the case. Eleven days later, three anti-Castro Cubans were arrested for illegal possession of explosives and firing the bazooka. The courts tossed the case out on the grounds that a confession had been obtained illegally. The general feeling in BOSSI headquarters, a feeling which I shared, was that the CIA had staged the whole incident in order to appease those Castro opponents who were still smarting from the CIA-sponsored disaster at the Bay of Pigs. As we all knew in BOSSI, the big brims from the CIA were capable of anything.

While in New York, Collier again made connections with Guevara who, in turn, told him to contact a French-Canadian woman named Michele Duclos, a television journalist from Montreal, who frequently traveled to New York. She spent a great deal of time hanging around the United Nations, making a special effort to socialize with representatives of the African delegations, especially those Third World African nations that were leaning toward the Soviet bloc. Behind her journalistic front, Duclos was a leading member of the terrorist unit of the Canadian Separatist Movement.

On the night of December 14, 1964, Collier invited Wood to come to his apartment in lower Manhattan. He told Wood that he wanted to find a way "to get close to this country" and that he wanted to target the greatest, most meaningful symbols of America so that the American people would finally understand the frustrations and discriminations of black people. "When the time is ripe," he said, "we will make our

159

move." Collier's statement triggered questions of just how dangerous this man was. How far was he willing to go, and what was Wood going to be exposed to? How long could we keep him undercover?

Wood's first reports revealed the conspiracy festering in Collier's mind: he had earmarked for destruction the Statue of Liberty, the Liberty Bell, and the Washington Monument, in that order. On January 19, 1965, Wood met Collier's other key associates in the Black Liberation Front, Bowe and Sayyed. Bowe was a judo instructor at the Henry Street Settlement House and a member of the Fair Play for Cuba Committee. Sayyed, along with Bowe, had attended Howard University. Sayyed had been previously arrested for assaulting a cop outside the UN while picketing for the Pan-African Student Movement. Even for a case-hardened cop like me, it was quite a jolt to learn the identity of their targets. When as a kid I had dreamed about doing police work, never once did I foresee that one day I might be using my shield to prevent the destruction of America's greatest symbol.

On January 24, Wood, acting on instructions from Collier, took the ferry out to the Statue of Liberty. Bowe and Sayyed were instructed to go there separately and on different days. Wood carried a brown lunch bag to see how carefully security guards checked packages or handbags that visitors were carrying. Bowe's assignment was to determine which location inside the Statue itself was best for planting explosives. In their earlier meetings Bowe had brought a souvenir replica of the Statute back to Collier's apartment. "We can break the lock on the door leading to the arm and put the explosives in there and knock the arm and head off the old bitch," Bowe said. He also said that if any lives were lost when the Statue blew up, it would be just those of "a couple of fancy pants marines." When Wood returned to Collier's apartment after scouting the Statue, Collier told him to buy some planks of wood, long spike nails, cotton wadding, and wide-necked bottles. They were needed for Collier's training sessions in the fine art of demolition. The bottles were to be filled with gasoline and capped with cotton or a cotton rag. The wider the bottle opening, Collier told Wood, the more cotton could be saturated with gasoline. That meant there would be a bigger explosion when the bottle was thrown against an unsuspecting target. There would be more shards of glass, more splinters of wood, more concrete landing on

160

heads. When Wood reported Collier's request for the materials, Theologes told me he asked Wood when he was supposed to bring them back to Collier. "Tonight," Wood answered. If it hadn't been clear how far Collier was willing to go to achieve his goal, it was now.

Five days after Wood's trip to the Statue to check out its security system, he headed north to Canada with Collier to make contact with Duclos and the radical wing of Quebec's Separatist Movement. Collier's aim was to come back with either a plan or an assurance that he would be able to obtain the necessary explosives. Whether to allow Wood to accompany Collier on this trip to Canada was an agonizing decision, for sending an undercover agent into another country was extremely dangerous. Until now, we had deliberately avoided telling the FBI anything about the formation of BOSSI's undercover unit, but now we realized that we were going to have to tell the agency about Wood because the conspiracy involved not only crossing state lines, but also citizens of another country. The task of informing the FBI was left to Kinsella and on up the line to the Office of the Police Commissioner. My job was to protect Wood's safety. Both Kinsella and I were concerned that notifying other authorities would risk blowing Wood's cover. If it was blown, the militants and conspirators would retreat deeper under their cover, only to come out exploding without further notice. Kinsella finally said, "Wood's going, and you're following, Tony."

The decision to allow Wood to go with the conspirators to Canada was also an acknowledgment that Wood would soon have to surface. The plot to blow up the Statue of Liberty was now beyond the talking stage. It was time to make connections in Canada, to buy explosives, and to plant them inside what Bowe called the "old bitch" in the harbor. Once we disclosed the fact that Wood had infiltrated the Black Liberation Front, he would soon be under surveillance by the FBI and the intelligence division of Canada's Royal Canadian Mounted Police. Even so, that wouldn't mean the end of my care or responsibility for his safety once he crossed the border into Canada. Someday Wood would be testifying about this journey, and his reports would be placed in other hands. I wouldn't be surfacing when this case ended, and neither would Mulligan nor Theologes. Our job was to remain undetected. Other undercover operators we trained were moving inside other radical groups, and I had

161

to shepherd them along with Wood. Since Wood was my first recruit, I had a special interest in ensuring his safety and didn't want that duty to go to any "Red Coat" in Canada or FBI agent. Kinsella didn't have to tell me that I would be the one to tail Wood to Canada; I accepted that job eagerly.

My last discussion with Wood concerned the car which he was directed to rent for the trip to Canada. I wouldn't talk with him again, although he knew I would be tracking his every move. Before he left, I gave him a series of different signals he was to use if he needed help. I packed a small suitcase, took my 38 calibre snubbed-nose detective special, and had my wife, Mary, make me six bologna sandwiches. I took along a six pack of Coke to wash them down.

In advance of Wood's departure from New York, I drove to the New York State Thruway rest stop near Harriman, New York. I then called Mulligan from a pay phone and told him to send Wood on his way. I gave Mulligan the number of the pay phone and then waited by the phone for him to give me the word that Wood was on the road. After estimating the time it would take Wood to travel from the city limits to the Harriman rest stop, I parked my car where I could clearly see every car that came in that direction. I made sure to park between other cars in order to avoid drawing attention. Wood was instructed not to stop to look for me. I checked my watch and waited. I ate two sandwiches and drank one Coke while I watched, like a marksman at a target, for Wood's car. My biggest concern, other than missing him when he passed, was the weather. A large low pressure system was moving into the area, and the farther north I traveled the worse I knew it would become. As the clouds thickened and darkened, I realized I didn't have any options. The mission couldn't be reprogrammed for a sunny day.

After I finally spotted Wood's car heading north, I let him get at least a mile ahead of me before I drove out of the rest stop and moved within sight of his wheels. North of Albany, Wood left the Thruway and switched to Route 9, the old two-lane route to Canada. Then the heavens broke open with heavy wet snow; sleet mixed with freezing rain; drizzle merged with fog. I could barely keep my windshield clear to see the road, let alone see Wood's car. I lost him once when I got sandwiched in between two trailer trucks that showered me in slush. I felt like I was driving inside a car wash. To keep my focus on Wood's car, I had placed some small pieces of black electric tape on the tail and headlights of his car while he and Collier stopped for something to eat. With the pieces of tape in place, I was then able to spot the partially obscured tail or headlight depending on whether I stayed in front or behind his car. I needed all the help I could get.

I arrived ahead of Wood and Collier at the Canadian check point near Rouse's Point and waited for them to cross the border. I positioned myself so that Wood could easily spot me as he passed through. The movement of cars entering and leaving Canada and the actions of Customs officers pulling cars over and spot checking their contents provided me with a perfect cover to wait for him. As soon as Wood and Collier entered Canadian territory, I called Kinsella and gave him the exact time they crossed the border. Wood's final destination was Montreal. The plan was for Kinsella to notify the Police Commissioner, who would then notify the head of Canadian intelligence operations that I was about to enter Canada on an extremely sensitive assignment. For security reasons, Wood's presence in Canada was to remain a secret. The Police Commissioner gave only my name and rank and said that if I asked for assistance, no further verification of my authority or the reason for my request was required. If I needed help, Canadian authorities were asked to be prepared to move quickly. My call for help would mean that a life was at stake. The police in Montreal were not notified of my coming because the feeling was that the more people who knew about my assignment the greater the chance of a screw up or a leak. I knew what I had to do to protect Wood; I couldn't afford to worry about another cop's trigger.

After Wood and Collier finally checked into a Canadian motel for the night, I found myself a place to stay and hoped my guess was right that Wood and Collier would now slow their pace. The trip to Montreal had been grueling. I was exhausted from the tension. Based on what Wood had reported before he left New York, apparently there was no plan in place to get the explosives and then high tail it back to New York. There was no guarantee that Collier would be able to buy anything. I bet on them sleeping a long time, cooling it for awhile, sizing up the situation, and also being thoroughly checked out themselves. I'm glad I won the bet. On occasion I had gone days without sleep, but I didn't want to test my endurance on this assignment. I finished off the last sandwich, drank a Coke, and fell into a deep sleep.

Wood and Collier left their motel late the following afternoon, January 30. It was dusk by the time they drove into a restaurant parking lot. I drove around the area for a while, and then decided to take a chance and remove the black tape from the lights on Wood's car. I didn't want Collier to become suspicious. After all, rental agencies don't give out cars with black tape on their head or tail lights. Before proceeding I checked the windows from other buildings facing the restaurant parking lot to see if I could be seen. When the coast was clear, I pulled off the tape as quickly as I could. Feeling confident, I decided that it was time to let Wood know I was in the area. I walked into the restaurant and sat at the bar until Wood turned his head just enough to notice me. He seemed to be having a ball; he was also, I hoped, taking care of business. At their table were also a woman later identified as Michelle Saunier and two other unidentified members of Quebec's Separatist Movement. Up until now, I had no idea when or where Collier would make contact with his prospective Canadian supplier. There was no way to arrange for a wiretap in Canada because I didn't know where Wood and Collier were going to stay when they arrived in Canada. Also, there would have been too much red tape with the Red Coats to plan in advance for wiretaps. I assumed that Collier called Saunier from the motel and that she selected this restaurant as the place to start talking business. I finished my drink and then headed outside into the Canadian night to wait for the next move.

Wood and Collier didn't meet anyone else until the next night when, at approximately 9:30 p.m. they entered Saunier's Montreal apartment. Waiting to meet them was Michele Duclos, their connection to the Canadian terrorist underground. Collier and Duclos had met once before, in New York when Castro sent his master terrorist, Che Guevara, to address the United Nations. Guevara, as it was commonly known, was in charge of exporting Castro's revolution. Collier had had dinner with Guevara, a meeting which Duclos knew about and helped establish Collier's credibility. Here in Canada Collier wanted to buy plastique, an explosive that is more powerful than dynamite and is easily molded to the target chosen. Duclos told Collier that plastique wasn't available; dynamite was all they had. As payment, she preferred access to apartments in New York to cash because her organization needed safe houses and hideouts for people coming in and out of the city. Apartments were also needed to entertain foreign diplomats who might be sympathetic to her cause (and maybe Collier's).

One way money was being raised for terrorist organizations was by persuading Third World countries to siphon off some of America's foreign aid and sending it to terrorist groups through back-channel intermediaries. BOSSI's intelligence apparatus, together with that of the FBI, CIA, and the State Department, had put together a much darker profile of opportunities which UN membership provided for supporting terrorist activities (and espionage) than was commonly known. Membership in the United Nations provided excellent cover for all sorts of illegal operations. (International money laundering started under the UN blanket, but the drug lords and their cartels that began forming in the 1960's needed a faster turnaround on their money. So they began going outside the United Nations' umbrella protection to bribe bankers and government officials, like Panama's Manuel Noriega, so that the flow of cash didn't have to trickle through any checkpoints.)

Saunier and Duclos had met alone at Duclos's Montreal apartment in the morning before meeting Wood and Collier that night. Saunier handed Duclos Collier's shopping list for ten blasting caps, 30 pounds of explosives, and 30 feet of primer cord that Collier had given Saunier the night before. Before he left New York, Wood reported to me that Collier had carefully calculated exactly what he needed to do the job. When Duclos was handed Collier's list, before giving the go-ahead for the sale she said that she had to meet Collier again and his friend and then talk with her people in the underground. Filling Collier's order meant stretching the lines of her organization; contacts might be exposed, covers blown, and the seal of a watertight terrorist group punctured. Just because Collier had met Che Guevara and was all charged up about what had happened to the black man in America didn't mean that every other terrorist organization had to climb on his wagon. There were plenty of buildings and monuments to blow up in Canada.

When Wood and Collier entered Saunier's apartment that night, I was watching and waiting in the dark. I had no idea how long Wood would remain inside or where he would go after he left. I was, of course, prepared to stay all night. Wood was neither wired nor armed. Even if he risked carrying a tiny gun in his crotch, if he were frisked or searched he'd be a dead man. The only instruction I gave Wood was to place himself where he could throw a chair out a window or to bolt for the door if he smelled danger. My job was to keep out of sight and be ready to save his life. I waited and watched for something to happen. The silence was oppressive and heavy.

Inside Saunier's apartment, as Wood reported later, Duclos grilled Collier on what type of organization he was trying to put together. Collier said it would be different, nothing like CORE or Martin Luther King's civil rights marchers. It would consist of three- and four-man teams trained in the use of explosives who would eventually hook up with other teams scattered around the country. They would make their move "when the time was ripe." It was to be a small and very secret operation designed to prevent infiltration by the police. Collier's plan was also designed to cure a disease that destroys most radical organizations when they get too big. Too many people like to hear themselves talk, and after they finish nobody can decide what to do because the agenda gets longer, everybody wants a priority seat on the radical plane, and most often it never takes off. Duclos asked Collier to describe how his organization could stay secret if it wanted to expand around the country. "That's a problem," Collier acknowledged. "How do you know you're not infiltrated now?," Duclos asked. Collier answered that he was sure Wood was a safe bet. Wood later reported that when that question was asked, he started measuring his distance from the door and picking out the chair he would throw out the window if things suddenly got too hot.

Duclos pressed Collier as to where he was going to get his weapons and other explosives to carry out his goals. He bragged that if one of his team got caught, he'd free him from the cops even if he had to kill every cop in town. He then went on to describe how to make a lot of noise and do a lot of damage with very few tools. "Take, for instance," Collier began his lecture, "two used gun shells, pack one with gunpowder, the other with a pin, shove them together and when someone steps on it they might lose some toes. If you want a bigger bang and maybe blow off a leg then use cans—old dog food or soup cans. Want to throw something at somebody? Put sugar in your Molotov cocktail and you'll see it burns longer. Put a pin and some powder in a pipe and you've got a homemade bazooka." Duclos chimed in that hair spray bottles were good, too, because there is usually a small curve in the inside bottom of the container so that if you turn it upside down, put a little bit of gasoline in it, stick in a wick, and then light it (and run like hell), you'll hear the biggest firecracker around. "Sometimes," Collier continued, "you don't have to kill or maim someone if all you want to do is deliver a message." (I wonder what the difference is between an enforcer working for the mob and a terrorist when they want to deliver a message.) "Put an oil slick by the front door or on the balcony and you'll find it's better than a banana peel, or pound some nails through a board and rap it around your arm so if the cop's German Shepherd gets too close you can nail him on the nose. Sometimes cops ride horses and try to run over people. Put some ammonia on the end of a stick and watch the horse toss the cop off his back when the horse gets a whiff."

After all this talk, Wood reported that they all had something to eat, turned on some music, and danced. To get out of the apartment and make contact with me to signal he was alright, Wood put on his coat and started to leave. "Where are you going?" Duclos asked. When Wood told her he was going on a tour of the city, she offered to drive him around. Being careful to stay in the shadows to avoid being spotted, I followed Wood until he returned to Saunier's apartment to pick up his own car. As Wood's car rolled south again, I trailed it until he crossed the border into the United States. I notified Kinsella at headquarters that Wood was on safe ground and then headed home.

It wasn't until Wood returned to New York that the FBI was fully brought into the picture. Privately, the FBI was embarrassed that it knew nothing about Wood's role as an undercover police officer—especially in a case involving the potential destruction of U.S. property—until he returned from Canada. The FBI was also brought up short with the knowledge that BOSSI was returning to the use of undercover agents in connection with radical political activity. It was a tough pill for them to swallow that they hadn't been told everything and wouldn't be in the future, if we felt there was any risk of exposure to any of our men or women (which was the flip side of the Galindez case). While coordinated plans were worked out between Kinsella, the Chief of Detectives, and the FBI to watch out for Duclos's expected trip with the dynamite into the United States, I met with FBI Special Agent Jim Brody. He and I had met when Brody was working the federal side monitoring the movements of the American Nazi Party. Brody and I met to develop a methodology as to how and under what circumstances the FBI was to learn whether someone they were keeping tabs on was in fact one of my men. The distinction between the use of information and the protection of an undercover agent was to be kept clear. I was the man Brody would contact. I would remain the final judge as to whether the disclosure or verification of an agent's presence inside a group under surveillance was without risk to his or her safety.

As she had promised Wood, Michele Duclos arranged to pick up and deliver enough dynamite to blow the head off the Statue of Liberty. Duclos told Wood she would bring it to New York herself. It was uncertain where she would attempt to cross the border into the United States. Besides the Canadian–U.S. Customs check at Rouse's Point, there were also the woods and old tote roads used by lumberjacks and hunters. Every possible route for her crossing was put under surveillance. The possibility also had to be considered that the dynamite would be shipped by some other means and that Duclos would act as a decoy. It soon became clear, however, that Duclos would keep her promise and deliver the dynamite herself. She left Canada on the late afternoon of February 15. As a ruse to get through Customs at the Canadian border, she brought along two young boys for the ride. When a Customs agent asked the usual question, "Where are you going?," Duclos let one of the kids answer. She remained silent. "We're going out for dinner," the boy answered. Smart. Duclos's car containing the dynamite for Collier was allowed through Customs without examination. But when Duclos left Canada, her every movement was tracked by Canadian intelligence, FBI agents, and some of our men from BOSSI. Squad detectives from the NYPD picked up the scent when Duclos got closer to New York City. These detectives, by prearrangement, were assigned to make the anticipated arrests when Collier made his move to pick up the dynamite.

When Duclos arrived in New York, she drove to 239th Street in the Riverdale section of the Bronx and pulled into a small parking lot. Her young companions were told to disappear. On the right side of the parking lot, looking from the street, was a garden. Duclos got out of her car and walked toward a fence that bordered the garden. She put the box containing the dynamite in a ditch near the fence and covered it with some branches and some snow left over from a storm. She then placed the blasting caps into two empty cigarette packs and wrapped them in newspaper. She put the caps in the wrapped packs under a fire bucket she took that was hanging on the fence. She then left the scene and went to the Colonial House on 112th Street from where she called Wood. "Please come, I need you," she told Wood.

Nobody had time to bug Duclos's room or to put a tap on her phone because we didn't know where she would stay until she arrived in New York. Wood, however, was wired when he arrived at Duclos's room at approximately 2:30 on the morning of February 16. Duclos thought she had been followed. "I've lost the tail," she said, "and I've gotten rid of the box, but I want you to be sure that box won't be there tomorrow morning." She was worried because she had left her footprints in the snow. "Please get in touch with Bob," she said, "or do something. Go and get it yourself or go and get Bob."

"What do you want me to do?" Wood asked.

"It's no longer my concern," Duclos answered anxiously. "It's yours. Now you have the box. That's what you wanted. Well, you keep it!"

On the morning of February 16, when Collier ever so briefly took possession of the box of dynamite, he was placed under arrest. Soon after, Bowe, Sayyed, Duclos, and Saunier were arrested and indicted for plotting to "commit depredations against the property of the United States." Collier, Bowe, and Sayyed pleaded not guilty and went to trial. Unlike the days when I sat in Judge Medina's courtroom during the communist conspiracy trial my first year in BOSSI, reporting back each day's proceedings, it was now my turn to receive daily reports on the trial. Bowe and Sayyed testified in their own defense that they were peace-loving and nonviolent. Wood, they said, was the cause of it all; it was his idea, they argued. When arrested, Sayyed had two M-1 carbines and several clips of .30 calibre ammunition in his possession. Those items weren't Wood's idea. Bowe said he was a judo instructor, and all he wanted to do was hold classes in the martial arts. He knew nothing, he said, about nothing. Collier didn't testify. Taken from his apartment and introduced into evidence at the trial were some of Collier's terrorist tools: planks of wood, long spike nails, bottles, cotton wadding, a funnel, and two plastic containers of gasoline and benzine. All of the defendants except Duclos were convicted as charged. Duclos, having pleaded guilty before the trial started, became a witness for the prosecution and verified everything Wood had reported.

As a result of his work, Ray Wood received New York City's highest award for heroism, the Medal of Honor. To preserve my anonymity, as well as that of my partners, our Citations for Excellent and Meritorious Duty were slipped into our personnel folders at Police Headquarters. The monthly bulletin of orders and awards was silent about our work. But when Wood received his medal, I was standing in the wings watching.

O N February 21, six days after the dynamite to blow up the Statue of Liberty was delivered in New York, Malcolm X, leader of the Organization for Afro-American Unity, was assassinated as he stood on the stage of the Audubon Ballroom to address the crowd. After Malcolm X was blown apart by a sawed-off shotgun, Gene Roberts tried mouth-to-mouth resuscitation to breathe life back into the man who had been Harlem's most articulate preacher of violent rebellion against the whites. Roberts was one of my undercover operators. He had been sent deep to measure how great a threat Malcolm X posed to the City of New York. In the Audubon Ballroom that day, there were members of his own race in the audience who didn't want to hear what he had to say. Opening his trench coat and running down the aisle, Thomas Hagan, also known as Talmadge Thayer, emptied both barrels of his shotgun into Malcolm X's chest just as he was telling the crowd to "cool it."

Malcolm X had always refused police protection. On the day of his assassination, he refused to have any police officers stationed inside the Audubon Ballroom, not wanting "pig cops" inside. No one entering the Ballroom was checked for firearms because Malcolm X wouldn't permit that either. But he had been a marked man ever since he broke away from Elijah Muhammad's Black Muslims. Just one week before his death, his home in Queens had been firebombed. The Black Muslims denied responsibility, saying it was their house anyway and that they had just gotten a court order to kick Malcolm out of it. "Why would we burn down our own house?" the Muslims asked. The day after Malcolm X was murdered, the Black Muslim Mosque on 116th Street and Lenox Avenue was burned down. Malcolm's followers denied having anything to do with it.

The frustrating part of the Malcolm X murder was that, inside his organization, Gene Roberts was as close to Malcolm X as anybody could get, but he couldn't stop his assassination. He didn't carry a gun, let alone his badge. If Roberts had opened his mouth and started screaming he was a cop and everybody hold it right there, he would have been shot and probably killed, too. My flock of undercover operators was formed to help stop violence, not to stand by helplessly and watch it happen. As it was, Roberts carried a bullet hole in his jacket when he went home that night. He was on stage with Malcolm X to keep us informed about what was going on inside his organization. While I had no quarrel with Malcolm X's desire to better the conditions of his race, I took his words at face value, and they were a threat to the safety and security of the people of New York. For his beliefs, he was silenced by his own race, and there wasn't a damn thing we could do about it. He charted his own course to get himself killed. Robert Collier touched the dynamite, and we saved the Statue of Liberty; Gene Roberts touched the face of Malcolm X but couldn't bring him back to life. Malcolm X's death was yet another lesson that intelligence work carries no guarantees, just goals. Many times there are no rules that govern the play of the game, no consistency in expectations as to how people will behave in any given situation. Malcolm X tested his chances of survival against his chances of martyrdom. If his murder triggered open warfare among blacks themselves or between blacks and whites, he no longer had anything to lose. He could inflict his revenge against the white man from his grave.

The same dose of fanaticism that poisoned Thomas Hagan into killing Malcolm X also affected the mind of one of my operators who had

171

infiltrated the Muslim organization. I was disappointed but not surprised when I learned I had a turncoat among my recruits. Teddy Theologes had become suspicious of him when he began noticing major discrepancies between what the operator was reporting and what our other undercover operator was saying about the same event. One day soon after we had grown suspicious of his motives he showed up outside one of our offices in downtown Manhattan and began pointing out our location to some other Muslims. I watched him from the window. He was in clear violation of our orders not to come near the office except when he was scheduled to report to us. Within minutes, I closed the office, left an extra month's rent on the desk, and disappeared into the streets. We soon flushed the turncoat operator into the open.

There was a danger that this operator would expose our undercover work if he was dismissed out of hand without an opportunity to explain why he had violated his instructions. Also, to avoid charges of discrimination, and the creation of an unnecessary hostile atmosphere, this operator and his lawyer were given a chance to appear before the Police Commissioner to clear the air. The matter was resolved by having the operator voluntarily resign from the Department.

B LACK radical activists were not our only concern. George Lincoln Rockwell and his American Nazi Party had proved that point. After Rockwell died, Robert Bolivar DePugh moved from his retreat in the Missouri woods and headed north to lead the Minutemen, a hard-hatted, two-fisted, righteous bunch of posturing white American extremists. DePugh said he was ready to clear out everybody's forest— black and white. His stated objectives were to stake the land for his own band of American guerrillas and to rid the U.S. government of its "bunglers and traitors." After he cleaned house, he said he was going to establish a "genuinely pro-American government here at home." His form of government, he declared, "could no longer be established by normal political means." To rid America of the disease he saw everywhere, his Minutemen began plotting in secret for armed conflict by holding paramilitary exercises at training sites throughout the metropolitan area. An arsenal of weapons, including machine guns, bombs,

172

mortars, rifles, bazookas, bullets, and hand grenades, was secretly stockpiled. Before DePugh and his troops pulled any triggers or launched any missiles, some of my flock blew the whistle on his plans. On October 31, 1966, nineteen Minutemen were arrested and charged with illegal possession of weapons and conspiracy to commit arson. Their arsenal for war was quickly confiscated. The Minutemen had planned to firebomb three locations in New York, New Jersey, and Connecticut which DePugh claimed were Communist Party training sites. Also in line for Minutemen arson was the Brooklyn campaign headquarters of Herbert Aptheker, an admitted member of the Communist Party who was running for Congress on the Peace and Freedom ticket.

By June 1967, the Revolutionary Action Movement finally got its radical act together and targeted Roy Wilkins, Executive Director of the National Urban League, for assassination. Before any bullets or bombs could be used, however, undercover operators I helped recruit and train surfaced from the field, and together with city, state and federal law enforcement officers, helped dismantle RAM's deadly conspiracy. On June 21, twelve men and four women were arrested on charges of conspiracy to commit murder, arson, advocating anarchy, and illegal possession of firearms. In pre-dawn raids in Brooklyn, Queens and Manhattan, rifles, shotguns, carbines, and over a thousand rounds of ammunition were seized along with fifteen of the sixteen conspirators. The sixteenth, described by the FBI as the head of RAM, was picked up in Philadelphia. By the time this conspiracy was defused, BOSSI, the FBI, and city, state and federal prosecutors were working together as a tightly knit team to protect the people and property of New York City.

Although the disclosure of these plots brought headlines and praise, it also caused a demolition of its own for the continued effectiveness of BOSSI undercover operations. Starting with the emergence of Ray Wood, radicals became increasingly cautious about admitting new members to their organizations. Wholesale changes occurred in the structure of radical groups when a conspiracy was defused and arrests were made. Some of the best radical minds as well as some of our best undercover personnel were tossed indiscriminately out the same radical door. Both had to be replaced. Once, after a big case made big news, a spokesman for the Department said that "BOSSI always loses some of its best people because of the publicity." In May 1969, without fanfare or notice, I had a heart-to-heart talk with Barney Mulligan and Teddy Theologes and told them that BOSSI was going to lose me, too. I was going to retire from the Police Department and was going to work as the personal private investigator for the President of the United States.

The President's Private Eye

M Y first opportunity to work for Richard Nixon came in August 1968 after the Republican National Convention nominated him to run for the Presidency. The convention had followed the violent demonstrations that accompanied the Democrats' convention in Chicago. Worried by the tense atmosphere in the nation, Nixon's campaign staff was convinced that the presidential race between Nixon and the Democratic candidate, Hubert Humphrey, would set records for campaign hostility. Nixon's campaign officials were especially anxious that pickets might start staging demonstrations at whistle stops and rallies, actions which in the violent climate of the times might easily get out of control. I got word of this concern from Jack Caulfield, a former BOSSI detective who had been given an official leave of absence to become head of Nixon's campaign security detail.

Caulfield's relationship with the Nixon campaign began in 1968 when former astronaut, now Senator, John Glenn came to New York when a ticker-tape parade was held to honor the Apollo mission astronauts who first orbited the moon. BOSSI had assigned Caulfield to Glenn's escort detail. Coinciding with Glenn's arrival was John Ehrlichman's trip to New York

175

to get political exposure for Nixon as well as to help him assess presidential campaign security procedures. Caulfield became Ehrlichman's contact with BOSSI, and through Ehrlichman, Caulfield met H. R. Haldeman, who would become Nixon's chief of staff after he was elected President. Both Ehrlichman and Haldeman were impressed with BOSSI's thoroughness in handling security, and at Ehrlichman's prodding, Haldeman persuaded the Police Commissioner to let Caulfield become head of Nixon's campaign security detail. Caulfield's assignment was classified as detached departmental service. Almost immediately after his appointment, Caulfield called to ask me to join Nixon's campaign train, but I turned him down. The job simply held no challenge for me. In my mind a campaign security assignment would mean nothing more than a lot of glitz and tinsel draped over a lot of travel, talk, and parties and too little sleep.

In March 1969, after Nixon had won and taken office, Caulfield again approached me about a possible assignment. It wasn't going to be what I thought, Caulfield said; it would be so different in fact that he couldn't talk about it over the phone. This time I was a bit more receptive, having in the last few weeks begun to think about retiring. In 1969, at age fifty-one, I was only seven years away from retirement on a full police pension, but setting myself up in business as a private investigator had begun to interest me. An affiliation with the White House would surely benefit the future of my own operation, and so I was ready to hear Caulfield out. We met at the Hofbrau, a bar and restaurant near 42nd Street which had long been a hangout for both New York's cops and reporters for the *Daily News*.

I hadn't seen Caulfield in over a year, and in an instant I could see that he had already become a tout for all the power that makes Washington move. He was just bursting with his news that he had found the Yellow Brick Road and was going to make a million bucks as a lobbyist when he finished working for Nixon. "The lobbyists in Washington run the whole show," he said. But I wasn't interested in his ambitions; all I wanted to know was what was so hush-hush that he couldn't tell me about it over the phone.

Over a few drinks, Caulfield outlined the big secret. He said the White House wanted to set up its own investigative resource which would be quite separate from the FBI, CIA, or Secret Service. "Vis-

a-vis the national situation, the predominant problem," Caulfield started
to tell me. I stopped Caulfield in his tracks. "What language are you
speaking?" I asked. In the place of the simple street lingo of a cop was
this dense, almost impenetrable patter. I didn't know what the hell he
was talking about. If he was looking for a vigilante, I wasn't it. Then
Caulfield explained that the White House, being deeply concerned about
the seemingly endless series of demonstrations and protests sweeping
the nation, wanted its own staff operation to monitor all such activities.
The new administration, Caulfield said, was finding government intelligence methods to be deficient. "Who said that?" I asked him; "it
certainly couldn't have been J. Edgar Hoover." Caulfield answered that
Ehrlichman, Nixon's Counsel at the White House, had assigned him to
check out what it would cost to set up an off the books, secret intelligence operation. As I listened to Caulfield ramble on, trying to make
himself sound more important with each syllable, I found it hard to
imagine that after only three months in office, the White House, from
the President on down, could have evaluated and concluded that U.S. intelligence wasn't good enough. I wondered who this guy Ehrlichman
thought he was to propose going behind Hoover's back to form a private
under-the-table intelligence unit? The suggestion was off the wall. I
reminded Caulfield that the President had not only the Secret Service,
the FBI, the CIA, and the State Department, but also the intelligence
units of the Army, Navy, and the Air Force at his command. Caulfield's
justification of the White House's position was that the President was
afraid of leaks and didn't want any Congressman to know that the
administration was pushing to learn more about the leaders of campus
protests, anti-Vietnam demonstrations, or which radicals had infiltrated
liberal organizations. I told Caulfield I didn't want any part of that. "If
you're suggesting I retire and use BOSSI as a source of information, let's
end it right here." Caulfield then tossed me his bait. "No, Tony, you're
job would be for the President. You'd be his own private investigator.
Your assignment would be to privately check out any person or situation
that could directly affect the President or his family." While that had a
better sound for me, in fact it was a tantalizing idea, I told Caulfield I
wanted a lot more specifics before making up my mind. "Then you'll
have to meet Ehrlichman," Caulfield said.

I flew down to Washington on April 9 for my meeting with Ehrlichman at the White House. All I ended up doing, however, was cooling my heels in Caulfield's office because some emergency had come up and Ehrlichman was closeted with the President all day. When I left Washington that day, I expected that to be the end of it. But to my surprise Caulfield called back and told me Ehrlichman wanted to meet with me as soon as possible. The meeting was rescheduled for May 9 at the VIP lounge at LaGuardia Airport.

As a BOSSI detective, I was generally known to be a tight-lipped guy, a trait that stood me in good stead with the Department but obviously seemed to bother Ehrlichman when I didn't say very much in response to what he said. "Your silence bothers me," Ehrlichman said. "It tells me you apparently feel quite confident about yourself. Do you have bouts of overconfidence?" "No," I answered, "I stay well sealed, like a clam." For my part, Ehrlichman bothered me, too. Working on BOSSI assignments protecting even kings and queens from all over the world, I had never felt uncomfortable in their presence. I respected but was never awed by the power they represented. I felt uncomfortable, however, in Ehrlichman's presence, sensing that he was trying to overwhelm me with his importance. For example, when we were first introduced inside the VIP lounge, he looked offended that I didn't jump to attention.

Ehrlichman finally described what my job would be. I was to make sure that nothing of a personal nature would unexpectedly arise to harm the reputation of the President, the First Lady, or any of their children during his term of office. I was also expected to make background checks on certain politicians within both parties, especially on individuals who might be in line for government appointment; to screen heavy Republican campaign contributors who wanted access to the White House; or occasionally to review a prospective visitor's credentials who was just trying to hustle a White House invitation to dinner. That was a far different assignment from dealing with Caulfield's "vis-a-vis the national situation" fixation.

Ehrlichman advised me that I was to observe the utmost confidentiality; that was obvious from his emphasis throughout the interview on the White House's desire for secrecy. He repeatedly mentioned that there were too many leaks and that the FBI and the Secret Service wrote too many reports. If I decided to take the job, he said my work would never be disclosed. Nor were any records of my employment to be kept. "If you're hired," Ehrlichman said, "you'll be allowed no mistakes. There will be no support for you whatsoever from the White House if you're exposed." As I listened to him, Ehrlichman's fascination with the secrecy and intrigue of intelligence work became increasingly obvious. Then we got down to the details of taking the job. I declined his first offer which was a trial period of six months, followed by a review of my work. A trial period would have been a waste of my time. Instead I asked for a guaranteed contract of at least a year. I wasn't going to risk my family's financial security by shooting craps with my future. I also insisted that my salary be a thousand dollars more a year than what I was then making as a first grade detective. With the added value of my pension (even though it would now be half of what it would be worth in another seven years), I'd have a solid financial footing when I left the Police Department. Ehrlichman promised he would talk with the President; others, he said, were being considered for the job.

Before the meeting ended, I set out other conditions for accepting the assignment. First, I told him that I would operate strictly as a loner and would report to only one man. If there was a leak, I wanted to know where it started. Also, there would be no written reports because I didn't want to get bogged down at a typewriter. Doing a solo as an investigator meant I had to be ready to move to the assignment's location and not worry about the method of transmitting my findings. Someone else at the White House could put it on paper. Too much typing could get me stuck in a chair, glued to a telephone. I was never a desk jockey detective and wasn't going to become one now. If Ehrlichman wanted confidentiality, then, I said, no evidence was to exist of my appointment. I would have the final word as to when to terminate an investigation if my cover was ever in danger. My functions and duties were to be private, not governmental in any way. There would be no gadget work, no taps, no doubling up on Secret Service work. Finally, I told him that with respect to the payment of my salary and reimbursement for expenses, I preferred working through an attorney—someone familiar with the affairs of the President, but unconnected with the administration. "That can be arranged," Ehrlichman replied. I then asked him if there was a need for concern about my conditions, and he said no. Our meeting ended with the understanding that he would discuss my terms with the President and give me an answer in a few days. I escorted Ehrlichman out of the airport. He stared at the traffic jam as if he thought his looking at it would make it go away. Watching him seethe with impatience, I decided I had better take advantage of my shield, and so I herded the cars out of his way. Three days later, Caulfield called from the White House with the news that I was being hired as the President's private eye.

A FTER twenty-seven years on the job, I couldn't exactly retire quietly from the New York City Police Department. I knew too many people; I was even one of the founders of the roastings we gave at retirement dinners for BOSSI detectives at Toots Shor's on 52nd Street. If I had tried to hide under Ehrlichman's confidential bush after turning in my shield, my friends would have found me and pinned it on my butt. Also, Caulfield was careless by leaving messages at BOSSI headquarters for me to call him at the White House. Ehrlichman's order for secrecy was shredded by knowing looks at "Tony Tens" on Mulberry Street and at the bar rail at Patrissy's Restaurant on Kenmore Street.

"Where's Tony?," I heard they asked about me.

"Going private—something to do with the White House."

"He'll be out there under the eagle."

"Skoal."

Barney Mulligan helped me complete the necessary paperwork and hurried through the background checks required to get my private investigator's license. He also helped me schedule the New York State licensing exam that I had to pass. The terminal leave and unused vacation time that had accrued during my years as a cop gave me until October 27 before my retirement would become permanent. I decided to use this period of time to test my relationship with Washington. I would survey my new territory and then stay with the White House or return to BOSSI. I resolved that the White House would be on trial during this period, and not the other way around as Ehrlichman originally proposed.

At 8:00 a.m. on June 29, 1969, I arrived in the lobby of the Madison

The Rookie Cop.

The "Buck Private."

Camera ready in the sky during
World War II.

On the Tarmac with Paul Robeson upon his return from Russia at La Guardia Airport, June 16, 1949 (*The News*).

Locking eyes with former Iranian Premier Mohammed Mossadegh at New York's Pennsylvania Station, October 22, 1951 (*UPI/Bettmann Newsphotos*).

With former Soviet Foreign Minister Andrei Vishinsky at the Soviet Consulate with BOSSI Detective Bill Taraska (far right) and two Soviet NKVD security guards in 1954 (*Alfonso Preindl*).

In the taxi escorting George Lincoln Rockwell away from the New York County Court House, June 23, 1960 (*The Bettmann Archive*).

On watch guarding Nikita Khrushchev upon his arrival in New York to attend the United Nations General Assembly, September 19, 1960 (*AP/Wide World Photos*).

Walking behind the Shah and Empress of Iran in a ticker tape parade up Broadway in 1962 (*UPI photo*).

First appearance before United States Senate Watergate Committee, May 23, 1973 (*AP/Wide World Photos*).

Explaining the use and identifying the location of the telephones used to make arrangements for the delivery of $219,000 in cash to the Watergate burglars and their attorneys (*UPI/Bettmann Newsphotos*).

Dike Bridge on
Chappaquiddick.

The bridge rail.

Explaining the money drops at Washington's National Airport (*UPI/Bettmann Newsphotos*).

The symbol of Watergate.

Rooster Sirica leading the way (*Watertown Daily Times*).

At the woodpile
(*Watertown Daily Times*).

Hotel in Washington and, as instructed by Caulfield, called the room of Herbert W. Kalmbach, personal attorney for President Nixon. "Mr. Kalmbach," I said when the phone was answered, "this is Tony Ulasewicz."

"Good morning, Mr. Ulasewicz," he said. "I've been expecting your call; my morning just started. I'm not quite dressed, but I'll meet you downstairs for breakfast in a few minutes."

"It would be better if I came up," I said to him. "I'll explain when I get there."

"Well, this is only a small bedroom," Kalmbach replied. "I don't want you to have to stand around up here."

"We could meet in a closet and it would be okay by me," I said, trying to break the ice and get him to understand that we couldn't meet in the wide open spaces.

"Oh, all right, come on up," Kalmbach said good-naturedly.

When Nixon was elected, Kalmbach was the major partner in the Newport Beach, California, law firm of Kalmbach, DeMarco, Knapp & Chillingworth. Shortly after the inauguration, Maurice Stans, Finance Chairman of Nixon's campaign, and H. R. Haldeman, Nixon's Chief of Staff, asked Kalmbach to take charge of the funds left over from the 1968 Republican primary campaign. The funds, all in cash, were stored away in two safe deposit boxes: one in a branch of the Riggs Bank in Washington, D.C., and the other in a branch of the Chase Manhattan Bank in New York City. The Riggs box held approximately $750,000, and the Chase another $400,000. The money was withdrawn and transferred to California, and then divided and put into two other safe deposit boxes—at the Crocker Citizens Bank in Los Angeles and in the Security Pacific National Bank at Newport Beach. A portion of this political nest egg was to be used to pay my salary and expenses.

When Kalmbach opened the door of his hotel room, he was still in his bare feet. While he finished dressing, I sat across from him in the only chair in the room. In contrast to Ehrlichman with his iron-jawed demeanor, Kalmbach presented a rather quiet Jimmy Stewart elegance. He seemed comfortable with himself, which made me feel relaxed, but still I spoke cautiously.

"Mr. Kalmbach," I said, "what I've been asked to do requires the utmost confidentiality. I told Mr. Ehrlichman that I preferred to work through an attorney associated with the President, who wasn't connected with the administration, for payment of any salary and the expenses involved in my work—my umbilical cord if you want to call it that. I'm not to be on any government payroll or have any records connecting me directly with the White House. I've dealt with all kinds of lawyers—D.A.s, federal prosecutors, Justice Department lawyers, defense lawyers, and I've always had personal admiration for what they do. I think you'll understand that it's necessary for me to make sure that my work for the President is never disclosed or jeopardized. If you don't mind my asking, Mr. Kalmbach, would you please verify for me just how you fit into the picture?"

"Mr. Ulasewicz, I'm the President's personal attorney," Kalmbach responded. "I'm not connected with the administration. I don't like the political life or even being here in Washington, but I do handle all the President's matters that relate to his status as a private citizen. The President called me and I spoke to John Ehrlichman and Jack Caulfield, and I understand I'm to help in any way necessary, but I don't know where to begin. I don't know anything about this sort of thing."

"Well," I said, "let's start with some statistics—who I am—like the Army—name, rank, serial number, family, then I'll explain how I think matters should be handled."

I sketched in my police background, told Kalmbach about my wife and kids, then outlined my method of operation.

"I'll be in charge of confidentiality," I told him. "You'll be in charge of payment for my services. You'll never know what I'm working on."

"That's good," Kalmbach interrupted with obvious relief in his voice.

"I'll keep exact records of all expenses," I continued, "and those will be sent to you. Because you'll be the only identifiable link between myself and the White House, I'll be using an alias. You'll use it if you want to reach me. What I'll need is a telephone credit card in my name and an American Express and telephone credit card in the name of my alias. The cards should be issued in the name of Edward T. Stanley. The credit card number for Stanley is to be blind so it can never be traced to me. All his bills are to be sent directly to you. I'll send you my own credit card charges separately for reimbursement."

"Every day at four o'clock I'll make a check with an answering service in New York. A message left for Ed Stanley to call California will be sufficient for me to call you. There will be no other personal contact between us. You'll mail my salary checks and any reimbursement to my home in Queens."

"I suppose after today I won't be seeing you again, Tony."

"I don't expect so, Herb."

We were both wrong, of course.

The alias of Edward T. Stanley was one I had always held in reserve for use in connection with my undercover work for BOSSI. The sensitive nature of my police work had made it necessary for me to have several identities. Edward T. Stanley stood ready if I needed him. But until I did, he only lived on a business card in my pocket. For my work for the President, I set up a mail drop and telephone answering service for Stanley in care of Alden Business Services, Inc., at 1 East 42nd Street in New York. I filed an application for an American Express card to be issued in the name of Edward T. Stanley. I already had an American Express card in my own name. When the credit cards arrived, I called Caulfield at the White House and gave him the credit card numbers. However, I had a problem with the cards. The letter to Kalmbach confirming that the cards would be issued gave my home address instead of the mail drop I had set up as the one to use for Stanley. That was a direct link to me that had to be eliminated. Ed Stanley had to go back in my pocket and disappear. I decided that whatever alias I would use in the future would only be known to me.

On July 7, I flew to Washington to meet Caulfield to discuss my first assignment for the President. My initial task was to check into Senator Hubert Humphrey's possible involvement with Bobby Baker, President Lyndon Johnson's former confidant and convicted swindler, in the Minnesota-based Mortgage Guarantee & Insurance Company. Although Nixon had beaten Humphrey in the 1968 Presidential election, he was already preparing for the next campaign. I was given a memo to read that was written and sent by Rosemary Woods, the President's personal secretary, to John Ehrlichman on June 25, 1969. Woods' memo summarized a telephone call she had received from Wiley Buchanan, who told her that Humphrey and Bobby Baker had set up the Mortgage

Guarantee & Insurance Company of Minneapolis with branches in all fifty states. Woods' memo also stated that Humphrey and Baker had taken a big chunk out of it. "Wiley says this is something we should have looked into," Woods wrote, "and get the facts looking to the time (and that might be even now) that we might want to have them ready for us if needed. This discharges my duty on this," Woods concluded, "but I would like to personally recommend that we have someone check into this and see whether there is anything to it." I was to be that someone.

After meeting with Caulfield, with some reluctance, I went to the office of Murray Chotiner, President Nixon's long-time political tutor and campaign strategist, who apparently was expecting me to stop by and see him. A little annoyed, I told Caulfield to stop playing fast and loose with my name; the more people who knew I was on the job for the President, the greater the risk of the very leak Ehrlichman was so paranoid about. I didn't see why my assignments had to involve meeting Chotiner anyway if my existence as Nixon's private eye wasn't going to receive any support from the White House if my identity was disclosed. But as Caulfield explained, Chotiner had files on people which I had to take a look at so I'd know the type of information the President was looking for when I got the call to go to work.

When I met with Chotiner, the first thing he did was to hand me a file he had been keeping on the Rand Development Corporation and its officers. He made it clear that he kept exhaustive records on everyone who played the political power game. He told me that if, instead of Nixon, I had gone to work for the Democrats, I'd probably be meeting with Larry O'Brien instead of him. "We'll get around to O'Brien," Chotiner said, "don't worry about that." Chotiner said that O'Brien, Chairman of the Democratic National Committee in 1968, still had some dues to pay from the 1960 election that Nixon had lost to Jack Kennedy. As a member of Kennedy's escort team of detectives during the 1960 campaign, I had briefly met O'Brien during one of Kennedy's stops in New York. I knew that Nixon campaign officials blamed O'Brien for leaking the story about a secret loan to Nixon's brother, Donald, of $200,000 that came from the late Howard Hughes. Chotiner claimed that this story cost Nixon the election. "O'Brien's nothing but a lobbyist for Hughes," Chotiner said. "His turn is coming."

Chotiner's file on the Rand Development Corporation disclosed that during the 1968 presidential campaign Rand was named as a defendant in a lawsuit started by some angry Minnesota businessmen. The charge was that the Small Business Administration and the General Services Administration were guilty of fraud and conspiracy in the way a government contract for some postal vehicles was awarded to a wholly owned Rand subsidiary named Universal Fiberglass Corporation of Two Harbors, Minnesota. The contract was for 12,714 three-wheel mail delivery trucks. Universal, the lawsuit charged, was born for the sole purpose of becoming a competitor with the plaintiffs and had no qualifications to do the job. The plaintiffs, with all the necessary qualifications, didn't get the contract which was worth millions. From ground zero, everyone involved in reviewing Universal's competence, financial backing, and plant capability to perform the contract voted against giving Universal a shot at the deal. The fix was in, however, and after every rejection slip was piled on the desk of the head man at the Small Business Administration (SBA), he went ahead and awarded the contract to Universal anyway. The SBA Administrator at the time was Eugene P. Foley, Humphrey's West Virginia primary campaign manager in 1960 when he made his first presidential bid. Republicans and the guys who brought the lawsuit yelled foul and claimed the Democrats were playing the shell game and had once again stolen the pea. Universal defaulted on the contract, in the process filling its till with government-backed loans it couldn't pay back, and disappeared under Rand's umbrella. Chotiner's file contained press clippings about the case and copies of memos from the Comptroller General's Office, the General Services Administration, and the Small Business Administration explaining how the contract had gotten into Universal's hands.

Chotiner's job was to keep this and other cases alive in the press, nationally if possible, and preferably with some editorial comment condemning the principals involved so that in the voter's mind they'd be branded as the bad guys. I was still too close to my work with the Police Department to bother thinking about the fix or the retaliatory process involved in American politics. I had no interest in political scandals. As a detective, my job had been to worry about terrorists and extremists retaliating with guns and bombs. Votes didn't interest me. I figured, however, that Chotiner was showing me all this stuff to give me a short course in how the money-power game was played in Washington. Players shifted and changed identities, but the game was always the same. Before I left his office, Chotiner said that Larry O'Brien was next on his list. "You'll be hearing more about that," Chotiner said as he stood up to say goodbye, "I can guarantee you that."

I went home with copies of Chotiner's postal vehicle file under my arm, but on July 14 I was back in Washington to pick up yet another assignment. Caulfield told me Ehrlichman wanted to know everything Senator Ted Kennedy was up to and that I was to get myself on Kennedy's mailing list. That was easy. I sent a note to Kennedy's Senate office and asked that Ed Stanley (my alias) c/o Alden Business Services receive any mailings that Kennedy would be sending out. In about a week I (Stanley) received a response that said Kennedy had no separate mailing list other than what the Massachusetts Democratic Committee sent to his constituents. I told Caulfield he didn't need Ed Stanley to get a copy of that material. In contrast, Caulfield told me Kennedy's office was trying to find out what he was doing in the White House through another retired detective from the NYPD (not a BOSSI man) named Jimmy King who, Caulfield said, was working at the time for Stephen Smith, Kennedy's brother-in-law. I knew King from my escort days at the Waldorf. If he was nosing around, I knew I had to downplay my role in this new job—especially if any of my old Police Department friends or contacts began asking too many questions or Caulfield kept announcing that I was on some kind of assignment for the White House.

While still organizing for the tasks to come and arranging the method with Kalmbach's office for submitting my expenses for reimbursement, I made preliminary inquiries by telephone to locate the exact address of the Mortgage Guarantee & Insurance Company in Minneapolis. Until Saturday, July 19, 1969, I was still putting my affairs in order. Those efforts were suddenly interrupted by a phone call.

Chappaquiddick

"**G**ET out to Martha's Vineyard as fast as you can, Tony. Kennedy's car ran off a bridge last night. There was a girl in it. She's dead."

This stunning directive from Caulfield, with all its implications, came less than two hours after the body of Mary Jo Kopechne, a former secretary to the late Robert F. Kennedy, was found inside his brother Ted's black Oldsmobile as it rested upside down in the waters of a pond on a place called Chappaquiddick. The shocking discovery was made on the morning of July 19, 1969. Two kids out fishing early that morning spotted the tires of Kennedy's car sticking out of the water. The President wanted to find out what happened, and I was sent to find the answer. I had never heard of Chappaquiddick, and neither had most of the world. I could hardly pronounce the word, much less spell it. It was just a sliver of the world minding its own business until Kennedy's accident made it famous.

When Caulfield called me I was in Spring Valley, New York, visiting my brother-in-law, Mike Dumiak, who had recently suffered a stroke. He knew my whereabouts every minute of the day, so there was no delay

187

in reaching me. As soon as he told me Ehrlichman wanted me to head for Martha's Vineyard, I left the hospital immediately, stopped at my home in Queens only to pick up a change of clothes, and then drove to LaGuardia. I grabbed the Eastern Airlines shuttle to Boston, rented a car at Logan, and then headed toward Woods Hole to catch the ferry to Martha's Vineyard. I didn't know much about this part of the universe; the sand and sail world just wasn't my territory. While driving to Woods Hole, I heard spot reports on the car radio describing Kennedy's accident. The car Kennedy was driving reportedly went off an unlighted bridge after he missed a turn in the road. The accident followed Kennedy's departure from a cookout on Chappaquiddick that was held for members of the late Robert Kennedy's presidential campaign staff.

When I arrived at Woods Hole and saw the ferry boat parking lot, I thought this first journey for the President would be stopped dead in its tracks before it began. The parking lot was jammed with cars and trucks waiting to board the ferry. When I walked down to the ticket office, I was told that reservations had to be made months in advance to get a car across to Martha's Vineyard or Nantucket in the summertime. Never one to give up easily, I approached a weather-beaten ferry boat attendant who was checking the load manifests of the trucks waiting on line. First, I told him I had an emergency, and before he could say so what, I showed him a hundred dollar bill I had cupped in my hand. (Ehrlichman had told me not to spare expenses, and I didn't.) "You got a manifest?," the attendant asked me. "No," I answered. "You got one now," he said as he handed me a yellow manifest sheet in exchange for the hundred bucks. "Your car is now a truck," the attendant said. "Get on line." When I finally drove on board the ferry, I passed the smiling attendant, who almost saluted. And why not? With the size of that tip, I could have sat with the Captain on the poop deck.

But instead of trying to get cozy with the Captain, I went up to the passenger deck and started studying my map of Martha's Vineyard. I also began organizing my mind for what lay ahead. All I had to go on were the radio reports about Kennedy's car plunging off a bridge. Kennedy survived and his passenger didn't. As a matter of habit, I drew myself a mental scenario of what might have happened the night before. Whatever answers I would find had to fall into one of three time slots:

the time of the party, the time of the splash, and the morning after. I didn't spend any time speculating on the relationship between the Senator and the girl. Kennedy was a married man driving in the company of an unmarried woman on a remote island in the middle of the night. Wherever they were going, they didn't make it to their destination. One of them had to explain why. The other person couldn't. She was dead.

Before sunset on July 19, I drove off the ferry at Vineyard Haven and started the final leg of my trip to Chappaquiddick. First, I drove to the village of Edgartown, Chappaquiddick's closest neighbor. On my way there, I felt tempted to pay a courtesy call on the Edgartown Police Department as Detective Tony Ulasewicz, NYPD, retired, just stopping by to find out what happened. Then I thought about what Ehrlichman's reaction would be: "Verboten. Nyet. You're fired!" Instead, I decided just to wander a bit to get my bearings and a sense of the place. Parking my car on the outskirts of Edgartown, I walked into town and found it packed with people on the sidewalks, the shops, the restaurants, and the narrow streets. Obviously, it was a place with a lot of history and a lot of pride in itself. The houses of old whaling captains were brushed clean; the white picket fences looked newly painted. Discovering that a small ferry connected Chappaquiddick with Edgartown, I decided to take it across without my car to get a feel for the distances I might have to travel to pinpoint the scene of the accident. Once I got there, however, I quickly realized I needed wheels, and so I went back to pick up my car. When I returned to board the Chappaquiddick ferry there was no waiting in line, but there soon would be. By tomorrow hordes of reporters from around the world would be here clamoring to find out why Kennedy's car went flying over a bridge. Because Kennedy's misadventure coincided with man's first landing on the moon, the world's media were preoccupied with reporting that event.

I began my investigation by retracing the route Kennedy had driven after leaving the cookout. Finding my starting point was easy because Chappaquiddick is sparsely populated with only a few roads. Nor did I have to ask a lot of questions to find out where the Kennedy campaign staff had held their party. From the ferry slip on Chappaquiddick, the main road runs east for about two and a half miles and then bends to the right like a coat hanger. At the bend, a dirt road extends straight ahead toward the waters of Nantucket Sound. Another dirt road, which looks like it goes nowhere, spurs off to the north of the main road. About half a mile southeast of this intersection, the cottage and grounds where I was told the cookout was held sat close to the road. When I arrived at the cottage and stepped out of my car, I was struck by an odd, strange silence about the place. The grounds were plucked clean, showing no signs that a party had ever been held here; there was no hint that a joyous, sharing evening had turned into a shocking, unexplained tragedy.

Around the back of the cottage I discovered a small hideaway studio I thought might have been used by a writer or an artist. It was separated from the main house by a fence. I looked through the windows of the studio but saw nothing important except a telephone. I couldn't tell if it was a working unit. I went back to my car and then drove southeast to explore Chappaquiddick a little more. The macadam pavement didn't last long; the road soon turned to dirt and sand. I then found the Chappaquiddick dump which was already under attack from legions of seagulls. They were having a grand time, swooping, dive bombing, and holding target practice on the refuse. I checked the dump but couldn't tell where any of the trash had come from. Plenty of it was fresh, including numerous empty liquor bottles and beer cans. Before the seagulls could carry me off, I left and headed to find the bridge that reportedly heaved Kennedy, his car, and his now dead passenger into the water.

I backtracked and drove past the party cottage again on the way to find the bridge. I slowed down and tried to imagine the weather and lighting conditions of the night before. According to the weather report, tonight would be the same kind of evening—clear and then foggy as an ocean mist rolled in with the tide. I tried to visualize myself behind the wheel of Kennedy's car. Even though it was dark and late at night when he left the party, I noted what he would have seen as he drove away from the cottage. Facing me (and I assume Kennedy) at the curve in the road was a three spot white reflector. Each reflector was approximately two inches in diameter. The turn for the bridge was impossible to see. The dirt road leading to it was almost perpendicular to the main road. I began second-guessing myself on the accuracy of what I had heard on the radio. Did the reports say Kennedy missed a turn in the road or the turn for the bridge? I decided that whoever was feeding information to the radio station had a casual attitude toward the truth. If you missed the turn for the bridge or failed to negotiate the bend in the road heading back toward the Chappaquiddick ferry, you would either drive into the bushes or slam against a telephone pole. Those were the choices unless you drove straight ahead onto the dirt road that stretched north from the intersection of the main road with the road to the bridge. If you made a mistake doing that, then you would have to back up and out onto the main road before heading in the right direction. "What was the right direction for Kennedy and his passenger?," I asked myself. The path of the main road was just too obvious, whereas the turn toward the bridge was just too sharp and unlighted.

I had also assumed from the radio reports that when Kennedy made his turn toward the bridge, he immediately plunged into the water. This couldn't be so for the bridge was a good half mile and more from the intersection of the main highway. When I came near the bridge, the last cottage closest to the bridge had a mailbox outside with the name "Dike Cottage" on it. Since nightfall was approaching I would wait until the next morning to pay a visit. No other cars were parked near the bridge when I finally pulled off the road and shut off the engine. I got out of the car and then walked back and forth, several times, over the length of the bridge. I carefully examined the various markings, scratches, and gouges that appeared on the bridge planking and on the right barrier rail the car reportedly flipped over. The wooden rail was no higher than a curb stone. Dike Bridge itself was a get-to-the-beach bridge, a hump-backed rock in the stream you stepped on to get to the other side. In the dark, you couldn't see it except with a flashlight or by the headlights of a car. As I walked the bridge, I noticed that several pieces of the rail's edge nearest the water had been freshly scalloped out, exposing sections of raw wood. There were also some black smudges and other narrow scratch marks which I guessed were probably caused by a scraping of the car's undercarriage. The distance between the first and last car mark on the bridge rail was greater than the length or width of any car. That meant to me that the car didn't just hit the rail in one spot and flip over the side but rather straddled the rail for a short distance with its tires groping for traction. If the car was going fast a direct hit on the rail would have caused the car to catapult into the water. If that happened, the markings, if any, would have been confined to one area. They weren't. While Kennedy might not have been speeding, why didn't he see where he was going? I couldn't help asking myself whether Kennedy jumped out of the car before it went over the bridge. Did the car stop, just for a second, and Kennedy got out causing a weight shift that tilted the car out of balance?

"Well," I thought, "I hadn't come here to reconstruct the accident" but I now had a lot more questions than the radio reports of the incident had even come close to answering.

Before the night and the fog could swallow me up, I left Dike Bridge to hunt for a phone to make my first report to the White House.

"I've been listening to the radio reports, too, Jack, but it's nothing like they say," I told Caulfield from a phone booth I found on the remotest end of Chappaquiddick.

"Tony, are you sure you're in the right place?," Caulfield asked with considerable concern in his voice. "This has to be right, Tony," he said. "Ehrlichman's breathing down my neck for a memo on what you're doing out there. He's in with the President right now, and I don't want this first report of yours to be wrong."

"Of course I know where I am!," I bristled. "I just drove the same route back and forth to the bridge. The road he took is dirt, washboard and directly right of the main road. That's a paved road, Jack, and it curves sharply to the left. You can't see the road to the bridge until you're right next to it. Before you get to it there's a telephone pole and some bushes. You'd never know the road was there unless you've been on it before. If Kennedy went for the bridge, it was deliberate, and I've never been here in my life. I'm not even sure Kennedy was in the car when it went over."

"Tony, none of the reports we've received agree with you," Caulfield interrupted me. There was a hot line from Chappaquiddick and Edgartown into the White House. I didn't know who was making the calls at the time, but whoever it was was sabotaging my credibility. I didn't like it.

"Jack, I'm certainly not comfortable with this whole job yet," I told him, "but I am comfortable telling you that was no accidental turn. The road to the bridge is a cloud of dust and the shakes. It's almost a mile long. And he's a sailor, Jack. Edgartown is west of Chappaquiddick. He was heading east, and if you're out there with the wind you better know east from west. This is a deck of cards I'm dealing you, Jack, one by one, and you better look at their faces. They don't lie."

After almost hanging up on Caulfield, I drove back to Dike Bridge. My mind was racing and in conflict. The radio reports said that Kennedy's car was first seen at about eight o'clock in the morning. It was trouble enough fathoming the reason for Kennedy's missed-turn-wicked-bridge story I was hearing without adding Caulfield's anxiety to the question about why the car wasn't found until daylight and then not by the police, but by two kids. Act I of this accident scenario took place in the dark; Act II was performed in daylight. The program didn't say what happened in between. That's what I wanted to know. "When were the police told? Where did Kennedy go after the accident?," I asked myself. I assumed others had to be asking the same questions. At first, it never crossed my mind that the authorities responsible for investigating this accident would not do it thoroughly and report accurately. Soon, however, I was nagged by the question of whether the police had handed out the information that was serving as the basis for the inaccurate radio reports. "If that was so," I asked myself, "then what justified the conclusion that Kennedy or anybody else could have missed such a turn? Hadn't the police checked out the route Kennedy said he took? Or had they?"

Just as the last of the daylight was disappearing, I found a stick, took off my shoes and socks, rolled up my pants to just above my knees and went wading into the channel waters of Pocha Pond. The pond, I discovered, was part tidal. With my stick, I measured how rapidly the water flowing in and out of the pond deepened away from the shoreline. I tried to imagine the position of the car and where the doors and windows would have been in relation to the height of the tide at the time of the accident. With my sleeves rolled up, I reached down with my hand to the level where I guessed the bumper was when the car was submerged. I speculated about what I would see if I held my nose and ducked under the water. I also tried to guess what Kennedy's condition might have

193

been at the time of the accident. I gave Kennedy several imaginary heads. One of them was healthy, rational and sober, attached to a wet and stunned body. I labeled another one irrational but sober, suffering from the effects of shock. I gave these heads the benefit of the doubt and assumed they were in the car when it went flying over the bridge. I gave Kennedy a third head. This one carried a good measure of alcohol, and I imagined it as being hopelessly confused. It didn't know where it was or what it should be doing after the car flipped out of control. This head of Kennedy's could have been either in the car or from the bridge watching the car gurgle to the bottom of Pocha Pond. I asked myself what actions were consistent with each of these conditions. The radio had reported Kennedy's statement describing how he had dived down again and again to see if the girl was still in the car. That struck me as rather odd. The reported statement didn't say anything about diving down to rescue the girl—only to see if she was still in the car. "If Kennedy didn't know the answer, why didn't he go and call for help?," I asked myself. I began to feel wary about my own thoughts. It was time, I decided, for me to sit down and sort things out.

The rush to get to Chappaquiddick in compliance with Caulfield's directive had barely given me time to pack a toothbrush, let alone think about what I might be getting into. I had no desire to be pulled into any paranoic tug of war between the Nixon and Kennedy camps. I was a professional investigator, not a head hunter. If it was Nixon's goal to pull a shroud over the remaining political life of the Kennedys, it certainly wasn't mine. My being here didn't make any sense either. What did Nixon have to worry about? He had been inaugurated just six months ago, almost to the day, and there was no race horse in front of him—no Kennedy, no Humphrey, no one he had to catch. Nixon had finally made it to the top and was finally free to enjoy being President. This Chappaquiddick business didn't need a private investigation. The accident was a liability on its own merits. The last of the Kennedys who might pose a challenge to Nixon had just destroyed his own presidential chances. Ted Kennedy had finally taken one detour too many in his personal life.

Memories of nine years earlier suddenly collided with the present reality. In the 1960 campaign I had walked in Jack Kennedy's motorcades as part of his security detail. As a detective during my escort days, I had also helped guard Nixon when he was Vice President. I heard the roar of Kennedy's crowds; I saw the silence of Nixon's determination. I remember once when Jack Kennedy stepped out of a hotel room shower—stark naked and soaking wet—yelling at my partner and me for someone, anyone, to find his goddam tuxedo. His aides had brought his tux to the Waldorf, but Jack was at the Biltmore. Now here I was, sitting in my bare feet in the Chappaquiddick sand gathering information for the White House tenant Kennedy thought he had whipped.

My trip to Chappaquiddick was also the first time in twenty-seven years that I was without my shield—my "potsy" as it's called among veteran detectives. I always had it with me before this, even if I couldn't show it in my undercover years with BOSSI. I used to put it on my dresser every night, and I would slip it into my pocket when I dressed in the morning. It had become part of me. I had turned it in for a pass to the White House I couldn't show to anybody. I thought of canceling this whole enterprise, disappearing with my memories intact, calling Barney Mulligan and telling him I was coming back to BOSSI. "Forget about it, Jack," I thought of telling Caulfield. "I'm going home."

But I couldn't. Who else, I asked myself, had ever been a President's private investigator? My chance to be the first in the nation wouldn't come again. Because of my career as a detective, I had an offer for my future wrapped in the imprimatur of the President of the United States. What more could I ask for? I couldn't turn tail and just leave Chappaquiddick. I had to admit, however, that here on Chappaquiddick I felt lost for the first time in my life. Sometimes mottos about never looking back don't match up with your feelings. Besides the love I felt for my wife and children, I had only one other love in life and that was my life as a cop. Having a shield, whether or not I could show it, was the symbol of my pride, my self-respect.

But I also felt uncomfortable with the idea of calling Barney Mulligan and telling him I was coming back to BOSSI. What would I tell my sheep? That I didn't have the nerve to keep working for the President? Ehrlichman said the President needed me. Should I quit before I start?

195

My reasons for returning to BOSSI wouldn't be sellable to anyone but myself. I couldn't look another cop in the eye at the bar in Patrissy's or at "Tony Tens" and tell them I had tried working for the President and didn't like it. I decided the time had come for me to quit riding the fence and to embrace my new career. It was time for me to start learning all about this land of the wicked bridge. It was time to go to work.

I spent the entire night of July 19 on Chappaquiddick, taking periodic cat naps in my car and moving it every so often so that some snoop wouldn't knock on my window or write down my license plate number. I had charged the car rental to my own American Express card rather than the one issued for my alias, Ed Stanley, because Stanley was my tie-in to the White House. I did have to use the telephone credit card issued to Stanley, however, because I hadn't had the time to obtain one in my own name. I resolved that after I finished this assignment, Stanley's name and the list of his calls would be eliminated from telephone company records. That was an assignment I intended to give to Caulfield. Using my own credit card on Martha's Vineyard or Chappaquiddick wouldn't link me to anyone. I also had a practical reason for charging the rental car to my own name: I had to account for my travel and expenses. On every investigation I eventually did for the White House, I always charged one item to my own credit card in order to prove I had been where I said I was in the event anyone in the White House ever raised any question about my expenses. I kept exact records.

As dawn broke over Chappaquiddick, I returned to Dike Bridge, confirming my thoughts of the night before and planning my next move. I had to act quickly. The media heavyweights would soon arrive from their coverage of the historic trip to the moon, and some of them would, of course, be from the New York press corps. I didn't need to hear a "Hey, Tony" or have my shoulder tapped by an old acquaintance.

I waited on Chappaquiddick until a decent hour and then went to "Dike Cottage." As I stood waiting for the door of the cottage to open, I became a man named Ferguson, a fictional investigative reporter for a doubly fictional feature writer's association I had made up. Ferguson wasn't exactly Clark Kent from the *Daily Planet*, but he wasn't a bad guy either. Answering the door of the cottage was Mrs. Pierre Malm. Dike Cottage was her summer home, she said, her permanent residence being in Lebanon, Pennsylvania. It was to her door that the two boys who spotted Kennedy's car had come to report their sighting. Mrs. Malm told me she was upstairs reading in bed on the night of the accident when she heard a car pass their cottage. The car, she said, was traveling rather fast as it headed for the bridge. She didn't hear it return. She didn't hear it hit anything or go crashing into the water. She stopped reading for a short while as she listened for further sounds. Hearing none, she continued reading until midnight, then put out the light and went to sleep. She told me that her two dogs would have barked and awakened her if anyone had come near the cottage. Nobody did. Only the two youngsters who came the next morning to tell her what they found.

Afterward, I headed back to Edgartown with a shopping list of questions in my head. Although I desperately wanted to go to sleep, I wanted to learn the official cause of death as well as the results of the autopsy I expected had been performed on the girl. So I went to the obvious place: the Edgartown Funeral Home. The first question I asked was who had been called to the scene to examine the body after it had been pulled out of the car. The owner and director of the funeral home, Eugene Frieh, told me that he had been called together with Dr. Donald R. Mills, an Associate Medical Examiner for Suffolk County. Mills had examined the body at the bridge. According to Frieh, Mills estimated that Mary Jo Kopechne had been dead for approximately six hours before being pulled out of the car. But the radio reports—if you could believe them—said that her body had been in the car at least nine hours before being brought to the surface. That left three hours of possible life to account for. I wondered if there was an air pocket in the car after it sank in the pond. I then asked Frieh about the autopsy.

"There wasn't any," Frieh said.

"No autopsy?," I asked in astonishment.

"No," Frieh answered. "They said it wasn't necessary."

"Who said it wasn't necessary?"

"Dr. Mills. He said she drowned."

"What kind of examination did he give her?"

"He checked her with his stethoscope, pushed against her chest and turned her over."

"What happened when he pushed her chest?"

197

"Mills said there was a lot of water in her. I didn't see much water. I saw a lot of foam around her nose and mouth."

"How long did the examination take?"

"Just a few minutes."

"That's all?"

"That's all."

I was dumbstruck that an autopsy hadn't been demanded. Where I come from, an autopsy would have been standard operating procedure. During the years I was assigned to Harlem's Twenty- fifth Precinct, the currents of the Harlem River frequently became the escort for bodies that floated up the river with other flotsam and jetsam and then got wedged up against the base of the Triborough Bridge. When a body was pulled out of the water, the amount of fluid pouring from it governed the intensity and the time the "brains" in the detective squad spent investigating the cause of death. The less saturation of the tissues, the more intense the investigation. Ordering an autopsy would have been automatic. As I talked to the Edgartown funeral director I also knew that the presence of foam around the nose and mouth was an indicator of oxygen starvation, not drowning. If the radio reports issued about the time of the accident were accurate and Mills' estimate of the time of death was on target, then there was a good chance that the girl had been alive in Kennedy's car for quite awhile after his car hit the water. For public consumption, Mills was quoted as saying, "The body was rigid as a statue, the teeth were gritted, there was froth around the nose, and the hands were in a claw-like position."

During my discussion with Frieh, I noticed that he kept twisting and turning his body to point out a casket as he talked. I didn't need a road map to tell me that it was the girl's casket. Frieh also told me that on Saturday afternoon, after the body had been placed in his custody and delivered to his funeral home, someone—Frieh couldn't remember his name—identifying himself as a Kennedy staff member said he was there to complete arrangements to fly the girl's body back home to Pennsylvania. When Frieh said he had already been in touch with a funeral director in Pennsylvania who had been hired by the Kopechne family to make the necessary arrangements to send the girl home, the Kennedy staff man left and headed for Mills' office. Kennedy's man,

Frieh told me, was also very interested in what Mills had to say about the official cause of death.

"Why?," I asked.

"I don't know," Frieh answered. "He left in a hurry."

After I left the Funeral Home, I headed for the Edgartown Police Station, disregarding Ehrlichman's warnings about the risk of disclosing my existence as President Nixon's private investigator. I had to know what, if any, conclusions the police had come to about the cause of the accident, the cause of death, and what evidence they had to support their findings. I didn't want to read about it in the newspaper. When I walked into the station I felt strange. I had a business card in my wallet for my alias as Ed Ferguson, but I couldn't stop thinking like a cop. Walking into the station made me think even more like a cop, and I still wanted to be thought of as a cop. Nobody in the station, however, was supposed to know who I was.

Looking at the police blotter, I immediately noticed an entry that said that the body of Mary Jo Kopechne had been flown off the island. But that wasn't true: I had just left the funeral home and her body was still there. I couldn't believe that Frieh's twists and turns toward the casket in the funeral home were just part of a physical affliction; nor could I get a straight answer as to why that entry had been made in the police blotter or who provided the erroneous information. I also asked whether anybody, including members of the Kopechne family, had requested an autopsy. The answer was yes. The District Attorney of Suffolk County, Edmund Dinis, had asked for one, but he apparently was told that the body was gone when, in fact, it was still in Edgartown. Like the disappearance of Jesus de Galindez many years before, the whereabouts of Mary Jo Kopechne's remains was becoming another case of the vanishing shuffle. Who, I asked myself, was trying to get rid of the evidence? The answer was obvious: Ted Kennedy.

The police blotter also contained a notation that someone had come over to pick up a pocketbook found in the back of Kennedy's car after it was hauled out of the water. Since the pocketbook didn't belong to Mary Jo Kopechne, I was told, there was no point in keeping it.

"Who did it belong to?," I asked.

"A girl named Rosemary Keough," I was told.

"Was she in the car?," I asked.

"We don't know," came another unsatisfactory answer.

Now I was really stunned. A potential piece of evidence was never tagged; it was simply turned over on request. The police had given it up without running any check as to whether the owner was with Kennedy and Kopechne at the time of the accident.

"Who came to pick up the pocketbook?," I asked.

"Someone from Kennedy's staff," was the answer. I wondered if it was the same person who had been at the Edgartown funeral home offering to help fly Kopechne's body off the island. If it was, then what time did he learn she was found inside Kennedy's car? Where was he when he got the word?

"Where is Rosemary Keough now?," I asked.

"She left the island with all the others."

"When was that?"

"Sometime yesterday afternoon."

"Where were they staying? They must have checked in somewhere?"

"At a motel, Katama Shores. Some call it the Dunes."

"Were any statements taken from any of them?," I asked.

"Kennedy gave one."

"You mean everybody else flew the coop without saying anything to anybody, like the police?"

"I guess so."

"Weren't any statements taken from anyone besides Kennedy?," I asked with a mix of hope and disbelief.

"No, he was the only one."

"Did he sign it?"

"No."

"Was he asked to sign it?"

"No, I guess not."

When I left the police station still shaking my head over the sloppy way this case was being handled, I went to find the motel where the Kennedy party girls had stayed, but it was Sunday and there was no staff available until the next day to show me the girls' registration cards. I wanted to get their home addresses and phone numbers. As a matter of habit, I checked the grounds around the motel and was surprised to see a plane sitting out in a field all by itself. Walking directly toward the plane brought me into a marshy area. Before getting my feet soaked again (this time with my shoes on) I looped around the field to take a closer look at the plane. It was a single wing, single engine plane tied down to a couple of blocks. I made a mental note to myself to check it out more thoroughly when I came back to the motel on Monday to check the registration cards. I couldn't help asking myself whether Kennedy had someone fly over to Edgartown during the night, or as soon as dawn broke, before his car was discovered by those two kids. If so, then instead of trying to find out whether Kopechne was dead or alive and could have been saved, Kennedy spent his time saving his own skin and planning his coverup. If the plane was tied to Kennedy, it wasn't parked at the airport where a record of its time of arrival would have been kept. I left the field and headed back to Edgartown. Although I was hungry for something to eat, I had a belly full of suspicion.

Despairing of finding any bologna in Edgartown, I settled for a mid-morning hot dog. I bought a Coke and a *Boston Globe* and found myself a place down by the water to sit, eat, and read what Kennedy had to say for himself. I knew Kennedy had given a statement from listening to the radio reports. Those reports, I had already concluded, were inaccurate except for the time of death. When a detective reads a newspaper, he never takes what he reads for granted. BOSSI's filing cabinets were stuffed with newspaper clippings, not because we believed everything we read, but because people like to talk and the only people running around in public recording what people say are reporters, television crews and correspondents trying to make a big scoop. Most stories you read you can take with a grain of salt; others are used as a means to an end; some, as we all know, are used to shatter myths and expose evil. My first reaction when I finished reading what Kennedy had to say about the accident was that whoever let Kennedy give that statement should have had his head examined. His statement was a disaster. It absolutely destroyed the credibility he so desperately needed to establish.

"I was unfamiliar with the road and turned right onto Dyke Road instead of bearing hard left on Main Street," Kennedy said. But he couldn't have been unfamiliar with the road if he was able to negotiate the right turn to the bridge without crashing into something. "After

201

proceeding for approximately half a mile on Dyke Road," I read on, "I descended a hill and came upon a narrow bridge." What hill, I asked myself as I took another bite of my hot dog. I didn't see any hill. There was a rise in the road but no hill. "The car went off the side of the bridge," I continued reading. "The car turned over and sank into the water and landed with the roof on the bottom." I had no problem with that statement. "I . . . had no recollection of how I got out of the car. I . . . dove down to the car in an attempt to see if the passenger was still in the car. I was unsuccessful in the attempt." Whether Kennedy was in the car when it went over the bridge was still an open question—at least to me it was. "I was exhausted and in a state of shock," the statement continued. "I recall walking back to where my friends were eating. There was a car parked in front of the cottage and I climbed into the back seat. I then asked someone to bring me back to Edgartown." What about asking someone to rescue the girl he knew he left in the car, I asked myself. "I remember walking around for a period of time and then going back to my hotel room." Where did he walk around? Who took him back to the hotel? What did he tell his friends back at the party? What did *they* do about trying to rescue the girl? "When I fully realized what had happened this morning, I immediately contacted the police," Kennedy went on to say. Nobody called the police before the morning after? It was unbelievable. What I did believe was that this statement was a coverup. Even if the plane I saw behind the motel wasn't linked to Kennedy, he wasn't going to be able to dig himself out of the hole he created with this statement. I had no doubt Kennedy was in shock. His statement fit right in with the second and third imaginary heads I gave him while I was examining the scene of the accident. But it seemed incredible to me that he would say that until he "realized what happened" nobody did anything about reporting the accident or trying to rescue the girl in the car. Kennedy's statement was food for sharks. Didn't anybody check out what he was saying before letting him put it on a piece of paper? I knew one answer as I folded my newspaper and started looking for a place to rent a camera and that was that the key to understanding this Chappaquiddick business lay somewhere in between the splash and the morning after.

Before I could unlock any mysteries, I just had to find a place to sleep.

There was no longer any point in trying to keep ahead of everybody else, even though members of the press were beginning to arrive in Edgartown like a school of piranha. Everybody connected with the accident had fled from Chappaquiddick, hightailing it out of town before anyone had a chance to ask them any questions. There was no autopsy, and by now the girl's body, too, was long gone. Souvenir hunters, I was sure, were carving slices out of the bridge so that the markings made by the car would be inseparable from those made by the scavengers. My suspicions about what happened to Kennedy's car after it was cranked up out of the water were proved correct when I tracked it down to its resting place at an Edgartown service station. It looked like a dead crow in a parking lot. It had been picked at by bounty hunters. Stripped. Efforts by the station attendants to shoo people away had been useless. By the time a warning sign was put up and the car covered, any story left for it to tell wouldn't be worth the paper it was written on. The possibility of any serious examination into the circumstances surrounding the death of Mary Jo Kopechne was as remote as this island was from my old beat in Harlem. Any careful debriefing of the fleeing Chappaquiddick partygoers would take place away from the jurisdiction of those who were responsible for collecting the facts about this case. And the debriefing undoubtedly would be done by professionals representing the very people who were involved.

But enough of this frustration. I felt it was time to put my body between some clean sheets and my head on a pillow. Wanting and finding are two different things, however. I couldn't find a room anywhere in Edgartown. When it began to look as if I'd be sleeping in my car again, I decided to head back to Woods Hole, get a motel room near the ferry, and return to Edgartown on the first boat in the morning. Luckily, the Nautilus Motel in Woods Hole had a room available. It cost Ehrlichman a bundle, but I slept like a rock.

In the morning, now Monday, July 21, I headed back to Chappaquiddick. After taking pictures of the bridge, I drove back to the cottage where the cookout had been held. I was surprised that I was the only one around when I knocked on the door. The owner of the cottage was there, a Mr. Sidney K. Lawrence, and I introduced myself to him as reporter Ed Ferguson. When I asked him what he knew about Friday night's events, he said he didn't know much. Lawrence said he came straight to Chappaquiddick from his home in Pennsylvania as soon as he heard about Kennedy's accident. Although he wasn't too happy about being dragged away from home or having his place or his name spread all over the newspapers, he was gratified that his cottage was left in fairly neat condition. There were some packaged foods, canned goods, eggs and snacks left in bags, but nothing that couldn't be put in the garbage. The only bottles in the cottage were empty Coca Colas. Lawrence didn't know who rented the cottage, only that a Joseph Gargan left his phone number with the rental agent who handled his summer rentals. Lawrence said his next door neighbor watched over the place when he wasn't around or when it wasn't rented.

I went over and knocked on the door of the neighbors, Mr. and Mrs. Silva. "It was a noisy party," Mrs. Dodie Silva told me about Friday night's gathering next door. "There seemed to be a lot of laughter and talk and things like that going on. We have four dogs and they kept barking because of the racket. My husband couldn't sleep. He kept getting up to quiet the dogs. Things at the party quieted down around 2:30 in the morning. I didn't know Senator Kennedy was at the party, but earlier in the day I saw a girl driving the car that was pulled out of the pond."

"Did you ever see Kennedy in this area before?," I asked.

"Well, I never met him, but my son used to work at the beach club here, and one summer about six years ago my son did some work for him. My son told me they once had lunch together."

Mrs. Silva's eyes then began to fill with tears. Her son, she said, had recently died. Seeing her distress, I told her I was sorry for her loss; I thanked her for her time and then left. My mind began to race again. Kennedy had said he was unfamiliar with Chappaquiddick. Had he forgotten about his lunch with the late son of Dodie Silva?

I then took a long walk down Dyke Road. Including the home of the Silvas and the Lawrence cottage, I made a count of the number of buildings between the bridge and the Lawrence cottage and between that location and the Chappaquiddick ferry slip. The biggest building in the neighborhood belonged to the Chappaquiddick Volunteer Fire Department. That was located near the coat hanger turn where Chappaquiddick's main street bends and heads south toward the Chappaquiddick dump. No one could miss the firehouse going or coming from Dike Bridge. I counted eleven cottages within eyesight of the road and fifteen other driveways with mailboxes at their heads situated between the Chappaquiddick Fire House and the ferry to Edgartown. In addition to the Malm cottage at the end of Dyke Road, I spotted two other cottages along that strip. I didn't check to see if they were occupied at the time of the accident. I also began a count of the available public phones that could have been used to report the accident. I saw two public phones on the grounds of the Chappaquiddick Beach Club and wrote down their numbers. I also saw a private phone on a desk when I looked through a window of the locked beach club's office. I called the club to learn its number.

I checked the Chappaquiddick Beach Club to see if any employees had worked late on the night of the accident who might have heard something. One of the employees, Lansing Burns, said that at 1:30 on the morning of July 19, after he had finished work, he was on the beach when he heard noises from the vicinity of the Beach Club phones. The Club was closed at the time. He had no idea who might have been trying to use the phones. When he heard the commotion a second time, he got up and went over to check the area but he didn't see anyone. It was strange, he said; he felt whoever was there didn't want to be seen. There was another phone in the waiting shed at the ferry slip on Chappaquiddick. Kennedy, and whoever was with him, had plenty of phones to use to report the accident the night it happened. Finding available phones raised the question of whether any of these phones were used by Kennedy or any of his pals to pass the word that the Senator had just blown any chance he had of becoming President and that a major scandal was about to erupt and what should be done to cover it up.

During my stroll down Dyke Road, I was stopped along the way by an attractive young blond driving a Cadillac who was looking for a lost dog. Seizing the opportunity, I asked her if she knew whether Kennedy had ever been on Chappaquiddick before. "Sure," she answered. "He knows it. All the brothers knew it." Continuing my walk with another confirmation of Kennedy's familiarity with the territory in mind, I found myself joined by a Russian wolfhound. It was Khrushchev coming back to haunt me with his bag of tricks, I thought. He began following me after I gave him part of a sandwich I bought in Edgartown. The dog wouldn't leave my side. I soon realized he was good cover. To those who might be checking me over, I tried to look like a man with his dog, just taking a stroll, enjoying the scenery, counting the birds and taking some pictures.

When I returned to Edgartown from Chappaquiddick on Monday afternoon, I felt I was becoming part of a huge disorganized posse. Edgartown had become a media zoo. Every newsman, photographer, curious tourist, and scavenger able to find transportation was descending like a new strain of plague. Most of the reporters stood in clusters outside the police station or near the courthouse. Chief of Police Arena was trying to hold everyone at bay by saying that as far as he was concerned the investigation was over. He had the badge, the uniform, and the authority and, well, wasn't that enough? "Everyone please back off and quit looking for the snake in the grass," he seemed to be saying. The Chief said he was going to issue a ticket for leaving the scene of the accident, and that, he added, was the end of the matter. There was no evidence of foul play, no criminal negligence. But one of the problems for reporters was that Arena's sources had long since left the island and he was the one who had let them go. In the case of Kennedy and the bridge, the Edgartown Police Department was in over its head.

"What about the pocketbook you let go at the police station?," I yelled from the back of a room across from the Edgartown courthouse where Chief Arena began to hold impromptu news conferences. The room stirred. It hadn't yet become common knowledge that Rosemary Keough's pocketbook had been found in the back seat of Kennedy's car. I didn't identify myself when I asked the question. My purpose was to get the reporters in the room starting to think about the information they were getting. Most of them were staying put outside Arena's police station because they didn't want to be scooped if the Chief suddenly let go with a headline when they were out on a field trip. There were deadlines to meet with this story, and yet, ironically, few reporters had time to check independently what they were writing about. My Ed Ferguson cover was perfect for the role I was playing. I didn't have to write any stories. I dug for facts and passed them along, and for a buck a line, I told anyone who wanted to know. I buzzed around clusters of reporters like a bee in a flower garden. I tried to drop suggestions as to what these reporters might start checking. I had a purpose: The only way I could counteract White House doubts about the accuracy of my reporting was to get others to start verifying the accuracy or inaccuracy of Kennedy's story on their own.

After mixing it up with a group of reporters standing around outside the courthouse, just down the street from the police station, I headed for the Harborside Bar. It was time for me to pause, have a belt, share a little bull, and stake out the territories of other people's minds. There's no better place to hear a reporter talk than in a bar. They like to talk as much as some of the people they interview. A line of reporters had formed to use the phone. I overheard one or two of them say they had a source of information who was the most reliable tipster on the island and who hadn't spoken to anyone else but them. New York City informants would have made a fortune off some of these guys. Other hardnosed reporters were beginning to act and react as if they'd been had. The Harborside Bar became a grumble pit. No one was happy with what was being dished out at Police Headquarters.

Standing at the bar was a man who looked like the replica of an old-time Lower East Side detective. He had the hat, the slouch, and the eyes of a man who didn't believe in much of anything except his own hunches. I nudged him into conversation and learned that he was Arthur C. Egan, Jr., chief investigative reporter for the *Union Leader* of Manchester, New Hampshire. This was William Loeb's paper, the arch-conservative publisher who had grown apoplectic over the influence and power of the Kennedy name. Egan, nicknamed Ace, joined the *Union Leader* in 1965. He started his newspaper career in Wyoming in the late 1940s and gradually moved eastward until he settled in New Hampshire. When he asked for my name, I told him I was "Ferguson, Ed Ferguson, Feature Writers Association. I do the digging, others do the writing." When Egan told me who he was with, I unexpectedly blurted out, "I know Loeb." I could have bitten my tongue off. The *Union Leader* had supported George Lincoln Rockwell when he made his bid to enter the New Hampshire presidential primary in 1964. I went to interview Loeb to see if he was serious about his newspaper's backing of Rockwell and

207

whether he ever considered the impact Rockwell's movement might have on New York streets.

To spread out our thinking after a few drinks, Egan and I left the bar rail and went over to a corner table. Within minutes we zeroed in on the question of whether the police were checking out the phone calls that Kennedy or anyone with him might have made. We both agreed that it wasn't credible that Kennedy associates had contacted no one after the accident until eight o'clock the next morning. The implication in Kennedy's statement was that until he realized what had happened, no one was contacted. We simply didn't believe that. What bothered us most was what the Kopechne girl was realizing as she slowly died with the rising tide. It had to be that way. There was no other way to explain the difference between the estimated time of death and the number of hours she had been submerged in the car. She starved without oxygen, succumbing when her chamber of horror could no longer keep her alive. We asked ourselves the natural question: why didn't Kennedy and his friends, having tried to rescue Kopechne and having failed, ask someone else to try—someone with experience and equipment? By this time, Egan and I both knew that at least two of Kennedy's friends, Joseph Gargan and Paul Markham, had gone back to Dike Bridge with Kennedy. Gargan dove in to see what he could do about finding the girl. Then, when his attempt proved fruitless, he and Markham went back to the Lawrence cottage and went to sleep. Kennedy said he went back to the Shiretown Inn and turned out the lights. Gargan and Markham said they thought Kennedy was going to report the accident after he returned to Edgartown. He didn't, although the police station was only a hop, skip, and a zig zag from the back of the Shiretown Inn.

If no phone calls were made before eight o'clock in the morning, Egan and I agreed that the arrival of a Kennedy associate at the funeral parlor shortly after the body was placed in the undertaker's care was an immaculate coordination. If Kennedy or someone on his behalf had made phone calls during the night, there were more nooks and crannies inside Arena's bare cupboard than he ever dared imagine. As we continued to talk, Egan finally said, "I can get the numbers that were called." I quickly responded with, "I can tell you where they were made." Egan suggested that we get together in another week or so to match cards. The time in between would give us a chance to digest whatever else might turn up and to learn what other steps Kennedy would take to counter the growing suspicion that a big coverup was under way. The holders of power seemed to have mesmerized the Edgartown Police Department.

My years with BOSSI had taught me that with the right contact within the telephone company Egan would have no trouble getting copies of Kennedy's phone records. BOSSI had its own contact inside the phone company, as did the FBI and the CIA. The telephone company had employees who were assigned to meet and cooperate with top-level law enforcement and intelligence agency personnel. Building plans, circuitry design, telephone installation records were all made available by the phone company when wiretaps were needed. I met with phone company employees on numerous occasions to obtain information vital to the placing of a tap by a BOSSI wireman. For instance, in the Galindez case, the FBI obtained records of the calls John Frank made from the National Republican Club as well as records of all incoming and outgoing calls made to Horace Schmahl's office before Galindez was abducted. Egan made it clear that he had the necessary connections to get inside the phone company. "We've got the compound covered— coming and going," Egan said, meaning the Kennedy compound in Hyannis. My eyebrows lifted when I heard that one because Egan seemed to be bragging (and I was a stranger to him) that anytime he wanted, he could check on the phone line activity coming and going from the home of the late President. Egan apparently sensed my skepticism and said, "I don't mean—er,—ah,—that we're spliced into it, I just mean that when we want to know what's going on, we've got a source to get the records." I didn't doubt him, but I did wonder why Egan was letting me in on his little secret so soon after we had met. I guess I just came across to him as the man I pretended to be, namely, a digging investigative reporter named Ferguson.

For my part, I let Egan know the location of the public phones on Chappaquiddick and about the phone in the Lawrence cottage; about the reflectors on the road near the cottage, the deliberate turn Kennedy had to have made onto Dyke Road; about the markings on the bridge and the number of cottages between the bridge and the ferry slip on Chappaquiddick; and about how close the firehouse was to the Lawrence cottage. I was miles ahead of other reporters in what I had checked. Egan seemed impressed, and while he was getting a con job, he was also getting the results of my work. I didn't press Egan to reveal his contact, for that would have shut him up like a clam. Also, the White House had its own contact inside the phone company, and if I needed that, Caulfield was the one to press the right buttons. For all I knew, the White House— maybe Ehrlichman or Haldeman—was already probing into phone company records. But I couldn't call Caulfield and tell him to have his boss do the checking. That was my job and I had to do it through Egan, not through the contacts I had developed as a BOSSI detective. That would have risked disclosing my role as the White House private eye. Egan gave his shoulders a confident shrug as he described his ability to make a much broader sweep of Ted Kennedy's telephone activity than what he or his friends might have engaged in on the night of July 18. Loeb was monitoring Kennedy's every move through the guy sitting next to me in the Harborside Bar. "We've got Kennedy surrounded," Egan said. "He can't get out of this one."

I reported my meeting with Egan to Caulfield at the White House and gave him the numbers of the available telephones Kennedy or his associates could have used. I cautioned Caulfield, however, not to interfere with whatever Egan was doing. I told Caulfield to make sure my calls didn't show up in a check of phone company records. I assumed that any check of these records would cover more than just the period between the reported time of the accident and the discovery of Kennedy's car. The printout of the calls would most likely cover at least a twenty-four hour period. The identity of anyone charging phone calls during this period would be easily established. That would include a man named Edward Stanley, also known as Tony Ulasewicz, investigator for a President. It was his credit card I had to use. "Don't worry about it, Tony," Caulfield reassured me, "it'll be taken care of."

After I left Egan, I went back to the Katama Shores motel and talked with two employees, Mrs. Helen Missud and Mrs. Debbie Millard. Nothing unusual turned up when I checked the reservation cards except that when they checked out on the afternoon of the 19th, the checkout was handled by a man described by motel employees as being about 5'11", medium build with dark blond hair. He brought all the keys to the desk and said: "They're checking out." His description appeared to fit the description of the man who went to the funeral home on the morning of the 19th to check on arrangements to fly Kopechne's remains off the island. His presence in Edgartown solidified my suspicion that Kennedy and/or his associates had been busy on the phone soon after the accident to put people in place to help in the coverup. I walked out of the motel and headed for the field where I had seen the airplane resting in the middle of nowhere. It was gone. What bothered me even more than its absence was that after seeing it the first time I asked around about ways to fly in and out of Martha's Vineyard. "There's only one way," I was told. "The airport, that's it and if it's fogged in, nobody goes anywhere." Well, someone knew about another runway on the island, and it was right behind the Katama Shores motel which, I subsequently learned, had once been a barracks for the Navy. The Martha's Vineyard airport was nowhere in sight. No one I talked to seemed to know whose plane it was or how long it had been there. I was never able to prove this plane was connected to the Kennedy/Kopechne tragedy, but its presence in such an odd place raised my suspicions even further that Kennedy forces were pulling out all the stops to save his skin.

I remained in the area until July 23. I had found a place to stay on Martha's Vineyard between Edgartown and Gay Head so I wouldn't have to run back and forth to Woods Hole. Before packing up and heading for home, I went to see John Farrar, the scuba diver who pulled Mary Jo Kopechne out of Kennedy's car. When I met him in his dive and tackle shop in Edgartown, he seemed anxious to talk. He gave me the feeling that he didn't think anyone except the press was really listening to what he had to say; that what he saw was starting to become a nightmare. When he entered the submerged vehicle, Farrar said, he saw the girl's head cocked back, her face pressed into the foot well, her hands gripping the front edge of the back seat, her body shaped for the struggle to get a last gasp of air. It appeared to him, Farrar said, that Kopechne had been trapped alive for several hours inside Kennedy's car.

I didn't head directly back home on July 23. Instead, on instructions from Caulfield, I went to Boston where I was to see a lawyer named Whitehead. Before Chappaquiddick broke, an appointment had originally been set up for me to meet Whitehead on July 16 to discuss what he might have known about the Humphrey-Baker tie with the Minnesota Mortgage Guaranty Company. Whitehead, a key figure in Republican Party circles in Massachusetts, was also a former Assistant Attorney General in the Republican administration of Governor Edward Brooke before Brooke decided to run for the U.S. Senate. One of Whitehead's cronies, Charles W. Colson, became Special Counsel to President Nixon in late 1969. But the July 23 meeting wasn't about Hubert Humphrey; Chappaquiddick replaced Humphrey's name like the swipe of a brush. "Mr. Whitehead," his secretary said as I was ushered into his office, "this is Mr. Ferguson." I really didn't need any name. The door had been opened, and the red carpet laid before I ever entered Whitehead's office. The White House already instructed him to tell Ferguson anything he wanted to know. I was intrigued by Whitehead's assumption that I would be able to feed whatever he said into the proper channels. I wondered if he was a Murray Chotiner protege. Whitehead said he was going on vacation until August 11 but that I should contact him on August 13 at which time he would have something solid to tell me about Chappaquiddick.

On July 24, I was back home in Queens. Rumors were flying that Kennedy would go on national television the next night and make a statement about Chappaquiddick. Meanwhile, Caulfield had passed me Ehrlichman's tip that, when he took to the tube, Kennedy would admit that Rosemary Keough was also in the car when it went over the bridge and that he was able to save her but not Kopechne. Ehrlichman's understanding was that Kennedy would explain that he did not want to expose Keough to a possible charge that she, too, had inexplicably failed to report the accident. But the failure to report the accident, I was now convinced, had an explanation that had nothing to do with Kennedy's shock, or blackout, or whatever he claimed had obliterated his mind until the morning after the accident. The failure to report it, I had no doubt, was deliberate.

I was home when Kennedy made his televised apologia to the nation claiming, in part, that "all kinds of scrambled thoughts, all of them confused, some of them irrational, many of them which I cannot recall, and some of which I would not have seriously entertained under normal circumstances, went through my mind during this period—including such questions as whether the girl might still be alive somewhere out of that immediate area—whether there were some justifiable reasons for me to doubt what had happened and to delay my report. . ." For me the answer to this scrambled reasoning rested with the phone calls. Were there any? And if so, who made them? Who was called and why? Although I had no interest in the political fallout this matter was generating, I was professionally and personally irritated that there had been a coverup in this case, a screw-up by the Police Department, and a body removal act that would have impressed Houdini. But I had to keep my mouth shut. If I opened it, I knew I'd get fired by an employer who was nevertheless waiting on every blip of the White House switchboard to hear my next report. I listened carefully to Kennedy's mea culpa for his conduct. Wrong turn. Bad bridge. Whoops! Sorry about that. End of case. Give me absolution.

"Not so fast, Senator," I said to myself. "Not so fast." His statement left too many questions unanswered. It was at this point that I realized that I was no longer thinking about this case as an investigator for a President, nor was I interested in what anyone did with the information I gathered on Chappaquiddick or what they thought of my opinions. What was important to me as an investigator was the accuracy in reporting what I had found. That included listening to and evaluating what Kennedy had to say on national television. In my twenty-seven years as a cop, I had heard just about every deviation from the truth ever invented, but this was a beaut! After Kennedy finished his statement, I matched my own findings against his version of what happened.

There was no hard evidence from any source except Kennedy's statement that when he and Mary Jo Kopechne left the party at the Lawrence cottage, they were going back to their respective hotels for the night. Who changed that plan? He was tired, and she apparently didn't feel too well. Did Kennedy and Mary Jo Kopechne argue on the way? Did she tell him it was the wrong way? Had they headed toward the ferry and then turned back? Did one of them forget something? Did Kennedy miss the curve in the road coming back the other way and just kept going straight ahead down Dyke Road? Was Kopechne the one Mrs. Silva said she saw driving Kennedy's car earlier on the day of the accident? A Dukes County deputy sheriff named Charles Look, Jr., was reported to have told the Edgartown Police Department that he believed he saw Kennedy's black Oldsmobile at approximately 12:40 a.m. on July 19—more than an hour after Kennedy said the accident had happened—turning down Dyke Road after hesitating about which way to go. Look said he didn't recognize the driver. Regardless of the time Kennedy turned onto the dirt road, why did he keep driving east for three-quarters of a mile? After the bridge tossed Kennedy and his companion into the water—if, in fact, he was in it—what was so terrible about sharing the news, if the accident was merely the tragic result of an innocent detour? What made the truth so unbearable? I wouldn't know the answer to this question until the phone company records were checked for calls Kennedy or his friends might have made before dawn revealed the tires of his overturned car.

I had trouble buying Kennedy's story that he was in the car when it went over the bridge. I couldn't swallow Kennedy's statement that he remembered trying both the door and the window of the car and then forgot how he got out. How was it that his license and his registration, which were in his pocket, never got wet? If Kennedy was soaking wet from getting dunked in the car when it went over and then he redrenched himself swimming across Edgartown Harbor, how could his friends and advisors rationally expect Kennedy to go to the police station in his waterlogged condition and report the accident? If they truly retained that assumption, then what was the real condition of Kennedy's scrambled head? Did they think he had the presence of mind to explain the accident coherently? Why would Kennedy's friends leave it to him to report the accident if there was still a question as to the whereabouts of the Kopechne girl? They went to the bridge and then quit the search. The failure to rescue, like the failure to report, was a deliberate act and not the hopeless abandonment of a difficult task.

The effort to rescue would have disclosed the true nature of Kennedy's condition at the time of the accident, and that was too high a price to pay. Someone standing on that bridge had to decide that neither Kennedy nor anybody else had an obligation to rescue Kopechne, even if Kennedy could be held responsible for causing the accident. Failing to report the accident wasn't the equivalent of pulling the trigger, even though it was a fair assumption that Kopechne could have been saved if her gripping effort to stay alive lasted several hours. The medical examiner's opinion as to the time of death seemed to confirm that she had a chance to survive. The description Farrar gave of her position in the car when he found her proved she had struggled to keep breathing. If Kennedy was found by the police to have been intoxicated at the time of the accident, he would face negligent homicide charges. But there was no point in Kennedy or his friends telling the police anything. Reporting the accident immediately would have boxed in their story and exposed Kennedy to far more serious charges. Kennedy's friends and advisors needed time to consider all the options; to develop a strategy; to plan answers to all the questions that were bound to follow. This was probably the time when Kopechne was digging her fingernails into the back seat of Kennedy's car. If Kennedy's associates had told the others back in the cottage about the accident before the car was found in the morning, wouldn't they have wanted to know if the police were notified? Kennedy's friends and advisors couldn't tell them anything because there would have been absolutely no justification in not reporting the accident. The option they chose was the one that closed the lid on Kopechne's life.

Kopechne's death brought back memories of how I once saved a boy from drowning. In the summer of 1953 at the start of my vacation, I was headed for the Adirondacks in upstate New York and stopped with my family for a breather at Hessian Lake near Bear Mountain. The boy was a black kid from a Harlem orphanage who was staying for a few days at a nearby camp. When the kid's ball rolled into the lake, he went in after it even though he couldn't swim. Seeing the boy struggling in the water, I dove in with all my clothes on and swam to him as fast as I could. My days as a kid swimming in the East River came in handy. By the time I reached the spot where I had last seen him, he was already on his way to the bottom of the lake. I dove deep. I tried to see and reach at the same time. Luckily, I was able to grab hold of his clothes and pull him up to the surface. My own clothes were beginning to drag me down. I brought the boy in unconscious to shore, but before I could get him breathing again, I had to push him over a five-foot embankment. Finally, I stretched him out on the ground and began artificial respiration. After some agonizing moments, he opened his eyes. "I lost my ball," he said as he coughed himself back to life. "Right, kid," I responded, "and almost your own life along with it." With this memory indelibly a part of me, I thought, how could anyone turn his back on someone in danger of dying.

The *Union Leader*'s "Ace" Egan and I had agreed that the next time we met, it would be on his turf. In early August, we met in the lobby of the Howard Johnson Motel in Manchester, New Hampshire. Egan had picked this spot because, he said, nobody would bother us there. Having arrived before Egan, I watched him approach the lobby accompanied by two other men. From a distance, I thought that one of the men might have been Loeb himself. However, the two men waited outside the lobby and I never got a good look at their faces. As Egan came toward me I wondered how far my con job of him could travel. I was still Ed Ferguson, investigative reporter and had nothing to give him except a repeat of what he already knew—namely, the numbers and location of the public phones on Chappaquiddick. Egan looked as confident and cocky as any reporter I had ever met. He was on a mission to prove something, and that apparently neutralized any doubt on his part as to who I was or what I could deliver.

"Here's the list," Egan said as he handed me three folded sheets of paper. The perforation marks on the edges of the paper reminded me of the teletype paper I used to see in the Twenty-fifth Precinct during my years in Harlem. The records were authentic all right. I had seen plenty of phone records in my time as a detective and knew what to look for. There were handwritten notations of the names of some of those who had received the calls, the time the calls were made, and the listed owners of the phone numbers. There were also notations of "Ch" and "Pot" in the margin. Egan said they were abbreviations for the Chesapeake and Potomac Telephone Companies, respectively, which had issued a credit card in Kennedy's name. The list showed that phone calls had been made from a variety of points on Martha's Vineyard which indicated that more than one person had been using Kennedy's credit card during the night.

What bothered Egan the most was trying to match a 21-minute call that was made before midnight to the time Kennedy claimed he arrived back at the cottage after the accident. This call was traced to a phone number at the cottage and was made to the Kennedy compound in Hyannis. If Kennedy showed up before midnight but didn't tell anyone what had happened except Gargan and Markham, both of whom then went back to the bridge with Kennedy, then whoever made the call, if you believed Kennedy's statement, couldn't have known about the accident. Kennedy had already said on national television that nobody at the cottage knew about the accident except Gargan and Markham. If someone else knew and got on the phone as soon as Kennedy returned to the cottage, they were keeping quiet about it. Egan told me that he didn't know whether the phone that was used was the one I saw in the studio behind the cottage or one that was in the cottage itself. While it was possible that someone just wanted to make a social call around midnight and charge it to Kennedy's credit card, the timing was all wrong to accept that proposition.

To make matters worse, Egan said that when he confronted the Police Chief, Dominick Arena, at Police Headquarters about the phone calls, Arena said he knew all about the calls from the cottage and the Inn. "Which Inn?," I asked Egan. "The Shiretown," Egan answered, "where Kennedy stayed." Checking the list I saw that during the night several calls were made from a pay phone at the Inn and charged to Kennedy's credit card. The timing of these calls fit the period Kennedy was at the Inn after he swam back to Edgartown from the Chappaquiddick ferry dock. "What's Arena doing about the calls,?" I asked Egan. "Nothing," he answered. "As far as he's concerned the case is closed." I wondered how Arena was going to deal with the calls when the coroner's inquest was held. Phone records were going to be subpoenaed and Arena was going to look like a fool for not questioning everyone who attended the Kennedy party about the calls.

I couldn't give myself away and tell Egan what I would have done with these phone records if I had had the chance, but if I did, I would have stuck everybody in a room and called them in one by one and kept rotating them in and out until somebody broke. If no one owned up to making any of the calls, then Ted Kennedy had himself one monumental problem. He had lied to the nation on television because the phone calls were certainly made, and only he could explain them away. If someone did admit to the calls, then Kennedy was still in trouble because he said

217

he didn't call or tell anybody about the accident (except Gargan and Markham) until the morning after. In any event, none of the calls that were made that night sought help for Mary Jo Kopechne.

The calls on the list Egan showed me continued throughout the night. Some of them were made from the phones whose numbers I had recorded and given to Egan. I didn't ask to have a copy of the list because I really didn't have anything more to give Egan in return. But Egan didn't press me. His greatest need was reassurance that someone else had information that conformed with his; that when likely denials surfaced from the phone company and the Kennedy group, there was a force behind him to take on the challenge. Little did he know that the Nixon White House would be behind him all the way. "I've still got four or five more days work on this story," Egan said, "and then I'll let it fly."

On August 13, the *Union Leader* published Egan's story about the phone calls he and I were certain Kennedy or his friends had made between the time of the accident and dawn. The number of these calls gave the lie to Kennedy's claim that he experienced a period of absolute silence after the accident before his mind woke up to report it. Egan's story began: "Although U.S. Senator Edward M. Kennedy claimed to be in 'a state of shock' after the traffic accident which took the life of a pretty female companion, he nevertheless had the mental fortitude to make a total of 17 telephone calls in the hours succeeding the accident."

Sure enough, within a few days of the *Union Leader*'s publication of Egan's story, the New England Telephone Company denied the existence of the records. It didn't surprise me a bit, for that was their job. Egan confirmed his story in a follow-up article by disclosing his source for the records as James T. Gilmartin, a friend of Egan's who was an attorney and real estate broker with an office at 147 East 230th Street in the Bronx. Gilmartin had the right connection inside the phone company. Egan also wrote that he had a conversation with a Richard E. McLaughlin of the Massachusetts Registry of Motor Vehicles in Boston who told Egan that Kennedy's license wasn't wet and showed no signs of being immersed in water. McLaughlin denied ever speaking to Egan. After threatening a lawsuit and filing a complaint with the Massachusetts Public Service Commission, the *Union Leader* published a story which printed, in full, a letter from the New England Telephone

Company confirming Egan's story about the calls to and from McLaughlin. Operator toll-tickets, as they are called, proved Egan's allegations.

For whatever reason, Egan's story about the phone calls never took off in the press. While his scoop carried here and there, the media didn't pick up the story and run with it as a challenge to Kennedy's claim that he never contacted anyone until the morning after the accident. That in itself wasn't surprising either. Since everyone knew that Loeb and the *Union Leader* were out to tar and feather any Kennedy they could find, Egan's story had less impact than it would have had coming from a less biased paper. Regardless of the story about the phone calls, reporters and journalists around the world were not buying the Kennedy version of what happened. Staff members of the Republican National Committee were kept busy clipping and pasting together every newspaper article and editorial that broke into print. The White House wanted a record of the attack on Kennedy's credibility to use if Kennedy ever sought the Presidency. A scrapbook of the articles and editorials was put together and given the title: "At an Appropriate Time."

On September 25, I was back in Boston to see Donald Whitehead. By this time, in addition to Egan's stories about the phone calls, the media had been hammering away at Kennedy's story until there was almost nothing left of his credibility. There had also been a lot of speculation on just how much Kennedy had been drinking before leaving the Chappaquiddick party. Kennedy had already admitted on national television that he had been confused ("scrambled thoughts"), might have been "irrational," couldn't remember many things (which happens when you have too much to drink), and wouldn't have "entertained" some of the thoughts he did have (even if he couldn't remember what they were) under normal circumstances. Whitehead told me that I should contact a lobsterman named Herbert Lovell from Barnstable on Cape Cod to get the name of a cop in Edgartown who told Kennedy long before he went to the party on Chappaquiddick that he should let someone else drive his car. When I went to see Lovell, he didn't have the cop's name to give me. I didn't pursue the matter further because I assumed Kennedy had had too much to drink that day and what this cop might have observed or told Kennedy in Edgartown was too remote in time from the accident itself. I wanted to know what happened in the car between Kennedy and Kopechne *after* they left the party on Chappaquiddick and *before* it flipped over the bridge. Only Kennedy could answer that and, up until now, he hadn't and probably never would.

What did it all mean? I thought about Kennedy swimming the channel back to Edgartown, not going to the police station to report the accident, and then, almost mysteriously, appearing fresh as a daisy; he was dressed and clean shaven as if nothing, *nothing!* had ever happened. How does a man live with himself if he doesn't know whether someone he was just with is alive or dead? How do you explain the fact he showed no feelings until *after* he was told the body was found and only then, according to witnesses, did Kennedy appear to realize what happened. Then my thoughts shifted to all those hours Kopechne was in the car, to her rigid, statue-like body, her claw-like hands, her terror, and then no autopsy to learn if water was in her lungs. No medical examiner in the world worth his salt would have signed off as quickly as Dr. Mills.

On Monday, January 5, 1970, the inquest into the death of Mary Jo Kopechne began in the Edgartown District Court for the Commonwealth of Massachusetts. I was there, along with many others, shivering in the cold outside the courthouse. Not only was the public barred, but also the press. The journey to the inquest was my fifth trip to Edgartown. For four days, I stood in the cold outside the courthouse. It looked like the World Series had come to town: reporters, law students in recess, camera crews, traveling court buffs, Edgartown residents, and myself, among others, stood cloaked with the same motive—to find a way to get inside. But there wasn't any. Every available electronic security gadget was in place to make sure no one got a piece of the evidential pie until Judge Boyle released the slices.

While waiting for the inquest to end, I mentally speculated whether Kennedy's own phone calls had also been taken out—eliminated by his contact within the phone company or, inadvertently, by the White House connection who might have caused an overlapping obliteration of *everyone's* records. The phone company could never deny that there were once records of my calls to the White House. Not only did I make them, but they were also paid for with funds provided by Herb Kalmbach, the President's personal attorney.

The transcript of the Kopechne inquest did not become available to the press until April 1970, three months after the inquest ended. All members of the press who wanted copies had to reserve and pay for them in advance. In signing up with the court clerk for two copies, one for Nixon and the other for Ehrlichman, I decided it was time to use another alias. Ed Ferguson had been too good to me. I didn't want him connected to my real identity; I wanted to reserve him for future use. So I decided to use the other alias the White House had arranged for me, Thomas A. Watkins. Watkins had an authentic press pass that had been issued by the office of California Governor Ronald Reagan. Lyn Nofziger was then working for Reagan, and Caulfield had called him to arrange for my press credentials in Watkins' name. The pass itself was given to me when I went to California in September on an assignment to check into the background of John Alessio, the owner of the Caliente Race Track in Tijuana, Mexico, who was angling for an inside position on the White House power track. President Nixon, I was told, was worried about how close he should let him get to the gate. (Alessio was under investigation by the IRS for tax evasion; he was eventually convicted and sent to jail.) I set Watkins up with a mail drop at 1170 Broadway in New York City, and I got him a phone number and a business card as a representative of my fictional Feature Writers Association of America.

When the transcripts of the Kopechne inquest were ready, they had to be picked up in person, in the same historic, ceremonial hall where Jack Kennedy had first announced his candidacy for the Presidency of the United States. Walking down the hall to pick up my copies, I was concerned that no matter how many aliases I carried around, some reporter in that hall from New York was going to recognize me. Luckily, no one did. I put my copies of the inquest in my briefcase, left the hall as fast as I could, and headed to catch the next plane to Washington.

My original assumption that the Edgartown police would thoroughly investigate Kennedy's accident on Chappaquiddick had been dispelled long before I began thumbing through the transcript of the inquest. I was still convinced, however, that the District Attorney would make good use of the list of phone calls I saw when he made his pitch to the judge. I would have been better off holding on to my doubts. The phone calls I

221

saw were not part of the record of exhibits introduced at the inquest. They were never made part of the evidence. The only calls that were made part of the record were the ones Kennedy made on the morning of July 18 at 10:30 a.m., on the afternoon at 12:30, on the early evening at 6:39—all before the accident—and another on the morning of July 19 at 10:57—long after the accident. A transcript of the key phone calls—the ones made after the accident but before the discovery of the car—was missing. Neither the prosecutor nor the presiding judge at the inquest was made aware of their existence. I was stunned by their absence. It meant the phone company was cooperating on both sides of the fence: getting Egan the list of calls through his contact and then hiding the same list from the power of a D.A.'s subpoena. Because the inquest wasn't a trial and no cross examination was allowed, nobody's credibility was put to the test, not even Kennedy's. The list of phone calls had fallen through the cracks or, better still, been piled over with a lot of deep cover.

The issue of the phone calls lay dormant until 1980, eleven years after the *Union Leader* published Egan's story of the seventeen calls. The existence of these phone calls was again an issue when *The New York Times* began conducting its own investigation into the missing list of calls. On Thursday, January 10, 1980, when my wife and I were settling down for the evening, we noticed the headlights of an approaching car in front of our house. Since we weren't expecting anyone and no one could find our home without directions, I figured someone in one of the local watering holes had picked up at least a sawbuck to help this stranger find his way to my door. I soon heard a knock.

"Mr. Ulasewicz?"

"Yes?"

"I'm Philip Taubman of the *New York Times*," the visitor announced himself. "May I please speak to you about something we're checking out."

"What's it about?"

"We're trying to crack the Kennedy-Kopechne case on Chappaquiddick. We don't believe Kennedy's story about the phone calls. Can I come in for a little while?"

222

It was a cold winter's night, and not having the heart to send him back down the hill without a little warmth, I let him in. I listened very carefully to what he had to say.

"All our leads are based on phone calls that were made late on the 18th and then the 19th from phones on Chappaquiddick, Edgartown and Hyannis," Taubman said. "Some of the phone records have been tampered with. They've either been destroyed or are missing and hidden away some place. I'd like to know if you ever saw them or had any list of them. I was told you'd be familiar with how to get records from a phone company. We also know about your meeting with Egan. But Egan's dead now and you're the only one left who might have seen the records."

Taubman said he knew all about me. "Not quite," I said to myself, "not quite."

Taubman said that he and a couple of other reporters had broken one of the men who was in the so-called power trust that operated from the Kennedy compound in Hyannis the night of the accident. He wouldn't identify the man but said that he was struggling with his conscience. Taubman claimed the man had broken into tears when he was confronted with the matter of the missing list of calls. Jackie Onassis' cottage had been used as a center for communications. Taubman said a man named Ed Martin who worked for Ted Kennedy acted as master of ceremonies.

Taubman wanted to know whether I would consider working for *The New York Times* as they pursued the story of the calls and whether it was worth their time to dig further. He also asked whether Ehrlichman might know something about the records. "You'll have to ask him," I said.

I declined the offer of employment but did acknowledge seeing the list of phone calls. Taubman stayed for two hours, asking a lot about the calls, especially why one call never showed up at an inquest that had lasted twenty-three minutes. I was as puzzled as he was and told him so. When he left, Taubman said he'd be in touch with me in a few days. On the night of January 15, Taubman called to tell me that the telephone people he had spoken with reluctantly admitted there were additional phone calls that had not been brought to the inquest, but they wouldn't explain why they were not. Phone company personnel refused to discuss the specifics of any calls. He also told me that he had been in touch with

223

Egan's widow. She didn't have the list he showed me, and it wasn't in the archives of the *Union Leader*. Taubman said he was beginning to run out of sources.

But on Wednesday, March 12, 1980, *The New York Times* finally published a lengthy front-page article headlined "Gaps Found in Chappaquiddick Phone Data." The story confirmed what Egan and I had known many years before that there had been a coverup.

"Records of Senator Edward M. Kennedy's telephone calls," *The New York Times* article began, "in the hours after the accident at Chappaquiddick were withheld by the telephone company from an inquest into the death of Mary Jo Kopechne without the knowledge of the Assistant District Attorney who asked for them." The first call on the list the phone company produced at the inquest wasn't made until almost 11 o'clock in the morning. That a coverup of the calls I saw had been set in motion was confirmed again when I read that a pilot called by a Kennedy associate had flown over Chappaquiddick while Kennedy's car was still in the water. The Times story claimed that the Kennedy associate who made the call had been on Nantucket, not Martha's Vineyard. Someone had to have called him first before he told the pilot to start up the engines of his plane. I regretted not having had the second chance to check the identification numbers of the plane I saw parked behind the Katama Shores Motel and learn the owner and when that plane had landed there. The Kopechne family deserves a boatload of answers to the questions left unanswered. If they want the case reopened, I sure wouldn't blame them.

The Road to Watergate

O N August 15, 1969, two days after Egan's story on the phone calls first appeared in the *Union Leader*, I completed another investigation for the President, which I had sandwiched in between my trips to Edgartown. To begin moving Larry O'Brien into the target zone, as Murray Chotiner had predicted would be the case, I was told to take a look at the structure of a privately controlled company named Dyson-Kissner and to profile its key officers. My report to the White House, with help from a contact I had inside Dun and Bradstreet, showed that the Dyson-Kissner Corporation was formed in 1961 as part of a reorganization of the Dyson-Kissner Holding Company. Dyson-Kissner's stock holdings, combined with those of its individual officers, controlled 58 percent of Kearney National, Inc. (the Board chairman, Charles H. Dyson, was also Chairman of Kearney's Board of Directors), 48 percent of Wallace Murray Corporation, 38 percent of the Esterline Corporation, and 78 percent of the Boldt Corporation. Dyson-Kissner's subsidiaries were the Unit-Rail Anchor Company of Pittsburgh and a real estate company based in Minneapolis, known as D. K. Properties, Inc. which owned the real estate where three operating divisions of

Dyson-Kissner were located: Northwest Automatic Products, Twin City Monorail, and K. P. Manufacturing.

My profile of Dyson-Kissner's key officers showed two common threads: all of them had served the government in various high-level capacities, and all had been involved on both an advisory and operational level in the postwar continuation of the U.S. military-industrial alliance. The founding father, Charles H. Dyson, served as a Special Consultant to Secretary of War Henry Stimson in 1941. In 1944 President Roosevelt appointed Dyson as the U.S. representative to the International Monetary Conference at Bretton Woods. After returning to public life, he became a member of Textron's Board of Directors and later Director of the Burlington Mills Corporation. In 1957, he joined forces with Franklin H. Kissner who had once served as a deputy director of the Economic Division of the U.S. military government in postwar Germany and later, with Dyson, as an executive with Textron. Another key executive with Dyson-Kissner was its Vice President, John F. Culp. Culp served in the United States Navy Supply Corps from 1941 to 1945. He resigned with the rank of Commander.

Over the next several months, I learned that, in addition to his powerful business and political connections, Dyson was a trustee of the Businessmen's Educational Fund (BEF), a nonprofit corporation with offices in Washington, California, and New York. The BEF sponsored a daily radio program called "American Forum," which was a propaganda arm of the Democratic Party and was broadcast nationally over 300 stations. The radio show was only five minutes long but featured prominent Democrats as key speakers. I passed this information on to Caulfield, who then summarized it and submitted it to Lyn Nofziger. Caulfield added a supplemental note stating that the radio show was being taped in advance and that a "covert copy" of the tape could be obtained. That last bit of information didn't come from me, so obviously I wasn't the only kid on the block working behind the scenes for the White House.

IN January 1970, while I was criss-crossing the country on other assignments (including shivering in the cold in front of the Edgar-

THE ROAD TO WATERGATE

town courthouse during the Chappaquiddick inquest), Larry O'Brien announced that he was forming a new public relations company to be called Lawrence O'Brien Associates. His office would be at 230 Park Avenue, the same address as the Dyson-Kissner Corporation. At least for awhile, it appeared that O'Brien and Dyson-Kissner were going to share the same phone number. O'Brien's long standing relationship with Dyson himself, a powerful Democrat, was designed to become stronger than ever.

In addition to his Dyson-Kissner connection, heading O'Brien's list of clients was Howard Hughes, whose many corporate interests included the Hughes Tool Company, a huge government defense contractor. O'Brien's competition for the rest of the Hughes empire account was controlled by the public relations firm of Carl Byoir and Associates. O'Brien's other important clients included the American Society of Composers, Artists and Publishers (ASCAP) which had offices in Beverly Hills and New York, and the Riker-Maxson Company, an electronics firm formed in April 1969 when Riker Corporation and Maxson Electronics Corporation merged. Riker operated in the manufacturing fields of electronics, communications, and computer programming, whereas Maxson functioned in three general areas: government business, industrial products, and computer services. The phrase "government business" was a catchall for Maxson's work in research and development and in the manufacture of missiles, drones, missile guidance systems, microwave, and radar systems as well as a large volume of pyrotechnic components—the stuff that makes bombs. Maxson Electronics' government contracts were worth millions.

On March 5 1970, O'Brien was once again appointed Chairman of the Democratic National Committee (DNC). A spokesman for him reported that he would remain in charge of his public relations firm, that his staff was going to be expanded, and that he was going to serve as Chairman of the DNC without salary.

In July 1970, some shifting took place in the White House power structure. Ehrlichman left his post as White House counsel to become chief advisor on domestic affairs for the President, and John Dean took Ehrlichman's place. Dean's office incorporated the report on Dyson-Kissner that I had prepared and delivered to the White House in August

1969 into a lengthy memorandum. The resumption of O'Brien's chairmanship of the DNC triggered the following question:

"Whether there is any conflict of interest or tie-in between the clients he (O'Brien) represents and his political activities as Chairman of the DNC. For example, he will be in touch with Democratic Members of the House and Senate, which Party is in control of Congress. This can affect legislation in which his clients may be interested. Furthermore, even though the Executive Branch is Republican, there are many holdovers in key places who can be helpful in the award of contracts."

The followup memo went on to list forty-three other questions about O'Brien's possible lobbying influence. The questions were worded as if O'Brien was going to be tried in a courtroom or at least be subpoenaed to testify at a Congressional hearing. "How do you happen to have offices with Dyson-Kissner," one of the questions started off, "with the same telephone number, instead of having your own office?" The other questions centered on what specific duties his public relations firm would perform for each of his clients, what he would get paid by each of them, what business his clients had with the federal government, how many people O'Brien had on his payroll hustling for these clients in the halls of Congress, how much money the Hughes Tool Company paid him, and, most fundamentally, why O'Brien and Dyson-Kissner shared the same address and phone number. The genesis date of the Watergate break-in was not 1972, but 1969. It started with the assignment to profile the structure of Dyson-Kissner, but the real target was Larry O'Brien. What was wanted was to expose the link between O'Brien, Dyson-Kissner and its subsidiaries, the Hughes Tool Company, and the lobbying power O'Brien's public relations firm tried to use on behalf of other Defense Department contractors.

B Y April 1971, my investigations for the White House had slowed down to a walk. The lack of work didn't concern me. I was on salary, hired to work exclusively for the President and my expenses were being reimbursed promptly. No situation had developed that threatened to expose my anonymous status as a private investigator, and no fault had been found with my work. Much of it was boring (except for coverups like Chappaquiddick) because it involved traveling to investigate events that had already happened or checking the accuracy of information that had already appeared in newspaper articles. Some of my assignments certainly proved that President Nixon obviously hated to be ridiculed or made the butt of jokes and cartoons, but those he should have known went with the territory of his office. Also, they weren't going to cost him any votes unless he really screwed up his office and, up until then, it never crossed my mind that that was likely to happen.

One of these trips ended up being more of an adventure than an investigation when I was sent into the Sierra Madre to track down President Nixon's nephew Donald Nixon, Jr., and find out what he was up to. Nephew Donald had become a pain in the butt to the White House, demanding things like a diplomatic passport so he wouldn't get hassled by Customs or Immigration officials, especially going back and forth to Mexico. Ehrlichman was worried that his antics might prove to be embarrassing for the President. I flew to Los Angeles, rented a car, and drove toward Donald's suspected hideout in the Sierra mountain village of Three Forks.

To start with, I stopped in a general store in the area and told the proprietor that I was looking for two runaway girls from New York who might be hiding out in the hills with a group of hippies. I figured that if the hippies were living anywhere near Three Forks, I'd find Donald. I used pictures of my daughters as part of the ruse. "Oh, sure," the proprietor said as he scanned the photos. "I saw one just the other day headed north." So much for his credibility. My daughters had never been west of the Hudson River. At one point on this journey, I stopped at a roadside stand to have a hot dog and a coke. Before I had a chance to get out of my car, a motorcycle gang, dressed in God knows what all, roared up out of nowhere and surrounded my car. Each cyclist carried a thick necked chain in his hand. One bearded, bull-chested gang member, who looked like he came from another planet, sashayed on his wheels to the driver's side of the car. I rolled down the window to hear what he had to say. "Now, mister," he said, "you would like to buy us all some hot dogs and some gas, *wouldn't* you?" I didn't like what I was hearing. I squeezed out of my car before answering. Each gang member checked his gas supply. "I think we *all* need gas, don't you," their leader said while slowly twirling his chain. I measured my chances of escape. I didn't have any. I wanted to break some heads but in my mind's eye I saw Ehrlichman again, and I could hear his "nyet." I carried the authority of the White House, a gun as a licensed private investigator, twenty-seven years experience as a cop, but I couldn't do anything except keep my mouth shut and buy the bums their hot dogs and gas.

With the help of a local sheriff I stopped to shoot the breeze with, I learned the whereabouts of the President's nephew. As far as the sheriff was concerned, the kid was just having a good time. "Yeh, he's here all right, the sheriff said, "hangin' out with those artsy characters up in the mountains, thinks he's a big deal." After I reported his whereabouts to the White House, Ehrlichman, still worried that Donald, Jr. might succumb to the temptation of drugs and start making promises he couldn't fulfill, personally went to fetch him out of his hideout. Ehrlichman turned him over to Robert Vesco (now a notorious fugitive) for safekeeping.

One of my assignments resurrected memories of my police career when I was sent to unravel a screw-up in communications between the Justice Department and a former police officer from Chicago named Bert "Crusader" Bielski who had gone to court to have "Crusader" officially made part of his name. Bielski was head of an outfit called "Operation Crimechex, U.S.A.," a civilian vigilante group that had more commandments than Moses about how to combat crime in America. Bielski had written a self-serving letter to the President about his crime-stopping movement. "Never knuckle under to criminals" was one of Bielski's lines. The President took the bait, but without checking Bielski's background, Egil Krogh, Ehrlichman's assistant, instructed the Justice Department to respond favorably to Bielski's letter. "President Nixon very much appreciates your recent communication concerning Operation Crimechex," Associate Deputy Attorney General Ronald E. Santarelli wrote to Bielski on behalf of the President. "Organizations such as yours possess a great capacity and a potential for effective crime reduction." But Santarelli, with the whole Justice Department apparatus available to him, didn't bother to learn that Bielski, while on the Chicago Police force, had been suspended at least three times for "questionable conduct" including beating up a motorist. That cost the city $40,000 in damages. Bielski made Santarelli's letter part of a new batch of promotional leaflets. It was too late to stop him. I went to see Bielski at his Crimechex headquarters. Although Bielski, like me, was Polish, that didn't stop me from telling Caulfield at the White House that Bielski had just gone haywire with his patriotism and that the best thing the White House should do is to ignore him.

The only trip out of the country I took for the President was to Mexico. The Mexican illegal alien problem was giving Nixon a real headache after he nominated Mrs. Romana Banuelos as Treasurer of the United States. If confirmed by the U.S. Senate, her signature would appear on all new greenbacks printed by the Treasury Department. Mrs. Banuelos, a Mexican by heritage and a U.S. citizen, owned a food processing plant just over the U.S. border from Tijuana. She also had a controlling interest in the Pan American National Bank. The press was hounding Nixon with stories that Mrs. Banuelos' tortillo factory was riddled with illegal aliens. Federal agents had raided the place several times *before* Nixon had put Banuelos' name in nomination. The charge was that Nixon was anti-American labor, and, of course, the Democrats loved the whole situation.

My job was to verify where the women working in Banuelos' plant were coming from and how they were being transported past customs and immigration officials. The President needed to know how long he could hold out as the backer for Banuelos' nomination. I checked into a hotel in Tijuana, bringing enough cash with me to make sure I could open up a lot of doors. Like I did in Edgartown, during my investigation of Chappaquiddick, I went hunting for information in the best place in the world—a bar. After spreading some greenbacks around, I was soon being called the "big amigo" instead of the "big gringo." Inside the bar, mustachioed villains came out of the woodwork. I was offered every kind of illicit deal you could think of—drugs, jewels, gold, broads, protection if I needed it. The tourist section of Tijuana was like a glittering blanket covering a grimy, no-holds-barred, rotten side of life that seemed to be crawling all around the edges. I found out that the women working in Banuelos' plant came from all over the backlands of Mexico. They were picked up by truck from remote villages and hauled

231

like vegetables into Tijuana. They stayed for a few days in one of the seedier hotels until arrangements were made to sneak them across the border. The women were managed by the equivalent of a bunch of pimps whose palms were well greased to make sure their cargo was smuggled safely across the border.

When federal agents raided Banuelos' plant once again, they found it loaded with illegal aliens. Banuelos said she knew nothing about it— which was a clumsy lie. She had already been put on notice by the Immigration and Naturalization Service to stop her hiring practices. President Nixon finally withdrew Banuelos' nomination, but the whole episode pointed to the sloppy way political appointments and political favors were being handed out. (Sticking the needle in a little further, news accounts reported that a U.S. Secret Service check failed to disclose that an illegal alien had been hired to work as a gardener at Nixon's Western White House in San Clemente, California). Again, there was nothing my investigation could do to change the outcome. I told Caulfield to let these stories die and not let them interfere with the big picture.

In early September 1971, my role as the President's private eye began to change dramatically. The first indication of this change came when Caulfield called me to Washington to check out the Brookings Institution. I started off with the public library where I read that Brookings was a think tank founded and funded by some of the largest corporations in America. Brookings' contributors and personnel were from both sides of the political aisle. When I went there, I had to pass through security, but the security guard didn't ask me for any identification. I took the tack that I was a tourist just like thousands of other people who visit Washington. When asked, "may I help you," I simply said yes and asked if there was an information center or any brochures I could pick up that would tell me about the institute. The guard sent me to the building's maintenance office where I spoke to several employees. I then went on to the personnel department where I asked about job opportunities, about how many people occupied the building, and about whether the firms listed as tenants were in any way interrelated. All the people I spoke to were glad to tell me whatever they knew. Brookings was a big place, and they were obviously proud of working there. I played their fiddle and had no trouble getting a thorough picture of how Brookings was set up. I spoke to one or two security guards and to a porter to find out the hours the building was open, how waste was removed, who was in charge of buying cleaning supplies, and the combined size of Brookings' land and building. I learned that television cameras scanned and monitored the hallways twenty-four hours a day, and that fire alarms were connected to both the Fire and the Police Department. After my report to Caulfield, I flew back home.

At the time I checked out Brookings, *The New York Times* had already published "The Pentagon Papers," the story of Defense Department plans and strategy for continuing the war in Vietnam. The "Papers" had been stolen from the Defense Department files by Daniel Ellsberg. The reporter for the Times who broke the story was Leslie Gelb, a former advisor to the National Security Council. Gelb had an office at the Brookings Institute. When I was given this assignment, I had no knowledge, nor did Caulfield indicate to me that he had any knowledge, that Ehrlichman's obsession over leaks had caused him to form his own covert "Plumbers" unit to plug them up.

Soon after my trip to Brookings and my return home, Caulfield called me back to Washington and asked me to meet him in a restaurant for lunch. When I arrived, I was irritated to find Caulfield sitting at a table with Joseph Woods, brother of President Nixon's secretary, Rosemary Woods. Caulfield had already told me that he and Woods were planning to form their own private intelligence agency and that I was to be in charge of the New York and New England area. I immediately nixed that idea because I had no intention of hooking up with anybody after I finished this job; I had plenty of contacts of my own. I was a loner and intended to stay that way. By having me meet him in the restaurant with Woods present, Caulfield was again violating the rules that we meet alone.

Since there was no point in storming out of the restaurant, I sat down and listened while Caulfield told Woods about a wild scheme that White House Special Counsel, Charles Colson, had just dreamed up. His plan was to stage a phony fire at Brookings and then have the FBI check it out. Colson was going to have Congress pass an ordinance that would permit the FBI to investigate any fire of suspicious origin that happened

233

anywhere in the District of Columbia. Colson, Caulfield explained, would then have the FBI (along with the Fire Department) seal off the area and use this opportunity to break into Gelb's office and grab whatever papers they could. "It's the leaks over the Pentagon Papers, Tony," Caulfield said. "Gelb is going to do a followup study on Vietnam and use Brookings as his cover. Colson wants to stop him."

"With a fire?," I asked, dumbfounded at the idea. Was he crazy, getting involved in such a wild scheme? I didn't want any part of it myself. I immediately got up and left the restaurant, not caring to hear another detail of Colson's bizarre plans. Little did I know that more was being planned. Caulfield looked miffed when I got up to leave. I suspected that he had told Woods I was going to be part of their plans and my abrupt departure made Caulfield look bad, but I couldn't help that.

At the end of September, Caulfield asked me to meet with him in Herb Kalmbach's office in California. "Now what?," I thought. I had straightened Caulfield out about not wanting to be part of whatever private operation he had had in mind, and I thought that Caulfield might now be trying to use the President's personal attorney for his own benefit. Caulfield said that Mitchell and Ehrlichman wanted me to meet with Kalmbach because my arrangement with him was going to change because of the reelection campaign. I asked Caulfield for more specifics, but even he didn't know the details of how I was supposed to fit into the campaign.

I hadn't seen Kalmbach since our first meeting at the Madison Hotel in Washington, D.C., in June of 1969. (We didn't think we would ever see each other again.) Arriving in Kalmbach's office, I was surprised to learn that he would no longer be sending me my pay checks. He told me this wasn't his idea but rather Ehrlichman's and Mitchell's. This proposed break with Kalmbach bothered me because we had had an efficient system going and it was a condition of my hiring that I work through an attorney. I had been very glad when it turned out to be the President's. Using Kalmbach to pay my salary and reimburse my expenses had assured my anonymity. Now Caulfield told me that once the Committee to Re-Elect the President (CREEP) was officially in business, I would be paid through them. The question that immediately came to mind was how my identity could be kept secret if I was going to be listed on a payroll or as a campaign expense? And who would I now be sending my expense vouchers to? The only answer I got was that I was to receive an advance against expenses from the funds Kalmbach still controlled until the financial arm of the reelection committee was established. Kalmbach would then turn over whatever remained in his special trustee account to Maurice Stans who was to become finance chairman. My feeling was that Kalmbach wasn't too sure of all the details and that he was just following instructions.

It all sounded too disorganized for me. From a straightforward salary/ expense payment system Kalmbach and I had established, I was now being asked to become Caulfield's paymaster without knowing who was going to be mine. Kalmbach and I had kept records of everything, and I wanted to make sure, cash or no cash, that someone besides me would be in charge of approving my payments as well as keeping good records of where and for what the money was spent.

The amount of my advance apparently involved some debate between Ehrlichman, Mitchell, and President Nixon's close personal friend, Bebe Rebozo. In Kalmbach's office, Caulfield placed a call to Rebozo who was then in Key Biscayne, Florida. After the call, Kalmbach left the office and went down to a bank vault in the basement of his office building. He came back with an envelope full of cash, and handing it to Caulfield, he told him to count it. We then went into an adjoining conference room where Caulfield counted out $25,000 and told me I was to get $20,000 of it as an advance against my expenses. The remaining $5,000 would be kept as an advance toward his campaign expenses. He also told me that I was to pay him $300 a month plus expenses that he charged to his American Express credit card on matters related to my assignments. He would send me his receipts.

If I was going to be working for Nixon's reelection committee, I knew the $20,000 wouldn't last very long. I didn't treat the advance as money I could use to support my family. I pressed Caulfield for an answer as to when I would be paid for my work and by whom. I had kids in college, a mortgage to pay, and a wife to take care of. Caulfield told me not to worry about it. He said Dean, Ehrlichman, and Mitchell wanted me to work on the campaign and that he had given them a summary of some of my investigations. Caulfield said that as soon as Nixon's reelection committee was open for business, my salary checks would start coming. In the meantime, the $20,000 advance would cover the costs of my job.

Toward the end of December 1971, Caulfield called me and told me that a lawyer from the reelection committee named "Mr. George" wanted to meet with me to check over my expenses and to talk about my future assignments. Caulfield was then working as an assistant to John Dean. Mr. George, Caulfield told me, had been recruited by Dean to work on the campaign. The meeting was set for January 4, 1972 in New York in an apartment I had been instructed to rent for the use of reelection committee officials when they came to the city to work on the campaign. I had rented it under the name of Thomas A. Watkins, the same name I had used when I ordered a copy of the inquest into the death of Mary Jo Kopechne. Caulfield accompanied "Mr. George" to the meeting only to take care of the introductions, but he ended up staying the whole time. Actually, I wanted Caulfield to remain in order to have Mr. George verify that I was to continue paying Caulfield out of the advance I had received in California at the end of September. It was my understanding that Caulfield was going to be placed on the election committee's payroll, and if so, I wanted to stop being responsible for paying him or anyone else.

I had a lot of misgivings about meeting this "Mr. George." On one level, I was glad that I would finally be able to talk to someone about my long overdue paycheck. The $20,000 cash advance was almost completely gone, and I had spent none of it for personal use. Right after meeting with "Mr. George," I was supposed to leave for Wisconsin to check out a guy named Don Simmons who was offering to disrupt the Democrats' campaign in that state, and after that trip I was scheduled to head to New Hampshire to report on the grass roots strength of California Representative Pete McCloskey's efforts to grab the Republican Presidential nomination from Nixon. My pockets would be completely empty by the time I returned from these trips. On the annoyance level, my job now required me to meet with total strangers, like Mr. George, who were going to check my records. That never happened when I was with the Police Department, and Kalmbach had never had to raise an eyebrow over the report of my expenses. Even though I was now supposedly part of campaign operations for Nixon's reelection, the more knowledge of my work that passed around the White House, the greater the risk of a leak. It wasn't the information being circulated that I developed that bothered me as much as the fact that my work as a private investigator for the President appeared to be known by too many people.

As Mr. George carefully checked my expense receipts, I had no reason to doubt he was exactly who he said he was—general counsel to Nixon's reelection committee. Initially, he appeared to have all his screws tightened in the right places. He was efficient and meticulous. After finishing his review of my records, he told me I would be continuing my work and that I would soon be getting my salary. That was certainly welcome news! He then gave me his stamp of approval, which I didn't really care about one way or the other.

"We have plans, big plans, and we intend to include you in them," Mr. George said. Then, he suddenly began talking about other subjects in the "vis-a-vis," multisyllabic jargon Caulfield had begun using after he became Ehrlichman's assistant. As if slipping off a disguise, Mr. George began talking about the ideas bubbling in his head on how to screw the Democrats. I thought his own screws were coming loose. He began using an intelligence jargon I had never heard before. I listened as he described his plans to "conduct operative surveillance" of the Democrats from a yacht he was going to dock in front of the Fontainbleau Hotel in Miami Beach. The yacht would be outfitted with the most sophisticated listening devices on the market and would monitor what was going on behind the scenes at the Democratic National Convention scheduled for Miami in July. Mr. George said he was also going to buy a truck, stuff it with equipment, and use it as another listening post. Lots of prostitutes would be recruited to get convention delegates into compromising situations. His intelligence plan would cover every contingency. "This was war," he said. "This is ridiculous," I thought.

"What the hell is this all about?," I asked myself. I was as astounded at Mr. George's disclosures as he was astonished at the exactitude of my financial records. "Will you be available for duty?," he asked me, his eyes fixed on me as if they could penetrate a wall. "I'm a licensed private detective," I told him, keeping my face as blank as I could as I tried to guess what he meant by the question. Did he mean to recruit me for one of his crazy plans? What else was going on, I wondered. "I'm available for assignments," I told him without revealing that my answer to whatever he had in mind for me would be "nyet." On the way out of the apartment, he told me to destroy my records. I didn't respond, because I had no intention of destroying anything.

I couldn't help wondering what records Mr. George was keeping on his own activities. If he wanted my records destroyed, I assumed he wouldn't want anyone knowing about his plans to provide yachts, surveillance trucks, and big time hookers to entrap and embarrass the Democrats. He was obviously using his role as counsel to the reelection committee as a cover for his other schemes for getting Nixon reelected. If anything, he gave me all the more reason to keep my records as accurate as possible. (It wasn't until after the Watergate break-in that I learned Mr. George was actually G. Gordon Liddy.)

After meeting Mr. George, I learned that the reelection committee's right hand didn't know what its left was doing. I found this out when I arrived in Wisconsin to check out what a guy named Don Simmons was up to. On December 18, 1971, Timothy Gratz, Chairman of Wisconsin's Republican Party College Organization, received a call from a man calling himself Don Simmons. Simmons said he had gotten Gratz's name from Randy Knox, an active Wisconsin Republican. Gratz and Simmons met that afternoon in the Park Motor Inn Lounge. Simmons told Gratz that he had come to Wisconsin to recruit people to help with President Nixon's reelection campaign, and specifically to do "opposition research." He told Gratz he had all kinds of proposals for conducting a "negative campaign" to insure Nixon's reelection. His goal was to create as much bitterness and disunity within the Democratic Party as he could. He wanted that disunity to surface during the Wisconsin and other primaries to be held in the coming months. Three of his suggestions were to plant agitators in student audiences, set up picket lines, and infiltrate the local campaign offices of Democratic candidates. Simmons also wanted to line up a few blacks to picket Senator Edmund Muskie, a potential Nixon rival, wherever he spoke. After Muskie fell, Simmons told Gratz, McGovern would be next. At this point Gratz asked Simmons who had sent him to Wisconsin. At first, Simmons said he was working for a consulting company from New York, but he finally admitted that this was all his idea and that he was working with his own

238

money. When Gratz reported his meeting with Simmons to top Republican officials in Wisconsin, who in turn passed the information along to the White House, it seemed nobody had ever heard of Don Simmons. I was given the assignment to blow his cover.

For the first time, this assignment required that the White House provide me with a cover story of its own. The connection between the White House and me had to be revealed to insure my credibility in Gratz's mind. After all, he had gone to the top level in Wisconsin Republican politics to report Simmons and so had a right to expect that someone from the top was coming to see him. Using another alias, I called Gratz and simply told him that I had been asked to conduct a discreet inquiry on Simmons's background for the White House. When I met with Gratz in his apartment, he seemed pleased to hear the words "White House." With his cooperation, I made preparations to record Simmons's voice when he called again. I wanted to give the tape to the White House so that it could figure out who Simmons might be working for. Gratz, it seems, had already made arrangements for Simmons to call him at a preassigned time. When Simmons finally called, he continued to be both bold and evasive, acting as if it didn't really matter who he was working for as long as Nixon was reelected. He had a job to do and he wanted help. If Gratz would help him with the recruiting, Simmons would provide the money. Simple as that: spread the dirt and pass the ammunition.

Gratz was disturbed, not knowing whether Simmons was legitimate, and whether he should refuse to cooperate with Simmons or play along with him to find out what else he was up to. Whatever he was doing, Gratz felt that Simmons was going about it mighty sloppily. Gratz even wondered whether Simmons might be working for the Democrats to find out whether the Republicans were planting spies in Democratic candidates' organizations. Gratz was convinced that the Nixon White House didn't know anything about Simmons because one of his associates, John MacIver, had called some Republican Party big wigs who said they didn't know who Simmons was. If Simmons was legitimate, MacIver would surely have known about him. So who was this guy? I told Gratz I intended to find out. But, first, I was going to call the White House. As I left Gratz's apartment, I told him to sit tight until I came back. Next, I

239

called Caulfield from a pay phone in the lobby of the motel where I was staying.

"Jack," I told Caulfield, "I'm going to pull the lid off this guy. He's throwing his weight around, and he claims he's got the bucks to back him up. I'm convinced someone in that White House of yours knows all about this. You better find out who it is. And quick. I'll give you an hour."

When Caulfield phoned back as scheduled, he said he had checked with both Ehrlichman and Dean and they knew nothing about Simmons.

"Check with the other side of the throne, Jack," I said, referring to H. R. Haldeman, the President's Chief-of-Staff.

"But I don't have a line into him," Caulfield said.

"Get one!," I demanded and then hung up.

In a few minutes, Caulfield was back on the line.

"You're right, Tony," Caulfield said. "Simmons is Haldeman's man. Get out of there. Back off. Simmons will be told to lay off Gratz."

When I returned to Gratz's apartment I told him that the matter had been taken care of and that he wouldn't be bothered again, but I couldn't believe Haldeman or anyone else would let a guy like Simmons loose on the streets. If anyone found out about him, he was bound to hurt Nixon's campaign. As I found out later, Simmons was actually Donald R. Segretti, recruited by Haldeman's appointments secretary, Dwight Chapin, for the political game of "dirty tricks." Payments for Segretti's services, described as "field operation expenses," were authorized by Haldeman and paid out of Kalmbach's trustee fund. The Simmons/ Segretti investigation made it clear to me that White House intelligence operations, at least those that were connected to Nixon's reelection campaign, were being directed by more than one hand. All of these hands appeared to have been dipping into the money on deposit in Kalmbach's trustee account. But with Ehrlichman not knowing what Haldeman was up to, no one hand seemed to be in charge of what was going on. Chaos was in the wind.

After traveling to New Hampshire and then assuring the White House that California Congressman Pete McCloskey's grass-roots primary campaign was not going to pose any threat to Nixon's renomination, I flew to Washington on March 21 to meet with Caulfield again. By this time, Caulfield had become a staff member of CREEP and was listed as an employee. I was still working in limbo, not knowing what arrangements had been worked out for the payment of my salary or what my status would be during the campaign. I had already made up my mind that, right after the election, I was finished with Washington. My career was going nowhere, private eye for the President or not. Too many people had become involved in my work, and most of them were amateurs regardless of their titles. I had thought that becoming the President's personal private investigator would be the culmination of my career. Instead, I began to feel that the role was meaningless.

I met with Caulfield in Lafayette Park across from the White House. To my surprise he told me he was leaving CREEP and would be working for the Treasury Department. He complained that Mitchell was treating him as simply a bodyguard, and that wasn't what he had had in mind when he took the job. He claimed that his connections with Dean, however, were as strong as ever and that Dean had arranged to get me another advance to cover my expenses. On instructions from Dean, Caulfield had called Kalmbach, who was then in Washington working as Stans's assistant at the Finance Committee. Caulfield asked Kalmbach for $30,000, $5,000 of which he said he would keep for expenses and the rest he would give to me. Although he said he was no longer going to work for the reelection committee, he would still remain my umbilical cord to the White House, primarily to Dean to whom Caulfield had given a summary of my assignments to date. Caulfield didn't tell me what the $5,000 he was keeping was for, and I didn't ask.

When Caulfield handed me $25,000, he said I was supposed to keep $5,000 for myself to help cover my personal living expenses. I asked Caulfield who approved this deal. "Dean," he answered. I again asked about my salary. He said it was coming, but in view of Caulfield's low status with Mitchell and his expected limited stay with CREEP, I began to doubt that he had the authority to guarantee me anything. Still, I was being asked to continue my work, and at this level, I thought that someone from CREEP, perhaps not Caulfield, would finally deliver on the promise. I had yet to meet Dean, but his name kept popping up. My impression was that he was pulling a lot of strings behind the scenes that involved far more than just his role as Counsel to the President.

241

On May 18, I flew down to Washington for yet another meeting with Caulfield who by then had already started his job with Treasury. He wanted me to go over some papers he had collected while working for Ehrlichman and Dean. He was in the process of clearing out his old office in the Executive Building and said he didn't want to throw out any memos or reports that involved my investigations before I had a chance to go through them. Caulfield also said John Dean wanted to see me. Caulfield left his office for awhile and when he came back, Dean was with him.

When I was introduced to him, there was something beyond his impeccably groomed appearance that bothered me. Maybe I didn't expect the President's White House lawyer to dress or look like a model or like a mannequin in a men's shop. Every crease in his suit was perfectly ironed, every hair on his head in place, and he had a smooth, almost hairless face. Everything about him appeared too delicate and too neat for me. I took an instant dislike to him and dismissed him as a slick operator.

Dean started off the conversation by telling me how impressed he was with my work. He said he knew about my meeting with "Mr. George" and that all my records checked out as being in order. (He didn't ask me whether I had destroyed them as "Mr. George" suggested, and I didn't volunteer that I hadn't and wouldn't.) Dean said he expected me to continue working, although he didn't specify what it was he had had in mind. In general, somewhat vague terms, he spoke about plans for the upcoming election campaign, the activities planned to stir up a few things at the Democratic National Convention (I hoped it wasn't Don Simmons), and the White House's interest in Larry O'Brien's activities at the offices of the Democratic National Committee in Washington. My ears perked up. Dean was putting O'Brien in the target zone. Murray Chotiner's prediction was coming true.

Before returning home, Caulfield asked me to go through his papers in his duffel bag and take out what I wanted. The first thing I sorted out and kept was the original White House memo Ehrlichman had written to Caulfield on April 29, 1969 stating that "The President has been told that the present intelligence system to provide the Federal government with advance warning of activities on campuses and among minorities is deficient. It is argued that conventional intelligence gathering simply are not applicable in the new contexts. I would appreciate your talking with people in whom you have confidence outside of the government and giving me your thoughts within the next five days on whether the present intelligence gathering system is adequate, and if not, what might be done to improve it."

In March 1969 when Caulfield first broached the subject of the White House's secret intelligence operation, I had made it clear that I thought the whole idea was ridiculous and that no matter what plan was put on the drawing boards, once Hoover found out about it, he was going to bounce it out the door on the end of his foot. Ehrlichman's memo was a direct challenge to Hoover's authority. The only sense I could make of it was that Ehrlichman and the President were either being coached by some old codgers from the intelligence wars of the 1940s and 1950s or by some hard hat arch-conservatives who didn't think Hoover was doing enough to end the protest sweeping the country. Fresh with victory and with more power than they knew what to do with, men like Ehrlichman went haywire trying to do Hoover's job. Caulfield, once a BOSSI detective, had become a gofer for the amateurs in the White House.

The next memo I picked out was from Caulfield to Ehrlichman and fingered Mario Biaggi as a potential "unsettling force in the '72 election if he stumbled onto the right issues." The memo was dated May 2, 1969, a week before I first met Ehrlichman at LaGuardia Airport. I was startled to see it because Biaggi had been a hero cop in New York and he was a friend of mine. Biaggi had joined the police force at about the same time I had. He spent a tour of duty in Harlem in the Twenty-third Precinct when I was working in the Twenty-fifth. We met many times over the years at various police functions, dinners at the Waldorf when I was escorting world leaders, and sometimes at police headquarters when we crossed paths working on an investigation. The memo to Ehrlichman stated that Biaggi might be not only a spokesman for a large Italian constituency, but also the Mafia's mouthpiece in Congress. I didn't believe that and was surprised to see how far the White House was prepared to go to try and nail Biaggi. (In 1988, when Biaggi went on trial for his part in the Wedtech scandal, he asked me if I ever did an investigation on him for the White House. I told him that I didn't and that

243

I would have refused the assignment. He said his own sources had told him he had been a White House target for a long time. All this is particularly strange because, in fact, Biaggi had a letter hanging on his wall from President Nixon thanking him for his support for legislation Nixon had wanted passed. I saw the letter in Biaggi's office shortly before he went to jail.)

Another memo which Caulfield sent to Ehrlichman was dated July 17, 1969, right before I headed for Chappaquiddick, and reported that a security survey had been completed at the offices of the Republican National Committee. In Caulfield's opinion "unless the recommendations are implemented on a continual basis, we run the formidable risk of opposition penetration at any time." He went on to say that a copy of the memo was being sent along to Haldeman "because of his expressed interest in this last February." That meant a month after Nixon's inauguration Ehrlichman and Haldeman were actually worried about "opposition penetration" at the Republican National Committee.

A series of other memos confirmed that Caulfield was reporting my assignments to Dean, if not acting on his directives. On April 19, 1971, Caulfield wrote a memo to Dean that recommended using Colson to "endorse Lyn Nofziger and Charlie Fagan getting together for optimum results with minimal White House exposure" on one of my assignments. This assignment involved looking into an already published story involving allegations that Maine's sugar industry was improperly funneling campaign contributions into Senator Muskie's election till. This story and others like it would occasionally blow into the news like a hot wind and then disappear without a trace. I found no substance to the story when I went to Maine and checked up on it, but Caulfield's memo meant he wanted to keep stoking its embers.

Dean himself sent a memo on one of my investigations to Haldeman. Dated October 26, 1971, the memo concerned a movie called RICHARD which was designed to be a "satirical spoof on the President." Playing the part of Nixon was to be an actor named James La Roe who had formally changed his name to Richard M. Dixon. The movie, scheduled to be released in February 1972, was also supposed to star Mickey Rooney. My assignment had been to see who was putting up the dough for the film and to see if La Roe/Dixon was a front for any political group opposing Nixon's policies, especially the Democrats. This investigation and a similar one I did on a movie produced by Emile de Antonio called *Millhouse: A White Comedy* showed me how paranoid the White House was about protecting Nixon's image. It all seemed such a waste of time to me because once Nixon was elected President he was more than fair game for anyone who wanted to ridicule or spoof him in any way they chose. The one difference in the case of the *Millhouse* investigation was that in a memo to Dean dated June 25, 1971, Caulfield recommended that "we watch the progress of the film taking particular note to determine if Larry O'Brien is stupid enough to get behind it. If so, we can, armed with the Bureau's information (I presumed Caulfield meant the FBI) do a Nofziger job on De Antonio and O'Brien, thereby losing the battle but winning the war." (I went to see the movie and found myself alone in the theatre except for the mice; or so I thought. A man sat down beside me and began stroking my shoulder. Without taking my eyes off the screen I told him to beat it or I'd break his arm.)

The only assignment I ever received directly from Dean was to find a more cost-efficient boat than the Presidential yacht, *Sequoia*, to float President Nixon's guests down the Potomac River. I don't know why Dean thought I would know anything about yachts. Maybe he didn't think I did but picked me anyway because he had to find somebody to do the job. The only boat I owned was a row boat that I took out on Sacandaga Lake during the summertime. To start looking for the *Sequoia*'s replacement, I went to the New York Yacht Club which has models of all types of schooners, frigates, yawls, ketches, and sloops resting inside glass cases. But the President, I was told, didn't want a sailboat; he wanted a sleek motor boat.

To find a bunch to choose from, I went to a firm of naval architects and then to the office of a yacht broker. I told the broker that I was making a discreet inquiry for someone who flies around a lot, "if you know what I mean," and is kind of tired of living on the run. I said my client wanted to get a little closer to the ground and still be able to move when he wanted to. I winked at the broker. I made the bucks my client was willing to pay sound big enough so that I had the broker prancing around his office like a peacock. The broker winked back. I dropped enough hints to make the broker think I was representing the billionaire recluse,

245

Howard Hughes, although I never mentioned Hughes's name. The yacht broker was in his glory as he gave me the specifications of every boat he could think of that would satisfy the cravings of a king. I sent Dean back a list of ten choices for the President. I didn't tell Dean where I got them. He didn't tell me how he did his job, and I wasn't about to tell him how I did mine.

I took the memos and documents from Caulfield's duffel bag home, and stored them in a box in my attic. I wasn't home very long when I got another call from Caulfield to come back to Washington.

"What for?," I asked.

"Dean wants you to check out the offices of the Democratic National Committee."

"For what?"

"He just wants a report on how it's set up."

Caulfield made no mention of plans to bug it or to break into it. I treated the assignment in the same way as I did the Brookings job. It also didn't escape me that the DNC's offices were the political headquarters of Larry O'Brien.

On May 28, 1972, I flew down to Washington to pay a visit to the offices of the Democratic National Committee (DNC). I took a cab from the airport, but when I arrived at the Watergate complex of buildings, I decided to check the general layout of the place before specifically going to DNC headquarters. I would do that the next morning. I showed up there around 10:00 o'clock on the morning of May 29. When I arrived, I was surprised to learn that the office just about had no security. The doors of the DNC were see-through glass, not heavy oak as one might guess to symbolize the heavy secrets locked inside. I opened the doors and walked in with a pleasant hello to the receptionist. When she asked if she could help me, I told her I was waiting for someone else to join me. That way I wouldn't have to tell her who I had come to see. I sat down, placing myself in a position where I could see everything that was going on. One thing I immediately saw was that there wasn't any heavy thinking going on there. It was more like a mail order office, with people stuffing and opening envelopes, typing letters, and answering the telephone. It quickly became apparent to me that this office was the headquarters for coordinating arrangements for fund-raising dinners and

246

breakfasts, mailing out invitations and solicitations, marshalling statistics, cutting out newspaper clippings, and updating records in order to keep track of the addresses of new delegates and key Democratic leaders. The Watergate offices of the Democratic National Committee simply served as a data center; the big political strategy was being planned in fancy restaurants and posh apartments or in the conference rooms of big-city lawyers and bankers. "There's nothing there, Jack," I told Caulfield after my visit to the DNC. They're not worried about security. It's as open as the sky."

W HEN Caulfield called me on the morning of June 18 with the news that five men had been caught inside the DNC's offices in the middle of the night trying to rifle files and photograph papers, he sounded like a beached fish, thrashing about, disappointed he hadn't been caught in the net. He had obviously been left out of the whole operation. If he had been kept on the inside, been made part of the planning, then, strangely enough, I think Caulfield felt he would have finally made his score. The yellow brick road, however, now led to jail and not to the Wizard. Caulfield told me the names of the men arrested: James McCord, Bernard Barker, Virgilio R. Gonzalez, Eugenio Martinez, and Frank Sturgis. All of them had past ties to the CIA, and all were active in the anti-Castro movement based in Miami. Of those arrested, the only name I recognized was Barker's, whom I knew as an old BOSSI informant. We rated him a "freebie"—an informant who was a spear carrier for pro-Batista interests, always volunteering information we already had and didn't need. Whenever Batista's advisor Manolo Benitoa was in New York with Mrs. Batista, I frequently saw Barker talking with Benitoa in the Batista suite at the Waldorf Astoria. Even with his CIA connections, any information Barker volunteered to give us about Cuba was regarded as slanted and was filed under a caution light. Caulfield said he was most worried about the fate of McCord, a retired CIA agent whom he had helped get hired as head of security for the Republican National Committee. Caulfield said he and McCord had become friends.

The first question I asked Caulfield was why an army of burglars had been sent to hit this beachhead. The operation had been downright stupid. Caulfield answered that he didn't know and neither did Ehrlichman. When Caulfield first heard about the break-in, he called Ehrlichman who had asked him "What's this all about?" Ehrlichman didn't know a thing about this operation. Caulfield said Ehrlichman asked him if I was involved. When Caulfield said no, Ehrlichman apparently sounded dumbfounded that he didn't know what was going on. This scenario sounded just like the Simmons caper in Wisconsin when Ehrlichman told Caulfield he didn't know anything about Simmons's (Segretti's) plan to disrupt the Democrats' campaign there. Haldeman hadn't bothered to fill Ehrlichman in on the action. Ehrlichman also didn't know that Dean, his successor as White House Counsel, had had Caulfield send me in to check out the DNC offices at the end of May. I couldn't help asking myself whether Haldeman knew in advance about the plan to hit the DNC or played a role, along with Dean, pushing this crazy plan through. I also wondered how Dean, counsel to the President, planned to extricate himself once this caper was fully exposed.

Putting two and two together, just to make some sense out of this fiasco (the burglars didn't even know enough to tape the door jam up and down instead of from front to back which exposed it), I assumed the break-in at the DNC had been orchestrated with an army in order to cover the real purpose of the effort—which the army itself didn't know—and that was to get information on O'Brien. The effort backfired. Until now, not a dent had been put in O'Brien's image, nor was he made to answer whether his role as chairman of the Democratic National Committee and as head of his own public relations company represented a conflict of interest. If McCord had been given specific instructions to find evidence of one or if any of the others had been told what to look for, then this assignment would have been a job for one man, not an army. The burglars had to have been instructed to gather up and photograph whatever they could without knowing what the hunt was all about. Whatever they found was going to be sifted and evaluated later at the White House probably, I figured, by Dean, Haldeman, and Colson.

Caulfield called me several times that day. When he first suggested that I should come down to Washington in case I might be needed, I told him to forget about it. I wasn't interested in any coverup. But then I got another call telling me that Dean wanted me in Washington as soon as I could get there. Caulfield told me that Dean was calling from San Francisco and wanted my telephone number so he could personally make sure I got the message. Caulfield also said that Fred Fielding had told Dean that he better get to Washington himself and get control of the situation. The Democrats weren't going to let this incident pass as just an ordinary nighttime office burglary. Caulfield asked me to check into the Roger Smith Hotel where I was to wait for Dean's call. I flew down to Washington that day and then cooled my heels for the next two days without ever getting a ding-a-ling on my phone. I went back home on June 20.

Shortly after I returned home, Caulfield called me again and asked me to come right back to Washington. I told him I was tired of being yanked like a yo-yo. Caulfield said he couldn't discuss the matter over the phone; it was personal, he said, and he didn't dare say anything until he met me. So I flew back to Washington on June 23 and met him for lunch. Caulfield told me that he wanted to contact McCord—to express his "sympathy" for his being caught in this mess. But I didn't believe that was the only reason Caulfield wanted to contact him; something else had to be going on. McCord had been disgraced by his arrest. Despite his clean record, this was a bad burglary. It was also a bad omen for the Republican Party. What the Republicans were proposing to do through men like Colson and "Mr. George," such as firebomb the Brookings Institute or eavesdrop on the Democrats at their Miami convention, would surely surface with a vengeance. McCord was caught breaking into the centerpiece of operations for the Democratic National Committee in a Presidential election year. I had no doubt McCord was going to end up doing time—probably more than a year—regardless of his clean record. I figured Caulfield was going to try to convince him that he wouldn't be forgotten.

Caulfield said he didn't know the best way to contact him. "That's easy," I told him. I asked Caulfield to think of something only McCord would know could connect up with him. Caulfield said he remembered that McCord had found a raincoat of his which he had misplaced. "That's it," I said. Caulfield said McCord had an unlisted telephone number and he didn't know it. "So what!," I said. "If he has a mailbox, put a slip of paper in it with a number on it and give him a time he should call it. Write a note to McCord and tell him a mutual friend would like to speak with him about a raincoat he recently left somewhere that McCord picked up for him." To help Caulfield make his contact, I drove to the area near McCord's home and looked for a phone booth. Spotting a pair of them next to the Blue Fountain Inn, I wrote down the telephone number of each booth, wrote a designated time next to each number, and left the note in McCord's mailbox. I called Caulfield, gave him the same information, and told him it was now up to him to make the connection with McCord. Then I went back home.

On June 28, ten days after the break-in, I received a phone call from Herb Kalmbach in California asking me to meet him at the Statler Hilton in Washington. This was going to be my third trip to Washington since the burglary. Kalmbach said it was urgent that I meet with him. He said Dean had told him something had to be done immediately to help those who had been arrested inside the DNC. The only details Kalmbach had was that arrangements had to be made for putting up bail, paying attorneys fees, and providing some cushion of living expenses for the burglars and their families. Because of the serious nature of this request and its implications, Kalmbach said he planned to check on Dean's authority to set everything up.

When I stepped inside Kalmbach's Washington hotel room on the afternoon of June 29th, what I saw was anything but a President's attorney bearing his former Jimmy Stewart elegance. Kalmbach was obviously uncomfortable with what he had to say to me. He began our conversation by asking me if I had been reading what was appearing in the newspapers. "How could I avoid it?," I answered. Kalmbach then described a meeting he had just had with Dean on a bench in Lafayette Park, across from the White House. It was through Kalmbach that I learned, for the first time, that others were involved in the burglary at the Democratic National Committee who hadn't yet been arrested. Kalmbach explained that a man named Hunt and his wife were exerting a lot of pressure to come up with enough money to cover the bail, attorneys' fees, and living expenses for the Watergate burglars and their families. With or without details, Kalmbach said he felt uneasy about becoming

250

involved in something like this. Sensing a lot of deception in what Dean was saying, he had decided not to accept what Dean told him until he had first checked it with the President. That made me feel better about the situation because Kalmbach was still the President's attorney and was a man I trusted without hesitation. In contrast, I didn't trust Dean at all. He was going to park himself in the most secured area he could find and deceive anybody he had to in order to save his hide. Kalmbach said that Dean wanted him to raise between $50,000 and a $100,000 for the Watergate burglars and their families. When Kalmbach told Dean he didn't want to be the only one responsible for trying to raise this money and that a committee ought to be established, Dean killed the idea, fearing the consequences of a leak. I told Kalmbach that if Dean was so worried about a leak he should start worrying about the five burglars in jail who were going to sing somewhere along the way, no matter what amount of money was paid out. Kalmbach said Dean insisted that there was to be no path anyone could follow that would lead near the White House. (At the time, neither Kalmbach nor I knew that McCord had an address book on him when he was arrested and that the names in it would ultimately tie the White House to the burglary.)

Kalmbach then looked at me and dropped a bombshell, "Dean thinks you're the man to deliver the money." (Dean later claimed that my involvement was Kalmbach's idea, but it was Dean, not Kalmbach, who wanted the money delivered and it was Dean, not Kalmbach, who knew what assignments I had already handled.) I was floored. There had to be some fast footwork going on behind the scenes to make sure the Watergate burglars had attorneys who would tell them to keep their mouths shut. Money would grease the way, but the investigation of the Watergate burglary wasn't going to stop at their level. Barker had to know that and so had McCord if he was any good at what he did as a former CIA agent. They had to know that the FBI would be in on this case. The Democrats weren't going to leave it in the hands of the District of Columbia Police Department. Pressure was going to build, and when money gets involved, big money, so does the possibility of blackmail. "If you're asking my advice, Herb," I told Kalmbach, "when you get into dealing with money this size, sooner or later, word of it leaks out.

251

More and more people want a piece of the action. From what the papers are saying, this Watergate thing is going to grow. Unusual things happen when you start talking about money."

Any thoughts I had of walking out of that hotel room were blunted because I was sitting across from the very man I insisted on working through when I first started working as the President's private eye. Kalmbach's voice, sputtering and agonized as it sounded, was drowning my own thoughts of quitting the job on the spot and going back home. Kalmbach said he had checked out Dean's request with Ehrlichman and that the White House was responding to a moral obligation. Dean didn't want the burglars to feel they had been abandoned. I didn't buy that story. At one point or another during their careers, the men arrested had been paid professionals in the intelligence field. A number of amateurs had cut the orders to send them into the DNC offices, and now it was time for the pros to cut the amateurs loose from this case as fast as possible and with the least amount of damage. Kalmbach said that Ehrlichman had told him that the payments to the burglars for their bail, their lawyers, and their families had been okayed at the highest level. Kalmbach had been given his marching orders, including a directive that there was to be no disclosure to anyone of what was afoot—especially not, Kalmbach made emphatically clear, to Caulfield. Dean was using Caulfield but didn't want Caulfield to know what was going on.

"Well," I said, "you've made one mistake already. You called Caulfield to get my phone number when all you had to do was call information." Kalmbach looked sheepish. He then told me that Maurice Stans had come over to his hotel room with $75,000 (actually $75,000 and a C-note) in cash. Kalmbach put it on a closet shelf. "Please take it, Tony," Kalmbach said. "I can't tell you what to do with it yet because I don't even know. All I know is that you and I have to wait for further instructions." Kalmbach had been told to use the name "Novack" whenever he called me. The phone calls we made to each other would not be traceable. Whenever I called about the money, I was to identify myself as "Mr. Rivers" and say that I was calling about the "price of the script" and "the cost of the players." Those were code words, respectively, for attorneys' fees and the amount each family was to receive. Kalmbach told me I was not to negotiate with anyone. Once I made

252

contact and was given the amount set aside for a particular "script" or "player," I was then to arrange a discreet location for its delivery. The strange thing about this meeting was that he and I were now switching roles. He was in charge of confidentiality; he was the one supplying the names of the aliases we would use; he was providing the "script" and the code words for communication. Kalmbach, I sensed, felt completely out of place. He was being given a part to play in a drama he had no business performing.

"You'd better not keep any records of this, Tony," Kalmbach said.

"It wouldn't mean anything if I did or didn't, Herb," I responded. "One way or another, this money business is going to come out in the open. If some of this money is for attorneys, then why all the secrecy?"

"They're afraid of the press."

"Herb, the press isn't that dumb to think these attorneys were hired and paid for by the burglars. Not when high ticket people start showing up to defend these guys."

"How do you intend to deliver it?," Kalmbach asked.

"I don't think you should know that, Herb," I told him. "If you don't know how I do it, then neither one of us can accuse the other of leaking it out. If it does come out, don't ask anyone else about the leak until you first speak with me."

I left the hotel room of the attorney for the President with $75,100 in cash stuffed in a laundry bag tucked under my arm. I didn't know where else to put it. I carted the money back home and waited for Kalmbach to tell me what to do with it. At first, nobody wanted the money. The "laundry" was a hot potato. I kept it in a bank vault—the "ice box," I told Kalmbach—until someone made up his mind to take it. I was first instructed to call a C. Douglas Caddy, a Washington attorney. When I did, Caddy acknowledged the code name "Rivers," but didn't know the price of the "script" or the cost of the "players." Caddy suggested a meeting at a restaurant in Georgetown where we could talk about the figures. I went to the bank and removed $45,000 from the "ice box" and put it in a brown paper bag. If I was to be stopped and asked about the contents I would have said I was carrying my "lunch." A paper bag was easier to fold inside a newspaper or to stick under my raincoat. If I carried a brief or attache case then, for security purposes, I would have

253

had to attach it to my wrist or my belt with a small chain and a lock. Somewhere along my journey I would have to unhook myself and that could have been an invitation to a disaster, however remote. The last thing I needed to do was attract attention to myself as I tried to deliver money to those involved in a burglary. A brief or an attache case was an invitation to a thief.

Waiting for Caddy to appear, "Mr. Rivers" was paged by the bartender. Mr. Caddy said he wasn't coming to the restaurant and wanted me to come to his office instead. I told Caddy that wasn't possible. "Hold everything," I said to myself. Caddy was obviously getting cold feet. I had to call Kalmbach back and find out what he wanted me to do. After I reached him and told him what Caddy said, I had to wait in the restaurant for a callback. He said he had to check with someone else to find out what he was supposed to do. This began a whole series of Kalmbach comeback calls. "Call Caddy back," I was finally told. "Try again." I did, but it wasn't sinking into Caddy's head that "Mr. Rivers" was a courier, not a negotiator. "Drop it," Kalmbach then ordered me. "Forget about Caddy," he said. Before I left the table in the restaurant for the last time (the waiters were beginning to give me funny looks), I overheard someone sitting near me complain that their expensive raincoat had been swiped off the coat rack. I chuckled to myself. My own raincoat was a six-dollar Canal Street special I had bought in 1960. When I went to the phone, I wrapped the paper bag inside my raincoat and left it on the seat next to me. If the raincoat thief had had x-ray vision, he would have skipped the coat rack, grabbed mine, and made himself a quick 45 grand.

After the expected delivery to Caddy turned into a bust, Kalmbach told me to go back home. My next call was to come back to Washington and to contact a Paul O'Brien. When I did, using a public phone booth again, O'Brien said he didn't want any part of the "script" or to know who the "players" were. O'Brien understood the code language I was using but hung up on me as fast as he could. So back home I went again. And then back to Washington for a call to an anonymous voice who told me to call the "writer's wife." I didn't know anything about a "writer's wife" at the time and didn't have any other phone number except

Kalmbach's. "Go back to New York, Tony," Kalmbach told me again. And so I did.

As I waited at home for further instructions, I began to realize that the delivery of my "lunch"—badly ripening—wasn't going to be the one-shot deal I was led to believe would be the case. "Call William C. Bittman," I was told after a few days at home. "He's the 'writer's attorney.' "

The "writer," as it turned out was E. Howard Hunt. When I called Bittman as "Mr. Rivers," Bittman hemmed and hawed about the price. He didn't know what it was. "I'll have to get back to you," he said. And again and again, it was back and forth to Kalmbach and then to Bittman. I was using public phone booths and so much change that to save my pants, avoid heavy bulging pockets, and an increasing dose of irritation, I bought myself a busman's money changer and hooked it on my belt.

The cost of the script for Bittman was finally settled on $25,000. I stayed out of the negotiations. Getting involved in that would have put me blindfolded in a mine field. To get the money in Bittman's hands, I called Bittman and told him to come down to the lobby of his office building. I asked him to describe what he was wearing. I then told him to walk over to the shelf next to the lobby telephones as soon as he got off the elevator where he would find a package waiting for him. I made sure he couldn't see me as I watched him pick up the brown envelope with the cash inside and head back upstairs to his office. Traveling to Washington to make this delivery, I learned that screening devices for checking travelers' personal belongings were being installed at airports because of the increase in the number of hijackings. To avoid detection of what I was carrying, I stepped out of line, had a coughing fit, and left the airport to take the train.

After delivering Bittman's "price," I began to have a series of long, tortuous conversations with the "writer's wife," Dorothy Hunt. On July 11, Kalmbach had called me to give me Dorothy Hunt's telephone number, instructing me to deal with her from now on. I don't know who put her in charge of arranging delivery of the rest of the money, but as soon as I spoke with her, the pattern and mood of the calls changed dramatically. She acted like a gambling casino pit boss, directing the dealer, counting

255

the chips, figuring the odds, making sure her cut was secure. She didn't want to listen to the strictures binding my position as the courier of the money. She also raised the ante each time I spoke with her.

At first, she told me that she had lost her job over the Watergate scandal including her medical benefits. She said somebody had to take care of those. She started calculating everybody's needs and came up with a minimum figure of $3,000 a month, but as she didn't want to worry about a monthly delivery from the post man, it was better, she said, to get a big chunk up front to relieve the pressure on everybody. "So let's start with $10,000 or $15,000 apiece to get this thing off the ground," she said. She wanted the advance to cover five months of living expenses. She said Barker, Sturgis, Gonzales, and Martinez needed at least $14,000 apiece and that Barker needed another $10,000 for bail, $10,000 more under the table, and $3,000 for "other expenses." Twenty-five grand apiece were needed for Sturgis, Gonzales, and Martinez's attorneys. I told Mrs. Hunt to slow down. Now she was talking about $400,000 or maybe $450,000. That wasn't even close to the amount Dean had told Kalmbach to raise when they met in Lafayette Park.

When I told Mrs. Hunt that I had no room to negotiate and that it was pointless to present me with a shopping list of who needed what, she said people were starting to get desperate. They felt they were being abandoned. She added a new name when she told me that one of those who needed money was a guy named Liddy. He was involved in the break-in along with the "writer" but hadn't yet been charged with anything. That was news. Hunt's name had been found in an address book kept by one of the Watergate burglars. So had the name Colson. Now Mrs. Hunt was adding another name to the stew. I was a stranger to Mrs. Hunt, and yet she was telling me something that proved Hunt's connection to Colson in the White House. With Liddy in the picture the ring of involvement was widening, and I was learning more than I wanted to know. That was the first time I heard the name Liddy. The way she spoke about him, however, made me feel that she was looking for a way to deal him out of the game as quickly as she could. Liddy had to get some of the money, but just one payment and that was it, she said. Others had to be covered, lots of others whom she said were more important than Liddy. Living expenses were high for all these other people. Money was needed over and under the table. (I doubted many people in Washington really knew the difference.) She said that her husband and the other defendants wouldn't have to go to jail for very long because meetings were going on about that and about pardons and immunity.

The pressure that was building behind the scenes for the payment of increasingly large sums of money to those connected directly and indirectly to the Watergate break-in was turning this "one-shot deal" into a multiheaded tapeworm. It had some appetite, and to feed it, I had to meet Kalmbach on four different occasions to pick up additional sums of money. The first installment was the $75,000 I took out of the Statler Hilton in a laundry bag. The next dump in my lap was at the Regency Hotel in New York where I walked out with $40,000. The third course of the burglars' meal, $28,900, was again given to me at the Statler Hilton in Washington. Kalmbach gave me the last amount off the menu as we sat in a car outside the Airporter Motel at the Orange County Airport in California. It consisted of $75,000 in cash.

I delivered a total of $154,000 to Dorothy Hunt in four separate installments: $40,000, $43,000, $18,000 and $53,000. She was never satisfied with the amount of money I gave her. She never believed that I didn't have (and didn't want) the power to determine the breadth of financial support she said was necessary to keep things afloat. Neither Kalmbach nor I knew whether she was delivering what those involved were supposed to receive. She kept telling me about Barker's problems down south; that he needed a lot of cash to keep the lid on things in Miami. Again, she talked about Liddy as if she was trying to give him the shaft. She told me she was worried that Liddy's wife might crack under the strain. Mrs. Liddy was a school teacher and was frightened that she might lose her job if it was discovered that her husband was involved. Dorothy Hunt seemed to want to help Liddy's wife and yet get rid of her at the same time.

When phone booth arrangements were made for me to contact Liddy, he told me he wasn't going to break. He said he wasn't running for cover; he was just not talking. He needed money for his lawyer, Peter Maroulis, in Poughkeepsie and for his family. He sounded frustrated that the

257

Watergate fiasco would never have happened if he had been better advised as to what the break-in was supposed to accomplish. Liddy was in it up to his eyeballs and felt that those in the White House who were responsible for shoving it down his throat were now going to try and cover it up and would end up selling the President down the river. Liddy said that if he was the only one left to protect the President, so be it. He said he had no intention of opening his mouth to anyone. Liddy made it very clear that he had no use for John Dean. He knew other people were demanding more and more money but he felt that he couldn't stop it. Liddy said he felt abandoned and that he was worried about his wife and kids. The more he stuck to his guns, he said, the less chance he had of getting the money he needed to live on or to pay his lawyer.

For my part I told Kalmbach that any money earmarked for Liddy should go directly to him and not pass through the Hunts' hands. I did this not to keep Liddy quiet, but to keep him from getting screwed. Kalmbach passed the word back and then called me with the okay to bypass Mrs. Hunt. I made two deliveries of money to Liddy, $8,000 and $18,000.

Except for Bittman's $25,000, I made all my money drops at Washington's National Airport. It was an ideal place because it had lockers, phone booths, lounges, and balconies where I could stand and observe the pickups without any fear of being spotted or identified. When Liddy picked up a key to a locker I left in an envelope on a window ledge across from the Eastern Airlines counter, I watched his movements from an airport balcony. Only then did I realize that Liddy was the "Mr. George" who had been sent from CREEP to check my records the previous January. His plans to spy on the Democrats were in shambles. ("I was on the bridge," Liddy testified some years later in the United States Tax Court, defending himself against the IRS, "when the carrier hit the reef.") At the time, I never acknowledged to Liddy that I had met him before as "Mr. George."

When I met with Kalmbach in California to pick up the last batch of cash for delivery, we had a heart to heart talk as we sat in his car in the parking lot at the Orange County Airport.

"Tony," Kalmbach asked me with a look of desperation on his face, "what's your opinion of all this?"

258

"Well, Herb," I answered, "something here sure isn't kosher." Kalmbach gave me a blank stare. He said he didn't know what "kosher" meant. "You might be the President's lawyer," I told him, "but you sure don't know anything about life in the streets." "This is definitely not your ball game, Herb," I said. "Whatever has happened, we started with no negotiations, then we got into negotiations; we started with $75,000 plus a yard and now we're into something like $220,000, and we're only approaching half of what they probably want. I know that in the next conversation with Hunt or whoever else I talk with, that figure has to go up. I know your feelings in the matter, Herb. I know how we started. What you said about it all being legal and moral and humanitarian, but it's leading in a different direction. It's a dangerous situation. It's time to quit." Kalmbach and I agreed it was time to do just that.

Soon after we parted company, Dean and Fred LaRue, a key assistant to John Mitchell, Chairman of CREEP, insisted that Kalmbach dig in and raise still more money. Kalmbach refused. On September 19, 1972, I flew to Washington and, without ever letting him see me, watched LaRue as he picked up all the remaining money I had in my possession. I was finished with the White House—or so I thought.

I N January 1973 Caulfield called me once again and asked me to play courier for the delivery of a message from Dean to McCord. According to Caulfield, I was to say the following: "A year is a long time, your wife and family will be taken care of, you will be rehabilitated with employment when this is all over." Telling Dean he didn't want to deliver the message himself, Caulfield said he then suggested that maybe I could call McCord over the telephone, anonymously, and just tell him that the message had come from Caulfield. According to Caulfield, earlier McCord had sent him a letter threatening to turn everything into a "scorched desert" and warning that "every tree in the forest would fall." Caulfield explained that McCord was apparently angry that the White House was trying to put the blame on the CIA for the break-in. When he got McCord's letter, Caulfield immediately called Dean but when he found that Dean wasn't available, he read the letter over the phone to Fred Fielding. Caulfield said he then headed over to the White House to deliver the letter in person, and by the time he got there, Dean was waiting for him.

There was a loud silence on my end of the phone as I listened to Caulfield again plead our friendship as the basis for asking me to deliver Dean's message to McCord. First I gave Caulfield a flat no, but before I could end the conversation, he spilled out his plea for help. He was in California at the time attending a conference of the Federal Drug Task Force at the San Clemente Inn. "Tony, I'm here for meetings," Caulfield said. "I'm very busy. I can't do a thing like this from here. I wouldn't ask you except I know you're a friend. I wouldn't ask anyone else. I don't know who else I can ask. Things are being pushed on me. I'll lose my job if I don't deliver on this. I don't want to get into it or I wouldn't ask you to do it." As he talked, he began to crack, almost sob.

"Jack," I spoke carefully, "you have to realize it is a very unusual request—and for a lot of reasons. This isn't the same situation as last June. McCord's trial is about to start. He could be a witness. This isn't something to tinker with. And McCord is a wireman. Whatever is delivered you can expect will be recorded."

"Tony, if this ever comes out," Caulfield responded, "I will definitely admit that I asked you to do this. As a friend."

Caulfield's claim of friendship was following me like a bad shadow. I finally agreed to deliver the message to McCord, but after this, I warned Caulfield, there would be no more collections, no more offerings at the White House rail. I was finished. At the time of Caulfield's call for help—just one more time—I was living in the town of Day in my home overlooking Great Sacandaga Lake. I was all through using code names for the White House, taping locker keys in phone booths and under window sills, keeping money "drops" under surveillance, carrying "lunch" bags and money changers. I wanted to be left alone to start my own business as a licensed private investigator in the Albany area, tend my chickens, and split my firewood. There wasn't any doubt in my mind of what would happen "if this ever comes out," as Caulfield put it. It was all surfacing, just as I had told Kalmbach it would when the money came on stage in June 1972. Any call now to McCord would bring the Day of Revelation that much closer, not postpone it. I tried to tell Caulfield that sending these words to McCord would backfire.

Rather than call from my house, I went to a roadside phone booth several miles away. When McCord answered the phone, I didn't identify myself; I simply said I had a message from Caulfield and told McCord to go to the phone booth (the same one he was instructed to use the previous June when Caulfield wanted to deliver his "sympathy" message to him). I waited a sufficient length of time to allow McCord to get to the phone and then called. When McCord answered, I delivered the message, at the end of which the barely audible McCord asked me if it meant he was supposed to plead guilty. I told him that all I was delivering was a message, not a promise, and that it was up to him to draw the inferences. But it didn't take a genius to read between the lines.

On March 20, 1973, Federal District Court Judge John J. Sirica sat in his chambers in the Federal District Court House in Washington, D.C., and read a letter McCord had sent him. As history now records, his letter blew the lid off the Watergate coverup. In just three days McCord would be sentenced by Judge Sirica for his part in the break-in. McCord had kept his silence during the trial, but since no moves had been made to save his skin or that of any of his fellow burglars on trial he broke his silence with a loud crash. In writing his letter, McCord had short-circuited the White House, refusing to wait until after he was sentenced to see if the White House would go over Sirica's head and pardon him. As he predicted in his earlier letter to Caulfield, the trees in the forest were falling. The White House Rose Garden was becoming a "scorched desert." Judge Sirica read McCord's letter aloud in open court, and the Watergate firestorm soon followed.

O N Easter Sunday night, April 22, 1973, I received another phone call from Kalmbach.

"Have you heard?," he began the conversation.

"Heard what?," I answered.

"Have you been down to the Court House?"

"No, I haven't. Not yet."

"Well, I've been down there. I met with the U.S. Attorney's office— with a man named Silbert and two others, Glanzer and a Mr. Campbell. I told the truth, Tony, and I know you will, too. They're going to call

261

you, Tony. They asked me to get your address and give them your phone number."

As predicted, Assistant United States Attorney Earl J. Silbert called me at home on Monday, April 23, and requested my appearance in his office in Washington the next morning. The call seemed extremely courteous, almost deferential. Outside the federal government's organized crime witness protection program, it was unlike a U.S. Attorney's office to give preferential treatment to anybody, and yet I felt that either Kalmbach or someone close to Nixon had paved a smooth way for my upcoming meeting with Silbert.

Entering the office of a U.S. Attorney was old hat to me. These offices were usually occupied by the elite graduates of top-level law schools who chose not to enter the law firms of Wall Street or the corporate law departments of the Fortune 500. These sharp-minded individuals had the awesome power of the federal government at their fingertips. When I entered Silbert's office, I expected a lengthy, carefully thought out debriefing of my entire career as an investigator for the President. I also expected that the basic underlying premise of all the interrogations would be honored with a vengeance. That is, nothing is disconnected until the mosaic is completed; nothing is discarded during an investigation until *everything* is known. Instead, the questions posed to me seemed peripheral, like dots on a circle. There were no arrows being shot at the bull's eye; maybe they didn't know there was one.

In contrast to what was happening outside this office—the press, Judge Sirica, and an aroused public sitting like owls on a branch ready to pounce—the atmosphere inside Silbert's office was docile, almost timid. My only irritation was having Silbert's associate, Donald E. Campbell, sit behind me taking notes like a fly on the back of my neck. Sitting behind a witness or a suspect is a standard interrogation technique. Its use is meant to keep the truth from running out the back of someone's head while an interrogator tries to pull it out the front. When I talk to a man, I want to look him in the eye. I waited for the hard questions, not because I thought the answers would uncover any criminal act on my part, but because I knew these men were paid to be thorough and uncompromising. But the tough questions didn't come. Although I didn't doubt the integrity of my interrogators, somehow I felt that a squeeze was being put on them not to go too far. What was Watergate all about? I wasn't sure Silbert's office was willing to find out. I kept telling them not to ask me what I thought about what someone else had said or what I thought about a particular event that didn't involve me. I wanted to be asked in the same way I conducted interrogations when I was with the Police Department: what, who, where, when, how—what did you *do*?, who did you *speak* with?, where did you *go*?, when were you *there*?, how did you *operate*? Get the details, then match the cards against what you learn from others. Don't start with answers and then expect the person you're questioning to give you back the questions. That's for game shows, not for criminal investigations.

My interview with Silbert and company lasted, with a break for lunch, from approximately 10:30 in the morning until 2:30 that afternoon. The subjects covered my hiring for the President by John Ehrlichman, my relationship with Caulfield, my meeting in January 1972 with "Mr. George" in New York, and the amounts and the delivery schedule for the payments made to the Watergate burglars, their families, and their attorneys. There was little, if any, discussion about John Dean. I wondered why. As far as I was concerned, Dean was up to his sleek cheeks in the whole Watergate affair—before and after the break-in. Why send me to check out the security of the offices of the DNC if he didn't know what information the White House wanted about O'Brien? It couldn't have been just his idle curiosity.

On April 28, I was notified that my appearance before the Grand Jury was scheduled for May 1. Anxious to know precisely what Silbert and his associates had asked me, Caulfield peppered me at home with a number of phone calls. He had no idea whether he was a target of the Watergate investigation or a witness without a problem. Caulfield knew nothing about my role in delivering the money to the Watergate defendants or to their attorneys, and I wasn't about to tell him. It was for his own good. Using arguments of our friendship again, Caulfield badgered me for inside information on the scope of Silbert's interrogation. I didn't tell him a thing. I didn't think he was calling just for his own benefit. Accordingly, whatever I said was not going to be kept in confidence. To verify my own suspicions about Caulfield's reliability, I decided to give

263

him a little test. I also had a feeling that Caulfield was about to lose control of his life. His vis-a-vis world was in ashes.

When I first joined BOSSI as a detective, Lieutenant Tom Crane taught me something I never forgot about how to test somebody's ability to keep things confidential. "Pick out something only you know," Crane said. "Leak it and wait until it comes back to you. Never tell your wife, your kids, your friends, anyone, what this piece of information is. Save it. After you use it, no matter how many times it is repeated afterwards, you'll know where the leak started." To test Caulfield, I asked him to meet me in a bar in Washington. When he pressed me with questions about what I told Silbert instead of what Silbert asked me, I made up a story about being in a closet in a hotel room while Mitchell and Haldeman discussed the amount of money to be given to the Watergate burglars. I told Caulfield I kept a pillow case over my head just in case the closet door was opened by mistake. I told him nobody was to know the face of the man delivering the money.

Less than twenty-four hours after I told Caulfield this story, I received a phone call from Silbert. "Ulasewicz," Silbert commanded, "I want you in my office tomorrow morning. Make sure you're there!" Traveling back to Washington as ordered, I was kept standing in the hallway outside Silbert's office for almost two hours. I felt like a coatrack. Everyone working in his office avoided looking at me. A hello became a grunt. When I was finally signalled to go inside, Silbert, Glanzer, and Campbell had an executioner's pall about them. "You're lying, Ulasewicz. You didn't tell us everything," Silbert shot out.

"Wait a minute," I said. "Before you go any further, I know why I'm here." Silbert looked puzzled. "You got a little story about a pillow case over my head in a hotel closet. Right?" Silbert began to smile. The tension in the room instantly evaporated. Silbert almost tripped over his chair as he sat back and laughed. "The story was a complete fabrication," I continued telling him. "I fed it to Caulfield. I hated to do it, but I had to check him out. I had to verify something I really didn't want to believe might happen. It did. I'm sorry about that. I'm sorry about him."

On May 17, 1973, the day the Senate Watergate hearings opened for business, I was sitting at home in my living room watching the event on television. I watched and listened to the proceedings more intently than to anything else I had ever done. And that covered a lot of territory! As I sat there transfixed, I knew my turn before the microphones and the television cameras and the klieg lights would be coming soon. Ehrlichman couldn't fire me now for surfacing in public. He had been discharged by the same President for whom he had hired me to work. When I sat down to testify, I expected an exhaustive public examination of my work for the White House. This expectation was based on my impression of what I saw and heard Senator Howard Baker of Tennessee promise on the opening day of the Senate hearings. He had told the audience that the Watergate Committee would "inquire into every fact and follow every lead." So I took Baker at his word.

After McCord testified, referring to me as "the mystery man with the New York accent," my phone at home began ringing off the wall. McCord didn't identify me by name, but he didn't have to. Senate Committee lawyers and investigators were having a field day leaking information to the press. The show was on. With the White House under siege, everyone was fair game, including me.

I made my first appearance before the Senate Watergate Committee on Wednesday, May 23. Before stepping into the spotlight, I waited alone in a room in the New Senate Office Building. Initially, I had no idea what I was going to be asked about when I sat down before the world. While waiting to be called before the cameras, I got hungry. When I found out that I had plenty of time before I went on stage, I left to get some lunch. To avoid the curious onlookers—"Who's that?"— lurking in the Senate cafeteria, I walked to the railroad station. Upon entering, I passed a newsstand, and there, on a rack, I saw something that made my heart sink. There in stone black and white blistering silence was my picture on the front page of the *Washington Star.* The picture was a close up, full face, and the headline, in bold black letters, read: *SPY.* Suddenly, I lost my appetite. I felt caged and expendable. I was no spy. I was a licensed private investigator who had broken no law and breached no confidence. I felt my guts harden like quick-drying cement. My picture had been leaked to the press. I had met with Lenzner and Assistant Majority Counsel Marc Lackritz on May 8 and again with Lenzner and Schure on May 19 to discuss my role as the President's

265

private eye. Nothing I had told any of them had remained, as promised, confidential. I had been worried about Caulfield leaking information. I should have been more concerned about the men leading the investigation into the Watergate scandal.

Before being called in to testify, Lenzner introduced me to Chief Counsel to the Senate Committee, Sam Dash, in front of a water cooler. Lenzner acted as if he was showing off a specimen, not a human being. The meeting with Dash was perfunctory. Dash said he was only going to ask me about the call Caulfield made to me about wanting to contact McCord right after the Watergate burglary and the call I made to McCord in January 1973 to deliver the veiled clemency message if McCord kept his mouth shut and plead guilty. That was it. Nothing more, nothing less. I understood immediately what Dash was trying to do: build a case against the President of the United States. If Nixon was behind the clemency offer to McCord, he was finished. I was just one small piece of Dash's case. He was going to try and present it like a trial lawyer in a courtroom, piece by piece, building block by building block. But I wondered how long he really expected his neat orchestration to last. No matter how serious, hard to believe, outrageous, and damning these Senate hearings would be, they were being held in a setting Hollywood couldn't match. None of the Senators were going to let Dash remain the director of the whole show. This was big-time politics, entertainment, and the headwaters of an impeachment proceeding rolled into one. The script for the show was the bringing down of a President. Dash wasn't going to be the only one allowed to direct its ending.

When I sat down to testify before the Senate Watergate Committee, I was broke. I had delivered over $200,000 in cash, filled my busman's money changer with enough quarters, dimes and nickels to fill ten piggy banks, turned over all my receipt and expense records to Senate Committee investigators that showed where all the money went, and now sat before the world with empty pockets. Everyone started diving for cover after the arrest of the Watergate burglars, and any hope I had of receiving my promised salary evaporated. Whatever money Nixon's reelection committee had left soon started rotting in the Watergate spotlight. Gordon Liddy, the man from CREEP who first appeared as "Mr. George" to check my records and approve my continued work had sealed his lips and as a result was powerless to rectify the financial damage done to me in the aftermath of Watergate. There was nothing he could do to help me, although I had made sure he wasn't stiffed by Dorothy Hunt when all that hush money was being passed around. Kalmbach, Mitchell, Ehrlichman, Haldeman, Dean, LaRue, and Stans— everyone who ever had a part, directly or indirectly, in paying my salary, providing expense money or dumping the hush money in my lap—were in such deep trouble they had no time for me. Because I was never listed as an employee with CREEP, those who were named to close the books on work of the reelection committee said they had no obligation to pay me. Look elsewhere, call the White House, ask the President, don't call us, we'll call you.

Beyond my police pension, I had no financial resources to support my family. My pension was too small to pay all my bills, and so I found myself taking out a mortgage on my home in Queens, borrowing from my insurance policies, and, in humiliating desperation, accepting a loan from a relative. My son, Peter, was in college, and my other boy, Tom, was in law school. I had daughters getting married and absolutely no funds available to fulfill my dream of opening up my own detective agency. The only money I had coming in aside from my pension was the small allowance the Senate Watergate Committee and the Special Prosecutor's Office provided me to help cover expenses traveling to and from Washington. I was now branded with the scar of Watergate. As far as my career was concerned, it didn't matter whether I was only to be a witness for the prosecution as Silbert had said or a defendant facing a conviction and probable jail. The greedy amateurs that President Nixon allowed himself to be surrounded by had torn the White House loose from its moorings. I felt a tidal wave about to pour over my life, and there wasn't anything I could do to stop it. For a minute, the choices I made as a kid not to stick up the pool hall instead of cleaning it didn't seem to make any difference. I began kicking myself for not walking off the bridge on Chappaquiddick and returning to BOSSI. But I knew I couldn't live the rest of my life looking over my shoulder or change who I was. Instead, I just looked up at the Senators with their faces all polished and ready to shine in the lights and said to myself "fire away boys, fire away. I've got nothing to hide."

Before being sworn in, one of the Committee Senators asked me if I had a statement I wanted to read. "Do I need one?" I asked him. "Should I go out and get one?" Starting off as planned, Dash's questions centered on my anonymous contacts with McCord; these were the only specifics he asked about. When Dash finished his questions, the rest of the Committee's questioning just filled time. I was surprised. Some of the things I said while answering Senator Howard Baker's questions triggered a lot of laughter, but comedy wasn't my intent. I was just being myself, as when Baker asked me if I thought my "wiremen were better than McCord's wiremen." I wasn't a wireman, but I told Baker that "any old retired man in the New York City Police Department who would become involved in a thing like that . . . would not have walked in with an army, that is for sure." Besides being a crime, the busted burglary at the Watergate offices of the Democratic National Committee was a farce. If my testimony pointed out how foolish that whole enterprise was, the packed house in the Senate caucus room was entitled to react in any way it chose.

When Baker asked me how I might have obtained the information being sought by the burglars, I answered in part that besides trying to bug or break into the place, one of the first things you do is to get yourself on a mailing list. In fact, one of the first things I did after being assigned to work for Nixon's reelection committee, was to join a Democratic fund-raising organization called the "'72 Sponsors Club." Using the name of my brother Leo and his home address in Queens, New York, I contributed $72 to the club and got on their mailing list. I mailed in this same amount each month and was soon notified that I had qualified as a sponsor. I told Baker that once you get yourself on a mailing list it's hard to get off of it. For the next several years—before and beyond Watergate—I was invited (through my good brother Leo) to attend every major Democratic fund-raising dinner in America, as well as several Democratic congressional black tie dinners in Washington. In fact, I received an invitation to attend the 1974 Democratic Congressional Dinner which honored, among others, Carl Albert, Speaker of the House of Representatives who had had some bad press thrown in his face a few years back when he tipped a few too many at the Zebra Lounge in Washington and got into a fight with his wife that spilled outside onto the sidewalk. I was asked by the White House to check out what happened *after* the fact. For his transgression, Albert got his absolution from his fellow congressmen in a hurry.

I (Leo) also received mail about the activities of the Finance Committee of the Democratic Party, together with several complimentary letters that thanked me for my support. My contribution was officially recognized in 1974 when "Leo" was invited to become a member of the Finance Committee of the Democratic Party. "You have always been instrumental in supplying the Democratic National Committee with the funds it needed," my invitation read, "to carry out its leadership role in administering and directing the course of the Democratic Party." In 1974, the year Richard Nixon resigned the Presidency, I, as his former private investigator, was invited to become a member of the Democratic Party's Finance Committee. Since I was busy at the time preparing to testify as a government witness in the Watergate conspiracy trial, I declined the invitation.

Neither Baker nor any other Senator asked me about the specifics of any of my investigations, although they must have known about them because Lenzner had made a list of them for the committee. My financial records, including receipts for all my travel and lodging expenses, were also turned over to the committee. I was never asked about my trip to check out the offices of the DNC at the end of May, who asked me to go there, or who was behind that request. Caulfield's call to me the afternoon after the Watergate break-in was never explored, although John Dean was the man who had ordered the call to be made. I expected to be asked about my meeting with Dean when Caulfield was clearing out his office in the Executive Office Building. Again I wasn't. Dean, I concluded, was obviously being protected for star billing as a witness. No one asked me if I had any documents or White House memos about any of my investigations. While I had no intention of playing cute with anybody, I wasn't going to volunteer information unless I was asked for it. I wasn't asked about meeting "Mr. George" or hearing his off-the-wall intelligence plans for the campaign, or about Colson and the Brookings Institution, or about Simmons in Wisconsin. I didn't mind not being asked; I just didn't understand why I wasn't.

The questions Lenzner, Shure, and Senators Daniel Inouye, Edward

269

Gurney, Joseph Montoya, and Herman Talmadge asked me focused primarily on how much money was involved and how I delivered it to the Watergate burglars and their lawyers. I was pressed to explain what I understood was the purpose of the money and the real purpose of the message I delivered to McCord. These "will you please look over your shoulder" questions were clearly designed to get me to admit whether I knew it was "hush" money when I delivered it or an offer of White House clemency to McCord, in exchange for his silence, when I called him. These efforts were now linked to proving that the White House (and the President) tried to sabotage the Watergate investigation. The delivery of the money was accomplished only after Kalmbach and I were satisfied it had been approved from the top as a gesture of help. When it turned sour, I quit, and I told Kalmbach to do the same. Passing the clemency message to McCord was accomplished the way Western Union would have done it. Senator Inouye asked me whether I considered the activities I was involved with "were completely legal." I answered "Yes, Sir," but when Inouye asked me whether I was aware that I was an accessory "to the crime of obstructing a criminal investigation" when I delivered the message to McCord, I answered "Yes, I knew that it was wrong." In hindsight of course it was and that's what I meant by my answer, but the message itself should have never existed.

After testifying, I flew to the Albany Airport to pick up my car. There, on the newsstands again, I saw—as I would for months to come—columns of ink pumped from the confidential well of the staff of the Senate Select Committee listing my investigations and linking me with Ehrlichman's "Plumbers" whom I knew nothing about. I was described as a "seducer" of women I never met or planned to meet and as a would-be "procurer" for prostitutes at the Democratic National Convention. I was also targeted erroneously as "the fat man who investigated Senator Muskie." Information I first gave in confidence to the staff investigators of the Senate Watergate Committee leaked like a broken faucet into the notebooks of reporters.

I decided to test Terry Lenzner and Senator Weicker's assistant, William Shure, to prove the point to myself just as I had tested Caulfield with the story about the pillow case. When I described my trip to the movie house to see Emile de Antonio's Millhouse, I changed the facts

270

just a hair and told Lenzner and Shure that "I had my pocket picked" instead of telling them that a guy started pawing me in the theater and that I had threatened to break his arm if he didn't leave me alone. Sure enough, what I told Lenzner and Shure showed up in the newspapers. "No, no," Lenzner pleaded with me when I confronted him after seeing it in print. "It wasn't me. It was Shure. He leaked it."

"A pox on both your houses," I told Lenzner.

After my first appearance before the Senate Watergate Committee, the press began a non-stop series of phone calls to follow up on what my testimony revealed and the leaks about my assignments they were getting from the committee itself. One reporter who called me was Bob Woodward of *The Washington Post*. He called me several times during the next several weeks. No matter how clever he tried to be, I could tell by his questions that he wasn't just calling me to verify what someone else had told him. Woodward was groping, trying to figure out where I fit in. He and his pal Bernstein (the siamese reporters I called "Woodstein") had the White House in the cross hairs of their pens, but Woodward told me he didn't know anything about me until I appeared before the Watergate committee. Before I testified, "Woodstein" only knew that there was an "unidentified source" who delivered some of CREEP's cash to the Watergate burglars. That meant the Deep Throat "Woodstein" later identified as being their big leak had a very short-term link to CREEP, or Deep Throat did know about me and was deliberately hiding my existence, or *I* was Deep Throat—which I wasn't. If Deep Throat really existed and operated from a base inside the White House, he or she didn't know very much. And if Deep Throat functioned outside the White House, then whoever kept Deep Throat informed wasn't connected to anyone inside the White House who really knew what was going on. Deep Throat didn't know anything about Tony Ulasewicz. Why not? I was there all the time.

On July 18, I was back again to testify in front of the Senate Watergate Committee. This time I had a lawyer. "What did you get a lawyer for?," Lenzner asked me. "So I'd have the pleasure of not talking to you anymore," I answered. I didn't like having a lawyer sit next to me, however, whispering in my ear how to answer a question. I do best when I'm on my own. But Lenzner, no matter how much he denied responsibility for the leaks to the press, had forced my hand. I got a lawyer because I didn't want to talk to him anymore or even with anyone connected to him. I had given my full cooperation to the Senate committee and had answered every question asked of me. I simply didn't like the games that were being played with the information I provided. I wasn't Lenzner's puppet, and I wasn't afraid of anything I had to say before the Watergate Committee.

Again, none of the Senators asked me about specifics. Inouye and Baker came close; they pressed against the edge, but they didn't step over the line. Senator Inouye asked me, "What sort of discreet investigations were you required to carry out?" I answered "they were of a various nature and ranged from investigations of backgrounds of persons to organizations and types of that." Inouye didn't push any further into the underbrush. Baker asked me to describe what Ehrlichman had told me in 1969 would be my "probable assignments" if I was hired by the White House. I answered in general that there would be confidential investigations of political figures in both the Republican and Democratic parties. There would be background checks on would-be visitors to the White House, on persons seeking or being sought for political appointment, and investigations into certain matters the White House didn't want the Secret Service or the FBI conducting.

I sensed that Senator Baker was itching to dig into the details of my investigations, but like a good, cautious trial lawyer who wanted to know the answer before he asked the question, he veered away from the temptation. I was surprised, however, that he began his questioning as if he were setting the stage for a vaudeville show and not an interrogation. Baker, it suddenly appeared, was to be the straight man to my comedian act. It was nice to know that, as Baker said, I had provided the committee "with at least a half dozen titles for books and novels" (he suggested The Ulasewicz Caper and I told him I'd probably have to pay for it). But when he asked, "Who thought you up?," and the audience burst into laughter, I felt my whole career sliding under the Watergate tidal wave as the spontaneous banter with Baker continued. When I answered Baker on the same wavelength—"I don't know, but maybe my parents,"—the audience roared again. The committee hearings had become a show called entertainment today. I'm no spoil sport, and maybe it was a healthy release in the gloom and doom to have that moment with Baker. However, I wanted Baker to get into the nitty gritty of what it all meant to me, what my story really was.

Baker asked me in general what my arrangement had been under the agreement I made with Ehrlichman in 1969, but when he asked me "of whom and about what" did I investigate, I didn't get a chance to open my mouth before Baker said, "Let me say this, Mr. Chairman. It is my understanding that Mr. Ulasewicz will once again return for further testimony in another category of testimony." I affirmed Baker's assumption and said, "That's correct." Baker then cut off the inquiry and said, "So we will abbreviate this inquiry at this point, with the full understanding that we can pursue that aspect of it later." Senator Weicker said he wanted Baker to continue the line of questioning he started, but Baker responded that Committee Chairman, Senator Sam Ervin, whispered in his ear that "if we don't get on with this hearing, we'll still be here when the last trembling tones of Gabriel's trumpet fades into ultimate silence." At that point I wished Baker, Ervin, and I could have found a nice quiet bar, had a couple of drinks together, and straightened everything out.

The one Senator on the Watergate Committee who wasn't interested in any humorous diversions, unintentional or otherwise, was the newly elected kid on the block, the millionaire moralist from Connecticut, Senator Lowell Weicker. In what I considered to be a cheap shot, he asked me if I "dealt in dirt at the direction of the White House." My attorney, John Sutter, leaned over at this point and whispered in my ear to say "allegations of it." And that, like a parrot, is what I answered. I didn't like being programmed to respond, but nevertheless I was stuck with the answer, even though I thought Weicker was driving down the wrong road. I never would have accepted the position as a private investigator for President Nixon if all I was supposed to do was slink around and find evidence to discredit or embarrass people. I didn't turn in my detective's shield to become a sleazy peeping tom. Besides that, if there was any "dirt" to be found in any of my investigations, I didn't put it there. I didn't drive Mary Jo Kopechne off the bridge at Chappaquiddick, lobby for government contracts like O'Brien or Dyson-Kissner, use the Small Business Administration as a front for patronage or funding politicians' campaigns, peddle my influence, break into the

273

offices of the DNC, make a fool of myself in the Zebra Lounge like Speaker of the House Carl Albert had done, or plan a fire bombing of the Brookings Institute. I ignored the one investigation where I was told I would find real dirt and that was reportedly in a black book floating around Washington that supposedly contained the names of politicians and White House officials involved in a call girl ring. I dismissed the assignment with a big "so what." Everybody was running around in circles with the story trying to make it bigger than it was. I had left it where I found it—in the garbage. If I had pursued the story, what I would have found would have been the equivalent of a skinned rabbit—someone got to it before I did.

Instead of probing me, Weicker chose to blast what he apparently—and erroneously—thought was my intentional act to be funny. He thought that somehow I was downgrading the significance of these Senate hearings rather than uplifting them to the tragic level of his perceptions. Weicker was making it clear, at my expense, that he had come to Washington and found the "dirt" in these Senate hearings and that I was rolling in it. He and he alone was "Mr. Clean." I resented being tarred and feathered like this. I was licensed by the State of New York to conduct my business. I paid money to the government for the privilege of working as an investigator, and I had no regrets or mea culpas to express for being hired as President Nixon's private eye. I didn't like the outcome, and maybe I picked the wrong President, but I wasn't about to apologize for my skills as an investigator.

Regardless of Weicker's efforts to stick me with his pins, I was excused from the witness chair after the Chairman of the Senate Committee, Senator Sam Ervin, thanked me for my full cooperation. I looked forward to my promised return to the witness chair when, I was told, the specifics of my work, other than as a courier of money and messages, would be explored in detail. I would then, I decided, come back alone, without a lawyer, sit across from Weicker and challenge him to name the assignments where I went hunting for his "dirt." I wondered what he'd have to say about Chappaquiddick. I never expected that I would not be called back to the witness chair, but that's exactly what happened after the Senate Committee, including Weicker, voted to end the hearings.

On March 6, 1974, a little less than a year after I surfaced as "the mystery voice with the New York accent" before the Senate Watergate Committee, I was back in Washington at the request of J. Fred Buzhardt, the Special Counsel to the President appointed by Nixon after John Dean sold out and jumped ship in May 1973. At the time of his appointment, Buzhardt, a West Point classmate of Alexander Haig, Jr. (they graduated a year apart), was general counsel to the Department of Defense. I met with Buzhardt in John Dean's old office. Buzhardt said he wanted to know my real feelings about Nixon and where I was going to stand when the impeachment hearings began. He said he couldn't find anything in any White House files that was stamped with my initials or any memos I prepared, or any hint that I had incriminating evidence against the President in my pocket. Since I never signed or initialed anything, there was nothing there to find. But lurking in the background was an apparent feeling on the part of General Alexander Haig, who took over as White House Chief of Staff after Haldeman was booted out, that I knew something about Nixon supposedly getting part of a storehouse of cash that was left in Vietnam after the United States scrambled out of there. Although appointed by President Nixon himself, Haig, I began to think, was actually turning against the President in the final days before Nixon resigned.

In June 1974, Haig ordered the U.S. Army's Criminal Investigation Command (CIC) to conduct a high-priority, classified investigation to determine whether Nixon had stuffed his pockets with cash contributions from leaders of Southeast Asia and the Far East. Haig even went so far as to ask for confirmation as to whether Nixon had connections with organized crime and had received payoffs from the Mafia. The State Department was contacted to see if I had a passport and, if so, whether I had used it to head for Vietnam. I didn't go, but if I had I certainly wouldn't have left a trace of how I got there and back. The Army CIC spent over a month trying to verify my nonexistent trip to Southeast Asia to pick up booty for the President. The investigation went nowhere, of course, but the timing of Haig's efforts to undercut the President meant that Haig—and perhaps others—wanted the President discredited long before this.

In November 1974 I traveled to Washington again to testify for the Special Prosecutor at the Watergate conspiracy trial for the obstruction

275

of justice—the main and last big event after President Nixon resigned the Presidency in August. I was named in the Watergate obstruction of justice indictment as an unindicted co-conspirator. The delivery of the so-called hush money and the message of clemency to McCord were said to be overt acts on the part of the indicted conspirators to block the Watergate investigation from continuing. I was not named as a defendant in the indictment. I did not ask for or receive immunity from prosecution when I testified. When I first repeated my story to Richard Ben-Veniste of the Special Prosecutor's Office in preparation for my testimony, I had a great sense of relief. That office operated with a team of skilled matadors. They knew how and where to strike at the heart of a witness. There were no leaks out of that office, no glad handing or cocktail talk while handing out confidential memos or photographs to the press. I was dealing with true professionals, appointed to do one of the most difficult jobs any prosecutor's office in the history of law enforcement has ever been handed. After he finished going over a list of my investigations, Ben-Veniste said to me, "Tony, just tell us what you didn't agree to do. Then we'll know somebody else tried to do it." I reminded Ben-Veniste that I wasn't a preacher but a detective and that whether I agreed to do something or not didn't make any difference to the clowns who created the Watergate whirlpool and then sucked everybody into it.

Stepping inside Judge Sirica's courtroom in the Federal Courthouse was like old home week for me. Bill Hundley and Plato Cacheris were there representing former Attorney General John N. Mitchell. I hadn't seen them since their days as government prosecutors during the first trial of former FBI agent John Frank. They were now partners in a private law practice. "Any surprises?," Cacheris asked me before I testified. "No," I told him. "I'll tell it like it is."

Again, my testimony at the Watergate conspiracy trial centered on the delivery of the money to the Watergate burglars, their families and lawyers. My busman's money changer was introduced into evidence and tagged as exhibit 112 under the watchful eye of Judge John Sirica. After the trial, when the appeals of those convicted for obstructing justice were completed (and denied), I wrote Judge Sirica and asked him if I could please have my changer back. He graciously complied with my request and instructed the clerk to return it. In its own way, as it now sits on a shelf in the den of my home, I think of it as the symbol of Watergate.

In the Spring of 1977, I paid a visit to ex-President Nixon who at the time was still living in his Western White House at San Clemente, California, not far from the home of my daughter Manya. Before leaving New York, I wrote to the former President and told him I'd like to stop by and say hello. I received a response from one of his aides to call when I arrived in California. The President, I was informed, would be glad to see me. When I arrived for my visit with him, President Nixon and I had a heart to heart talk. In the middle of it, he asked me how the whole Watergate episode had affected my career. My answer could have taken all day. Before I could form a short response to his question, he asked me, "What was it, Tony? What did it? What do you think caused Watergate?" I paused for a moment to catch my breath. The dimension of the question was bigger than any answer I could give. I thought for a moment and said I thought it was something called greed. "You had a lot of guys around you," I told the former President, "who were trying to protect their own future at your expense." I didn't try to tell him what mistakes I thought he had made. He had enough problems.

I left California and drove to Arizona. I stopped by to pay John Ehrlichman a visit in the Federal Prison at Safford where he had been sent after his conviction in the Watergate obstruction of justice trial. The haughty demeanor, the I have the power look, once the trademark of his office, had been erased from his face. He had completely lost his sense of superiority. A plastic surgeon couldn't have done a better job. Ehrlichman told me that he had begun to search within himself to find a better way to live. He said he was also working on a book about his White House years. Before I left him, he gave me an apple, telling me that it was one of a rare strain that grew in the mountains in his native state, Washington. A friend, it seemed, had brought him a bagful and he had plenty to spare. I didn't eat the apple. I carried it out of the prison and gave it to my wife, Mary, who was waiting for me in the car in the parking lot. (She hadn't accompanied me inside because prison rules prohibited more than one visitor at a time.) We took the apple back to our hillside home in upstate New York and kept it for two weeks. Mary moved it around the house as if by doing so the apple would become immortal. Instead of eating it or just throwing it away, we watched its skin shrivel and pucker and then begin to sag. We buried it in our garden, hoping it would reproduce itself, but it didn't. It was one of a kind. As far as I'm concerned, so was Watergate. For the first time, it made a President of the United States, the one I went to work for, resign from office.

Epilogue

In November 1974, shortly before I testified in the Watergate conspir-acy trial, Richard Ben-Veniste asked me during an interview whether my income taxes were all in order. "Sure," I answered. "I don't have any problems." "Well, Tony," Ben-Veniste said, "somebody's asking questions about your tax returns and I don't know why. Do you?" "No," I answered. "I paid my taxes. I don't owe the government a penny." And I didn't. But what followed Ben-Veniste's question soon became my own Watergate nightmare.

Because so much money had passed through my hands by the time Watergate broke, on the advice of John Sutter, the lawyer who sat with me the second time I testified at the Watergate hearings, I went to see a tax specialist, Murray Kaplan, in June 1973. Sutter wanted an opinion as to whether any of the money I delivered to the Watergate burglars, their lawyers and families could be considered taxable income. During my meeting with Kaplan, he suggested that I file amended tax returns for the years 1971 and 1972 and report the expense money I had received in cash after my salary payments were cut off (but promised to resume once CREEP was formally organized). I couldn't understand how the cash advances could have been considered taxable income since I had to spend every nickel of it on my assignments—traveling, for example, back and forth to Washington, flying to Wisconsin to check out the Simmons/Segretti caper, driving to New Hampshire to check out the strength, if any, of Pete McCloskey's Presidential primary campaign, staying in hotels and renting cars.

When I sat in Kaplan's office, I was still—almost hopelessly— waiting for my salary from CREEP even though it had stopped functioning after the '72 election. I didn't think this expense money and my salary, if and when I received it, could both be taxable. I had kept exhaustive, accurate expense records of what I had spent on behalf of other people—and at their direction. Kaplan said I was wrong in not reporting the cash advances I had received. I couldn't understand how, since I was also the conduit for advancing expense money to Caulfield as well as paying his American Express charges. But I went along with Kaplan's advice and let him prepare amended tax returns for 1971 and 1972. I spent my last dime paying for taxes on money I never used for myself. Kaplan said it would all work out when I finally got my back pay. "Fat chance of that," I thought at the time.

To the amended tax returns themselves, Kaplan added a note of his own:

> Taxpayer received monies during the year to compensate him for his future services and expenses to be incurred and disbursed by him in carrying out his assignment. Taxpayer was under the erroneous impression that such monies received need not be reported in income until his services are completed and expenses fully accounted for. Taxpayer has been advised by counsel that such monies received should have been included in gross income in the year received. Accordingly, they are being included in this Form 1040X.

The amended tax returns for 1971 and 1972 were mailed on July 25, 1973, and I thought that was the end of the matter. In fact, in early 1974, I received a form letter from the IRS telling me that everything had been accepted as filed for 1971 and 1972.

But in July 1974, I found myself sitting in front of two IRS agents in an IRS office in Brooklyn, where I had been asked to come for an interview. The agents were assigned to the criminal investigation division of the IRS. One of Sutter's assistants, F. Dana Winslow, went with me. I had no concern about what I said to the agents; I wanted someone on my side of the fence to hear what *everybody* said at this conference. Winslow said he wanted to tape record the session, but the IRS agents, to my astonishment, refused to permit that to be done because it was against their policy. They said a summary of the interview would be typed up and given to me if the case ever went to trial. I felt the IRS was maneuvering me into position to be pushed off a cliff.

The atmosphere in Brooklyn was nothing like the one I had experienced in the Special Prosecutor's Office during the Watergate investigation. In Washington, I had won the respect and appreciation—at least for my credibility (and you can't invent that)—of·people in charge of one of the most serious criminal prosecutions in the history of this country. In contrast, in the Brooklyn office, I had the distinct feeling that the two agents had harpoons ready to throw at me with instructions not to miss. I couldn't understand why the government had begun to move against me. Before this interview, no one had ever asked to see my records or had notified me that there was any deficiency in any of my tax payments. When these agents told me that I was the subject of a criminal investigation, I simply couldn't fathom what the government wanted from me. This criminal investigation was way outside normal channels. Why single me out, I wondered, when so much money had exchanged hands between CREEP and the White House to cover up Watergate? I was the only one who wasn't running for cover. Who, I questioned, was really calling the shots? Probably some young turk who wanted to make a name for himself or someone who still had me mixed up in his head with the wrong people.

Piecing things together, in response to the agents' questions, I told them that from January 1 through September of 1971 my salary was being paid through the office of Herb Kalmbach, Nixon's personal attorney. It was duly reported on my tax return. After that time, in place of my salary, I received the $20,000 cash advance to cover expenses. The year 1972, I told them, was the year I received no salary at all; all I got was another cash advance—this one for $25,000—which Caulfield handed me in Lafayette Park during one of my trips to Washington. As authorized by John Dean, $5,000 of that advance was used for personal living expenses and was duly reported as income on my 1972 tax return. I was strictly a conduit for the money earmarked for the Watergate burglars and their lawyers. No one has ever claimed I owed taxes on that money. I was authorized to use $1,000 of that money to cover airline, lodging and phone booth usage (filling up my money changer). I duly accounted to the government for the use of that money and for everything else I had done during my years as an investigator for the President and later for the Committee to Re-Elect the President. All my financial records were first in the hands of the Senate Watergate Committee and then with the office of the Watergate Special Prosecutor.

Incredibly, in May 1975, I was indicted for failing to include on my *original* tax returns the expense money I had been handed in Kalmbach's office and in Lafayette Park in Washington. The indictment charged that I signed income tax returns for 1971 and 1972 "in which I did not believe to be true and correct as to every material matter." I never signed anything in my life in which "I did not believe." There was no question about the payment of any back taxes: they had been paid already. If the government was going to collect any money, it would be after my trial, in the form of penalties and interest—not in the form of taxes! If the taxes were all paid, however, why indict me? It didn't make sense. The case was too bizarre to justify all this effort and expense.

The most depressing day of my life, aside from the time my mother died, was the day I stood in a basement room of the Federal courthouse in Brooklyn waiting to be booked, photographed, and fingerprinted, accused of a felony by the United States of America. That's what the indictment said. My heart stopped when they hung a card around my neck with a criminal ID number on it. In earlier years I had proudly worn the badge of a cop and the uniforms of both a soldier and a sailor. The only other numbers I had ever carried around my neck were those on the "dog tags" issued by the Army and Navy. For the first time in my life I tasted bitterness.

At my trial, neither the government nor my lawyer introduced into evidence either the financial records that I had turned over to the Senate Watergate Committee or to the Watergate Special Prosecutor. I sat in disbelief as I heard arguments by the prosecution that the reason I didn't report the cash advances on my original '71 and '72 tax returns was that I was trying to protect the President. But I had already turned over my records, expenses receipts, and had made full disclosure to Senate Watergate Committee investigators *before* I filed the amended tax returns. I wasn't covering up or protecting anybody. It didn't help matters much when I found myself in the middle of a dispute between Sutter and Winslow as to whether or not I should testify. Winslow said that I had to take the stand to explain the business purpose of the money; that I kept records and receipts of my expenditures and that they were all incurred at the direction and for the benefit of others. Sutter, on the other hand, said that I didn't have to testify because the government hadn't proven its case. For my part, I wanted to take the stand because I was convinced of my innocence and wanted to prove it. I didn't have anything to hide, and I didn't owe the government a dime. During the trial I got the terrible feeling that maybe Sutter didn't know what to ask me; that he was just going through the motions and that he had never examined any of my records. Insisting that I didn't have to take the stand to explain anything, he said the jury wouldn't believe the guy from the IRS. I was at war with my own lawyer, at war with myself, and watched my own lawyers have a war with each other.

The only good feeling I had during my trial came when Richard Ben-Veniste took the witness stand. When my attorney asked him for his "reaction to the news of Mr. Ulasewicz's indictment," he made the following reply:

> In view of the all the circumstances which include Mr. Ulasewicz's relative role, the time in which he came forward to cooperate, the extent of his cooperation, our analysis of his reliability as a witness, the pardon of one of the principals involved in the Watergate cover-up, the commutation of the sentence of many others who had pleaded guilty and were more seriously involved, I was surprised, frankly, and somewhat disappointed that this indictment had been returned.

I didn't take the stand, however, and that is something I will regret the rest of my life. We all lost. I was convicted as charged.

My case was tried in the Federal District courthouse in Brooklyn. Adding insult to injury, when I walked out of the courthouse one day during the trial, I got hit in the back of the head with a custard pie. Whatever missed me hit Chris Borgen, a newsreporter with CBS, who was in the middle of interviewing me on the courthouse steps. Right after I got hit, someone shouted, "That's for Special Services!" Turning around quickly I saw Aaron Kay, the leader of an organization called Youth Against War and Fascism, running into the streets. At one time, BOSSI along with the FBI had kept this group under surveillance as a possible Communist-front organization. Kay was apparently getting even for that surveillance. Stunned as I was by Kay's pie, the trauma was nothing compared to the shock I felt when I heard the jury say "guilty."

After I left the courthouse on the day of my brutal conviction, I made up my mind that it was time to go it alone again. When I picked up my records from Sutter's office, I discovered that the box of material I left with him was still tied with the same string and with the same knot. The box had never been opened! I was so depressed and disgusted I didn't even bother to ask Sutter why he hadn't looked at my records. He didn't seem worth the effort. Back home, I began working with my wife to gather up as many receipts as I could from the Special Prosecutor's Office and from whatever other cubbyhole in Washington they might have been resting. My day of sentencing had been scheduled for the first week in February 1977. After I collected as many receipts as I could and made a list of all my expenses for the years in question, I delivered them to a Federal probation officer who had been assigned to prepare a pre-sentence report for Judge Edward R. Neaher. I also wrote the Judge a letter that summed up all my feelings about what had just happened to me.

"I am almost stunned over how events, beginning with the Watergate break-in up to the present, have enmeshed me in a web from which I seemingly cannot free myself," I wrote the Judge. "On the one hand, there is sworn testimony in this case by top Justice Department officials—U.S. Attorney Silbert, Special Prosecutor Ben-Veniste and others associated with them, of my complete co-operation with them,

284

honesty and with full disclosures of the monies and their disbursement. On the other hand, from within the same Justice Department, I am selected for this prosecution.

"I have been 'hanging by my thumbs," I continued writing, "slowly twisting in the wind' since Watergate broke in June 1972, and now am about to be cut down. With Your Honor's understanding, I hope to make a soft landing, then hasten back to try and resume and recoup a somewhat normal life. So much has been taken away from me in terms of time—54 when Watergate broke, 58 now, and I'm broke. Even my fondness for coconut custard pie was taken away from me."

Judge Neaher sentenced me to one year's unsupervised probation—which in effect was saying go home, Tony, and don't come back. There was no fine, no jail sentence, just the scar of a conviction branded on my life.

Only after my trial and conviction did the IRS conduct a civil audit of the original and amended tax returns for 1971 and 1972. They ruled that I was subject to fraud and interest penalties on top of the effects of my conviction. Armed with the receipts and records my wife and I had gathered for the benefit of Judge Neaher, I went head to head with an IRS auditor. After all the heat generated by my prosecution had turned to ice, the only deficiency the IRS could come up with was less than a hundred bucks—including penalties and interest.

From all parts of the country, including jails in Arizona and California, the government had paid for transporting Dean, Ehrlichman, Kalmbach, Justice Department personnel, IRS Agents, U.S. Attorneys, television monitors, stenographers, marshals, grand jurors and trial jurors to come to Brooklyn to testify and to listen to my case. All to collect less than a hundred bucks? That was too ridiculous a reason. More than ever I became convinced that someone with powerful connections was out there determined to push the exit button on me.

One goal I persisted in—getting my long overdue salary paid by CREEP—was finally reached, at least partially, in 1984. After Watergate it was hard even to identify who was in charge of CREEP. When I learned that CREEP had put itself into the hands of a group of trustees (Maurice Stans, Finance Chairman of CREEP was originally one of them) I tried writing to them but CREEP's trustees had no official place for doing business. They had no official address, no secretary to answer letters or phone calls. In September 1973 an accountant for CREEP wrote *me* that his office "has been requested by the Finance Committee to Re-Elect the President to prepare a report to be filed with the Clerk of the House of Representatives of the United States showing the receipts and disbursements of the Finance Committee to Re-Elect the President, and all related committees for the period January 1, 1971, through April 6, 1972 . . . If you have any accounting or other records which will assist my office in the preparation of this report, would you kindly notify me. I will be glad to meet with you at your convenience to discuss this matter." By the time I received the letter, all my records were in the hands of the Senate Watergate Committee. If I wasn't connected to CREEP then why write me? When I wrote back requesting information about the payment of my back salary, my letters went unanswered. In effect, I was being told to get lost. I had become the phantom of Watergate, and to those controlling the purse strings, I simply didn't exist.

Although I had to sue in Federal Court in Washington to get my money, it was my lawsuit that broke the back of the warfare that was going on between other claimants who were fighting over CREEP's remaining funds. These claimants, including John Mitchell, Maurice Stans, Kenneth Parkinson and Robert Mardian, had to settle their differences or be forced to join my lawsuit in order to have the court decide who would get what. (Richard Galiher, the lawyer for CREEP's trustees in the case told the court there was "internecine warfare" going on among these other claimants.) Since there wasn't enough money to go around, everybody had to take a cut. These claimants didn't want the court deciding what it was going to be. A settlement of everyone's claim, including mine, was achieved in principle in the fall of 1984.

Shortly before the settlement documents were to be signed, however, G. Gordon Liddy suddenly appeared with a claim of $66,000. At my request, Liddy had signed a statement verifying that I did in fact work for Nixon's reelection committee and was entitled to my salary, but my claim apparently prompted Liddy to conclude that maybe he ought to get a piece of CREEP's pie before it all disappeared. He threatened to block the proposed settlement in court unless his claim was paid. The basis of Liddy's claim was that the IRS was after him because he failed to report as income the cash he got from CREEP that he used to finance his intelligence plans for the 1972 election campaign. But Liddy, I soon learned, hadn't been criminally prosecuted by the IRS as was my case. He was being charged civilly. All he received from the IRS was a "deficiency notice" in the mail that claimed he owed the government more money. Liddy denied he owed the government anything. At his trial before the U.S. Tax Court, Liddy said he didn't report this money because it wasn't his to keep. He testified he was merely the bagman, the paymaster for whatever CREEP's bosses had approved for his use developing intelligence schemes to defeat the Democrats. He testified that he carried out his intelligence assignments when he was General Counsel to CREEP and that the trustees of CREEP were obligated to help him out. None of the money was spent for his own personal use. (That tack sounded mighty familiar.) He had destroyed his financial records in order to protect the President. My records were in the hands of the Senate Watergate Committee and then with the Special Prosecutor's office. Liddy wanted some of CREEP's money to pay for what it cost him to defend his case in court.

At this time I also learned from the transcript of Liddy's Tax Court trial that, during the Watergate investigation, the IRS and the Special Prosecutor's Office together obtained a court order from Judge Sirica that set the guidelines for releasing information to the IRS on anyone caught up in the Watergate investigation. At Liddy's trial a key IRS agent testified that the criminal prosecution of any target of the Watergate investigation had first to be cleared through the Special Prosecutor's Office. That revelation meant that my criminal prosecution hadn't been orchestrated through the established channels. The cash advances I received in 1971 and 1972 to continue my investigations came from the same source as Liddy's. I kept my records and cooperated fully with the Senate Committee and the Special Prosecutor's Office. In contrast, Liddy stonewalled everybody and destroyed his records. And what was the result? I was served with an indictment, but Liddy was given a bill. I was convicted, but Liddy was exonerated by the U.S. tax court except for taxes on money he agreed he couldn't account for. The judge agreed with Liddy that the bulk of what he received from CREEP wasn't taxable income.

287

Most people don't want to talk about their troubles with the IRS, but I've talked about mine because someday I hope to clear my name. I want that felon's identification number off my neck, and I want to know why and who ordered it put there in the first place. Just as I was honorably discharged from the Army and the Navy, I want to be honorably discharged from this life when my time comes. I want the American flag draped on my coffin or over the jar or on a pole in the garden or wherever they decide to put me or my ashes when I'm gone. But I'm not finished yet. I still have a ways to go.

Ciudad Trujillo,
Distrito de Santo Domingo,
22 de abril de 1953.

Señor
Anthony Ulasewicz,
New York.

Estimado señor:

          Ya en mi país, de regreso de mi
viaje a los Estados Unidos, deseo por este
medio expresarle mi gratitud por los eficien-
tes servicios prestados por usted y sus com-
pañeros durante mi permanencia en esa ciudad
de New York.

                    Muy atentamente,

                  Rafael L. Trujillo Molina

ah
c

                    TRANSLATION

Dear Sir:

          Having returned now to my country from my

recent trip to the United States, I wish to express

my appreciation for the efficient service rendered

by you and your associates during my stay in New

York City.

                    Sincerely,

APPENDIX 1   Letter to Senor Anthony Ulasewicz from Rafael L. Trujillo dated
April 22, 1953.

- - - - - - - - - -

Q. Will you tell me your name, shield number and command?
A. Det. Anthony T. Ulasewicz, Shield #1719, Bureau of Special
Services. Appointed Feb. 17, 1943 and assigned to the 25th
Precinct. Temporarily assigned to the Bureau of Special Ser-
vices Feb. 3, 1949; permanently assigned to the Detective
Division, Bureau of Special Services, May 2nd, 1949.

Q. Do you know John Frank?
A. I do.

Q. How long do you know him?
A. I know him since January 1956 or December 1955.

Q. Where did you meet him?
A. I met him in my office, when he was presented to me as a former
F.B.I. agent and an attorney, and that he might have information
relative to the activities of Dominican exiles residing in this
city as well as organizations interested in Dominican affairs.

Q. Do you recall what was the type of information that Frank was
giving to you at that time?
A. On this occasion and on two or three other times he gave information concerning a German Ornes Coiscu, the former editor of
a Dominican newspaper. His information tended to link Ornes
with established anti-Trujillo groups in this city. It is my
recollection he also mentioned Alberto Aybar, Jose Espaillat
and Nicholas Silfa, the Dominican Revolutionary Party and the
Casa Dominicana, as persons and groups opposed to Trujillo and
with whom Ornes might become associated. He also indicated an
interest as an attorney in the criminal prosecution of Ornes,
pointing to the alleged missing funds belonging to the newspaper "El Caribe", and it was my impression that he either had
or intended to take the matter up with a District Attorney.

Q. Did he give you this information all at once or did he give it
to you piecemeal?
A. Piecemeal, on several different occasions.

Q. And what you have just outlined to me is your recollection
generally of what he had given you in one interview or in a
number of interviews?
A. In a number of interviews.

Q. Did Frank at any time indicate to you what his connection was
with the Dominican Republic?
A. Well, it was my impression that he was an attorney connected
with a law firm which was doing business with the Dominican
Republic.

Q. Did he ever definitely state to you that he was employed by
the Dominican Government?
A. No.

Q. Did he at any time tell you that he lived in the Dominican Republic?
A. Yes, that he had visited the Dominican Republic.

APPENDIX 2   Galindez Case—Statements of Anthony T. Ulasewicz, Arthur E.
Schultheiss and Edward B. Fitzpatrick.

Q. Did he ever say anything to you about having a home or a residence there, that you can recall?

A. Well, I had the impression that he had been living in the Dominican Republic from time to time, whether as a guest or that he had a home established, I can't recall.

Q. What was the chief interest of Frank in his various conversations with you?

A. The individual German Ornes and the possibility of his tying in with anti-Trujillo groups in this city.

Q. We have a record here of Frank calling your home FLushing 7-9211 on 9/19/56. Can you tell me what the nature of that call was?

A. I recall receiving a phone call at my home, at which time Frank in general terms established a friendship between Ornes and Nicholas Silfa and advised for the information of my office that Silfa had in the past few months traveled abroad in connection with some world labor movement. This information, like most of the previous, was already known and on file in my command, having been verified through the United States State Department and given to the 4th Squad and the F.B.I.

Q. Then most of the information that Frank gave you was of a corroborative nature, is that correct?

A. That is correct.

Q. We have other calls listed to the Bureau of Special Services. There was one on 1/19/56. Do you recall whether you received that one?

A. By the date I can't, but I can recall receiving one or two, possibly two telephone messages from Frank to my command, in which he offered information similar to that mentioned previously.

Q. Another call on Feb. 29th. Do you know if you received that one?

A. I can't be sure.

Q. There is another call on May 6th, two calls. Do you recall if you received that one?

A. No, I didn't receive those calls.

Q. Why are you so sure?

A. I was on vacation at that time.

Q. There was a call on May 14th and May 15th. Do you recall having received either one?

A. No, I was on vacation until returning to work on May 16th.

Q. Also a call on June 11, 1956. Do you recall if you received that one?

A. I don't know.

Q. Can you say whether you did or did not?

A. No, I can't say.

Q. Were you working that day?

A. Yes, I was working on that day.

Q. In the office?

A. Yes, in the office, assigned to my regular work. I may have gotten the call but I have no recollection of it.

Q. There was another call made on Jan. 11, 1957. Do you recall whether you received that call or not?
A. No, I didn't receive that one.

Q. Why are you so sure?
A. I was on investigations the larger part of the day and I don't recall receiving that call.

Q. In going back to Frank's conversations with you, did he indicate to you in any way the nature of his association with the Dominican Republic?
A. No, only as an attorney for a law firm.

Q. Did he indicate to you in any of the conversations, either by phone or in person, what his activities had been in the Dominican Republic or for the Dominican Republic?
A. No, he never did.

Q. And that is your complete recollection of the context of the calls that you have received from Frank?
A. That is correct.

- - - - - - - - -

STATEMENT TAKEN BY DEPUTY CHIEF INSPECTOR FRANCIS J.M.ROBB,
COMMANDING OFFICER, CENTRAL OFFICE BUREAUS & SQUADS, on WEDNESDAY,
April 10, 1957

- - - - - - - - - - - -

Q. Will you tell me what your name and rank is, please?
A. Arthur E. Schultheiss, Lt., Commanding Officer of the 14th Det.
Squad.

Q. Lt. Schultheiss, do you know John Frank?
A. I do.

Q. Will you tell me something of the nature of your association
with him?
A. I have known John Frank since the days that I was a detective
assigned to what was then called the Criminal Alien Squad, now
known as the Bureau of Special Services, in Police Headquarters.
At that time, I believe it was during the years of World War II,
around 1941 and 1942, while assigned to that command under Act.
Capt. James Donnelly, we would receive daily assignments with
agents of the F.B.I. During those days I got to know Mr. Frank
as such. He was an agent for the F.B.I., working on those security matters to which we were assigned together. Primarily these
duties consisted of the execution of Presidential Search Warrants
in the homes of German and Japanese nationals and the subsequent
investigations in the office of the F.B.I. I got to know Mr.
Frank very well in those days in that my assignment with him was
more or less on a permanent basis and through the years since
then we have retained this acquaintanceship.

Q. What were the years in which you had this close association with
John Frank?
A. It was during the World War II years. I would say between 1941,
1942 and 1943.

Q. When did this close association as partnership in the execution
of police and F.B.I. matters cease, can you tell me?
A. It definitely ceased as of October 1944, at which time I was
promoted to the rank of Sergeant in the Police Department. It
had ceased some time around the year 1943, perhaps even in 1942.
This was more or less the beginning of World War II insofar as
the Germans were concerned and later when the Japs entered the
war, during the beginning of that war.

Q. Did you maintain this friendship and association with Frank after
your transfer from the Criminal Alien Squad?
A. Yes, I did retain that friendship with Mr. Frank. I would say
acquaintanceship rather than friendship, with Mr. Frank through
the years following.

Q. Do you know the present day business of Mr. Frank?
A. I know him to be an attorney, practicing out of the city of
Washington, D.C.

Q. Is he connected with a law firm there that you know of?
A. No, I don't know whether he is connected with a law firm or has
been in business for himself. I don't know his business that
well.

Q. Does Mr. Frank ever call you on the telephone?
A. Yes, I would say Mr. Frank calls me on the telephone whenever he
comes to New York. I have been in the habit of hearing from him
through the years on the telephone and occasionally we would meet
and have dinner together.

Q. Has he ever discussed with you any of his business connections, primarily with reference to the Dominican Republic?
A. No, he has not.

Q. Has he indicated to you in any way that he had business with or business in the Dominican Republic?
A. Yes.

Q. Can you tell me what he explained to you or has told you of his connections in the Dominican Republic?
A. I never carefully questioned him and he never told me about his business in any detail. He merely indicated that he had business or clients that took him into the Dominican Republic, because he had told me of business there on several occasions. I had received cards from him, postcards to my office, I believe during the winter of 1954 and 1955. I received postcards from down there from which I gathered that he was living there.

Q. In these telephone conversations with you, what was the nature of these calls?
A. He would call and speak to me, ask about how I felt, how my family was, some of whom he got to know, and I would ask about his wife Frances whom I got to know through the years, having visited his home in Jackson Heights during the days of our assignment together in 1941, 1942 and 1943. There was more or less just small talk along those lines.

Q. Do you know where Mr. Frank lives at this time?
A. I know he lives in the suburbs of Washington, D.C. Just exactly where, I couldn't tell you. I believe it is in the State of Virginia.

Q. Did he at any time discuss his business with you?
A. No, not in detail. Just generally that he was handling a civil practice and we had nothing in common in that field, in the civil field.

Q. I have here a record showing that John Frank called you, or called WA 9-5746 on the following dates:
        Jan. 17, 1956 - 2 calls
        March 5,   " - 1 call
        March 7,   " - 2 calls
        March 8,   " - 1 call
        April 20, " - 1 call
        April 18, " - 1 call
        May 7,   " - 1 call
        May 11,   " - 2 calls

and a call listed to GI 7-3357 on May 6, which telephone is listed to G. J. Schultheiss. We also have another call to PE 6-2888, which is the 14th Squad office, on September 20th. Can you tell me from your best recollection what the context of these calls was? We have assumed that because of Frank's friendship with you, that you were the one he was calling at these locations. Do you know of any other person in that squad whom he would call?
A. No, I'm sure it was to no one but me. He had no acquaintance-ship with anyone else in the squad.

Q. Can you tell me the context of these conversations?
A. I don't remember these specific calls on these specific days because as I have previously stated, our telephone conversations were of an unimportant nature, generally just small talk conversations, but I do believe that these calls were all made to me. I do know that the call he made to GI 7-3357 was to me, because I have specific recollection of that call. It was the only time he had ever called me at this number, which is the home of my mother and father at 129 Targee St., Stapleton, Staten Island. On this occasion he told me that he had just come to town and wondered whether I was free for dinner that evening, and I suggested that he join me at my mother's home, which I believe he did on that occasion because I remember having him to my mother and father's home for dinner. I suggested that he visit with me with my mother, father, brother and my wife, I believe, but I'm not too sure.

Q. Do you know where Frank lived on the occasions of his visits to New York?
A. As far as I know, he always stayed at the National Republican Club, on West 40th St., between 5th and 6th Avenues.

Q. Again, I repeat, did he ever discuss with you any of the business that he was conducting while he was in the Dominican Republic or with Dominican clients?
A. I have no specific recollection of anything concerning his business there.

Q. Then your association with Frank was more of a social nature, emanating from the time that you met him when you were both assigned to the execution of Presidential warrants in the years 1941, 1942 and possibly 1943?
A. Strictly social.

Q. Will you again, just for the record, explain to me the conditions that existed at that time with reference to the assignment of F.B.I. special agents and policemen as so-called partners?
A. The F.B.I. would send various Special Agents daily at 9 A.M. to Special Squad 1

Q. Where was that?
A. Special Squad 1 was located on the third floor of 400 Broome St. under the command of Inspector George Mitchell. I was assigned to the Criminal Alien Squad which was located on the 6th floor of the same building, 400 Broome St. Detectives from Special Squad 1 and from the Alien Squad were picked daily at 9 A.M. to be present in their offices and to be assigned with these agents as they appeared in Special Squad 1 with their warrants, for the purpose of investigation and subsequent execution of these warrants. We would then be paired off, an agent with a detective. The agent had the choice of selecting the particular detective if he so desired, and having been assigned with me on a few occasions, Mr. Frank usually chose me and thereby we worked together for the most part quite regularly, and this is more or less how the subsequent acquaintanceship or friendship was struck up. We got to visit each others homes on several occasions. He was a member and swam at that time at the N.Y. Athletic Club. I would go up there with him on our time off, off duty, and he having been athletically inclined, having played basketball at Georgetown University, and I was a basketball fan, he played basketball at the N.Y. Athletic Club. I would go with him to watch some of their games and in that way our friendship grew.

Q. Do you know when Mr. Frank severed his connections with the
F.B.I.?

A. I don't know exactly but it was subsequent to the end of the
war, because I remember during this time I had met Mr. Frank at
that time and he had told me of working on communists, of his
intense hatred and dislike for them, and just general talk about
his duties in connection with such assignments.

Q. Did you know whether Mr. Frank worked for any other federal
agency?

A. I have a recollection that when he severed his connections with
the F.B.I., he went with another agency, possibly the O.I.A., and
following that, the O.P.A. in Detroit, Michigan. I'm not too
sure about this. I never paid enough attention to his assignments any more than I know of his assignments in recent years.

Q. Did you know John Frank when he worked for the Pier security
Bureau in New York?

A. I never heard of the Pier Security Bureau before this.

Q. That is the agency which was headed up by Ed Conroy, who was
the Special Agent in Charge of the New York Office of the F.B.I.

A. Oh, I have heard of Mr. Conroy and his connection subsequent to
his severance with the F.B.I., as having been connected at that
time with a security bureau. I never heard of it as the Pier
Security Bureau.

Q. Did you know that Frank worked for him?

A. No, I never did.

Q. During your period of acquaintanceship and friendship with Mr.
Frank, what kind of a fellow did he appear to be to you?

A. John Frank impressed me as being a good Christian. I knew he
was of the same faith as myself, we both being Catholics. I
knew he was devoted to his folks who were located some place in
Connecticut. He was married to a woman, who was previously a
nurse, her first name as I recall was Frances. I know John Frank
to be a good American citizen because of the way he conducted his
duties while he was an agent for the F.B.I. and the manner he was
performing his duties as an American and because of his complete
hatred at all times for communists and anything having to do with
communism. I know him to be a man of high moral standing and of
good character.

Q. Do you know whether he was a member of the bar during your association with him?

A. I never did question him as to whether he was admitted to the bar
in any particular state. I presumed him to be an attorney, based
on the fact that he was an agent for the F.B.I. and that he subsequently practiced law.

Q. Did he practice law in this state, do you know?

A. I don't know of any one particular case that he handled. I just
generally felt that he was a practicing attorney.

Q. You stated before that he had led you to believe that he was practicing law in Washington, D.C.

A. That's right. That's where I presumed he was practicing law,
based on what he told me, that in recent years he was practicing
law in Washington, D.C.

Q. Did he ever mention any law firm that he was connected with?
A. No, he did not. At one time he gave me his address on N.W. 15th
Street but I don't remember the exact number or location, or
whether he was associated with anyone or was alone. I had no
occasion to contact him so I don't know where he was.

- - - - - - - - - -

Q. Will you give me your name, rank and shield number?
A. Det. Edward B. Fitzpatrick, shield #1936, Bureau of Special services. I was appointed Sept. 28, 1938 and temporarily assigned
to the Bureau of Criminal Alien Investigation on July 20, 1939
and permanently to the Detective Division, Bureau of Criminal
Alien Investigation on Oct. 24, 1941.

Q. When were you transferred to the Bureau of Special Services,
which is known as B.S.S.
A. On May 13, 1945 when the Bureau of Criminal Alien Investigation
was consolidated with Special Squad 1, the name was changed at
that time to the Public Relations Squad. It was subsequently became
known as the Bureau of Special Services, its present name.

Q. Do you know John Frank?
A. Yes.

Q. Do you recall when you met him?
A. I met him in the latter part of 1955 or the early part of 1956
at the Bureau of Special Services. However, I knew him by sight
in 1942 or 1943 when he and other agents of the F.B.I. visited
our offices and together with detectives from this Department
executed Presidential Search Warrants. However at that time I
was not assigned with him on any of those occasions.

Q. Were you assigned with other agents of the F.B.I.?
A. Yes.

Q. But never specifically assigned with Frank?
A. No.

Q. However, your next recollection of meeting John Frank was in the
office of the Bureau of Special Services in December 1955 or
January 1956?
A. Yes.

Q. Do you recall what he was doing in the office of the Bureau of
Special Services at that time?
A. Frank visited the office of the Bureau of Special Services, giving
information on one German Goiscu Ornes, a former editor of the
Dominican newspaper "El Caribe". He stated that Ornes had absconded with a large sum of the newspaper's funds and was possibly
dealing with Latin-American communist groups in this city.

Q. Did you make a record of the information which he had given you?
A. Whatever information he furnished was taken, since it was deemed
pertinent to an investigation then in progress, due to the newspaper articles concerning Ornes.

Q. Did Frank at any other time give you any other information that
you can recall?

A. He offered information concerning Nicholas Silfa, Tulio Arvello
and Jose Espaillat, who were Dominicans opposed to the Trujillo
regime. He also mentioned the Dominican Revolutionary Party,
of which Silfa is the leader, and the Casa Dominicana, of which
Jose Espaillat was the leader. He said that he felt that Ornes
might be connected with these persons and groups.

Q. The people that Frank was telling you about, all seem to have
some connection with the Dominican Republic, either pro or con.
Did Frank ever explain to you any of his connections with the
Dominican Republic?

A. No, he said that he was a member or was connected with a law firm
in Washington, D.O.; that it represented the government of the
Dominican Republic in some manner, but he did not elaborate.

Q. Did his connections seem to be in any particular case?
A. The Ornes case - he was particularly interested in the Ornes case.

Q. Did he tell you how much money Ornes was supposed to have absconded
with?
A. As I recall, it was something around $80,000.

Q. Can you tell me if you know what subsequent steps he took in the
Ornes case?
A. He had mentioned that he was going to a District Attorney, but
whether it was a local or federal D.A. I don't recall, to make
a complaint concerning Ornes having absconded with the funds of
the newspaper, and in later conversation with me - the time of
which I can't place - he related that the case was eventually
turned over to the United States District Attorney in New York
City. I don't know what happened from then on.

Q. John Frank called you at your home, at TA 9-1313 on January 17,
1956. Can you tell me what that call was about?
A. I remember him calling me at home - the date may have been January
17, 1956, and on that occasion he wanted to know if I would be
in the office the next day as he had something to discuss concerning Ornes.

Q. And did he visit the office the following day, after that call?
A. Yes, and gave information already mentioned, concerning Ornes.

Q. There were a number of phone calls made by Frank to the Bureau
of Special Services, namely January 19, 1956. Did you receive
that call?
A. I recall having answered a phone call from him on one or possibly
two occasions.

Q. There was another call made to the office on February 29, 1956.
Did you receive that call?
A. That may have been one of the calls I received, because I was
) working in the office that day and may have answered the phone.

Q. There was another call, two calls, on May 6, 1956. Can you tell
me if you answered the phone that day?
A. May 6th was a Sunday and I was off that day.

Q. There was another call from Frank on May 14, 1956. Did you receive
that call?
A. No, at that time I was assigned to escort duty to the Vice-President of Brazil.

Q. There was another call on May 15, 1956. Did you receive that call?
A. No, I was still on escort duty and I was not in the office.

Q. There was another call on June 11, 1956. Did you get that one?
A. I was in the office but I have no recollection of answering any such call.

Q. There was still another call on January 11, 1957. Do you recall receiving that call?
A. No, I don't believe I received that one because I did night duty on January 10, 1957 to 8:30 A.M. on January 11th and then I went home.

Q. On the calls that you recall having received from Frank, can you give me your recollection of the context of these phone calls and the things that were discussed?
A. As I stated before, his information principally concerned Ornes and activities of other persons already mentioned, such as Silfa and Jose Espaillat. Most of his information was previously known to my command and required no investigation. It merely tended to corroborate information already known.

Q. Can you tell me, and again I repeat, did Frank at any time tell you of his interest in Dominican affairs?
A. No, only his deep interest in the Ornes case.

Q. Did he at any time tell you that he had lived in the Dominican Republic?
A. No, never.

- - - - - - - - - -

IN THE UNITED STATES DISTRICT COURT

FOR THE DISTRICT OF COLUMBIA

UNITED STATES OF AMERICA)

v.) Criminal No. 493-57

JOHN JOSEPH FRANK)

Defendant)

THE TESTIMONY OF ANTHONY ULASEWICZ IS ADMISSIBLE

Anthony Ulasewicz, a detective assigned to the Special Bureau of the New York City Police Department will testify that he first met the Defendant in January 1956 when Frank came to his office to report on the activities of certain anti-Trujillo Dominicans residing in New York City. The Defendant told the witness that German Ornes had left the Dominican Republic and had unlawfully taken with him a large sum of money. In the course of other conversations the defendant told the witness that Ornes might attempt to join up with certain exiles and anti-Trujillo groups which had a Communistic background. The defendant told Ulasewicz that the reason he was furnishing this information was that he was connected with a law firm, who had offices in Washington, D. C. and he was doing business with the Dominican Republic.

The defendant makes a statement in his memorandum of law on this witness which seems to imply that he told detective Ulasewicz about a plot to assassinate Generalissimo Trujillo in December, 1954 and January and February 1955. Obviously if the witness first met the defendant in January 1956, as he testified at the first trial the defendant could not have provided him with any information of this alleged plot.

It is a reasonable inference from the nature of the information supplied to detective Ulasewicz that the primary objective of the defendant was not to provide information regarding

APPENDIX 3   Memorandum of Law regarding admissibility of testimony of Anthony Ulasewicz in the case of United States of America v. John Joseph Frank.

violations of New York State law but to harass and injure
German Ornes and other anti-Trujillo.Dominicans in the New
York area pursuant to and in furtherance of his agency relation-
ship with the Dominican government and Generalissimo Trujillo.

At this juncture it should be noted that the defendant
at his first trial raised this same claim of privilege about
detective Ulasewicz testimony which was rejected by Judge
Kirkland. Counsel for the defendant now asserts the same claim
in his Memorandum of Law and cites three reasons whereby the
informer's privilege renders the testimony of detective Ulasewicz
inadmissible.

I

Defendant claims a formal letter of waiver must be obtained from the office of the Mayor of the City of New York.
While we do not agree with this contention, nevertheless we
have been informed that such a Notice of Waiver will be provided. Therefore, the defendant cannot argue that the City
of New York, the employer of detective Ulasewicz has not formally
waived any privilege which it might have asserted in this matter.

II

The defendant claims that under the law of New York State
there are two privileges; i.e. the Government's privilege (which
has been waived) and what he denotes as a qualified informer's
privilege which belongs to the informer alone. As authority
for this proposition he cites Pecue v. West, 233 N.Y. 316, 135
N.E. 515 (1922) and Application of Langert, 173 N.Y.S. 2d 665
(App. Div. 1st Dept., 1958). These cases do not substantiate
the proposition for which he asserts them, namely that when an
informer makes admissions in providing information to a police
officer which admissions are subsequently sought to be used
against the informer when he is prosecuted for a crime, the
testimony of the police officer would be privileged.

Pecue v. West, supra, was a suit for damages by a saloon keeper against a man who had written the district attorney accusing the plaintiff of keeping girls for immoral purposes. The charges were untrue and plaintiff sued for damages for the libel. The case had no relation to the admissibility of testimony against a defendant in a criminal trial but discusses the degree of protection to be afforded a defendant who is sued for defamation on the basis of his false accusations of criminal activity. The decision discusses the New York law of defamation and distinguishes between those situations where there is no absolute privilege against civil suit as opposed to those where a qualified privilege is afforded whereby the defendant can be held liable for damages if the plaintiff can prove malice. The case decides that a complainant to a district attorney has only a qualified privilege and that if he acted wantonly or with a reckless disregard of the rights of others he is liable in a civil suit to respond in damages.

The petitioner in Application of Langert, 173 N.Y.S. 2d 667, in order to commence a defamation action sought to compel the Commissioner of Investigation of the City of New York to reveal the person who had made a complaint against the petitioner. The Commissioner refused to reveal the informant claiming such information to be privileged and therefore he could not be forced to reveal it so Langert could commence a defamation action against the informer. The Court held that the matter was privileged from disclosure as "[t]he concern here is with the privilege of the public officer, the recipient of the communication, rather than with the privilege of the maker of the communication." (173 N.Y.S. 2d at 668).

From the above analysis of the New York law it is evident that the cases cited by the defendant have no bearing on the issue of the admissibility of the defendant's admissions made to a police officer and the informer cannot claim he has a right

to prevent the introduction of such evidence when it is sought
to be used against him.

III

The defendant's last argument for the exclusion of
detective Ulasewicz testimony is based on a claim that an informer has a Constitutional right both to inform and to have
his admission as an informer to a police officer held to be
privileged when they are sought to be used against him at his
criminal trial. As authority for this novel proposition is
language quoted from In re Quarles and Butler, 158 U.S. 532, 537.
In this case a man who had reported an illegal still to the
authorities was set upon and attacked by the defendants because
of his action in reporting the presence of the still. The
defendants were indicted and convicted of having deprived a
citizen of the United States of a right and privilege protected
by the Constitution. The defendants in their appeal claimed
that their attack on the informer had not constituted a violation of any right which would be actionable under United States
law. The Supreme Court held there was a right protected by the
Constitution to be free from a conspiracy to injure and threaten
a citizen who has reported a violation of the law to the proper
authority. The Court did not say that a person has a constitutional right to have his statements to a law enforcement official
held to be privileged when he is prosecuted for a crime. In
fact, the Court specifically stated that the informer's privilege
belongs to the Government and can be waived by it.

> "It is likewise his right and his duty to communicate
> to the executive officers any information which he has
> of the commission of an offense against those laws;
> and such information, given by a private citizen, is
> a privileged and confidential communication, for which
> no action of libel or slander will lie, and the disclosure

of which cannot be compelled without the assent of
the government." (158 U.S. at 535-536) (Emphasis
supplied)

See also Vogel v. Gruaz, 110 U.S. 311, 316; Scher v. United

States, 305 U.S. 251, 254; Worthington v. Scribner, 109 Mass.

487, 488. This view that the informer's privilege, in the

limited instances where it may be asserted, is in reality

the Government's privilege to withhold from disclosure the

identity of a person who reports violation of the law to the

authorities was recently reaffirmed and restated by the Supreme

Court in Rovario v. United States, 353 U.S. 53, 59.

Professor Wigmore in volume 8 On Evidence, S 2374 (3rd

ed. 1940) states the following concerning the informer's privilege:

"The privilege applies only to the identity of the in-

formant, not to the contents of his statement as such * * *"

(page 753)

"If the identity of the informer is admitted or known,

then there is no reason for pretended concealment, and the

privilege of secrecy would be merely an artificial obstacle

to proof." (page 755)

"Even where the privilege is strictly applicable, the

trial court may compel disclosure, if it appears necessary in

order to avoid the risk of false testimony or to secure useful

testimony." (page 756) (Emphasis in original)

In conclusion, the City of New York, having waived any

privilege which it might have asserted, there is no rule under

either New York State or Federal Law which holds a defendant

can claim his admissions made to a police officer are not

competent as evidence when sought to be introduced against him

in a criminal action.

- 5 -

Careful research has failed to find any case in which a court has held that an informant has a right or privilege to prevent the introduction into evidence of his admissions made to a police officer in a subsequent prosecution against the informant.

Nathan B. Lenvin
Attorney for the United States

Edward N. Schwartz
Attorney for the United States

Jerome Avedon
Attorney for the United States

United States District Court

FOR THE

District of Columbia

UNITED STATES OF AMERICA

v.

No. 493-57

JOHN JOSEPH FRANK

To   Mr. *FRANCIS SULLIVAN*,   BUREAU *OF* SPECIAL SERVICES, or his authorized representative, Custodian of Records for the Police Department of the City of New York, State of New York, Broom and Center Streets, New York, New York

You are hereby commanded to appear in the United States District Court for the

District of   Columbia   at   3rd & Constitution Ave., N. W.   in the city of 4th Floor, Courtroom 8.

Washington   on the   10th   day of   March   19 59 at   2:00   o'clock p. M. that is, forthwith,

to testify in the case of United States v.   John Joseph Frank   and bring with you

the following documents:

1. Reports and memoranda of the Bureau of Special Services of the Police Department of the City of New York, State of New York, relating only to the investigations conducted by police officers of the squad of which Detective Anthony T. Ulasewicz was and/or is a member, with regard only to reports or memoranda relating to an alleged plot to assassinate Generalissimo Rafael (or Raphael) Trujillo of the Dominican Republic

This subpoena is issued upon application of the¹ Defendant   (see attached page for continuation)

March 9,   19 59 .

Attorney for   Defendant 15th Street, N.W.

Address   Washington 5, D.C.

HARRY M. HULL   Clerk.

By _____

Deputy Clerk.

¹ Insert "United States," or "defendant" as the case may be.

RETURN

Received this subpoena at   on and on   at served it on the within named by delivering a copy to h   and tendering to h   the fee for one day's attendance and the mileage allowed by law.²

Dated:

_____, 19___   By _____

Service Fees

    Travel _____$

    Services _____

    Total _____$

² Fees and mileage need not be tendered to the witness upon service of a subpoena issued in behalf of the United States or an officer or agency thereof. 28 USC 1825.

Continuation of Subpoena Duces Tecum attached hereto:

by persons within the City of New York on the next occasion that the said
Generalissimo Trujillo came to the United States, together with reports and
memoranda relating to an alleged plot to assassinate Generalissimo Rafael
(or Raphael) Trujillo as aforesaid, supplied to the said Bureau of Special
Services of the City of New York Police Department by an informant or informants.
All of said reports and memoranda being dated between the period October 1, 1954
and February 26, 1955 and the majority of which are presently in the files of
the said Bureau of Special Services.

2. Any report or memoranda relating to the investigation or checking of an
apartment of or house of, Mr. Manuel R. Blanco, also known as John R. Blanco,
at 155 Audubon Avenue, New York, New York by an informant or informants
of the Bureau of Special Services of the New York City Police Department,
the informant's name or one of the informants' names being Mr. Jones, or a
report or memoranda relating to the above which involved only a discussion of
said activities by said informants or informant, during the period November 1,
1954 to February 28, 1955.

3. Any report or memoranda of the substance of conversations had between
John Joseph Frank of Washington, D.C. and Detective Anthony T. Ulasewicz of the
said Bureau of Special Services of the Police Department of the City of New York,
during the period December 1, 1955 to March 15, 1956.

May 22, 1958

Mr. Sydney Baron
515 Madison Avenue
New York, N. Y.

Personal and Confidential

My dear Syd:

The chore is at an end. It's been a good adventure, and I want yo
to know how deeply I appreciate all of your cooperation. I know
that you are really not offended because I always thought it wise t
keep you in ignorance during the long and dreary path of digging f
evidence. I would like you, particularly, to extend my thanks to
Ambassador De Moya, and to all of his associates, and especiall
Otto Vega. I have no doubt that at many times, they thought I was
a tough nuisance. I have said in my report, with all honesty, that
the cooperation I received, as called for under the retainer agree
ment, is, without exception, the fullest that any lawyer could eve
expect.

As I made clear before I took on the job, all of my subconscious
prejudices which might have affected my open mind, were forces
acting against your client. You will recall that I dictated a memo
indicating that even though I bitterly opposed Communism, I had
defended Communists. I had differed with the position of the
Catholic Church in birth control and divorce, even though, as I
explained, I am entertained by the Cardinal at his home for lunch.
I made clear that I was emotionally in favor of a quickening pace
throughout the world in the reduction of powers in executives of
each nation, an accomplishment that was, in my opinion, depende
on the expansion of literacy and communication.

I know you have had consideration in the attacks made on me by
honorable people in our society. I tried to explain to you that a
lawyer acting in the classic tradition of the Bar, must satisfy

APPENDIX 4   Letter to Sydney Baron from Morris Ernst dated May 22, 1958.

his own conscience rather than the passing attitudes of any particular group in a society, even though it is always more pleasant
if society agrees with one's own prejudices.

I am sending to you herewith copy of the legal opinion called for
under the retainer agreement; also letter and final bill, the amount
of which I fixed even before I knew the ultimate conclusion which I
would reach. I wanted to guard against my own subconscious cor-
ruption. By that I mean that if the facts in my opinion would be in
terms agreeable to your client, that I would not weight the bill because of that fact. I would appreciate early payment, since the
retainer was paid nearly a year ago.

I previously sent you a memorandum in regard to libel immunity
and explained that I see no danger other than the nuisance from
psychopathic people like Silfa.

I now write in terms of highest secrecy, except between you and
your client. I must ask your pledge that what I am about to write
will never be made public without my prior consent.

As you know, you and your associates conferred, as I did, in
Washington, with persons in important positions in our government. I never asked permission to accept this controversial retainer, but I was told by fast friends of mine at the White House,
FBI, and others whom I respect at State Department and Justice,
that my government would welcome my going into this enterprise.
Within a week after the announcement of my retainer, a complete
uranium curtain was dropped between me and my government. As
you know, I have been treated like a leper.

For a time I concluded, and I now confess, wrongly, that I thought
this shift attitude arose because Edgar Hoover was afraid that with
my little staff I might get the answer to the Galindez case before he
did. The FBI, I am told, spent well over a half million dollars in
extra outlays on the Murphy-Galindez matter. Although this observation in a way was flattering, I was deeply hurt that Hoover would not
see me, that our Attorney General would not allow his people even to
talk to me when I offered to turn over material to my own government.
I was practically dismissed by the State Department.

Through luck, of which my life is quite full, I discovered the real
reason for the shift. The reason is quite frightening. For a time
I felt like the little boy who peeked through the keyhole and saw
some things he regretted having seen.

What I have seen is far more important than any contribution my
staff and I may have made, of what, comparatively, is minor importance, the disappearance of Galindez. I have in my possession
an overwhelming mass of material which leads me to conclude with
complete assurance, that Galindez was an agent of the United States
Government. I have been told by a high and respected official, who
name shall never pass my lips, that four hundred lives were at stak
if I told all I knew.

The operation for which Galindez was an agent, in brief, was to spy
on the Spanish Republican Committee in exile, so as to help our
nation and the free world in the event of the death of Franco. This
seems to me like a reasonable and valid operation, since, as I have
intimated in my opinion, the free world is in peril if, on the death
of Franco, the Communist infiltration of the Republican government
in exile puts that organization in a position to seize power in Spain.
The monies that Galindez received were only to a minor extent, as a
kind of cloak, monies flowing from Basque adherents. I have no
evidence, but I would not be surprised to learn that two nations belonging to the free world in Europe, worked with our government
in the financing of the Galindez operation.

I do not know whether Galindez was told to go underground because
the Communists had found that he was a double agent. He may have
been killed either by Communists, or even by our government, since
our government might have felt that they could not run the risk of a
double agent who failed, circulating freely even under disguise.

I am in no position to suggest more to you and your client. I reached
a point where I was faced with a conflict of loyalty to a client and
loyalty to my government. As you know, I offered my government
to eliminate such minor facts as I have incorporated in my opinion,
particularly in Part 5, all of which will, fortunately or unfortunately
alert the minds of men to get the real answer. I cannot imagine the
present Spanish Government being so unimaginative as not to pursue
the inquiry. As you know, I want no part of such project if anyone
is interested in carrying it on. I have had my fill, and at my age, I

nt to go back to a practice at the Bar less full of cloaks, daggers
l filthy human beings.

om the point of view of your client, I suggest that the entire
eign policy of that nation vis-a-vis the United States must
p the above in mind. What I really suspect has happened
that our government, on a risk for risk basis, felt compelled
choose the disturbance of relations with your client, rather
a divulge an operation which might, in historic terms, be an
ment in the maintenance of freedom from Communism in
rope.

der these circumstances, it may not be impertinent for me to
ggest that the best defense for your client is an objective, dynamic,
l idealistic offense. To this end, you and I have, together, developed
least four measures which not only would shift public opinion, but
ght even create a change in the attitude of the State Department
pite the feelings of any other agency of our government. I refer to
the series of books; b) the aerial survey to discover resources in
Dominican Republic; c) the visual education survey already under
y; and d) the development of cohesion in the Caribbean by the creation and
anizing of a new form of boat transportation which is cheaper than
nes and has such speed as to reduce costs called for by refrigeration
the shipping of produce. The survey and the boat program can be
eloped with small amounts of capital outlay, but with a clear
sibility of becoming income producing entities.

m off to Nantucket and my sailboat. Since the proposals for future
ps are mainly the product of your fertile mind, I end merely by
ing good luck and God bless, and of course, you can see me in
ntucket where you can fly in one hour by plane.

                    Yours,

                    Morris L. Ernst

e/eg

SON OF JESUS DE GALINDEZ LIVE IN SANTO DOMINGO?

A boy, who Trujillo wanted to disappear from his mother's womb, because he was the son, as evidence shows, of one of his most ardent critics, the Spanish writer Jesus de Galindez, is today a healthy youngster who demands, in all his innocence, that the authorities undertake some action to definitely determine his origin.

Having lived ten years, the same amount of time since the mysterious disappearance of the professor from his residence on Fifth Avenue, in New York, Jesus Manuel never felt the warmth of his mother, since she was assassinated by paid Trujillian assassins twelve days after his birth

However, the element of maternal love has never been missing, at any time from Manuelcito. His grandmother, Confesora Marte, and his aunt, Thelma Viera de Michel, together with her husband, Dr. Rafael A. Nichel Suero (Yuyo), have given him an adequate and happy life.

Although the paternal status of Manuelcito has not been made clear, numerous coincidences have been made known which indicate that he is the true son of Jesus de Galindez.

Relatives, with whom the mother lived a long time asserted that on one of her frequent trips to the United States, Gloria Estebania Viera Marte, was employed as bait, because of her beauty, to attract de Galindez, investigate him and inform on his movements, and that she had stayed with the professor in his apartment in New York.

Optimistic and radiant with happiness, the beautiful Trujillian spy, Gloria de Jesus Viera, told her aunt, on one occasion that "if I stay with him I will triumph".

According to her aunt, her niece described Galindez as "a man of fine tastes, an intellectual, and handsome, with a beautiful office and apartment".

"THE MISSION"

The "mission" that took Gloria Marte to meet de Galindez, according to what has been affirmed, commenced in November, 1955. From this date on, Marte traveled constant

APPENDIX 5   Memo from files of FBI indicating Galindez may have fathered a son.

rom Santo Domingo to New York, with brief stops in Puerto
ico. This suggests that Gloria, a graceful young woman
l years of age, whose cadaver was found dejected from a
recipice near the Villa Altagracia, on the Duarte Road,
imilar to other gloomy links that make up the macabre chain
onstructed by Trujillo to eradicate all those associated
ith the assassination of de Galindez, informed on the
ovements of the Spanish professor.

In spite of this, the charm and appeal of Galindez
ttracted the restless young Puerto Rican, and what was
imply a love adventure for the "service" was converted to a
rofound sentiment of passion and affection.

This sentiment separated "Gogi" from what she con-
racted to do, and what she was entrusted to do, which made
ne tyrant suspicious, and without disregarding this, the
ssassin, obeying the desires of Trujillo, erased all traces
f the crime committed against de Galindez, especially when
he FBI and the North American authorities commenced an
fficial investigation of his death.

The North American Pilot, Gerard Murphy and the
ominican Octavio de la Maza, who apparently were involved
ith the disappearance of de Galindez, were also assassinated
y Trujillo.

ODYSSEY

When de Galindez was rubbed out, on March 12, 1956,
here started what is considered an Odyssey for Gloria Marte.

The secret agent of Trujillo, now several months
regnant, had to abandon North American territory presumably
o avoid the intense investigation by the American authori-
ies. Believing that she would be secure on Dominican soil,
he returned to Santo Domingo, but immediately intense per-
ecution by the informants of Trujillato (followers of Trujillo)
as let loose upon her.

Perhaps this would explain why she did not stay
n the United States, eventhough she had the knowledge that
he bloody hands of the dictator would reach her on North
merican soil, at least the possibilities of her death were
ar reduced, if she had taken into account that de Galindez
ould not escape from Trujillo eventhough he was on American
erritory.

In her home on the expanded Espaillat, her aunt

spoke with deep nostalgia, about how "Gogi" was a prisoner
of her unusual nervousness, which was provoked by the in-
tensive surveillance which she was the object of, and by
the advanced stage of her pregnancy. This behavior contrastc
strongly with the youthfulness and happiness she demonstrated
on previous returns from New York.

SHE CRIED

Her aunt, who had the same name as she, was the
sister of "Gogi's" father, Pedro Viera (Perucho). She (aunt)
stated that her mother told her that the assassinated spy
(Gloria) had told her that "she was with Galindez in his
apartment". According to what she said, this occured when
both of them were in Mayaguez, Puerto Rico.

She stated that when her niece returned from the
United States, never to return, she seemed very suspicious
and isolated. "She didn't want anything to happen to us on
her account". It was when she moved next door to her parents,
in an apartment on Villa Mella, that she became happier. She
never talked about her pregnancy. I believe not even with
her own mother. She only told me on one occasion, while she
was crying, that Trujillo had asked her to have an abortion.

SHE GIVES BIRTH

Gloria Estebanis Viera Marte gavé birth in the publi
Maternity Hospital on July 22, 1956. If one alZigns this
date with her first trip to "conquer" de Galindez in New York,
one can easily note the normal time (9 months) for the ges-
tation and birth of a child.

Viera took the precaution of annotating, by hand,
on the "Registry of Birth" (which appears on the records of
the Court) the information concerning the pre and post
pregnancy data of the baby. All this information was verified
by her family. On the line which corresponds to "Father's
Name" Gloria wrote "Jesus". She did not write the last
name because of the pressure the Trujillian agents, who did
not want her to write the last name.

CRITICAL STATE
THEY KILLED HER IN HER YOUTH

Gloria's aunt stated that before her (Gloria's)
dramatic death, she (Gloria) visited her at her home located
in Mujoramiento Social, in "a state of extreme nervousness
and with the child in her arms; at times she vomited and

howed signs of having serious setbacks in her health".
t this same time she (Gloria) told a friend "Aida if some-
hing happens to me take care of the child"... Days later
e found out about her violent death.

"They killed her in her youth. She had just
ecome 21". She stated with deep mourning, furthermore she
aunt) stated "Serving Trujillo was what did her great harm."

During her childhood, Viera lived a long time with
er aunt. "She would constantly travel to Puerto Plata"...
he (aunt) expressed some fear, eventhough her husband was
police officer, "when the news came about Gogi's death".

Until now the exact place where the horribly mutil-
ted cadaver of Viera was buried is not known. Eventhough,
t has been said that she was buried by the Trujillian Regime
n Villa Altagracia, and it is believed that the cadaver was ex-
umed and transferred to a common grave in the cemetery at
arahona.

On different occasions, Gloria's aunt has been
uestioned by North American investigators, but she has re-
used to answer their questions. This is the first time she
poke about the tragic death of her niece.

LOAK OF MYSTERY

A cloak of mystery has shrouded the disappearance
f the Spanish author. The silence of the witness has
hwarted the efforts to clarify what happened. On one occa-
ion "Dominican Justice" declared itself incompetent to solve
hat has been considered one of the most "perfect political
rimes" in the history of Latin America. North American
ongressmen and authorities have been interested in discover-
ng the assassins of de Galindez but have also failed.

De Galindez was a strong opponent of the Trujillian
egime. Although he was born in Madrid, he considered himself
citizen of the Republic of Autonoma Vasca, which was abo-
ished by Franco after the Civil War. De Galindez was deported
o France together with other Spaniards who fought at his side.
n 1939 he came to the Dominican Republic. He became a pro-
essor in the School of Diplomatic Rights which functioned in
he Secretariat of Foreign Relations, and held special classes
or Ramfis Trujillo, the son of the tyrant. In December 1945
nd in the following year, he helped to favorably resolve
he strike conflicts between the workers and the North Ameri-
an sugar plantation owners. At this time he was in charge

of the functions of the Secretary of the Commission of Minimum Salary of the Secretary of Work. Considered to be a suspicious person, he had to leave for New York where he started to criticize the Dominican dictator. There he mysteriously disappeared on March 12, 1956. Years later the North American courts pronounced him officially dead, and gave his possession which were about some 50 thousands dollars, to his father in Madrid, Spain.

Another witness to the crime, was ex-general Arturo Espaillat, but he has not returned from his exile from the country.

According to another Spanish professor, whose name is Daniel Diaz Alejo; de Galindez was a man who manifested his disagreement with the exploitation of the Dominican Worker, as well as the cruel despotism and oppression which Trujillo had subjected the country to.

Diaz Alejo stated that on one occasion de Galindez was with a group of Spanish refugees, in Puerto Plata, and was given the advice that if he continued to conduct himself in this way he might gain the antipathy of the regime. "But de Galindez was a restless, stubborn, and forceful man".

He stated that in a meeting held in the Casa de Espana, located on Padre Billini Street, in Santo Domingo, that there was a discussion on the opportunity to "protect" the son that de Galindez had left. It was also discussed that his son be sent to a foreign land to study. This is according to what Diaz told the guardian of the boy, Dr. Michel Suero (Yuyo).

THE ONLY INTEREST

For his part, Dr. Michel Suero, who, together with his wife, Thelma Viera de Michel, took charge of the boy in 1959 (the previous three years the boy was with his grandmother in Puerto Plata) stated that his only interest is to definitely clarify the paternal origin of Manuelcito.

He stated that the silence which guarded this during the Trujillian period was obvious. He stated that when the investigations reached their most interesting point, in 1962, "We did not talk because we did not want them to think we were doing this for commercial (monetarian) interests".

"Now, in spite of this, we believe that this is the opportune moment to reveal the things that induce us

o think that this is the son of Jesus de Galindez", he
tated.

RENEWING INVESTIGATIONS

The inconclusive investigation of this misty case
has been renewed, starting with a visit by men, who identified themselves as "public officials of Justice", to the
home of Gloria's aunt.

Possibly the case was reopened to complete the
legal records, since March 12th, was the Tenth anniversary of
the assassination of de Galindez.

The matter, in spite of this, has not progressed.
The torpid and impregnable veil of mystery covering the
death of the Spanish intellectual has not been removed, not
even in its most elementary aspects.

Meanwhile, a ten year old blonde boy, with restless eyes like those of de Galindez, and when he was seven
years old without anyone asking him, said he wanted to be a
writer, waits for the authorities to definitely clarify his
paternal existence.

Manuelcito lives with his aunt and uncle in a modest
house, located on Luis E. Delmonte No.39 of Barahona, 204 kilo-
meters south of Santo Domingo. His refined characteristics
and his speech, appeal like those of de Galindez.

His aunt and uncle are interested in an official
explanation of the child's origin, because in the future this
might have some psychological affect, which might impair his
mental and physical growth.

The Dominicans have a debt to Jesus de Galindez
because he was a Spaniard, and "felt" the deep Dominican
drama, which he transcribed in his relentless opposition to
Trujillo. This moral debt can be repaid. Nevertheless, the
time has come to repay the eternal homage which we owe this
Spanish writer.

How? Reaffirm his virtues by supporting the investigations proving the paternal status of his presumed
son.

POLICE DEPARTMENT

CITY OF NEW YORK
NEW YORK 18, N. Y.

MPB - 5254 - PB

JESUS DE GALINDEZ

MISSING since 10.30 P.M.
March 12th, 1956, last time
seen when subject was to take
subway from 57th Street & 8th
Avenue, to his home at 30
Fifth Avenue, New York, N.Y.
Subject is described as a
white male, 41 years of age,
6'1", 160 lbs., slim build,
fair complexion, light brown
hair (slightly bald in front),
brown eyes, good teeth; may be
wearing a dark grey overcoat
with belt in back and grey-
green fedora and was carrying
a dark brown briefcase.
Subject is a lecturer in
International Law and Spanish
at Columbia University, New
York, N.Y. Special attention
to all hospitals.
Any information call Missing
Persons Bureau CAnal 6-2000.

APPENDIX 6   Missing Persons Bulletin.

MEMORANDUM

THE WHITE HOUSE
WASHINGTON

CONFIDENTIAL

APRIL 29, 1969

TO: JACK CAULFIELD

FROM: JOHN EHRLICHMAN

The President has been told that the present intelligence system
to provide the Federal government with advance warning
of activities on campuses and among minorities is deficient.

It is argued that conventional intelligence gathering methods
simply are not applicable in the new contexts.

I would appreciate your talking with people in whom you have
confidence outside of the government and giving me your thoughts
within the next five days on whether the present intelligence-
gathering system is adequate, and if not, what might be done to
improve it.

Would you please also give me a memorandum setting out the precise
costs that would be involved in the retention of the personnel we
discussed the other day?

CONFIDENTIAL

APPENDIX 7   White House Confidential Memorandum to Jack Caulfield from
John Ehrlichman dated April 29, 1969.

May 2, 1969

TO   JOHN EHRLICHMAN

FROM   JACK CAULFIELD

SUBJECT   Freshman Democratic Representative Mario Biaggi

The attached article indicating the emergence of Biaggi as a political spokesman should, in my view, be given continued attention by those concerned in the Administration. Biaggi commands a large nation-wide following among Italian/American groups. He could be an unsettling force in the '72 election if he stumbled onto the right issues.

My intelligence concerning him is that he is in fact close to some of the New York Maffia families. Indeed, I strongly suspect that he may well be a paid spokesman.

Some years ago I recall FBI leaders in New York became quite upset when it was rumored that Biaggi might become Chief Inspector of the New York City Police Department. I have reason to believe the FBI has considerable derogatory information concerning Biaggi and it is suggested that John Mitchell or Dick Kleindienst make it available to the Administration.

attachment

APPENDIX 8   White House Confidential memo to John Ehrlichman from Jack Caulfield regarding Mario Biaggi dated May 2, 1969.

June 18, 1969

John Ehrlichman

Wiley Buchanan called and talked with me about
the MORTGAGE GUARANTEE & INSURANCE COMPANY, Minneapolis, Minnesota.

He said it apparently is a company that was set
up by HHH and Bobby Baker in all fifty states and they take a
big chunck out of it.

He further said that the other day a newspaper
man called him and asked about this fact -- said a Republican
had told him he knew something.

Wiley says this is something we should have looked
into and get the facts looking to the time (and that might be
now even) that we might want to have them ready for us if needed.

(This discharges my duty on this -- but I would like to personally
recommend that we have someone check into this and see whether
there is anything to it).

RmWoods
6/25/69

APPENDIX 9   Memo to John Ehrlichman from R.M. Woods regarding Hubert
Humphrey, Bobby Baker and the Minnesota Mortgage Guarantee & Insurance
Company dated June 18, 1969.

FILE: J.D.E. - Edward T. Stanley   Date: July 7, 1969

                                        To: File

                                        From: Herbert W. Kalmbach

                                                 Caulfield

At 8:00 a.m. on Sunday morning, June 29th, Mr. Anthony T. Ulasewicz came to my room at the Madison Hotel in Washington, D. C. to discuss the mechanics of his intelligence work as an independent contractor for the Administration. This meeting had been set up by my earlier conversations with both John Ehrlichman and Jack Call-field.   *Caul-*

Ulasewicz will be performing special work for the Administration in various areas reporting to Jack Callfield and to John Ehrlichman. He will use the alias of Edward T. Stanley from time to time but when we call him at his home in Flushing, New York, we are to use his proper name. His full name and home address in New York City are as follows:

                Anthony T. Ulasewicz
                5316 195th Street
                New York, New York 11365
                Telephone: (212) FL7-9211

                (Social Security No. 091-01-8090)

Ulasewicz is married and has five children. His wife's name is Mary (S.S. No. 055-10-6650); son, Thomas A. - Marist College; daughter, Mary J. - Molloy Catholic College for Women; son, Peter D. - Archbishop Molloy High School. The two other children are married and are living away from home, i.e., non-dependents. They are Alice, age 23 and Antonette, who is 25 years of age.

Ulasewicz is to be paid at the annual rate of $22,000 a year with his first day on the job being July 7th. We will pay him on the 15th and on the 30th of each and every month with the first payment to be posted to him on Tuesday, July 15th for the period from July 7 to and including July 15. Inasmuch as we will be sending the checks from here, we will be posting the checks by air mail on the 14th and on the 29th of each month. Either Marilyn or I will sign the checks.

In addition to the aforementioned payments, we will reimburse him for expenses, including payment of all travel, meals, entertainment, etc.

In talking with John Ehrlichman, it was agreed that we would get credit cards in both his real name and under his alias

APPENDIX 10   Memorandum: law offices of Kalmbach, De Marco, Knapp & Chillingworth from Herbert W. Kalmbach regarding hiring of Anthony T. Ulasewicz dated July 7, 1969.

and that I would guarantee payment of same. Also, we are to get
him telephone company credit cards which I will arrange through
John Davies at The White House.

John and I were in agreement that $20 a day is a fair
per diem arrangement when he is on the road but that in the event
that such will not cover the costs involved, such can be modified
at a later date.

LAW OFFICES
KALMBACH, DE MARCO, KNAPP & CHILLINGWORTH

MEMORANDUM

FILE: J.D.E. - Edward T. Stanley   Date: July 8, 1969

To: File

From: Herbert W. Kalmbach

I talked to John Davies at The White House this morning and he agreed to have someone from A.T. & T. contact me relative to a telephone credit card for Ulasewicz. Also, a card will be issued under the name of Edward T. Stanley.

The cards, when issued, will be sent to Ulasewicz' address in New York with all bills to come to the law firm to my attention.

Ordinarily, the procedure is to issue cards against the party's home telephone number but in this instance, I have asked John to issue blind card numbers (i.e., where such cannot be traced back to Ulasewixz' home phone number).

HWK

Appendix 11   Memorandum: law offices of Kalmbach, De Marco, Knapp & Chillingworth from Herbert W. Kalmbach regarding telephone credit cards dated July 8, 1969.

AMERICAN TELEPHONE AND TELEGRAPH COMPANY

2000 L STREET, NORTHWEST

WASHINGTON, D. C. 20036

202   466-5561

BEN F. GIVENS
ASSISTANT VICE PRESIDENT

July 9, 1969

Mr. Herbert W. Kalmbach
Kalmbach, DeMarco, Knapp & Chillingworth
550 Newport Center Drive - Suite 900
Newport Beach, California   92660

Dear Mr. Kalmbach:

My secretary, Mrs. Elizabeth Thaden, received a call from John Davies, Special Assistant to the President, requesting that two credit cards be issued to Mr. Anthony T. Ulasewicz and Mr. Edward T. Stanley of 5316 195th Street New York, New York   11365, with the bills being sent to you.

It is my understanding that you have fully approved these credit cards. We are proceeding on the basis that you will be fully responsible for the calls placed on these credit cards.

Yours very truly,

B. F. Givens

APPENDIX 12   Letter to Herbert W. Kalmbach from American Telephone and Telegraph Company regarding telephone credit cards.

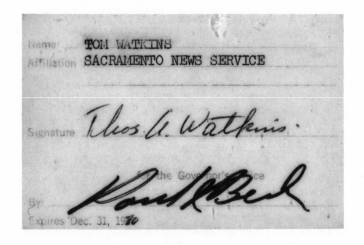

APPENDIX 13   Press Pass of Thomas A. Watkins (alias of Tony Ulasewicz)

TESTIMONY OF JOHN D. EHRLICHMAN IN THE CASE OF
UNITED STATES OF AMERICA V. ANTHONY T. ULASEWICZ
IN THE UNITED STATES DISTRICT COURT FOR THE
EASTERN DISTRICT OF NEW YORK/DOCKET NO. 35-CR-330
DECEMBER 21, 1976

"Q. Mr. Ehrlichman, do you know the defendant in this case, Anthony Ulasewicz?

A. Yes, I do.

Q. When did you first meet Mr. Ulasewicz?

A. Well, the first and only time that I met him was in the Spring of 1969.

Q. And that was in connection with what?

A. It was in connection with his possible employment to do political chores and investigations and errands for President Nixon.

Q. Now, do you have a present recollection of that conversation with Mr. Ulasewicz?

A. Yes.

Q. Okay. Would you tell us what he said to you and what you said to him?

A. Well, I can't---I obviously have a general recollection of our conversation in that sense. We met very briefly at LaGuardia Airport, by appointment. Mr. Caulfield arranged for us to meet there, as I was travelling from Washington to New York and some other---some other piece of business and the purpose of our getting together was to demonstrate to Mr. Ulasewicz that the President, through me, was indeed interested in having him making himself available for this employment and we discussed generally whether or not he would be available to do these non-governmental chores that the President wanted done and then we also discussed generally his past experience with the New York City Police Department as an undercover person.

Q. Do you have a present recollection of discussion about a private detective agency?

A. No, Not as such.

APPENDIX 14 Testimony of John E. Ehrlichman dated December 21, 1976.

Q. When you say "as such"?

A. Well, the work that we discussed Mr. Ulasewicz doing was of a private nature, not the creation of an agency but the employment of him as an individual.

Q. Was Mr. Ulasewicz to be paid for his services?

A. Yes.

Q. Thereafter---after that point in time, did Mr. Ulasewicz perform services at your direction?

A. Well, at my direction in the sense that I was the conduit through which the President's requests were passed and yes, he did ultimately perform services in that chain of requests, so to speak. The President would want some piece of information, or you know, something checked into and it would be something that it was inappropriate to have someone in the Government employed do.

It would be of a purely individual or political nature, and he would say something to me in the nature of a request and I in turn during the time that I was counsel to the President, which was in 1969, I would then pass that along to Mr. Caulfield and then he in turn would pass it along to Tony Ulasewicz.

Q. When you say "the President", you are referring to whom?

A. President Nixon.

July 17, 1969

FOR: JOHN D. EHRLICHMAN

FROM: JACK CAULFIELD

SUBJECT: Security Survey (RNC)

Following your endorsement of my recommendation for a
security survey at the Republican National Committee, I
put Jack Ragan in touch with Bob Hitt. The result is
the attached survey report. To say the survey was needed
is a gross understatement. In my opinion, unless the recommendations are implemented on a continual basis, we
run the formidable risk of opposition penetration at any
time. Unless I hear from you to the contrary, I will
suggest to Bob Hitt that Ragan be used in such connection.

Because of Bob Haldeman's expressed interest in this area
last February, I have sent him a copy of the report.

APPENDIX 15   Memo to John D. Ehrlichman from Jack Caulfield regarding
Security Survey at Republican National Committee dated July 17, 1969.

LARRY O'BRIEN

When Larry O'Brien became Chairman of the National Committee, he stated he would serve without salary and would continue with his public relations business.

The Wall Street Journal of March 10 carried a story that O'Brien planned to continue the operation of his New York public relations concern and would remain its president. "A spokesman said the staff of Lawrence O'Brien Associates, Inc. is being expanded."

The question, therefore, is whether there is any conflict of interest or tie-in between the clients he represents and his political activities as Chairman of the DNC. For example, he will be in touch with Democratic Members of the House and Senate, which Party is in control of Congress. This can affect legislation in which his clients may be interested. Furthermore, even though the Executive Branch is Republican, there are many holdovers in key places who can be helpful in the award of contracts, etc.

It is my understanding that the following are facts:

(1)   In the latter part of January 1970, O'Brien announced he was forming a public relations company at 230 Park Avenue, New York City.

(2)   His offices are part of the Dyson-Kissner Corp., which is a private investment company that uses the same address and same telephone number -- MU 6-9270.

        The Dyson-Kissner Corp. is a holding company engaged in manufacturing. Its affiliates are: Northwest Automatic Products Division, Screw Machine Products, Twin City Monorail Division, and K. P. Manufacturing Division, which makes conveyors and lubricating equipment. Its tangible net worth is in excess of $10 million.

        As of August 15, 1969, a report showed that the corporation was seeking profitable companies with experienced management.

        There are other subsidiaries, such as Unit-Rail Anchor Co. of Pittsburgh, Pennsylvania which manufactures rail anchors, railroad tools, agriculture implements and lock washers; D.K. Properties, Inc. which bought real estate at three Minneapolis locations leased to and occupied entirely by the three divisions of Dyson-Kissner Corp.

(3)   The principals in the Dyson-Kissner Corp. are:

        a) Charles H. Dyson, 58-60 years of age. He and his wife, Margaret M., reside at 24 Thompkins Road, Scarsdale, New York.

APPENDIX 16   Confidential Memo regarding Larry O'Brien.

Former residences were: 19 Ridge Road, Bronxville, New
York; 34 Crawford Street, Bronxville, New York, a nd 3133
Connecticut Avenue, Washington, D. C.

He is Chairman of Dyson-Kissner, with which he has been for
15 years, and is a man of independent means.

b)   Franklyn H. Kissner, 60 years of age. He resides at 24
Gramercy Park, New York City and has lived there for about
15 years; is married and highly regarded. He has an account
with First National Bank of Boston.

(4)   Also sharing office space with Dyson-Kissner, or a part of their
organization, are the following:

> Six-Fifty Nine Associates
> Varlen Corporation
> Berban Properties
> Cornwall Management Corp.
> WEFOUR Communications, Inc.
> H. M. Industries
> Hubbard and Co.
> Pat Erson Planning and Services

Individuals listed as part of the same organization are:

> F. W. Beck
> John F. Culp
> John C. Harding III
> Edward L. Hoffman
> Glenn O. Kidd
> M. M. MacGregor
> James A. McLean
> John A. Moran

(5)   As of March 1, before he became Democratic National Chairman,
O'Brien listed four clients:

a) Howard Hughes (corporate interests). It should be noted
that Carl Byoir and Associates has been public relations counsel
for Hughes and continues to hold the account; it is now expanding
its staff.

b) The American Society of Composers (ASCAP), with a branch
office at 9301 Wilshire Boulevard, Beverly Hills, California. Its
main address is 575 Madison Avenue, New York City.

The organization engages in promoting the interests of composers, authors and publishers.

It was involved many years ago in litigation with the Federal Government in connection with alleged restraint of trade and monopolies.

c) Riker-Maxson, an electronics firm. The company was formed on April 1, 1969 by a merger of Maxson Electronics Corp. into Riker Corp.

Riker Corp. operated in three basic areas -- electronics (64% of 1967 sales); communications (32%) and computer programming (4%).

Maxson Electronics operated in three basic areas: Government business (86% of fiscal 1967/8 sales); industrial products (12%) and computer services (2%).

SUBSTANTIALLY ALL OF NET INCOME IN RECENT YEARS CAME FROM THE GOVERNMENT BUSINESS GROUP, WHICH IS ENGAGED IN ADVANCED ENGINEERING AND MANUFACTURE OF MISSILES AND DRONES, MISSILE GUIDANCE SYSTEMS, MICROWAVE AND RADAR PRODUCTS, AND RELATED ORDNANCE, AS WELL AS VOLUME PRODUCTION OF PYROTECHNIC COMPONENTS.

The company is located at 280 Park Avenue, New York City. The President is R. Dressler.

d) Dukor Industries, Inc. We have received no information concerning this company.

(6)   The Evans-Novak column in the Los Angeles Times of March 3, 1970 stated that clients of O'Brien were Hughes Tool Company and Dukor Industries, Inc.

Personal matters concerning O'Brien are:

Born: Springfield, Massachusetts, July 17, 1917.

Married to Elva Lena Brassard on May 30, 1944; one child, Laurence Francis III.

Received his LL.B. from Northeastern University and several honorary degrees from other colleges.

He participated in various political campaigns in 1946, 1948, 1950, 1952, 1958, 1960 and 1964.

He was Special Assistant to the President for Congressional
Relations from 1961 to 1965; Postmaster General from 1965
to 1968 and former Democratic National Chairman.

Business and professional positions were: former manager
of family business enterprise; board president and business
manager of the Western Hotel fund (1952-58); public relations
1958 to 1960.

Served in the Army from 1943-45; is an Elk and belongs to
the American Legion.

POSSIBLE QUESTIONS

1. Who were O'Brien's clients just before he accepted the post of Chairman of the Democratic National Committee?

2. What were his specific duties for each of them?

3. What was his compensation from each of them?

4. Did any of them have any business dealings with the Federal Government?

   If so, what was the nature of them?

5. The Wall Street Journal of March 10, 1970 carried a story that you (O'Brien) would remain President of your public relations firm and that "a spokesman said the staff is being expanded." Has the staff been expanded?

6. How many people do you have on your staff now?

7. What are their duties?

8. How many people did you have on your staff just before becoming Chairman of the Democratic National Committee?

9. Has your firm obtained any new clients since you became Chairman of the Democratic National Committee?

10. If so, who are they?

11. What services are you expected to perform for them if there are any new clients?

12. What is your compensation from each of the new clients, if there are any?

13. Do you have any association of any kind with Dyson-Kissner Corp.?

    If so, what is it?

14. How do you happen to have offices with Dyson-Kissner Corp. with the same telephone number, instead of having your own office?

15. Do you represent the Dyson-Kissner Corp. or any of its subsidiaries or affiliates?

16. Do you represent any of the people or firms who share office space with Dyson-Kissner?

17. The Evans-Novak column of March 3, 1970 in the <u>Los Angeles Times</u> stated that some of your clients were the Hughes Tool Co. and Dukor Industries, Inc.

    How long have you represented Hughes Tool Co.?

    Isn't it true that Carl Byoir and Associates is the public relations firm for Hughes?

18. What have been your duties for the Hughes Tool Co.?

19. What compensation have you received from Hughes Tool Co.?

20. What have you done for the Hughes Tool Co.?

21. Have you made any contact with any Member of Congress or any Governmental agency in behalf of Hughes Tool Co. before you became Chairman of the Democratic National Committee?

22. Have you made any contact with any Member of Congress or any Governmental agency in behalf of Hughes Tool Co. after becoming Chairman of the Democratic National Committee?

23. As of March 1, 1970, before you became Democratic National Chairman, you listed The American Society of Composers (ASCAP) as one of your clients.

    How long have you represented ASCAP?

24. What have been your duties for ASCAP?

25. What compensation have you received from ASCAP?

26. What have you done for ASCAP?

27. Have you made any contact with any Member of Congress or any Governmental agency in behalf of ASCAP before you became Chairman of the Democratic National Committee?

28. Have you made any contact with any Member of Congress or any Governmental agency in behalf of ASCAP after becoming Chairman of the Democratic National Committee?

29. As of March 1, 1970, before you became Democratic National Chairman, you listed Riker-Maxson as one of your clients.

  . How long have you represented Riker-Maxson?

30. What have been your duties for Riker-Maxson?

31. What compensation have you received from Riker-Maxson?

32. What have you done for Riker-Maxson?

33. Have you made any contact with any Member of Congress or any Governmental agency in behalf of Riker-Maxson before you became Chairman of the Democratic National Committee?

34. Have you made any contact with any Member of Congress or any Governmental agency in behalf of Riker-Maxson after becoming Chairman of the Democratic National Committee?

35. The Evans-Novak column of March 3, 1970 in the <u>Los Angeles Times</u> stated that Dukor Industries, Inc. was one of your clients.

    Where is this company located?

36. What business does it conduct?

37. Who are the President and principal officers?

38. How long have you represented Dukor?

39. What have been your duties for Dukor?

40. What compensation have you received from Dukor?

41. What have you done for Dukor?

42. Have you made any contact with any Member of Congress or any Governmental agency in behalf of Dukor before you became Chairman of the Democratic National Committee?

43. Have you made any contact with any Member of Congress or any Governmental agency in behalf of Dukor after becoming Chairman of the Democratic National Committee?

# # #

April 19, 1971

MEMORANDUM FOR JOHN W. DEAN, III

FROM: JACK CAULFIELD

SUBJECT: MUSKIE'S ASSOCIATION WITH MAINE SUGAR INDUSTRY
                 FIRM ABOUT TO GO BANKRUPT

With respect to this matter, be advised that Lyn Nofziger
is most knowledgeable in this area. I have worked with
him on certain segments of it.

You should also be aware that considerable newspaper publicity
has already been given to Muskie's involvment in this matter.
Such publicity is a matter of record in the research division
of the RNC.

The only new development here is that the subject firm is
about to go bankrupt and we have Charlie Eagan in good
position regarding the current development.

Because of the information available, because of the hazards
of the White House pursuing this inquiry, I wish to strongly
suggest that Chuck endorse Lyn and Charlie Fagan getting
together for optimum results with minimal White House exposure.

APPENDIX 17   Memorandum for John W. Dean, III from Jack Caulfield regarding Muskie/Maine Sugar Industry dated April 19, 1971.

October 26, 1971

MEMORANDUM FOR H. R. HALDEMAN

FROM: JOHN W. DEAN, III

SUBJECT: JAMES LA ROE ALSO KNOWN AS RICHARD M. DIXON

Pretext inquiry in New York has resulted in contact with
Dixon's agent, Murray Becker of G. W. Purcell Associates,
150 East 52 Street, Manhattan 10022, #212-753-7600. The
results are as follows:

    A) Dixon is alleged to have legally changed his name
from James La Roe to Richard M. Dixon. As the attached
material indicates, he is 44 years of age, married with
two daughters and resides in Brooklyn. The F.B.I. has no
record based upon a name check.

    B) All contact with La Roe is restricted to his agent,
La Roe is presently in Philadelphia working on a movie with
Mickey Rooney to be entitled, "RICHARD". According to
Becker, the film, scheduled for release in February, is to
be a satirical spoof on the President. Becker asserts the
film will not be insulting.

    C) Harpers Bazaar magazine will publish an article in
January on this subject.

    D) Following the release of the film, Becker will be
seeking night club and dinner engagements for his client.

Attachment

APPENDIX 18   Memorandum for H. R. Haldeman from John W. Dean, III
regarding James La Roe dated October 26, 1971.

THIS REPORT SHOULD BE CONSIDERED CONFIDENTIAL, FOR YOUR EYES ONLY.

I received a telephone call at my apartment on Saturday morning, December 18th, 19 , from a man who identified himself as Mr. Don Simmons. He said he wanted to find a young person in the Madison area to do work for the reelection of the President, for about ten to fifteen hours per month, and wanted to put this individual on a retainer basis. He said the work involved opposition research, etc.

He said he was from a political consultant firm in New York. He said he received my name from Randy Knox. We set up a meeting in the Park Motor Inn Lounge for that afternoon.

Simmons said he was interested in running a "negative campaign" in Wisconsin. He explained that the purpose of the campaign was to create as much bitterness and disunity within the Democrat primary as possible. He suggested doing things such as planting questions in student audiences before which the Democrat candidates were working, getting students to picket the Democrat candidates, e.g. a black student to picket Muskie regarding his remark on a black V.P. candidate, etc. He also said he was interested in planting spies in the Democrat candidate's offices. He said that he wanted to concentrate on Muskie, and give second priority to McGovern.

Simmons said he wanted to pay someone $100.00 per month, plus expenses, to co-ordinate these projects. He also said he was willing to pay a salary of up to $50.00 per month to a person we could plant in Muskie headquarters.

I asked him if he was working for the CCREP or the RNC. He replied he was working on his own, with his own money. (He implied that he was saying this because he did not want anyone to be able to trace his activities to the Nixon campaign or the Party officially.) I asked him how I could establish his credentials, and he was, frankly, evasive, although I got the impression that he was implying this evasiveness was deliberate.

Although the whole incident seemed strange, I tentatively agreed to work on his project (as most of the ideas he suggested seemed like they were worth doing anyway). He gave me $50.00 in advance payment, and said he would call back in early January. He said I should concentrate initially on finding someone to plant in Muskie HQ. He said that we would communicate only by telephone, for security reasons.

Mr. Simmons registered at the Park Motor Inn on Dec 16, 1972, and checked out on Dec. 19th. He listed his home address as 1400 Olympic Avenue NW, Wash DC. He paid his bill in cash. He made approximately twelve local phone calls, and three long distance calls. One of the long distance calls was to Randy Knox' home in Fort Atkinson; one was to a Madison area (884 exchange) number, and one was to Peoria, Ill., 309-674-2143. (We are checking this number out through contacts in Illinois.)

APPENDIX 19   Confidential Memo of Timothy Gratz regarding Don Simmons (alias for Donald Segretti).

The only persons that I have discussed this matter w. h, all of
whom promised to keep it confidential, are: John Ma Iver, head
of the Nixon campaign in Wisconsin,; Karl Rove, Exec ive Director
of the College Republican National Committee; Mike I ren, Administrative Assistant to Sen. Devitt and a political ass iate; and my
parents. I discussed it in sketchier details with Randy Knox and
Doug Nelson of the Attorney General's office.

The following possibilities suggest themselves:

1. Don Simmons is legitimate.

    A. He is acting completely on his own, and has not informed
        anyone of his activities.

    B. He is acting as an agent of the Party or the Nixon campaign,
        but for security reasons, very few people know of his opera-
        tions. (This seems implausible, as Karl checked with high
        leaders of the Nixon operation in Washington, and they were
        unaware of Simmons. It also seems implausible that Mr.
        MacIver would not be aware of his presence in Wisconsin if
        he were legit.

2. Don Simmons is not legitimate.

    A. He is working for the Democrat Party or a Democrat candidate,
        or for a newspaper, or on his own, in an attempt to trap
        Republicans in embarrassing acts.

    B. He is working for a Democrat candidate (presumably other than
        Muskie or McGovern) and is attempting to use Republicans to
        accomplish his own ends.

    C. He is working for the Democrat Party or a Democrat candidate,
        the idea being to discover in advance if the Republicans are
        planning on planting spies in the Democrat candidates opera-
        tions.

The one thing which would argue against him being working for the
Democrats, it seems to me, is his free dispersal of funds. If the
news accounts are true, most of the Democrat candidates, and especially
the Democrat Party, are very short of funds. It would not seem logical
for them to be paying Simmons for his operations. (How could an
embarrassing story regarding Republicans help during the Wisconsin
primary?)

I would be interested in your thoughts on this matter: What should
I do, refuse to co-operate with Simmons any further, play along with
him to find out more about what he is up to, etc?

Also, if Mr. Simmons is not legitimate, and if his activities could
hurt the Nixon campaign, other Nixon organizations should be alerted
to his actions. (He implied he was concentrating on primary states,
I think.)

Would be interested in your comments on this matter.

HENRY M. BUCHANAN, C.P.A., P.A.
CERTIFIED PUBLIC ACCOUNTANTS
7979 OLD GEORGETOWN ROAD, SUITE 311
BETHESDA, MARYLAND 20014

HENRY M. BUCHANAN
GEORGE F. LYNCH, JR.

TELEPHONE
(301) 652-0580

September 4, 1973

Mr. Anthony T. Ulasewicz
Star Route (Saratoga County)
Hadley, New York 12835

Dear Mr. Ulasewicz:

. My office has been requested by the Finance Committee to Re-elect the President to prepare a report to be filed with the Clerk of the House of Representatives of the United States showing the receipts and disbursements of the Finance Committee to Re-elect the President, and all related committees for the period January 1, 1971, through April 6, 1972. This report is required by the order of Judge Joseph Waddy dated July 24, 1973, in the action entitled, Common Cause, et al vs. the Finance Committee to Re-elect the President, et al.

If you have any accounting or other records which will assist my office in the preparation of this report, would you kindly notify me. I will be glad to meet with you at your convenience to discuss this matter. Copies of any accounting records or other records which have a bearing on this report may be forwarded to my office. My report must be finished on or before September 28, 1973. If you have no records or information which is of assistance in the preparation of this report, kindly indicate this fact to me. I appreciate your prompt reply to my inquiry. A self-addressed, stamped envelope is enclosed. You may telephone me at 301-652-0580 during business hours, if you desire.

Very truly yours,

Henry M. Buchanan

Authorized:

Paul C Barrick

Henry M. Buchanan
Certified Public Accountant for
    The Finance Committee to Re-elect
    the President

HMB:da

Enc.

APPENDIX 20   Letter from Henry M. Buchanan to Tony Ulasewicz regarding report of receipts and disbursements of the Finance Committee.

TO: Terry Lenzner
FROM: Marc Lackritz
DATE: September 20, 1973
SUBJECT: Anthony T. Ulasewicz

          Tony Ulasewicz has testified before the Select Committee on two occasions: May 23, 1973, and July 18, 1973.

          On May 23, 1973, Ulasewicz testified as to his role as intermediary in the alleged clemency offer made to James McCord.

          Mr. Ulasewicz did not discuss his investigative role in the White House except under questioning by Senator Inouye. At page 708 of the transcript Mr. Ulasewicz testified that he was paid $22,000 a year from the payroll of Mr. Kalmbach and that his work involved being an outside supporting investigator for Mr. Caulfield. On the following page of the transcript, Ulasewicz states that he did investigative work in support of whatever Mr. Caulfield related to him. There was no other mention at this time of Ulasewicz' investigative role.

          Mr. Ulasewicz returned to testify before the Committee on Wednesday, July 18, 1973. On this occasion, Ulasewicz' testimony focused on his role as an intermediary in making payments to the defendants from Herbert Kalmbach. At page 4544, Senator Montoya questioned Ulasewicz briefly about the kinds of investigations that he was doing on individuals. These questions were only of a very general nature and did not get into the specifics of the investigations. Later that afternoon, during the questioning of Senator Weicker, a few of the specific investigations done by Ulasewicz were inquired into. Beginning on page 4550, Senator Weicker questioned Mr. Ulasewicz about his salary as a private investigator, the direction coming from Mr. Caulfield in the White House, and the nature of the investigations. Senator Weicker's line of questioning developed that Ulasewicz' investigations included inquiries into the sexual habits, drinking habits, domestic problems, and personal social activities of the individuals, corporations and organizations to which Ulasewicz was assigned. On the following pages, Senator Weicker developed the information that many of Ulasewicz' investigations were of potential political opponents of the President as well as other political figures. At page 4557, Ulasewicz described how he would develop the investigations requested by Mr. Caulfield as well as how he would keep these investigations discreet. Ulasewicz described interviewing individuals to find out information that was not a matter of public record as well as going into public records for matters such as financial contributors to past campaigns.

          Senator Weicker's examination of Mr. Ulasewicz did not delve into the relevance of Ulasewicz' investigations to the political espionage conducted in the 1972 campaign.

APPENDIX 21   Memorandum to Terry Lenzner from Marc Lackritz regarding Tony Ulasewicz's testimony dated September 20, 1973.

The importance of some of some of Mr. Ulasewicz' specific
investigations is that they lay a foundation for the pattern of espionage
that emerged in the 1972 presidential campaign, and provide a link to
many of the activities and events that other witnesses will testify about.

For example, Ulasewicz was asked by Caulfield to investigate the
group of Quakers who were protesting daily in front of the White House.
Ulasewicz did a discreet investigation of the financing and legitimacy of
the group and reported back to Caulfield some time in 1970. Later on in
1972, Jeb Magruder asked Ken Rietz to get someone to infiltrate the Quakers
in front of the White House to gather information concerning their proposed
activities for the 1972 political conventions.

Similarly, in December, 1971, Ulasewicz was asked to go out to
Wisconsin to investigate an individual who was trying to recruit Young
Republicans for pranks in the 1972 campaign. Ulasewicz flew out to
Wisconsin to try to arrange a face-to-face meeting with this unidentified
individual. Ulasewicz failed in his efforts to meet the unidentified individual
and was then told by Caulfield to stop the investigation because apparently the
individual was all right. This individual later turned out to be Donald
Segretti in the midst of his travels of late '71 and '72 recruiting a network
of agents for the presidential primaries.

A third example of how Ulasewicz' testimony would link up with
other incidents in the hearings was his investigation of the Brookings
Institute. Ulasewicz was given instructions to investigate the background
and structure of the Brookings Institute in the summer of 1971, at about
the same time that Charles Colson was proposing to Jack Caulfield that he
might start a fire in the Brookings Institute in order to secure valuable
papers from one of the offices inside.

Many of Ulasewicz' other investigations relate directly to the
1972 presidential campaign. Ulasewicz did more than one investigation of
Larry O'Brien, who was later to become the object of electronic surveillance
in the break-in itself. Ulasewicz did a variety of investigations on
Senator Edmund Muskie. He checked all the newspaper files in Augusta and
Bangor, Maine, on Muskie's past campaigns, secured lists of contributors to
the past campaigns of Muskie, did an investigation into the Maine sugar
industry to determine if favorable treatment for SBA loans was given to this
industry because of the intervention of Senator Muskie, and finally,
Ulasewicz did an investigation into the background of Muskie's youth
co-ordinator, Lanny Davis, to determine whether or not he was a Communist.

Ulasewicz also did some investigations into the background of
Senator Humphrey which included an investigation into the purchase of his
home (the financing end of it), and a list of the past contributors to his
campaigns.

In addition, Ulasewicz was sent up to New Hampshire to do an
investigation of the Ashbrook and McCloskey campaigns to determine how well
staffed and how well financed they were. Ulasewicz was also sent down to

Miami during the Florida primary, and one of his assignments down there was to check out the Miami Beach Convention Hall, and learn of the financing arrangements made with the tourist development agency.

Finally, Ulasewicz was asked to investigate Don Nixon, Jr., when he was in the Sierra Madre of California and allegedly living like a hippy and throwing his weight around. This investigation of Ulasewicz could well link up with the wiretapping of Donald Nixon, Sr., by the Secret Service in 1970.

DEMOCRATIC
NATIONAL COMMITTEE   *1625 Massachusetts Ave., N.W.   Washington, D.C. 20036   (202) 797-5900*

Lee Kling
Finance Chairman

February 6, 1974

Mr. Leo Ulasewicz
85-27 57th Avenue
Elmhurst, New York   11373

Dear Mr. Ulasewicz:

Our good friend Robert Strauss has seen fit to appoint me Finance Chairman of the Democratic National Committee. I am, of course, delighted and honored to accept this post and look forward to my duties and responsibilities with great enthusiasm.

You have always been instrumental in supplying the Democratic National Committee with the funds it needed to carry out its leadership role in administering and directing the course of the Democratic Party. I want to personally express my thanks for your past, present, and hopefully, future support.

As a means of creating both financial and leadership support for the DNC, we have created a "Finance Committee of the DNC". This committee will be limited in size and will be the spearhead and bullwark of financial support for the DNC. I would like to personally invite you to join me as a member of this committee. We would contribute $100 monthly, or if you prefer, $1,200 annually.

As a means of expressing our appreciation for your generosity, we would like to outline on the attached sheet what we plan to offer the Finance Committee members for this coming year.

I sincerely hope that you will seriously consider joining us as a member of the Finance Committee. If you should desire to discuss the Finance Committee, please call me here at the Democratic National Committee Headquarters. Also, when in Washington, please drop by and say hello.

Sincerely,

Lee Kling
Finance Chairman

P.S. A card is included to acknowledge your acceptance. Please merely check it, sign and return it. You will notice that we would further appreciate your preliminary thoughts as to whether you are contemplating attending the Mid-Term Conference and if we can assist you.

APPENDIX 22   Letter to Leo Ulasewicz from Democratic National Committee inviting him to become a member of the Finance Committee.

MARIO BIAGGI
TENTH DISTRICT
NEW YORK

July 13, 1982

Dear Tony:

You look great! Keep chopping those trees.

No one can stop a good cop...........

Give me a call; I'd like to hear from you.

Sincerely,

MARIO BIAGGI, M. C.

Mr. Tony Ulasewicz
Star Route - Day
Hadley P.O., N.Y.
12835

APPENDIX 23   Original letter to Tony Ulasewicz from Mario Biaggi dated
July 13, 1982.

RICHARD NIXON

May 22, 1979

Dear Tony,

Your letter of May 14 with the enclosed
Letter to the Editor of the Glens Falls
Post-Star was most thoughtful.

I want you to know how much I appreciate
your loyal friendship and support.

With best wishes,

Sincerely,

Mr. Tony Ulasewicz
Town of Day
Box 151 Star Route
Hadley P. O.,
New York 12835

APPENDIX 24   A thank you from the former President.

CHRONOLOGICAL HISTORY OF BOSSI

Dates:

1904	Italian Squad.
October, 1912	Radical Bureau formed.
1915	Neutrality Squad.
1924	Renamed the Radical Bureau which consisted of three additional units, i.e. Bomb Squad, Industrial Squad and Gangster Squad.
January 1, 1931	The Bureau of Criminal Alien Investigations was formed.
May 13, 1945	The Bureau of Criminal Alien Investigations was changed to Public Relations Squad.
October 22, 1945	Special Squad #1, and Public Relations Squad consolidated, to be known as Public Relations Squad.
April 15, 1946	The Public Relations Squad was changed to the Bureau of Special Service and Investigation.
1951	Bureau of Special Service and Investigation changed to Central Office Bureaus and Squads.
August 1, 1955	Name changed to Bureau of Special Services (Department Directive #80)

April 21, 1969 Bureau of Special Services was changed to Special Services Division.

December 1, 1970 Special Services Division abolished. Incorporated into the Intelligence Division of the Inspectional Services Bureau of the Office of the First Deputy Commissioner. (No longer under the Detective Bureau. TOP 332 dated December 1, 1970.)

December 23, 1970 Now known as the Security and Investigation Section, Intelligence Division. Authority: Assistant Chief Arthur Grubert, Intelligence Division.

November 14, 1972 Organized Crime Section and Security Investigation Section formally merged into the Intelligence Division. The Intelligence Division will have five Sections, namely: Liaison, Analysis, Investigations, Records & Administration.

September 21, 1973 The Intelligence Division reorganized to have two Sections: Operations and Analysis, plus a Staff Unit. Operations Section includes Special Projects Unit, Technical Unit, Liaison Unit and Information Control Unit. Analysis Section to include Syndicated Crime Unit, Principal Crime Unit, Security Unit, Special Interests Unit and Records Unit.

February 25, 1974 The Intelligence Division reorganized into three Sections: Operations, Criminal and Public Security, plus a Staff Unit. Operations Section includes Special Project Unit, Liaison Unit. Criminal Section includes Syndicated Crime Unit, Principal Crime Unit and Records Unit. Public Security Section includes the Security Unit and the Special Interests Unit.

NOTES

SURFACING.

Page 6: The taped conversation between President Richard Nixon and John Dean occurred on the morning of March 13, 1973 between the hours of 12:42 P.M. and 2:00 P.M. See THE PRESIDENTIAL TRANCRIPTS, Dell Publishing Co., Inc., New York, 1974, page 89.

Pages 15–16: In reporting the execution of Demetrius Gula and Joseph Sacoda on January 11, 1940, *The New York Times* quoted from *The Angriff*, a Berlin, Germany newspaper that published an article recommending to President Franklin D. Roosevelt that he stop criticizing Germany and start paying attention to the "terrorists and gangsters in his own country." Suggesting that Roosevelt turn his eyes on the depressing reality of his own country, *The Angriff* defined that reality as consisting "of a hungry farmer's family having to leave its home, strikers playing cards instead of working, youth never having jobs, bread lines with baby carriages, and 'shanty' depression homes."

At his trial, Demetrius Gula testified that he was beaten up by FBI agents after his arrest. "Get up, you son-of-a-bitch, get up. Talk," Gula claimed the agents yelled while they smacked him around. In rebuttal, an FBI agent testified that all he did was "jammed my gun into his ribs and told him (Gula) to keep his mouth shut." J. Edgar Hoover testified to bolster the credibility of the agents who worked on the case. Gula and Sacoda were convicted as charged, their sentence of death affirmed without opinion by the New York State Court of Appeals (281 NY 827), and their execution carried out without further appeal.

Pages 20–24: The Harlem riot of August 1, 1943. See *The New York Times,* August 2, 1943 and also *The New Yorker,* July 20, 1981, "That was Harlem" by Jervis Anderson (fourth part of a series of four articles).

351

BOSSI

Pages 33–35: For additional background information see *Police Intelligence, The Operation of An Investigative Unit*, by Anthony V. Bouza, AMS Press, Inc., New York, 1976.

Pages 56–57: Mrs. Oksana Stepanova Kosenkina's leap to freedom August 12, 1948. See *The New York Times* for August 13, 1948.

Pages 62–66: The death of Andrei Vishinsky November 22, 1954. See *The New York Times* November 23, 1954.

GALINDEZ

Page 83: *The Era of Trujillo* was originally written by Professor Jesus de Galindez in Spanish. It was then translated into English, abridged and revised, and became the thesis Professor Galindez submitted for his doctorate degree at Columbia University. In 1973, the University of Arizona Press published the English version of Galindez's book.

Pages 113–126: The prosecution of John Joseph Frank was made under indictment No. 493-1957 filed in the United States District Court for the District of Columbia on May 13, 1957. The opinion and decision of the United States Circuit Court of Appeals for the District of Columbia reversing John Frank's conviction and ordering a new trial was reported in 262 Fed 2d.695

Page 127: The United States Department of Justice, together with the Office of Records Administration, National Archives and Records Administration, Washington, D.C. has docketed the permanent historical value of the Galindez case under classification 109 (kidnapping). The records of this case, however, are still in the process of being classified or declassified, as the case may be, by Justice Department and National Archives officials. In addition, the FBI and the CIA maintain separate records on the case. FOIA litigation has been commenced against the FBI and the CIA in the U.S. District Court for the District of Columbia to force release of Galindez case records maintained by these agencies. The case is docketed as Fitzgibbon v. Central Intelligence Agency and Federal Bureau of Investigation, Civil Action Number 79-0956.

Pages 127–128: The records of Morris Ernst are stored in the National Archives in Washington in Record Group 200, National Archives Gift Collection— records of the Ernst-Schwartz collection (Galindez investigation).

Page 127: The book, *Trujillo: The Last Caesar,* by Arturo Espaillat, was published by Henry Regnery Company, Publishers, in 1963.

ROCKWELL: The American Nazi

Page 135: Rockwell permit hearing June 22, 1960; see *The New York Times,* June 23, 1960 and the *New York Daily Mirror* June 23, 1960

Page 140: Rockwell announcing his entry into the New Hampshire Republican Primary, see *The New York Times* of November 16, 1963.

GOING DEEP

Page 157: See *The New York Times,* July 16, 1964; article and photograph of Herbert Callender and Ray Wood, alias Raymond Woodall, for being arrested for disorderly conduct as they tried to effect a citizens arrest of Mayor Robert Wagner. See also *The New York Times,* July 19, 1964 reporting the riot in Harlem that followed the killing of black teenager, James Powell, by a white police officer, Lieutenant Thomas Gilligan. This article also reports on the type of pamphlet then being circulated on the streets of Harlem by the Progressive Labor Movement and the Revolutionary Action Movement urging violence.

Page 169: Walter August Bowe, Robert Steele Collier, Michelle Duclos, Michelle Saunier and Khaleel Sultarn Sayyed, were indicted for violating Sections 1361 and 545 of Title 18, United States Code for plotting to "commit depredations against the property of the United States." The case is docketed in the United States District Court for the Southern District of New York as 65 CRIM 189. The United States Circuit Court of Appeals affirmed the convictions of the defendants in its opinion reported in 360 Fed 2d. 1 See *The New York Times,* February 17, 1965.

THE PRESIDENT'S PRIVATE EYE

See appendices for exhibits.

CHAPPAQUIDDICK

Pages 218–219: See *Manchester (N.H.)The Union Leader* editions for August 13, 1969, August 16, 1969, August 21, 1969, January 7, 1970, January 8, 1970 and January 9, 1970. On August 13, 1969, the day Arthur C. ("Ace") Egan Jr.'s article about the phone calls first appeared, *The Union Leader* reported that District Attorney Edmund S. Dinis had "formally requested the exhumation and autopsy of the body of Mary Jo Kopechne."

A recent forensic laboratory analysis by Wolf Technical Services, Inc., Indianapolis, Indiana of the photographs Tony Ulasewicz took shortly after his arrival on the scene of Dike Bridge and the markings on the bridge rail reports that "the markings show that the car left the bridge at the same angle as the road enters the bridge and that little or no steering corrections were made. Further, the marks show some braking just prior to hitting the bridge rail but that the car continued over the edge without stopping or 'hanging' on the bridge edge. Finally, the car was redirected to the left as a result of impacting the bridge railing, but continued on over the edge after scraping the under carriage of the car."

Kennedy's plea of guilty to leaving the scene of the accident did not answer the question whether he had a duty to try and rescue Mary Jo Kopechne the night she died. In his decision following the inquest, Judge Boyle concluded, in part, that: "The failure of Kennedy to seek additional assistance in searching for Kopechne, whether excused by his condition, or whether or not it would have been of material help, has not been pursued because such failure, even when shown, does not constitute criminal conduct." (report of Judge Boyle, page 9). At the time of the accident, the law of Massachusetts did not require affirmative action to save a person known to be in peril. See *Osterlind v. Hill* 263 Mass. 73; 160 N.E. 301 (1928). Based upon the evidence presented at the inquest into the death of Mary Jo Kopechne, Judge Boyle concluded, in part, "that Kennedy did *not* intend to drive to the ferry slip and his turn onto Dyke road was intentional." Judge Boyle also concluded that the bridge on Chappaquiddick constituted "a traffic hazard." However, Judge Boyle stated that: "If Kennedy knew of this hazard, his operation of the vehicle constituted criminal conduct." (report, page 12.)

THE ROAD TO WATERGATE

See PRESIDENTIAL CAMPAIGN ACTIVITIES OF 1972
PHASE I: WATERGATE INVESTIGATION
Testimony of Anthony T. Ulasewicz May 23, 1973 and July 18, 1973. U.S. Congress Hearings 93:1 No. 1333-1335 and 1336-1338. See also The Final Report of The Select Committee on Presidential Campaign Activities United States Senate
Pursuant to Senate Resolution 60, February 7, 1973.

354

On February 10, 1974, the former publisher of *Women's Wear Daily* and *Harper's Bazaar,* James Brady, appeared on the David Susskind Show on WNEW/TV in New York. During his interview with Susskind, Brady made the following comment:

"I'm working on a story, and if I were writing it tonight, that Tony Ulasewicz, who was probably the most colorful and kind of cuddly figure of the Watergate hearings—do you remember him, the ex-cop who did the undercover work for the plumber's unit—has not yet hung up his spikes. He is shadowing Lowell Weicker, trying to catch Senator Weicker in some naughtiness, and it's very interesting. I haven't yet developed my thesis. I'm working on it now. But the point is that Weicker, who was very, very harshly critical of the Nixon administration during the hearings, surprised everyone recently by voting against a resumption of the hearings. He had been voting with the Democrats, and suddenly he switched. And one wonders whether Tony U has come up with some information of perhaps some Polaroid photographs that might possibly bring a little pressure to bear on the good Senator, I don't know. I think it's a lovely story that Tony, six or eight months after the hearings began, is still out there doing his number. I love it."

On March 23, 1974, Senator Weicker requested Emily Sheketoff, a Republican minority staff investigator for the Senate Watergate Committee, to examine the file, records and exhibits that had been developed and maintained on me by the Committee. On March 24th, R. Scott Armstrong, a staff investigator for the Committee's Democratic majority, was also requested to act on Weicker's behalf to have my file made available to the Senator. "For Weicker," the sign out sheet reads.

On April 7, 1974, *Newsday* published a story by Martin Schram headlined "Weicker to Bare White House 'Spying'." In part, the *Newsday* article reported that when Senator Weicker appeared before a Senate sub-committee "probing the misuse of federal agencies facilities and files" he would "outline intelligence operations conducted for Nixon men by Anthony Ulasewicz, a retired New York City detective . . . An aide to Weicker said the Senator had obtained records of the Ulasewicz investigations, the White House memos relating to the use of the IRS and military intelligence for spying on political groups, and other documents . . . Weicker is expected to try to show how the White House tried to use the IRS to retaliate against individuals or organizations which carried or aired news stories that angered Nixon men . . ."

In July 1983, ten years after I sat across from Senator Weicker during the Watergate hearings, Washington D.C.'s public television station WETA broad-

355

cast a retrospective look at the hearings in a program called "SUMMER OF JUDGMENT." Senator Weicker was one of those interviewed for the telecast. At one point during broadcast, Weicker said: "If Ulasewicz is funny, then politics in America is going to get dirtier and dirtier. That's why I blew the whistle on him."

At no time did I ever conduct an investigation of Senator Weicker, was I ever a member of John Ehrlichman's "plumbers unit," use government agencies to develop information designed to discredit anyone opposing President Richard Nixon, or get the IRS to retaliate against anyone who attacked Nixon in the media. When Weicker was requested to make available for inspection any documents, memoranda or other types of written communications generated by his office concerning my alleged involvement in the activities he described in the *Newsday* story, he refused. "The Congress," Weicker wrote, "for the purposes of the Act (FOIA), is not an agency subject to the Act's disclosure provisions."

See also appendices for exhibits.

EPILOGUE

Page 287: G. Gordon Liddy, after having maintained his silence all the way to jail, finally broke his silence in his autobiography, *WILL,* that was published in 1980 by St. Martin's Press. On November 15, 1983, Liddy testified on his own behalf in the United States Tax Court against the IRS claim that he owed taxes on the money he received and was required to spend on behalf of the Committee to Reelect Richard Nixon (CREEP). In part, Liddy testified:

"I was the man on the bridge when the carrier hit the reef. Damage control was my responsibility." (trans. p. 106.)

* * *

When questioned about his intelligence operations, Liddy testified:

"Q. And in your final budget, how many of these separate activities did you include?

A. Well, let's see, there were four breakings and enterings, bag jobs, black bag jobs that were in there. There were—let's see. There was—I'm trying to think of, you know, so many things got cancelled, your Honor, over the period of time.

There was for infiltrating down there at the Democratic Campaign thing in Miami, there were the activities of the prostitutes who were to frequent the watering holes down there where the junior and mid-level people in the Demo-

356

cratic party, would meet them and start—they weren't to represent themselves as prostitutes. But they would be pretty girls, would be picked up, and they would start telling them how important they were. And if you don't think I'm important, why you just watch tomorrow. This is going to happen. That's going to happen.

We had that all budgeted in there. All kinds of things like that, counsel. I mean, you know—I could sit here and tell you these things all night to the extent you want. But that's the kinds of things that we were budgeting and doing.

Q. And you made the determination to decide on this break-in.

A. Well, Mr. Hunt and I—no, no. I was supposed to be the person who would decide where we would go in. In other words, the way I understand this task when I was first recruited was, I would be held responsible for a valuable end product. And how I obtained that would be up to me. They would finance it and that would be it.

Then came all this bureaucratic business, you've got to have the budgets and the flow charts, and all the rest of it.

And then I found that I not only had to put up with that, but then they would run things in on me that they wanted me to do that were not budgeted, that I would have to take out of the budget.

They would decide—they would decide, you know, go in here, go in there.

After all, we had budgeted to go after O'Brien on a technical surveillance basis down in Miami. Later on, where it would presumably get us some really good intelligence.

Instead, they want us to go in up here, and he's not even there any more. That sort of business. I did not have the discretion that I was led to believe I was going to have." (trans. pgs. 158–160.)

Index

359

365

WTR
2150